Wissenschaftliche Untersuchungen
zum Neuen Testament

Herausgeber / Editor
Jörg Frey

Mitherausgeber / Associate Editors
Friedrich Avemarie · Judith Gundry-Volf
Martin Hengel · Otfried Hofius · Hans-Josef Klauck

176

James A. Kelhoffer

The Diet of John the Baptist

"Locusts and Wild Honey"
in Synoptic and Patristic Interpretation

Mohr Siebeck

James A. Kelhoffer, born 1970; 1991 B.A. Wheaton College (IL); 1992 M.A. Wheaton Graduate School (IL); 1996 M.A., 1999 Ph.D. University of Chicago; Assistant Professor of New Testament and Early Christian Literature, Saint Louis University.

ISBN 3-16-148460-6
ISSN 0512-1604 (Wissenschaftliche Untersuchungen zum Neuen Testament)

Die Deutsche Bibliothek lists this publication in the Deutsche Nationalbibliographie; detailed bibliographic data is available in the Internet at *http://dnb.ddb.de.*

The book was printed by Gulde-Druck in Tübingen on non-aging paper and bound by Großbuchbinderei Josef Spinner in Ottersweier.

Printed in Germany.

almis parentibus:

Janet Elsie Kelhoffer

Daniel Jay Kelhoffer

Acknowledgments

On one stiflingly hot August evening in St. Louis, I was walking the dogs when a large insect buzzed past. The dogs wanted to chase it—whether for amusement or an evening snack (or both), I do not know. The next morning I noticed the same (or at least a very similar) insect lying dead on the ground. I looked closer and saw that it was a locust. My stomach turned as I thought of John the Baptist. "Who would ever want to eat *that*?" I mused.

The question remained with me throughout the day. With syllabi prepared for the coming term but classes not yet in session, I spent a few hours in the library to put an end to the query. Over the next couple of days, I searched several dozen commentaries on Mark and Matthew and monographs on the Baptist. In the secondary literature I read then (and in much I have encountered since), I was dismayed not to find a satisfying answer. I was, in fact, astonished to see the same half-dozen or so references to locusts in Greco-Roman antiquity recycled in one discussion after another without reflection on what such passages reveal about the Baptist's diet. I thus decided then that an article on John as a locust eater would be part of my research in Fall 2002.

Soon thereafter, my attention was drawn to patristic interpretations of John's diet, which take on a life of their own in construing John as a non-locust eating 'vegetarian' and model of ascetic simplicity. Since a systematic treatment of these assorted interpretations had also not been done, I made a mental note to return to these materials when my work on the historical John was done. Two articles.

As fall slowly gave way to winter, it became apparent to me that two separate examinations of the historical Baptist and the patristic literature would leave certain gaps in the analysis. What to do with the Synoptic tradition, in particular Matthew's expanding upon Mark's claim about the Baptist's diet and, moreover, Luke's omission of it? Is it conceivable, as Matt 3:4c asserts, that John could have survived on *only* "locusts and wild honey"? During the 2002 SBL Meeting in Toronto, I was encouraged in conversations with potential publishers that a monograph on the subject would be a welcome contribution. It is hoped that the present study accomplishes its purposes of adding to our understanding of the historical Baptist, his presentation in the Synoptic gospels, and early Christian biblical interpretation.

Without the help and encouragement of many people, the timely completion of this study would not have been possible. I would first like to thank Professor Dr. Jörg Frey for encouraging me to publish this work in WUNT, for suggesting that I include a chapter on the Baptist's "wild honey," and for offering constructive feedback on each chapter. Paul A. Patterson was my research assistant in 2002–04 and offered invaluable help on this project from inception to completion. I am also grateful to Clare Komoroske Rothschild and Matthew A. Gilbertson for reading the entire manuscript and offering numerous helpful suggestions. Additionally, Charlotte M. Ridley, a nutritionist on faculty at Saint Louis University, was of great help in suggesting resources pertinent to the analysis of the nutritional aspects of "locusts and wild honey" in chapter 4. A number of other friends and colleagues, including Wendy Love Anderson, Bernhard (Ben) A. Asen, François Bovon, Sebastian Brock, Robert Matthew Calhoun, Phuichun Richard Choi, Ronald W. Crown, Robert I. Curtis, Frederick W. Danker, Rich Garella, Cornelia B. Horn, Brett A. Huebner, F. Stanley Jones, Laura Ann Lewellyn, Clarence H. Miller, Michael G. Morony, William L. Petersen, Jill Rasmussen-Baker, Mark Reasoner, George J. (Jack) Renard and James V. Smith, have also offered suggestions, feedback or assistance with various parts of this work. My thanks are also due to Mary L. Boles and Linda R. Ritter, who have shared their laser printer with me more times than any of us can count.

Portions of this study were presented at meetings of the Society of Biblical Literature, the North American Patristics Society, the Chicago Society of Biblical Research, and the Early Christian Studies Workshop at the University of Chicago; my thanks to those in attendance, whose responses helped sharpen the arguments offered here. Part of chapter 1 appeared in *Currents in Biblical Literature*, and parts of chapters 2 and 3 have been accepted to appear, respectively, in *Dead Sea Discoveries* and *Greek, Roman and Byzantine Studies*; these preliminary studies have been reworked, corrected and augmented for this monograph. I am grateful for the feedback that I received from the editors and blind reviewers of these journals. Once more I am indebted to Ilse König for overseeing the production of my book, and to others at Mohr Siebeck, with whom I am honored to be publishing again. Any remaining errors or infelicities in this work are, of course, my own.

This book is dedicated to my parents, Janet and Daniel Kelhoffer. Their devotion to family and commitment both to each other and to their children's happiness and dreams are an inspiration to me, and to my sisters and their husbands.

St. Louis, December 2004   James A. Kelhoffer

Table of Contents

Abbreviations and References

The Greek New Testament is cited from *Novum Testamentum Graece*, the Nestle-Aland 27th Edition. Abbreviations used in this work correspond to those listed in *The SBL Handbook of Style* (1999); the *Oxford Classical Dictionary* ([3]1996); Liddell, Scott, Jones, McKenzie, *A Greek-English Lexicon*; and G. W. Lampe, *A Patristic Greek Lexicon*, and include the following:

1 Clem.	*1 Clement*
1 En.	*1 Enoch*
2 En.	*2 Enoch*
AB	Anchor Bible
ABD	D. N. Freedman (ed.), *Anchor Bible Dictionary*
AbrN	*Abr-Nahrain*
ACNT	Augsburg Commentaries on the New Testament
ACW	Ancient Christian Writers
Ael., *NA*	Aelian, *De natura animalium* (*On the Characteristics of Animals*)
Ael., *VH*	Aelian, *Varia historia* (*Miscellany*)
Aesch.	Aeschylus
Agathar., *De mar. Eryth.*	Agatharchides of Cnidus, *De maris Erythraei* (*On the Erythraean [Mediterranean] Sea*)
AJP	*American Journal of Philology*
AJT	*American Journal of Theology*
AnBib	Analecta biblica
ANF	Ante-Nicene Fathers
AnOr	Analecta orientalia
ANRW	*Aufstieg und Niedergang der römischen Welt*
ANTC	Abingdon New Testament Commentaries
Apocrypha	*Apocrypha: Revue internationale des littératures apocryphes/ International Journal of Apocryphal Literatures*
Apul., *Met.*	Apuleius, *Metamorphoses*
Ar., *Ach.*	Aristophanes, *Acharnenses* (*Acharnians*)
Ar. Byz.	Aristophanes of Byzantium
Aratus, *Phaen.*	Aratus Solensis, *Phaenomena*
Arist., *Aud.*	Aristotle, *De audibilibus* (*On Things Heard*)
Arist., *GA*	Aristotle, *De generatione animalium* (*On the Generation of Animals*)
Arist., *HA*	Aristotle, *Historia animalium* (*History of Animals*)
Arist., *PA*	Aristotle, *De partibus animalium* (*On the Parts of Animals*)
As. Mos.	*Assumption of Moses*
Asen.	*Joseph and Aseneth*
ASTI	*Annual of the Swedish Theological Institute*
Ath., *Deip.*	Athenaeus, *Deipnosophistae* (*The Learned Banquet*)

AThR	*Anglican Theological Review*
August., *Conf.*	Augustine, *Confessiones* (*Confessions*)
August., *De cons. evang.*	Augustine, *De consensu evangelistarum* (*On the Harmony of the Gospels*)

b.	born
b.	Babylonian Talmud
BA	*Biblical Archaeologist*
BBR	*Bulletin for Biblical Research*
BDAG	W. Bauer, F. W. Danker, W. F. Arndt and F. W. Gingrich, *A Greek-English Lexicon of the New Testament and Other Early Christian Literature* (^{3}2000)
BDF	F. Blass, A. Debrunner and R. W. Funk, *A Greek Grammar of the New Testament and Other Early Christian Literature*
BETL	Bibliotheca ephemeridum theologicarum lovaniensium
BHT	Beiträge zur historischen Theologie
Bib	*Biblica*
BJRL	*Bulletin of the John Rylands University Library of Manchester*
BMI	Body Mass Index ($= kg/m^{2}$)
BN	*Biblische Notizen*
BNTC	Black's New Testament Commentaries
BR	*Biblical Research*
BSac	*Bibliotheca sacra*
BT	*The Bible Translator*
BWA(N)T	Beiträge zur Wissenschaft vom Alten (und Neuen) Testament
BZ	*Biblische Zeitschrift*
BZNW	Beihefte zur Zeitschrift für die neutestamentliche Wissenschaft und die Kunde der älteren Kirche

c.	century
c.	*circa* (approximately)
CAD	I. J. Gelb et al. (eds.), *Assyrian Dictionary of the Oriental Institute of the University of Chicago*
CBQ	*Catholic Biblical Quarterly*
CCSL	Corpus Christianorum, Series Latina
CD	Damascus Document
CGTC	Cambridge Greek Testament Commentary
CGTSC	Cambridge Greek Testament for Schools and Colleges
CH	*Church History*
Clem., *Paed.*	Clement of Alexandria, *Paedagogus*
Clem., *Str.*	Clement of Alexandria, *Stromateis*
CMG	Corpus medicorum Graecorum
CNT	Commentaire du Nouveau Testament
ConBNT	Coniectanea biblica: New Testament Series
CQ	*Classical Quarterly*
CSEL	Corpus scriptorum ecclesiasticorum latinorum
CurTM	*Currents in Theology and Mission*

d.	died
DDD	K. van der Toorn et al. (eds.), *Dictionary of Deities and Demons in the Bible*
Din.	Dinarchus
Dio Chrys., *Or.*	Dio Chrysostom, *Orationes* (*Discourses*)
Diod. Sic.	Diodorus Siculus
Diss.	Dissertation (unpublished)
DNP	H. Cancik and H. Schneider (eds.), *Der Neue Pauly: Enzyklopädie der Antike*
DUJ	*Durham University Journal*
ÉBib	Études bibliques
EKKNT	Evangelisch-katholischer Kommentar zum Neuen Testament
Ep(p).	*Epistula(e)* (*Letter[s]*)
Epiph.	Epiphanius
EpRev	*Epworth Review*
EstBib	*Estudios bíblicos*
ET	English translation
ETR	*Etudes théologiques et religieuses*
ETS	Erfurter theologische Studien
Eur., *Bacch.*	Euripides, *Bacchae*
Euseb., *Demonstr. evang.*	Eusebius of Caesarea, *Demonstratio evangelica* (*The Proof of the Gospel*)
Euseb., *Hist. eccl.*	Eusebius of Caesarea, *Historia ecclesiastica* (*Church History*)
Euseb., *Praep. evang.*	Eusebius of Caesarea, *Praeparatio evangelica* (*Preparation for the Gospel*)
EVie	*Esprit et Vie*
EvQ	*Evangelical Quarterly*
ExpTim	*Expository Times*
FC	Fathers of the Church
FRLANT	Forschungen zur Religion und Literatur des Alten und Neuen Testaments
FS	Festschrift
Gal., *De alim. fac.*	Galen, *De alimentorum facultatibus* (*On the Properties of Foodstuffs*)
Gal., *De loc. aff.*	Galen, *De locis affectis* (*On the Affected Parts*)
Gal., *De simp. med. temp.*	Galen, *De simplicium medicamentorum temperamentis ac facultatibus* (*On Temperaments*)
Gal., *In Hipp. aph.*	Galen, *In Hippocratis aphorismos* (*On Hippocrates's Aphorisms*)
Gal., *Nat. fac.*	Galen, *De naturalibus facultatibus* (*On the Natural Faculties*)
Gal., *UP*	Galen, *De usu partium* (*On the Usefulness of the Parts* [*of the Body*])
GCS	Die griechische christliche Schriftsteller der ersten [drei] Jahrhunderte
Gk.	Greek
Gos. Bart.	*Gospel of Bartholomew*

Gos. Eb.	*Gospel of the Ebionites*
Gos. Nic.	*Gospel of Nicodemus*
Greg	*Gregorianum*
Haer.	*Adversus haereses* (*Against Heresies*)
Heb.	Hebrew
Heph.	Hephaestion
Herod.	Herodotus
HeyJ	*Heythrop Journal: A Quarterly Review of Philosophy and Theology*
Hippol., *Ref.*	Hippolytus of Rome, *Refutatio omnium haeresium* (*Refutation of All Heresies*)
HNT	Handbuch zum Neuen Testament
HNTC	Harper's New Testament Commentaries
Hom., *Il.*	Homer, *Iliad*
Hom., *Od.*	Homer, *Odyssey*
HSem	Horae Semiticae
HTKNT	Herders theologischer Kommentar zum Neuen Testament
HTR	*Harvard Theological Review*
HUT	Hermeneutische Untersuchungen zur Theologie
IBC	Interpretation: A Bible Commentary for Teaching and Preaching
ICC	International Critical Commentary
IDB	G. A. Buttrick (ed.), *Interpreter's Dictionary of the Bible*
IEJ	*Israel Exploration Journal*
Int	*Interpretation*
ISBE	G. W. Bromiley (ed.), *International Standard Bible Encyclopedia*
ITQ	*Irish Theological Quarterly*
JBL	*Journal of Biblical Literature*
JECS	*Journal of Early Christian Studies*
Jer., *Adv. Iovin.*	Jerome, *Adversus Iovinianum* (*Against Jovinian*)
JETS	*Journal of the Evangelical Theological Society*
JHS	*Journal of Hellenic Studies*
JNES	*Journal of Near Eastern Studies*
Jos., *Ant.*	Josephus, *Antiquitates Judaicae* (*Jewish Antiquities*)
Jos., *B.J.*	Josephus, *Bellum judaicum* (*Jewish War*)
Jos., *Vita*	Josephus, *Vita* (*The Life*)
JQR	*Jewish Quarterly Review*
JSNTSup	Journal for the Study of the New Testament: Supplement Series
JSSSup	Journal of Semitic Studies: Supplement Series
JTS	*Journal of Theological Studies*
Jub.	*Jubilees*
Justin, *Dial.*	Justin Martyr, *Dialogus cum Tryphone* (*Dialogue with Trypho*)
Lampe	G. W. Lampe, *A Patristic Greek Lexicon*
Lat.	Latin

LCC	J. Baille et al. (eds.), Library of Christian Classics
LCL	Loeb Classical Library
Let. Aris.	*Letter of Aristeas*
LSJ	Liddell, Scott, Jones and McKenzie, *A Greek-English Lexicon*
Lyd., *Ost.*	Joannes Laurentius Lydus, *De ostentis et calendaria graeca* (*On Portents and the Greek Calendar*)
m.	Mishnah
Mart. Ascen. Isa.	*Martyrdom and Ascension of Isaiah*
MS(S)	manuscript(s)
NAC	New American Commentary
NAS	National Academy of Sciences
NCB	New Century Bible
Neot	*Neotestamentica*
NHL	J. M. Robinson (ed.), *The Nag Hammadi Library*, Revised Edition
NHS	Nag Hammadi Studies
Nic., *Ther.*	Nicander, *Theriaca*
NICNT	New International Commentary on the New Testament
NIGTC	New International Greek Testament Commentary
NovT	*Novum Testamentum*
NovTSup	Novum Testamentum, Supplements
NPNF	Nicene and Post-Nicene Fathers
NTAbh	Neutestamentliche Abhandlungen
NTApo	W. Schneemelcher (ed.), *New Testament Apocrypha*, Revised Edition
NTOA	Novum Testamentum et Orbis Antiquus
NTS	*New Testament Studies*
OCD	Hornblower and Spawforth (eds.), *Oxford Classical Dictionary* (^{3}1996)
OECT	Oxford Early Christian Texts
Or.	*Oratio* (*Oration*)
Or., *Mat. Cat.*	Origen, *Catenis in Matthaeum* (*Catenas on Matthew*)
Or., *Luc. Hom.*	Origen, *In Lucam homiliae* (*Homilies on Luke*)
OrChr	*Oriens christianus*
OTL	Old Testament Library
OTP	J. H. Charlesworth (ed.), *Old Testament Pseudepigrapha*
Palladius, *De vet. med.*	Palladius, *De veterinaria medicina de insitione* (*On the Veterinary Medicine of Grafting*)
PG	J. Migne (ed.), *Patrologia graeca*
Philo, *Det.*	Philo, *Quod deterius potiori insidari soleat* (*That the Worse Attacks the Better*)
Philo, *Fug.*	Philo, *De fuga et inventione* (*On Flight and Finding*)
Philo, *Leg.*	Philo, *Legum allegoriae* (*Allegorical Interpretation*)
Philo, *Opif.*	Philo, *De opificio mundi* (*On the Creation of the World*)
Philo, *Praem.*	Philo, *De praemiis et poenis* (*On Rewards and Punishments*)

Philo, *Spec.*	Philo, *De specialibus legibus* (*On the Special Laws*)
Philostr., *VA*	Philostratus, *Vita Apollonii* (*Life of Apollonius*)
PL	J. Migne (ed.), *Patrologia latina*
Pl., *Phdr.*	Plato, *Phaedrus*
Pl., *Ti.*	Plato, *Timaeus*
Plin. (E), *HN*	Pliny (the Elder), *Naturalis historia* (*Natural History*)
Plut., *Amat.*	Plutarch, *Amatorius* (*Dialogue on Love*)
Plut., *De soll. an.*	Plutarch, *De sollertia animalium* (*On the Cleverness of Animals*)
Plut., *Quaest. conv.*	Plutarch, *Quaestiones convivales* (*Table Talk*)
Plut., *Sull.*	Plutarch, *Sulla*
PO	Patrologia orientalis
Porph., *De antr. nymph.*	Porphyry, *De antro nympharum* (*On the Cave of the Nymphs*)
Prot. Jas.	*Protevangelium of James*
Ps. Arist., *Mir. ausc.*	Ps.-Aristotle, *De mirabilibus auscultationibus* (*On Marvellous Things Heard*)
PW	Pauly-Wissowa, *Real-Encyclopädie der classischen Altertumswissenschaft*
RAC	T. Klauser (ed.), *Reallexikon für Antike und Christentum*
RB	*Revue biblique*
Rust.	*De re rustica* (*On Agriculture*)
SANT	Studien zum Alten und Neuen Testaments
SBB	Stuttgarter biblische Beiträge
SBT	Studies in Biblical Theology
SC	Sources chrétiennes
ScotJT	*Scottish Journal of Theology*
Sen. (Y)	Seneca (the Younger)
Sib. Or.	*Sibylline Oracles*
SIDIC	*SIDIC* (Journal of the Service internationale de documentation judéo-chrétienne)
SJLA	Studies in Judaism in Late Antiquity
SL	The Scribner Library
SNTSMS	Society for New Testament Studies Monograph Series
SNTSU	Studien zum Neuen Testament und seiner Umwelt
Soph.	Sophocles
SP	Sacra pagina
SPCK	Society for Promoting Christian Knowledge
ST	*Studia Theologica*
STDJ	Studies on the Texts of the Desert of Judah
StPatr	*Studia patristica*
StudBT	Studia Biblica et Theologica
Tatian, *Or.*	Tatian, *Oratio ad Graecos* (*Oration to the Greeks*)
TB	Theologische Bücherei: Neudrucke und Berichte aus dem 20. Jahrhundert
TBl	*Theologische Blätter*

TDNT	G. Kittel and G. Friedrich (eds.), *Theological Dictionary of the New Testament*
Tert., *Adv. Marc.*	Tertullian, *Adversus Marcionem* (*Against Marcion*)
Theoc., *Id.*	Theocritus, *Idylls*
Theophr., *Sens.*	Theophrastus, *De sensibus* (*On the Senses*)
TLZ	*Theologische Literaturzeitung*
TNTC	Tyndale New Testament Commentaries
TPI	Trinity Press International
TPINTC	Trinity Press International New Testament Commentaries
TSK	*Theologische Studien und Kritiken*
TU	Texte und Untersuchungen zur Geschichte der altchristlichen Literatur
TynBul	*Tyndale Bulletin*
TZ	*Theologische Zeitschrift*
UF	*Ugarit-Forschungen*
USDA	United States Department of Agriculture
VC	*Vigiliae Christianae*
VCSup	Supplements to Vigiliae Christianae
VD	*Verbum domini*
Verg., *Ecl.*	Virgil, *Eclogues*
Verg., *Georg.*	Virgil, *Georgics*
VT	*Vetus Testamentum*
VTSup	Vetus Testamentum Supplements
WBC	Word Biblical Commentary
WC	Westminster Commentaries
WMANT	Wissenschaftliche Monographien zum Alten und Neuen Testament
WUNT	Wissenschaftliche Untersuchungen zum Neuen Testament
Xen., *An.*	Xenophon, *Anabasis*
ZAW	*Zeitschrift für die Alttestamentliche Wissenschaft*
ZDPV	*Zeitschrift des Deutschen Palästina-Vereins*
ZKG	*Zeitschrift für Kirchengeschichte*
ZNW	*Zeitschrift für die neutestamentliche Wissenschaft* und die Kunde der älteren Kirche
ZTK	*Zeitschrift für Theologie und Kirche*

Chapter 1

Introduction and the *status quaestionis* concerning the Diet of John the Baptist

"Insects are an important element in human diet in many
parts of the world, but they have long been taboo in
European civilizations."[1]

A. Introduction:
The Baptist's Diet in Synoptic Tradition

1. The Problem

Why do two NT authors present John the Baptist as eating "locusts and wild honey" (ἀκρίδες καὶ μέλι ἄγριον, Mark 1:6c‖Matt 3:4c)? Satisfactory explanations for this attribution with regard to the historical Baptist, the author of Mark and the author of Matthew have yet to be given. The present study seeks an answer not only for the historical John and the Synoptic tradition, but also for the patristic literature, much of which reflects a fascination with John's diet, as well as the desire to emulate John as an example of simplicity.

Much scholarly attention has been devoted in the modern period to four actions attributed to John the Baptist in the NT gospels—most famously, his baptizing in the Jordan River, but also his preaching a message of repentance, having disciples and wearing clothing made of camel's hair. Considerably less consideration has been devoted to the peculiarities of another deed credited to John, namely his eating "locusts and wild honey" (Mark 1:6c‖Matt 3:4c). John's diet has been largely or completely overlooked in many fine monographs[2] and articles[3] on the Baptist, as well as in commentaries on Mark

---

[1] Marston Bates, "Insects in the Diet," *American Scholar* 29 (1959–60): 43–52; here, 43.

[2] Any number of studies of John or exegetical analyses of the Markan or Matthean passages, including the following monographs, have little or nothing to say on this issue: Knut Backhaus, *Die "Jüngerkreise" des Täufers Johannes: Eine Studie zu den religionsgeschichtlichen Ursprüngen des Christentums* (Paderborner Theologische Studien 19; Paderborn: F. Schöningh, 1991); Jean Daniélou, *The Work of John the Baptist* (Baltimore: Helicon, 1966); Carl R. Kazmierski, *John the Baptist: Prophet and Evangelist. Metaphor and Social Context in Matthew's Gospel* (Collegeville, MN: Liturgical Press, 1996); Marcus L. Loane, *John the Baptist as Witness and Martyr* (Grand Rapids: Zondervan, 1969); Heinrich

1:6 and Matt 3:4.[4] Given this omission in so many prominent studies, it is understandable not to find mention of John's diet in reviews of scholarship on

---

Peter, *Johannes der Täufer in der urchristlichen Überlieferung* (Marburg: H. Bauer, 1911), 11–14, 60–7; Adolf Schlatter, *Johannes der Täufer* (ed. W. Michaelis; Basel: Friedrich Reinhardt, 1956); Roland Schütz, *Johannes der Täufer* (ATANT 50; Zurich/Stuttgart: Zwingli, 1967), 28–30, 40–5; Jean Steinmann, *Saint John the Baptist and the Desert Tradition* (New York: Harper, 1958); Robert L. Webb, *John the Baptizer and Prophet: A Socio-Historical Study* (JSNTSup 62; Sheffield: JSOT, 1991), 51–2; cf. Michael Hartmann, *Der Tod Johannes des Täufers: Eine exegetische und rezeptionsgeschichtliche Studie auf dem Hintergrund narrativer, intertextueller und kulturanthropologischer Zugänge* (SBB 45; Stuttgart: Katholisches Bibelwerk, 2001); Christoph Gregor Müller, *Mehr als ein Prophet: Die Charakterzeichnung Johannes des Täufers im lukanischen Erzählwerk* (Herders biblische Studien 31; Freiburg: Herder, 2001).

[3] For example, Ernst Bammel, "John the Baptist in Early Christian Tradition," *NTS* 18 (1971–72): 95–128; Colin Brown, "What Was John the Baptist Doing?" *BBR* 7 (1997): 37–50; Knox Chamblin, "Gospel and Judgment in the Preaching of John the Baptist," *TynBul* 13 (1963): 7–15; idem, "John the Baptist and the Kingdom of God," *TynBul* 15 (1964): 10–16; Michael Cleary, "The Baptist of History and Kerygma," *ITQ* 54 (1988): 211–27; Anthony C. Deane, "The Ministry of John the Baptist," *The Expositor* 8 (1917): 420–31; Eberhard W. Güting, "The Relevance of Literary Criticism for the Text of the New Testament: A Study of Mark's Traditions on John the Baptist," in: *Studies in the Early Text of the Gospels and Acts: The Papers of the First Birmingham Colloquium on the Textual Criticism of the New Testament* (ed. D. G. K. Taylor; Text-critical Studies 1; Atlanta: Society of Biblical Literature, 1999), 142–67; Paul W. Hollenbach, "Social Aspects of John the Baptizer's Preaching Mission in the Context of Palestinian Judaism," *ANRW* 2/19/1 (1979): 850–75; idem, "John the Baptist," art. *ABD*, 3.887–99; Archie W. D. Hui, "John the Baptist and Spirit-Baptism," *EvQ* 71 (1999): 99–115; S. Lewis Johnson, Jr., "The Message of John the Baptist," *BSac* 113 (1956): 30–6; James L. Jones, "References to John the Baptist in the Gospel according to St. Matthew," *AThR* 41 (1959): 298–302; Edgar Krentz, "None Greater among Those Born from Women: John the Baptist in the Gospel of Matthew," *CurTM* 10 (1983): 333–8; Jan Lambrecht, "John the Baptist and Jesus in Mark 1.1–15: Markan Redaction of Q?" *NTS* 38 (1992): 357–84; John P. Meier, "John the Baptist in Matthew's Gospel," *JBL* 99 (1980): 383–405 (but see idem, *A Marginal Jew: Rethinking the Historical Jesus* [Vol. 2: *Mentor, Message and Miracles*; New York: Doubleday, 1991], 2.46–9); J. Ramsey Michaels, "Paul and John the Baptist: An Odd Couple?" *TynBul* 42 (1991): 245–60; John W. Pryor, "John the Baptist and Jesus: Tradition and Text in John 3.25," *JSNT* 66 (1997): 15–26; John A. T. Robinson, "The Baptism of John and the Qumran Community," reprinted in: idem, *Twelve New Testament Studies* (SBT 34; Naperville, IL: A. R. Allenson, 1962), 11–27; cf. 28–52, 61–6; D. Brent Sandy, "John the Baptist's 'Lamb of God' Affirmation in Its Canonical and Apocalyptic Milieu," *JETS* 34 (1991): 447–59; A. H. Snyman, "Analysis of Mt 3.1 – 4.22," *Neot* 11 (1977): 19–31; Wolfgang Trilling, "Die Täufertradition bei Matthäus," *BZ* 3 (1959): 271–89; Jeffrey A. Trumbower, "The Role of Malachi in the Career of John the Baptist," in: *Gospels and the Scriptures of Israel* (eds. C. A. Evans and W. R. Stegner; JSNTSup 104; Sheffield: Sheffield Academic, 1994), 28–41; Christian Wolff, "Zur Bedeutung Johannes des Täufers im Markus-evangelium," *TLZ* 102 (1977): 857–65.

[4] The following commentaries on Mark 1:6 have little or nothing to say about John's diet of "locusts and wild honey": Paul J. Achtemeier, *Invitation to Mark: A Commentary* (Doubleday NT Commentary Series; Garden City, NY: Image Books, 1978), 34–5; idem,

the Baptist.[5] The same omission is evident in an important study of the Baptist in (mostly Western) art through the centuries.[6] The disinterest of so many

---

Mark (Proclamation Commentaries; Philadelphia: Fortress, [2]1986); Edwin K. Broadhead, *Mark* (Readings: A New Biblical Commentary; Sheffield: Sheffield Academic, 2001), 21–3; Larry W. Hurtado, *Mark* (New International Biblical Commentary; Peabody, MA: Hendrickson, 1989), 16–18; August Klostermann, *Das Markusevangelium nach seinem Quellenwerthe für die evangelische Geschichte* (Göttingen: Vandenhoeck & Ruprecht, 1867), 22–3; Paul Lamarche, *Évangile de Marc: Commentaire* (ÉBib n.s. 33; Paris: Gabalda, 1996), 38–9; Dennis E. Nineham, *The Gospel of St. Mark* (Pelican Gospel Commentaries; New York: Seabury, 1968 [1963]), 61; Vincent Taylor, *The Gospel according to Saint Mark* (Grand Rapids: Baker, [2]1966), 156; C. H. Turner, *The Gospel according to St. Mark: Introduction and Commentary* (London: SPCK, 1928), 12; Julius Wellhausen, *Das Evangelium Marci* (Berlin: G. Reimer, [2]1909), 4–5; Ben Witherington III, *The Gospel of Mark: A Socio-Rhetorical Commentary* (Grand Rapids: Eerdmans, 2001), 73. Similarly, concerning the relative lack of attention given to John's diet in commentaries on Matthew: James Montgomery Boice, *The Gospel of Matthew* (Vol. 1: *The King and His Kingdom: Matthew 1–17*; Grand Rapids: Baker, 2001), 49; Margaret Davies, *Matthew* (Readings: A New Biblical Commentary; Sheffield: JSOT Press, 1993), 41–2; David E. Garland, *Reading Matthew: A Literary and Theological Commentary on the First Gospel* (Reading the NT; New York: Crossroad, 1993), 33; Donald A. Hagner, *Matthew* (WBC; Dallas: Word, 1993), 1.48–9; Douglas R. A. Hare, *Matthew* (IBC; Louisville: John Knox, 1993), 18–20 (but see idem, *Mark* [Westminster Bible Companion; Louisville: Westminster John Knox, 1996], 15); Daniel J. Harrington, *The Gospel of Matthew* (SP 1; Collegeville, MN: Liturgical Press, 1991), 51; Albert Kirk and Robert E. Obach, *A Commentary on the Gospel of Matthew* (New York: Paulist, 1978), 37–9; Daniel Patte, *The Gospel according to Matthew: A Structural Commentary on Matthew's Faith* (Philadelphia: Fortress, 1987), 48; Eduard Schweizer, *The Good News according to Matthew* (Atlanta: John Knox, 1975), 46–7; Donald Senior, *Matthew* (ANTC; Nashville: Abingdon, 1998), 52–4.

[5] E.g., Gösta Lindeskog, "Johannes der Täufer: Einige Randbemerkungen zum heutigen Stand der Forschung," *ASTI* 12 (1983): 55–83; Jerome Murphy O'Connor, "John the Baptist and Jesus: History and Hypotheses," *NTS* 36 (1990): 359–74; John Reumann, "The Quest for the Historical Baptist," in: *Understanding the Sacred Text* (ed. J. Reumann; Valley Forge, PA: Judson, 1972), 181–99. Given that Mark 1:6c‖Matt 3:4c has been overlooked by such a great number of exegetes, it is perhaps not surprising that ἀκρίς was not deemed to be of sufficient theological significance to merit inclusion in G. Kittel and G. Friedrich, eds., *Theological Dictionary of the New Testament* (Grand Rapids: Eerdmans, 1964–76). There is also no entry for "locust" in the *Dictionary of Jesus and the Gospels* (ed. Joel B. Green et al.; Downers Grove, IL: InterVarsity, 1992).

[6] Alexandre Masseron's study, *Saint Jean Baptiste dans l'art* (Paris: Arthaud, 1957), Figures 4, 12, 15, 16, 56, 60, etc., contains any number of paintings and statues of John's hairy clothing, but none of his 'locusts' or 'wild honey.' This does not detract from the importance of Masseron's work, however. As is discussed in chapters 2 and 5, the common omission among artists is perhaps not surprising, because this diet was unremarkable in an ancient Near Eastern context and perceived as either extravagant or unpalatable by so many Christian interpreters through the centuries. Additionally, more recent studies highlight the scarcity of artistic depictions of Mark 1:6c‖Matt 3:4c: Friedrich-August von Metzsch, *Johannes der Täufer: Seine Geschichte und seine Darstellung in der Kunst* (Munich: Callwey, 1989), 102, fig. 93; cf. 189; E. Weis, "Johannes der Täufer (Baptista), der Vorläufer

fine scholars in John's food does not, of course, dismiss the value of their studies. It does, however, show that Mark 1:6c‖Matt 3:4c is a commonly overlooked biblical passage.

Various passages in the NT gospels offer additional anecdotes about the diet of John the Baptist.[7] This monograph focuses in particular on Mark 1:6c‖Matt 3:4c, according to which John's food regularly included (ἦν ὁ Ἰωάννης ... ἐσθίων, Mark 1:6) or was comprised of (ἡ δὲ τροφὴ ἦν αὐτοῦ, Matt 3:4) "locusts and wild honey." The remainder of this chapter surveys these assorted Synoptic passages on John's food before reviewing the secondary literature on Mark 1:6c‖Matt 3:4c.

2. "Locusts and Wild Honey" in Mark 1:6 and Matt 3:4

As already mentioned, Mark 1:6 and Matt 3:4 present John in peculiar clothing and eating a particular diet of "locusts and wild honey:"

Mark 1:6	Matt 3:4
καὶ ἦν ὁ Ἰωάννης ἐνδεδυμένος τρίχας καμήλου καὶ ζώνην δερματίνην περὶ τὴν ὀσφὺν αὐτοῦ καὶ ἐσθίων ἀκρίδας καὶ μέλι ἄγριον.	αὐτὸς δὲ ὁ Ἰωάννης εἶχεν τὸ ἔνδυμα αὐτοῦ ἀπὸ τριχῶν καμήλου καὶ ζώνην δερματίνην περὶ τὴν ὀσφὺν αὐτοῦ, ἡ δὲ τροφὴ ἦν αὐτοῦ ἀκρίδες καὶ μέλι ἄγριον.

John's *clothing* is readily understood as an allusion by Mark (or his source) to the OT prophet Elijah.[8] Despite the attempts of certain scholars, a connec-

---

(Prodromos)," art. *Lexikon der christlichen Ikonographie* (ed. Engelbert Kirschbaum et al.; Rome/Freiburg: Herder, 1968–76), 7.164–90; here, 170.

[7] The primary sources to be surveyed in this chapter are preserved in the Synoptics: Mark 1:6c‖Matt 3:4c; Mark 2:18‖Matt 9:14‖Luke 5:33; Q/Luke 7:31–35‖Matt 11:16–19; Luke 1:15b. The descriptions of John the Baptist in Josephus (*Ant.* 18.5.2 [§§116–119]) and the Fourth Gospel (John 1:6–8, 15, 19–42; 3:22–30; 4:1–3; 5:32–33; 10:40–41) make no mention of John's food.

[8] Compare Mark 1:6b with 2 Kgs 1:8 (LXX): ζώνην δερματίνην περιεζωσμένος τὴν ὀσφὺν αὐτοῦ. Additionally, Zech 13:4 assumes clothing like that described in Mark 1:6a‖Matt 3:4a as prophetic garb: "On that day the prophets will be ashamed, every one, of their visions when they prophesy; they will not put on a hairy mantle (אַדֶּרֶת שֵׂעָר) in order to deceive." On this point see Eve-Marie Becker, "'Kamelhaare... und wilder Honig': Der historische Wert und die theologische Bedeutung der biographischen Täufer-Notiz (Mk 1,6)," in: *Die bleibende Gegenwart des Evangeliums* (FS Otto Merk; ed. R. Gebauer and M. Meiser; Marburger Theologische Studien 76; Marburg: Elwert, 2003), 13–28; here, 15–20; Paul Joüon, "Le costume d'Elie et celui de Jean Baptiste," *Bib* 16 (1935): 74–81; Philipp Vielhauer, "Tracht und Speise Johannes des Täufers: Bisher unveröffentlicht," in: idem, *Aufsätze zum Neuen Testament* (TB 31; Munich: Chr. Kaiser, 1965), 47–54; here, 48–53; cf. Eberhard Nestle, "Zum Mantel aus Kamelshaaren," *ZNW* 8 (1907): 238. In the patristic literature, the connection between John's clothing and Elijah is recognized already by Clem., *Str.* 3.53.5; Or., *Mat. Cat.* 39.

tion with Elijah or, more broadly, a 'biblical' origin for John's *diet* is not as readily discerned.[9]

A subtle but significant difference between Mark 1:6c and Matt 3:4c, alluded to above, has been overlooked in previous studies of John's diet. On the one hand, in Mark 1:6 the imperfect ἦν forms a periphrastic with the perfect participle ἐνδεδυμένος and the present participle ἐσθίων. Accordingly, Mark 1:6 claims simply that "John had been clothed (ἦν . . . ἐνδεδυμένος) with hair from a camel" and that he "was in the habit of eating (ἦν . . . ἐσθίων) locusts and wild honey."[10]

On the other hand, Matthew's version of this Markan material makes the more far-reaching claim that John ate *only* such things: "And his food consisted of (ἦν) locusts and wild honey."[11] Matthew takes over the verb ἦν from Mark, but the subject of this verb in Mark 1:6c and in Matt 3:4c is different. In Mark 1:6c, the subject is John (ὁ Ἰωάννης), but in Matt 3:4c it is his food (ἡ δὲ τροφὴ . . . αὐτοῦ). With Matthew's deletion of Mark's ἐσθίων, the claim attains the level of exclusivity in Matthew. Studies of Matt 3:4 have noted the parallelism achieved by Matthew's stylistic editing of

---

[9] Against Catherine M. Murphy, *John the Baptist: Prophet of Purity for a New Age* (Collegeville, MN: Liturgical Press, 2003), 129; R. Alan Cole, *The Gospel according to Mark: An Introduction and Commentary* (TNTC 2; Grand Rapids: Eerdmans, ²1989 [1961]), 107–8; Elizabeth Struthers Malbon, *Hearing Mark: A Listener's Guide* (Harrisburg, PA: TPI, 2002), 14–15 (emphasis added): "[A]lthough this [Mark 1:2–8] is a very short section, we hear a bit about what John wears—camel's hair and a leather belt—and what he eats—locusts and wild honey. . . . [John] dresses like Elijah . . . , *he eats like Elijah*, and we know that Elijah is coming before the end time (Malachi 4:5)." Additionally, Josef Ernst, *Johannes der Täufer: Interpretation, Geschichte, Wirkungsgeschichte* (BZNW 53; Berlin: de Gruyter, 1989), 6, initially seems to favor a symbolic interpretation of John's diet and a connection to Elijah: "Die Wüste (V. 4) und die absonderliche Kleidung und die Speise (V. 6) erhalten einen symbolischen Sinn. Markus illustriert am Beispiel des Johannes erzählend das Dogma des Elias redivivus." Elsewhere, however, Ernst seems less sure of a symbolic connection of all of Mark 1:4–6 with Elijah: "Die Angaben über Kleidung und Speise des Johannes erzählen also von den außergewöhnlichen Lebensformen eines Mannes, der um seine hohe Sendung wußte. Ob und in welchem Maße der Elias redivivus-Komplex mitschwingt, ist schwer zu sagen" (9; cf. 8).

[10] See BDF §353 and Mark 1:22, 33; 2:18; 10:22; 13:25; John R. Donahue and Daniel J. Harrington, *The Gospel of Mark* (SP 2; Collegeville, MN: Liturgical Press, 2002), 63: "The periphrastic *ēn . . . esthiōn* (lit. 'was eating') is used of customary action."; C. E. B. Cranfield, *The Gospel according to St. Mark* (CGTC; Cambridge: Cambridge University, 1959), 47: "The force of the imperfect here is to indicate habitual action."; Erich Klostermann, *Das Markusevangelium* (HNT 3; Tübingen: Mohr [Siebeck], ⁵1971 [1919]), 7.

[11] Craig S. Keener, *A Commentary on the Gospel of Matthew* (Grand Rapids: Eerdmans, 1999), 119, is notable for construing correctly the assertion of Matt 3:4: "[L]ocusts sweetened with honey constituted John's *entire* diet" (emphasis original). So also R. T. France, *The Gospel according to Matthew: An Introduction and Commentary* (Grand Rapids: Eerdmans, 1986), 91: "His diet, though limited, was nutritious and readily available in the wilderness."

Mark 1:6.[12] Yet much as Augustine did,[13] scholarship has overlooked the different claim made in Matt 3:4c, as compared with that of Mark 1:6c. In this reorganization of Mark's syntax, the author of Matthew is to be seen as playing a rather active, and not a passive, role.[14]

As a result, Mark 1:6c and Matt 3:4c offer not one but *two* different claims about John's diet. These claims merit analysis in connection with depictions of locust eaters in Jewish and Greco-Roman antiquity (chap. 2), ancient conceptions of "wild honey" (chap. 3) and the significance imputed to John's diet in the Synoptic gospels (chap. 4). Additionally, the history of interpretation of Mark 1:6c‖Matt 3:4c is arguably as interesting as these two Synoptic passages. A peculiarity stemming from Mark 1:6c‖Matt 3:4c concerns early Christian reflections on John's (alleged) asceticism and, sometimes, 'vegetarianism.' Chapter 5 assesses the assorted patristic (and later) interpretations of John's "locusts and wild honey," including the following persons and works: the *Gospel of the Ebionites* (*Gos. Eb.*), several witnesses to Tatian's *Diatessaron*, Clement of Alexandria, Origen, John Chrysostom, Jerome,

---

[12] E.g., Karl L. Schmidt, *Der Rahmen der Geschichte Jesu: Literarkritische Untersuchungen zur ältesten Jesusüberlieferung* (Darmstadt: Wissenschaftliche Buchgesellschaft, 1969 [1919]), 22: "Der Parallelabschnitt aus dem Mt Ev (3. 1–6) ist in der Sache und in der Form im ganzen mit der Mk-Fassung identisch. . . ."; W. D. Davies and Dale C. Allison, Jr., *A Critical and Exegetical Commentary on the Gospel according to Saint Matthew* (ICC; Edinburgh: T. & T. Clark, 1988), 1.296: "For Mark's καὶ ἐσθίων Matthew has substituted 'the food of him was'. This makes for better parallelism between [Matt 3:]4a and [3:4]b. The final four words are from Mark, with the necessary adjustment in case ending."; Robert H. Gundry, *Matthew: A Commentary on His Handbook for a Mixed Church under Persecution* (Grand Rapids: Eerdmans, [2]1994), 45: In Matt 3:4, "'He had his clothing from hair' replaces Mark's 'was clothed with hair.' The replacement prepares for parallelism (a characteristic of Matthew's style) between 'clothing' and 'food.'" So also Alan H. McNeile, *The Gospel according to St. Matthew* (London: Macmillan, 1915 [= Grand Rapids: Baker, 1980]), 25–6; Gerd Häfner, *Der verheissene Vorläufer: Redaktionskritische Untersuchung zur Darstellung Johannes des Täufers im Matthäus-Evangelium* (SBB 27; Stuttgart: Katholisches Bibelwerk, 1994), 22: "Die mk Conjugatio periphrastica . . . wird in eine substantivische Konstruktion umgewandelt, die zwei parallele Hauptsätze ergibt (εἶχεν τὸ ἔνδυμα αὐτοῦ . . . ἡ δὲ τροφὴ ἦν αὐτοῦ); so wird der Notiz ein größeres Gewicht verliehen als in der Fassung des Mk." Häfner is on the right track in noting that in Matt 3:4 the statement has "a larger weight" than in Mark 1:6, but he does not make the case that the parallel construction is the reason for the heightened statement in Matthew. Indeed, Häfner's analysis of Matt 3:4 (22–3) and excursus on John's "hairy mantel" (23–31) otherwise ignore John's diet.

[13] August., *De cons. evang.* 2.12 (2.25), on Matt 3:4c: "Mark also gives us this same statement almost in so many words. But the other two evangelists omit it."

[14] Against Hans Windisch, "Die Notiz über Tracht und Speise des Täufers Johannes und ihre Entsprechungen in der Jesusüberlieferung," *ZNW* 32 (1933): 65–87; here, 67: "Die entscheidenden Bezeichnungen sind aber identisch. . . ."; Vielhauer, "Tracht und Speise," 47, that Mark 1:6 "ist bei Matthäus (3,4) stilistisch geglättet, aber sachlich unverändert erhalten" (47).

Gregory of Nyssa, Chromatius of Aquileia, Hilary of Poitiers, Peter Chrysologus, Theodore of Mopsuestia, Theodore of Pelusium, the Karshuni *Life of John*, the Slavonic additions to Josephus, and Theophylactus of Ochrida. A brief epilogue on the Baptist's deed of eating "locusts and wild honey" as a witness to the historical John and on early Christian biblical interpretation and conceptions of asceticism completes this volume. The remainder of this chapter surveys other Synoptic traditions about John's diet and assesses the history of scholarship on this subject.

3. Other Synoptic Traditions Pertaining to John's Diet

a) The Question about Fasting (Mark 2:18 par.)

Since Mark 1:6c‖Matt 3:4c is commonly discussed in relation to other Synoptic passages that touch upon John's diet, a few comments about these passages will offer some clarification (and, hopefully, justification) for the assessment of scholarship to be given below. Elsewhere in the gospel of Mark, which is followed by both Matthew and Luke, one learns that John's disciples practiced fasting:

Matt 9:14	Mark 2:18	Luke 5:33
	Καὶ <u>ἦσαν</u> οἱ μαθηταὶ Ἰωάννου καὶ οἱ Φαρισαῖοι <u>νηστεύοντες</u>.	
Τότε προσέρχονται αὐτῷ οἱ μαθηταὶ Ἰωάννου λέγοντες· διὰ τί ἡμεῖς καὶ οἱ Φαρισαῖοι <u>νηστεύομεν</u> [πολλά],	καὶ ἔρχονται καὶ λέγουσιν αὐτῷ· διὰ τί οἱ μαθηταὶ Ἰωάννου καὶ οἱ μαθηταὶ τῶν Φαρισαίων <u>νηστεύουσιν</u>,	Οἱ δὲ εἶπαν πρὸς αὐτόν· οἱ μαθηταὶ Ἰωάννου <u>νηστεύουσιν</u> πυκνὰ καὶ δεήσεις ποιοῦνται ὁμοίως καὶ οἱ τῶν Φαρισαίων,
οἱ δὲ μαθηταί σου οὐ νηστεύουσιν;	οἱ δὲ σοὶ μαθηταὶ οὐ νηστεύουσιν;	οἱ δὲ σοὶ ἐσθίουσιν καὶ πίνουσιν.

The question in Mark and Matthew is predicated upon John's disciples' and the Pharisees' discipline of fasting, as compared with the lack of such a practice on the part of Jesus' disciples. Mark again uses a periphrastic construction of an imperfect form of εἰμί with a present participle to describe dietary practice (ἦσαν ... νηστεύοντες, Mark 2:18; cf. 1:6). Yet in Mark's account it is not clear whether those who "come" (ἔρχονται) to Jesus are from John's disciples, the Pharisees, both groups, or some other group.[15]

---

[15] Cf. A. Schlatter *Johannes der Täufer*, 88: "Markus [2:18] hat ein ganz unbestimmtes Subjekt." The NRSV attempts (in my view, implausibly) to clarify Mark 2:18 by inferring yet a third group in addition to John's disciples and the Pharisees: "and *people* came and said to him." So also C. H. Turner, *Mark*, 19 (emphasis original): "*they came*: not John's

Matthew and Luke clarify the Markan ambiguity in different ways. In Matt 9:14, the dropping of Mark's periphrastic (cf. Matt 3:4) is not nearly as remarkable as Matthew's clarification that it was John's disciples who asked Jesus the question about fasting. In Luke 5:33, however, the subject of εἶπαν is not John's disciples but rather "the Pharisees and their scribes" (Luke 5:30; cf. mention of only Pharisees in Mark 2:16∥Matt 9:11). Despite these differences, the depictions of the diet of John's disciples in Mark 2:18 par. may be seen as complementary (*pace* the different claims made in Mark 1:6c and Matt 3:4c [no Lukan parallel]).

Taken as a whole, this pericope (Mark 2:18–20 par.) trumpets the superiority of the bridegroom Jesus to those who practice fasting. This presumed preeminence explains why John's disciples fast and Jesus' do not (or at least did not during Jesus' lifetime). Such an underlying motivation does not, however, cast doubt upon the pericope's central claim that John's disciples, like the Pharisees (and many other pious Jews), fasted.[16] Additionally, that embarrassment could have arisen from Jesus' disciples' abstention—whenever and for whatever reason—from fasting (*pace Did.* 8.1) adds to the credibility of this testimony concerning John's disciples' habit of fasting. Since this practice is assumed for the Baptist's disciples, it may plausibly be inferred for John as well.

For the present study, it is noteworthy that the testimony of Mark 2:18∥Matt 9:14∥Luke 5:33 neither sheds any light on nor is to be connected to Mark 1:6c or Matt 3:4c. The one witness involves the consumption of particular foods (Mark 1:6 par.), and the other mentions occasional refraining from all foods (Mark 2:18 par.). Because the two Synoptic testimonies neither support nor refute one another, they *should not be harmonized.*[17]

---

disciples, nor those of the Pharisees, but 'people came.' Mark is fond of this impersonal plural. . . ."

[16] With Michael Tilly, *Johannes der Täufer und die Biographie der Propheten: Die synoptische Täuferüberlieferung und das jüdische Prophetenbild zur Zeit des Täufers* (BWANT 7/17; Stuttgart: W. Kohlhammer, 1994), 49; E. P. Sanders, *Jesus and Judaism* (London: SCM/Philadelphia: Fortress, 1985), 92: "[John] and his disciples fasted, while Jesus and his disciples did not (Mark 2.18f. and par.). Jesus was known as 'a wine-bibber and a glutton' (Matt. 11.19 and par.), and his mission was to include sinners (ibid.). While it is possible that these contrasts have become schematized, there is no particular argument to be brought against any of them, and they probably point to remembered differences between the two men. . . ."

[17] Against Tilly, *Johannes der Täufer*, 48–51; here, 48, who offers "Die Fastenfrage (Mk 2,18) als Beleg für die Authentie von Mk 1,6." Nor should one infer, e.g., that John or his disciples fasted (Matt 9:14) because they needed a break from constantly eating "locusts and wild honey" (as Matt 3:4c might suggest)!

b) Q/Luke 7:31–35 and Q/Matt 11:16–19: John and Jesus

A third Synoptic passage concerning John's diet stems from Q/Luke 7:31–35. This Q saying condemns "(the people of) this generation" (Luke 7:31‖Matt 11:16) for listening to neither John nor Jesus, despite these two individuals' different *modi operandi* with regard to food and drink:

Q/Luke 7:32b–34	Q/Matt 11:17–19a
ηὐλήσαμεν ὑμῖν καὶ οὐκ ὠρχήσασθε, ἐθρηνήσαμεν καὶ οὐκ ἐκλαύσατε. ἐλήλυθεν γὰρ Ἰωάννης ὁ βαπτιστὴς μὴ ἐσθίων <u>ἄρτον</u> μήτε πίνων <u>οἶνον</u>, καὶ λέγετε· δαιμόνιον ἔχει. ἐλήλυθεν ὁ υἱὸς τοῦ ἀνθρώπου ἐσθίων καὶ πίνων, καὶ λέγετε· ἰδοὺ ἄνθρωπος φάγος καὶ οἰνοπότης, φίλος τελωνῶν καὶ ἁμαρτωλῶν.	ηὐλήσαμεν ὑμῖν καὶ οὐκ ὠρχήσασθε, ἐθρηνήσαμεν καὶ οὐκ ἐκόψασθε. ἦλθεν γὰρ Ἰωάννης μήτε ἐσθίων μήτε πίνων, καὶ λέγουσιν· δαιμόνιον ἔχει. ἦλθεν ὁ υἱὸς τοῦ ἀνθρώπου ἐσθίων καὶ πίνων, καὶ λέγουσιν· ἰδοὺ ἄνθρωπος φάγος καὶ οἰνοπότης, τελωνῶν φίλος καὶ ἁμαρτωλῶν.

Jesus' "eating and drinking" is contrasted with John's refraining from the same. In both Luke 7:33 and Matt 11:18, John's abstinence is attributed to his possessing power from a demon (δαιμόνιον ἔχει); it is not specified whether this is a result of some affliction or, perhaps, by a shaman's or magician's cunning.

As noted with Mark 1:6c and Matt 3:4c, the depictions of John's diet in this Q material, as preserved in Luke 7 and Matthew 11, are to be differentiated. Q/Luke 7:33 makes the historically plausible claims that John refrained from food(s) (ἄρτον; cf. לֶחֶם) eaten by most (Palestinian) Jews and that the Baptist did not partake of alcoholic beverages (οἶνον). By contrast, Matthew (again) makes a more far-reaching claim about the Baptist: Jesus ate and drank like other Judeans, but John did not eat or drink *anything* (Matt 11:18–19).

However desirable, the attempt to reconstruct the original content of this Q saying may not be possible. By analogy to the heightened claim of Matt 3:4c over against Mark 1:6c, one could infer that an analogous redactional principle governed Matthew's heightening the claim of Q/Matt 11:18.[18] The

---

[18] But see Maurice Casey, *An Aramaic approach to Q: Sources for the Gospels of Matthew and Luke* (SNTSMS 122; Cambridge: Cambridge University, 2002), 105–45; here, 132: "I have supposed that Matthew's μήτε ἐσθίων μήτε πίνων reproduces his Greek source. . . . Luke expanded this because it could not be true if interpreted too literally." So also I. Howard Marshall, *The Gospel of Luke: A Commentary on the Greek Text* (NIGTC 3; Grand Rapids: Eerdmans, 1978), 301; Joseph A. Fitzmyer, *The Gospel according to Luke: Introduction, Translation, and Notes* (AB 28; Garden City, NY: Doubleday, 1981–85), 1.678; K. Backhaus, *Die "Jüngerkreise" des Täufers Johannes*, 68–9, who likewise maintain that ἄρτον and οἶνον were not present in Q but added by Luke as a clarification. Cf. Luke 5:33 (that Jesus' disciples ἐσθίουσιν καὶ πίνουσιν), instead of οὐ νηστεύουσιν (Mark 2:18‖Matt 9:14).

discussion will return to this Q material after considering briefly a final Synoptic passage, Luke 1:15b.

c) *John the Nazarite (L/Luke 1:15b) in Relation to Q/Luke 7:31–35 and Q/Matt 11:16–19*

Attempts have sometimes been made to interpret the Q material discussed immediately above (Luke 7:33‖Matt 11:16–19) in light of Luke 1:15b, according to which John "must never drink wine or beer."[19] Such interpreters take the Q material as an example of John's Nazarite asceticism. This interpretation does not satisfy for several reasons:

1. The quasi-Nazarite vow imputed to John prior to his birth (Luke 1:15b) stipulates abstinence from alcohol but no other dietary restriction. By contrast, Q/Luke 7:33 highlights John's refraining not only from alcoholic beverages but also from the type(s) of food commonly eaten by other Judeans.
2. The Nazarite vow, taken by adults (!), was temporary and not a life-long commitment.[20] Whatever *may* have been expected of the unborn John would not necessarily have remained in practice during John's adult life.
3. Like virtually all of Luke 1–2, Luke 1:15b is peculiar to this gospel and was thus either composed by this evangelist or drawn from special Lukan tradition (L). It is thus tenuous at best to interpret Q/Luke 7:33 in light of a different tradition that was either composed by Luke or drawn from L (not "Q," since Matthew reflects no interest in John's birth).

Given that Luke 7:31–35‖Matt 11:16–19 differs also from the Markan passages examined above (Mark 1:6c par.; Mark 2:18 par.), it follows that the two versions of this Q saying must also be interpreted independently of other Synoptic traditions pertaining to John's diet.

d) *Synoptic Traditions Pertaining to John's Diet: The Case against Harmonization*

The flawed tendency in scholarship toward the harmonization of two or more of these Synoptic passages (Mark 1:6c‖Matt 3:4c; Mark 2:18‖Matt 9:14‖Luke 5:33; Luke 7:31–35‖Matt 11:16–19; Luke 1:15b) cannot be over-

---

[19] Gk.: οἶνον καὶ σίκερα οὐ μὴ πίῃ. Concerning the translation of σίκερα, Danker, BDAG, 923, calls attention to a cognate Akkadian term for "barley beer" and notes, "It is not possible to determine whether σ[ίκερα] was considered any stronger than wine; the rendering 'strong drink' (in so many versions) may be misleading." Cf. Lev 10:9; Num 6:2–5; Judg 13:4–7; 1 Sam 1:11 (LXX); 4QSam*ᵃ* 1:3.

[20] With E. Schweizer, *Luke*, 22; J. P. Meier, *Marginal Jew*, 2.48, against a Nazarite interpretation of John's diet: John is never depicted "abstaining from cutting [his] hair, perhaps the single most striking sign of a nazarite."

emphasized.[21] It has been argued, rather, that no two of these distinctive traditions lend themselves to such harmonization.[22]

To summarize, the discussion has noted the plausibility of three *different* claims, namely that John's disciples, and presumably also John himself, fasted from time to time, perhaps with some regularity (Mark 2:18‖Matt 9:14‖Luke 5:33), and that John's food was somehow distinctive (Mark 1:6c; Q/Luke 7:33):

1. The gospel of Mark states that John's diet regularly included "locusts and wild honey" (Mark 1:6c).[23]
2. Mark also makes the rather unremarkable claim that John's disciples sometimes fasted (Mark 2:18 par.).
3. The version of the Q saying preserved in Luke 7:33 states that John's diet was unlike that of most Palestinian Jews. One might expect at least a somewhat different diet from a prophet who spent much time "in the wilderness" (Mark 1:3a par.), removed from the rest of society.

Because these three Synoptic traditions (Mark 1:6; Mark 2:18 par.; Luke 7:33) make substantially different claims and are quite plausible, they need not rely on each other for "proof."

By contrast, three other Synoptic depictions of John's diet offer much more extraordinary, if not legendary, assertions:

4. Only Luke 1:15b makes the (unverifiable) declaration that John was forbidden to imbibe alcoholic beverages.
5. Through a subtle rewriting of Mark 1:6c, Matt 3:4c (δὲ τροφὴ ἦν αὐτοῦ κτλ.) claims that John's wilderness food consisted *exclusively* of "locusts and wild honey."
6. The version of the Q saying in Matt 11:18 makes the super-human claim that John survived without eating or drinking anything at all. Moreover, some

---

[21] E.g., François Bovon, *Luke 1: A Commentary on the Gospel of Luke 1:1–9:50* (Hermeneia; Minneapolis: Fortress, 2002 [1989]), 1.191, on Luke 5:33–35; C. F. Evans, *Saint Luke* (TPINTC; London: SCM/Philadelphia: TPI, 1990), 357; L. W. Hurtado, *Mark* (Good News Commentary; San Francisco: Harper & Row, 1983), 9–10; Leon Morris, *Luke: An Introduction and Commentary* (Grand Rapids: Eerdmans, [2]1988 [1974]), 159; John Nolland, *Luke* (WBC 35; Dallas: Word, 1989–93), 1.345; Walter Wink, *John the Baptist in the Gospel Tradition* (SNTSMS 7; Cambridge: Cambridge University, 1968), 2–3: "Mark tells us almost nothing of John's preaching or activity. Instead he mentions John's diet and clothing (1:6). Why such unimportant details? Because they build progressively to a confirmation of John's role as forerunner. . . . [H]is diet [is] that of the strict Nazarites of old." So also David Hill, *The Gospel of Matthew* (NCB; London: Oliphants, 1972 [= Grand Rapids: Eerdmans, 1981]), 91: "The food mentioned would be found in the wilderness, and it may indicate (if abstention from flesh is implied) Nazarite asceticism." Additionally, see below on O. Böcher, "Ass Johannes der Täufer kein Brot (Luk. vii. 33)?" *NTS* 18 (1971–72): 90–2. Notably, the purported connection to the Nazarites does not explain *this particular diet*, or how characterizing John as a Nazarite might support John's role as forerunner.

[22] Yet this tendency is attested already, e.g., in Euseb., *Demonstr. evang.* 9.5 (430B–D).

[23] See chapters 2 and 4 for arguments affirming the historical plausibility of Mark 1:6c.

people inferred that the Baptist was sustained by his mastery over, or the affliction of, an other-worldly being (δαιμόνιον ἔχει).[24] By analogy to Matt 3:4c, it is plausible, but by no means certain, that Matthew deleted ἄρτον and οἶνον from the Q material he inherited (cf. Luke 7:33).

The impossibility of verifying the quasi-Nazarite vow attributed to John prior to his birth (Luke 1:15b) and its (un)likely relevance for the adult John have also been noted. Moreover, the spectacular claim of Matt 11:18, that John could perpetually refrain from food and drink, is also not open to historical verification.

From these disparate anecdotes preserved within the Synoptic gospels, it can readily be inferred that the early Christians were fascinated by the diet of John the Baptist. Matthew was so intrigued that his incorporation (and editing) of two different traditions from Mark and Q culminated in a contradiction: Matt 11:18 (from Q), which states that John did not eat or drink anything at all, is impossible if John ate only "locusts and wild honey," at least while in the wilderness (Matt 3:4c, following Mark 1:6c). One is left with the general impression that John's status as a holy man and figure of significance for the origins of the Jesus movement was thought to be bolstered because of his choice of (Mark 1:6c‖Matt 3:4c), or his refraining from (Luke 7:31–35‖Matt 11:16–19; Luke 1:15b; cf. Mark 2:18‖Matt 9:14‖Luke 5:33), certain foods. After surveying the history of scholarship concerning John's diet in the rest of this chapter, this study will evaluate in greater detail the characterizations of John the Baptist in Mark 1:6c and Matt 3:4c (chap. 4) and in subsequent interpretations of these two Synoptic passages (chap. 5).

B. The *status quaestionis (si autem est quaestio)* concerning John the Baptist's Diet

An astonishing variety of answers, sometimes based on little evidence, has been proffered by scholars who have considered the literary or socio-historical interpretation of Mark 1:6c‖Matt 3:4c. What follows is a mostly diachronic summary and critique of what scholars have argued concerning either or both of these Synoptic passages. Occasionally, adherents to certain representative interpretations of John's diet—for example, John as prophet, wilderness dweller, ascetic or 'vegetarian'—are grouped together, however. As has already been mentioned, many fine biblical commentaries and studies of the Baptist completely overlook this deed attributed to John (Mark 1:6c), or this characterization of his food (Matt 3:4c). Those who attempt to address the issue merit praise for at least recognizing the potential significance of two

---

[24] With Carl H. Kraeling, *John the Baptist* (New York: Scribner, 1951), 11–13.

Synoptic passages explained by neither the NT evangelists nor (as far as we can tell) their sources.

1. Preliminary Observations concerning Locusts as Human Food: Erasmus, Wettstein, Bochart, Alford, Zahn, and Strack and Billerbeck

Writing in the sixteenth century, Erasmus (1466–1536) notes that the Mosaic law permits eating locusts and that certain Greco-Roman authors confirm that the consumption of such insects was indeed a culinary practice in antiquity.[25] Writing in the eighteenth century, Johann Jakob Wettstein and Samuel Bochart likewise reflect an awareness of locusts as human food.[26] If nothing else, Henry Alford's influential NT commentary made the passages mentioned by Erasmus, Wettstein and Bochart more accessible to the English-speaking world.[27] Alford knows also two patristic comments concerning John's diet, namely those of Jerome concerning locust eaters in late antiquity[28] and Epiphanius on *Gos. Eb.*[29] Like many scholars before and after

---

[25] Erasmus von Rotterdam, *Novum Instrumentum, Basel 1516* (ed. H. Holeczek; Stuttgart-Bad Cannstatt: Fromman-Holzboog, 1986), 242, 296; idem, *Desiderii Erasmi Roterodami, Opera Omnia* (ed. J. Le Clerc; Lugduni Batavorum [Leiden]: Petri Vander, 1703–06 [= Hildesheim: Olms, 1961–62]), 6.18–20; idem, *Paraphrasis in Marcum* (1523/24 C.E.); ET: *Paraphrase on Mark* (trans. Erika Rummel; Toronto: University of Toronto, 1988), 17. Conversely, J. Enoch Powell, *The Evolution of the Gospel: A New Translation of the First Gospel with Commentary and Introductory Essay* (New Haven: Yale University, 1994), 62, apparently overlooks Lev 11:20–23 when stating incorrectly, "Wild honey was kosher but 'locusts' (ἀκρίδες) scarcely would be."

[26] Wettstein, *Novum Testamentum Graecum* (Amstelaedam: Ex officina Dommeriana, 1751–52 [= Graz, Austria: Akademische Druck- u. Verlagsanstalt, 1962]), 1.258–9; Bochart, "Iohannem, Baptistam, veras locustas habuisse pro cibo," in: idem, *Hierozoicon, sive De animalibus Sanctae Scripturae* (3 Vols.; ed. E. F. C. Rosenmüller; Leipzig: In Libraria Weidmannia, 1793), 3.326–33.

[27] Alford, *The Greek New Testament* (Vol. 1: *The Four Gospels,* [4]1859 [1849]; London: Rivingtons, Waterloo Place/Cambridge: Deighton, Bell and Co., [4]1859–66), 1.18, on Matt 3:4: "There is no difficulty here. The ἀκρίς, permitted to be eaten, Levit. xi. 22, was used as food by the lower orders in Judæa, and mentioned by Strabo and Pliny as eaten by the Æthiopians, and by many other authors as articles of food." The witnesses of Strabo and Pliny to locust eating in antiquity will be examined in chapter 2. Concerning Mark 1:6, Alford (1.294) refers the reader to his notes on Matt 3:4.

[28] Ibid, on Jerome, *Adv. Jov.* 2.7. Christopher Wordsworth, *The New Testament of Our Lord and Saviour Jesus Christ: In the Original Greek, with Notes and Introductions* (London: Rivingtons, [2]1861–62), 1.12, is likewise aware of locusts as food in antiquity and of Jerome's testimony.

[29] Alford, *Greek NT*, 1.18, on Epiphanius, *Panarion* 30.13.4–5. The attention that Epiphanius calls to *Gos. Eb.* is also noted by Heinrich August Wilhelm Meyer, *Critical and Exegetical Hand-book to the Gospel of Matthew* (New York: Funk & Wagnalls, 1884 [[6]1876; 1858]), 76–7; and Constantin von Tischendorf, *Novum Testamentum Graece: Ad Antiquissimos Testes Denuo Recensuit* (Leipzig: Giesecke & Devrient, [8]1869), 9. These patristic interpretations, among others, will be discussed in chapter 5.

them, Erasmus, Wettstein, Bochart and Alford seem interested primarily in the veracity of these evangelists' characterization(s) of John as a locust eater. Yet even if this ascription was 'true' for the historical Baptist, one may further ask what this detail reveals about John, or at least about Matthew's and Mark's portrayals of John.

Without evidence, moreover, Alford states that such food "was used . . . by the lower orders in Judæa," thus positing for John a particular (albeit undefined) place in ancient Palestinian society. Such a generalization of locusts as a food of Bedouins or nomads is common in the secondary literature and will be criticized in chapter 2.[30] Writing before the dawn of form criticism, Alford and his predecessors reflect little interest in the origin of this gospel tradition.[31]

Despite the limitations of these early analyses, it is remarkable how many subsequent interpreters have mentioned the same handful of passages from the likes of Strabo and Pliny, Jerome and Epiphanius without attempting to elucidate what these and other ancient parallels mean for the historical Baptist or his legacy in early Christianity. It is only a slight overstatement for the present inquiry to note that scholarship on John's diet has not progressed significantly in the last century and a half since Alford's rather modest observations.

In his classic but still important commentary on Matthew, Theodor Zahn notes that locust eating was not simply an ancient practice but continues "still today" among certain Middle Eastern and African peoples:

> Die Heuschrecken, welche noch heute in Palästina, besonders im Ostjordanland, auch in Arabien und Äthiopien nicht selten gegessen werden und armen Leuten, zumal in Zeiten der Hungersnot, auch als eigentliches Nahrungsmittel dienen, pflegen im Frühjahr oder bei Gelegenheit von Heuschreckenschwärmen ohne Mühe in Masse gefangen, gedörrt oder geröstet, dann eingesalzen und teils in diesem Zustand aufbewahrt, teils gemahlen und zu einer Art von Brot verbacken zu werden.[32]

Zahn is absolutely correct to note that locusts regularly do serve as food, and not simply in a time of need. As is discussed in chapter 4 on the historical Baptist, locusts constitute a regular food staple of contemporary peoples, who

---

[30] E.g., Eduard Schweizer, *The Good News according to Mark* (Richmond, VA: John Knox, 1970 [[12]1968]), 33: "[John's] diet simply corresponds to the diet of poor nomads. Therefore, he was not one of those hermits among whom Josephus lived between A.D. 53 and 56 and of whom [Josephus] reports that they despised everything of human creation and denied themselves meat as well as clothing."

[31] In his introduction to the Synoptic gospels, Alford (*Greek NT*, 1.2–12) maintains that the three Synoptic evangelists wrote independently of one another. When commenting on Mark 1:6, however, he writes, "rec ην δε (from Mt iii. 4)" (1.294).

[32] Theodor Zahn, *Das Evangelium des Matthäus* (Leipzig: A. Deichert, [4]1922 [1903] = Wuppertal: R. Brockhaus, 1984), 132–3; cf. idem, *Das Evangelium des Markus* (Leipzig: A. Deichert, 1910), 41–2.

oftentimes dry or roast locusts and preserve them with salt, or mix the dried and ground locusts into bread.

Zahn is also aware that the second-century Christian Tatian was a vegetarian and that, differently from Mark 1:6c‖Matt 3:4c, certain witnesses to Tatian's gospel harmony (the *Diatessaron*) describe John's food as milk and mountain honey.[33] Numerous other commentators, including M.-J. Lagrange and H. B. Swete, may well pick up on, but do not add much to, Zahn's two central points concerning contemporary locust eaters and certain early church traditions of a 'vegetarian' John.[34] Other interpreters who have called attention to the function of locusts as human food in antiquity and in the present include Alfred Loisy,[35] C. S. Mann,[36] Sherman E. Johnson,[37] James R. Edwards[38] and Joel Marcus.[39] In chapter 4, ethnographic studies by archaeologists and anthropologists of contemporary peoples will be brought into the discussion of the historical Baptist's food.

Complementing Zahn's calling attention to contemporary locust eaters are H. L. Strack and P. Billerbeck, who highlight a plethora of Mishnaic commentaries on locusts as food.[40] Although contemporary NT scholarship

---

[33] Zahn, *Matthäus*, 133 n.33, referring to Tatian, *Oratio ad Grecos* 23 and the *Diatessaron*. The possible connection between Tatian's vegetarianism and this distinctive tradition concerning John's diet is examined in chapter 5. Cf. William L. Petersen, *Tatian's Diatessaron: Its Creation, Dissemination, Significance, and History in Scholarship* (VGSup 25; Leiden: Brill, 1994), 121-2.

[34] Lagrange, *Évangile selon Saint Marc* (ÉBib; Paris: Gabalda, [5]1929 [1911], reprinted 1966), 7–8; Swete, *The Gospel according to St. Mark* (London: Macmillan, [3]1913 [1898] = Grand Rapids: Kregel, 1977), 5–6.

[35] Loisy, *L'Évangile selon Marc* (Paris: Émile Nourry, 1912), 57. Noteworthy is Loisy's suggestion that John's "wild honey" may have been left by bees in tree trunks and rocks: "soit le miel déposé par les abeilles dans les troncs d'arbres et les fentes des rochers" (57).

[36] Mann, *Mark* (AB 27; Garden City, NY: Doubleday, 1986), 1.196, notes that locusts were "[a] common item of diet then and now in the Near East, high in vitamin content." So also W. F. Albright and C. S. Mann, *Matthew: Introduction, Translation, and Notes* (AB 26; Garden City, NY: Doubleday, 1971), 25. As is discussed in chapter 4, locusts/grasshoppers are a good source for certain vitamins (e.g., B_1 and B_2) and are also extremely high in protein.

[37] Johnson, *A Commentary on the Gospel according to St. Mark* (HNTC; New York: Harper, 1960 [= Peabody, MA: Hendrickson, 1990]), 37.

[38] Edwards, *The Gospel according to Mark* (Pillar New Testament Commentary; Grand Rapids: Eerdmans/Leicester: Apollos, 2002), 32: "Although offensive to some modern Western tastes, the eating of locusts fell within Jewish dietary regulations . . . and provided a high source of protein and minerals."

[39] Marcus, *Mark 1–8: A New Translation with Introduction and Commentary* (AB 27; New York: Doubleday, 2000), 151. See also Thomas Staubli, *Die Bücher Levitikus, Numeri* (Neuer Stuttgarter Kommentar, Altes Testament 3; Stuttgart: Katholisches Bibelwerk, 1996), 100; Hans Gossen, "Heuschrecke," art. PW 8/2.1381–6; here, 1386; BDAG, 39.

[40] Strack and Billerbeck, *Kommentar zum Neuen Testament aus Talmud und Midrasch* (Munich: Beck, 1922–61), 1.98–100 (on locusts), 100–1 (on honey).

appropriately calls for caution in using these later Jewish materials for interpreting (especially pre-70 C.E.) NT passages, it is significant for the present
study that the discussion of locusts in Jewish dietary practice was a living issue for Judaism in late antiquity. Later in the twentieth century, scholarship
would be blessed with the discovery of the Dead Sea Scrolls, which, like the
later Mishnaic materials, offer instructions for how to eat locusts.[41] In chapter
2 it will be argued that witnesses to locust eating not simply in the Pentateuch
(Lev 11:20–23), but in material roughly contemporary with the Baptist (Damascus Document 12:14–15) and, later, in the Mishnah and certain
midrashim, support the plausibility of the claim in Mark 1:6c that lo-
custs/grasshoppers comprised part of John's diet.

2. Form Criticism and John as Prophet: Dibelius (and Others)

Arguably the greatest legacy Martin Dibelius left for subsequent NT
scholarship concerns the application of form criticism to the study of the Synoptic gospels. Yet even before the appearance of his classic study,[42] one can
see glimpses of Dibelius's form-critical program in his work on the Baptist:

> [S]eine . . . Heuschreckenspeise und wildem Honig dient nicht dem Interesse an den
> Lebensgewohnheiten des merkwürdigen Mannes, sondern will dem Leser zeigen, daß
> Johannes mehr ist als ein Prediger der Bußtaufe. Die einfache Speise weist auf den
> Bewohner der Einöde, der außerhalb aller Kultur steht, sich aber engeren Zusammen-
> hangs mit Gott rühmen darf . . . — dies alles erwähnt Markus, um zu sagen: Johannes ist
> ein Prophet.[43]

Dibelius is to be credited with attempting to distinguish between the historical
John and how the author of Mark wishes to depict John. For Dibelius, al-
though the historicity of Mark 1:6c is to be denied,[44] the characterization in
Mark serves instead to highlight "that John is more than just a preacher of re-
pentance (Bußtaufe)." Rather, Mark wishes to present John as "a prophet."
Others who follow this line of interpretation—that John's diet bolsters his

---

[41] Damascus Document[a] (CD–A) 12:12–15. The Heb. and an ET are conveniently available in: F. García Martínez and E. J. C. Tigchelaar, eds., *The Dead Sea Scrolls Study Edition*
(Leiden: Brill/Grand Rapids: Eerdmans, 2000 [1998]), 570–1. Unless otherwise noted,
translations of the Dead Sea Scrolls are from this edition. On this passage see the discussions
in chapters 2 and 4.

[42] *Die Formgeschichte des Evangeliums* (Tübingen: Mohr [Siebeck], [2]1933 [1919]); ET:
From Tradition to Gospel (SL 124; New York: Scribner, 1965).

[43] *Die urchristliche Überlieferung von Johannes dem Täufer* (FRLANT 15; Göttingen:
Vandenhoeck & Ruprecht, 1911), 48. Dibelius (49–50) does not discuss the editing of Mark
1:6 in Matt 3:4.

[44] Additionally, Josef Ernst, *Johannes*, 6, also dismisses the historicity of the presentation
of John in Mark 1:4–6: "Geschichtliches ist von der Verkündigung absorbiert worden."

identity as a prophet—include Alfred Plummer,[45] Erich Klostermann,[46] Dieter Lührmann[47] and Michael Tilly.[48]

Dibelius's interpretation of John as a prophet in Mark by virtue of his food is equally intriguing and vexing. For one thing, Dibelius's judgment against historicity is stated rather than argued. More problematic is the contention that locust eating would somehow validate John's credentials as a prophet to Mark's audience, since neither Dibelius nor others who advocate this interpretation offers any ancient evidence to support this conclusion. Of course, the earliest interpretations of John as a prophet are preserved within the Synoptics themselves (Mark 11:32||Matt 21:26||Luke 20:6; Q/Luke 7:26||Matt 11:9 [*pace* John 1:25]; Matt 14:5), but only a hermeneutic of harmonization can justify the use of any of these Synoptic passages to interpret Mark 1:6c||Matt 3:4c. Nevertheless, even if Dibelius's solutions are not compelling, this pioneering scholar merits praise for raising for the first time traditio-historical questions to be addressed also in the present study.

3. John as Ascetic: McNeile, Gnilka, Pesch (and Others)

Looking to the context of Matt 3:1–6 for understanding John's diet, Alan H. McNeile argues that Matthew intends to connect John with the OT citation of "a voice of one crying in the desert" (Matt 3:3; cf. Mark 1:2–3).[49] His observation has merit, especially in so far as Matthew bends conventional rules of grammar to make this connection.[50] One may fairly ask, however, whether before Matthew the author of *Mark* also intended to connect John's diet in

---

[45] Plummer, *The Gospel according to St. Mark* (CGTSC 2; Cambridge: Cambridge University, 1915), 55: "It is neither said nor implied that it was his asceticism which attracted the crowds; the belief that he was a Prophet did that."

[46] So also E. Klostermann, *Das Markusevangelium* (HNT 3; Tübingen: Mohr [Siebeck], [5]1971 [1919]), 7: "In bezug auf Tracht und Nahrung erscheint das zugleich als eine Anknüpfung an das alte Prophetentum."

[47] Lührmann, *Das Markusevangelium* (HNT 3; Tübingen: Mohr Siebeck, 1987), 35: "es geht nicht allein um die Wüstentypologie, sondern um die Darstellung des Täufers als Prophet. . . ."

[48] Tilly, *Johannes der Täufer*, 38: ". . .Nahrung und Kleidung des Täufers gemeinsam als Erkennungszeichen eines Propheten gesehen werden müssen und nicht als feste Attribute des Elijah. . . ."

[49] McNeile, *Matthew*, 26: "Mt. transposes Mk.'s order, in describing the person of the Baptist before his success. The description (absent from Lk.) of his person, ascetic and prophetic, is thus made to carry on the thought of the prophecy 'a voice of one crying in the desert.'" McNeile also refers to H. B. Swete's commentary on Mark—McNeile's commentary is dedicated to Swete—for additional notes on John's food.

[50] Ibid, 25, on Matt 3:3: "The masc. ὁ ῥηθείς is unique in the N.T., but the formula is analogous to that in [Matt] 1. 22."

some way with Isaiah 40 and, additionally, whether Matthew highlights to a greater extent an element already present within Mark. Accordingly, McNeile makes a contribution in the interpretation of Matt 3:3–4 but does not make a compelling case for Matthew's novelty in this regard.

This criticism applies also to McNeile's characterizations, without argument, of John's alleged asceticism and prophetic identity because of eating "locusts and wild honey." Ascetic interpretations of Mark 1:6c or Matt 3:4c—that John is somehow presented as an ascetic by virtue of his clothing or food (or both)—are also advocated by numerous other scholars. These scholars include: Bernhard Weiss,[51] A. E. J. Rawlinson,[52] Hugh Anderson,[53] W. D. Davies and Dale C. Allison, Jr.,[54] Joachim Gnilka,[55] Rudolf Pesch,[56] Craig L. Blomberg,[57] Robert H. Gundry,[58]

---

[51] Weiss, *A Commentary on the New Testament* (Vol. 1: *Matthew–Mark*; New York: Funk & Wagnalls, 1906 [⁸1892]), 13.

[52] Rawlinson, *St Mark* (WC; London: Methuen, ⁶1960 [1925]), 8–9.

[53] Anderson, *The Gospel of Mark* (New Century Bible; Greenwood, SC: Attic, 1976 [= Grand Rapids: Eerdmans, 1981]), 72: "John's asceticism, as a datum of the tradition (attested also in Lk. 1:15), is of very small moment to Mark, and so the Evangelist hastens on forthwith to the Baptist's preaching."

[54] Davies and Allison, *Matthew*, 1.296–7: "If John's dress characterized him for Christians as a prophet and particularly as one like Elijah, his diet pointed to asceticism and poverty. . . ."

[55] Gnilka, *Das Evangelium nach Markus* (EKKNT II/1–2; Zurich: Benziger/Neukirchen-Vluyn: Neukirchener, ³1989), 1.47: "Heuschrecken, die im Salzwasser gekocht und auf Kohlen geröstet werden, und wilder Honig gehören zur Nahrung des Wüstenbewohners. Weil keine anderen Nahrungsmittel genannt werden, ist damit die asketische Lebensform des Täufers gekennzeichnet (Mt 11, 18)."

[56] Pesch, *Das Markusevangelium I. Teil: Einleitung und Kommentar zu Kap. 1,1–8,26* (HTKNT 2.1; Freiburg: Herder, ⁴1984), 82: "Die asketische Existenz des Täufers (die in täuferischer Überlieferung auch Lk 1, 15 hervorgehoben ist) entspricht seiner Rolle als Bußprediger und Prophet." Cf. Pesch, "Anfang des Evangeliums Jesu Christi: Eine Studie zum Prolog des Markusevangeliums (Mk 1, 1–15)," in: *Das Markus-Evangelium* (ed. R. Pesch; Wege der Forschung 411; Darmstadt: Wissenschaftliche Buchgesellschaft, 1979), 311–55; here, 321–2.

[57] Craig L. Blomberg, *Matthew* (NAC 22; Nashville: Broadman, 1992), 75: "Both clothing and food point to an austerity and asceticism appropriate to his stern calls for repentance."

[58] R. H. Gundry, *Matthew*, 45: "Even in his diet John portrays true discipleship. For that diet, Matthew uses 'food' rather than Mark's 'eating' and so makes John exemplary in his unconcern for food. . . . Locusts and wild honey not only indicate a sparse diet appropriate to the desert, but also a specially holy one devoid of flesh from which blood has had to be drained (hence locusts) and devoid of wine (hence honey)." Gundry does not, however, specify in what way John's diet exemplifies discipleship.

Craig S. Keener,[59] Francis J. Moloney,[60] Rudolf Schnackenburg,[61] Andrew Dalby,[62] and an aggregate majority of voting members of The Jesus Seminar.[63] This interpretation will be discussed critically in chapter 4 (on Matt 3:4c) and chapter 5 (on John's legacy in early Christianity). At present it suffices to note that most characterizations of the Baptist as an ascetic, like McNeile's, are of limited value because they are offered without evidence that ascetics chose these foods[64] and without a definition of asceticism.[65] These assessments of John as an ascetic because of his diet are also deficient for not clarifying what significance Mark and Matthew attach to John's alleged asceticism.

4. A 'Vegetarian' Historical Baptist? (Pallis, Kieferndorf and Eisler)

The depiction of John as a (non-locust eating) 'vegetarian' as early as the second century in *Gos. Eb.*—and, possibly, in Tatian's *Diatessaron* as well—has already been mentioned in passing. Certain studies of the Baptist have actually argued that John himself was a 'vegetarian.' For example, Alexandros Pallis supports the notion that "common sense" tells us that John

---

[59] Keener, *Matthew,* 118–19 (emphases original): "*John's diet* also provides Matthew's community a model of commitment. . . . [L]ocusts sweetened with honey constituted John's *entire* diet. The sort of pietists that lived in the wilderness and dressed simply normally ate only the kind of food that grew by itself. . . . This was not the only lifestyle to which God called his servants, but Matthew believed that God called some disciples to it (Mt 11:18–19), and their lifestyle challenges all disciples to consider whether they have staked everything on the kingdom. . . ."

[60] Moloney, *The Gospel of Mark: A Commentary* (Peabody, MA: Hendrickson, 2002), 33: "He lives as an ascetic, neither eating meat nor drinking wine. Such behavior is typical of late Jewish prophets."

[61] Schnackenburg, *The Gospel of Matthew* (Grand Rapids: Eerdmans, 2002 [1985–87]), 30: "His food . . . underscores his life of renunciation" (cf. 105).

[62] Dalby, *Food in the Ancient World: A–Z* (London/New York: Routledge, 2003), 199.

[63] According to W. Barnes Tatum, *John the Baptist and Jesus: A Report of the Jesus Seminar* (Sonoma, CA: Polebridge, 1994), 11, the conclusions that John "was an ascetic" and "lived on locusts and raw honey" received an overall judgment of "probability" (pink; .5001–.7500/1.0 scale). Cf. the Scholars Version's (SV) mistranslation of Mark 1:6: "And John . . . lived on locusts and raw honey" (29). So also Yizhar Hirschfeld, "Food: Christian Perspectives," art. *Encyclopedia of Monasticism* (ed. William M. Johnston; Chicago: Fitzroy Dearborn, 2000), 1.483–5; here, 483.

[64] In fact, there is no evidence to connect asceticism with locust eating. An example to the contrary is Augustine's argument that John was not tempted by eating meat (i.e., locusts) so frequently. On these points, see the discussion of the Synoptics in chapter 4 and of August., *Conf.* 10.46–47 and other patristic interpretations in chapter 5.

[65] For a discussion and definition, see Teresa M. Shaw, *The Burden of the Flesh: Fasting and Sexuality in Early Christianity* (Minneapolis: Fortress, 1998), 5–10. Shaw defines asceticism broadly as "a way of life that requires daily discipline and intentionality in bodily behaviors" (6).

did not eat locusts: "This observation derives considerable support from the fact that, in other instances where Jewish tradition represents men as having been driven into the desert either by stress of circumstances or by a passion for asceticism, their food is said to have been what the soil produced."[66] Pallis concludes that "the archetype [of Mark 1:6] read ἔσθων . . . ῥίζας καὶ καρπὸν ἄγριον, that is, *eating roots and wild fruit*."[67] Likewise, Philipp Kieferndorf maintains that John was a 'vegetarian' (Jesus too) on the grounds that ἀκρίς in Matt 3:4c should actually be rendered ἄκρα.[68]

Robert Eisler also argues that the original Synoptic tradition as preserved in Mark 1:6c‖Matt 3:4c has become corrupt:

> I am myself much more inclined to believe that the word ἀκρόδρυα = 'tree fruits' was maliciously distorted into ἀκρίδας by the hand of an enemy of the Baptist's sect, desirous of making the Baptist appear as one feeding on vermin, naturally loathsome to Gentile Christians of the educated classes.[69]

---

[66] Pallis, *A Few Notes on the Gospels according to St. Mark and St. Matthew: Based Chiefly on Modern Greek* (Liverpool: Liverpool Booksellers, 1903), 3–6; here, 3. So also Victor Hehn, *Kulturpflanzen und Haustiere in ihrem Übergang aus Asien nach Griechenland und Italien sowie in das übrige Europa: Historisch-linguistische Studien* (ed. Otto Schrader; Berlin: Gebrüder Borntraeger, [8]1963 [1870]), 456–60; ET: *Cultivated Plants and Domesticated Animals in Their Migration from Asia to Europe: Historico-linguistic Studies* (Amsterdam: John Benjamins, 1976 [1885]), 340–2.

[67] Ibid, 6, emphasis original. In following the reading ἔσθων (B ℵ* L* Δ 33 W), rather than ἐσθίων (A ℵ[c] G[sup] D K L[c] M P U Θ Π *f*[1] *f*[13] 2 28 565 579 700 1071 1424 𝔐), Pallis may be following the text of C. von Tischendorf, *Novum Testamentum Graece*, 218, who also prefers ἔσθων in Mark 1:6c. Cf. Reuben J. Swanson, ed., *New Testament Greek Manuscripts: Variant Readings* (Vol. 2: *Mark*, 1995; Sheffield: Sheffield Academic, 1995), 2.8.

[68] Neut. Pl. of ἄκρος, α, ον, apparently referring to the "tips" or "extremities" of vegetable 'shoots.' Given the title of the journal in which it appears, the argument is not surprising: P. Kieferndorf, "Seine Speise war Heuschrecken?" *Vegetarische Warte* 54 (1921): 188–9. Similarly, in the same journal another author identified simply as Dr. Marx, the Duke of Saxony and a university professor (Dr. Marx, Herzog zu Sachsen, Universitätsprofessor, "Die Nahrung Johannes des Täufers: Eine Antwort auf den Artikel von Philipp Kieferndorf," *Vegetarische Warte* 55 [1922]: 1–5) argues that both locusts *and* wild honey are corrupt traditions (p. 1) and calls attention to (much) later Christian interpretations of John the 'vegetarian' in Migne's *PG* (pp. 2–5).

[69] Eisler, "The Baptist's Food and Clothing," in: idem, *The Messiah Jesus and John the Baptist according to Flavius Josephus' Recently Rediscovered 'Capture of Jerusalem' and Other Jewish and Christian Sources* (New York: L. MacVeagh [Dial], 1931 [1929–30]), 235–40; here, 236; cf. 614–15. Note also the recent inquiry of Richard A. Young, "Didn't John the Baptist Snack on Locusts?" in: idem, *Is God a Vegetarian? Christianity, Vegetarianism, and Animal Rights* (Chicago: Open Court, 1999), 90–101. In the Lukan Parable of the Prodigal Son (Luke 15:11–32), Young calls attention to carob pods (κεράτια, v. 16), mentioned as the pigs' food desired by the wayward son who was down on his luck, as a possibility for John's food. Nonetheless, Young acknowledges that the Baptist probably did eat locusts and that "There is no clear evidence that John the Baptist or the early apostles were vegetarian and if they were what their reasons might have been" (100).

A common bias running through these studies, to which the present author must also confess, is the European prejudice against eating insects.[70] Given that such food is regarded as strange by most people of European descent and that John's locust eating was repudiated by certain early patristic testimonies about John, the logical inference made by these scholars is that John himself did not eat locusts. *Ergo*, a corresponding non-arthropod proto-gospel tradition must (!) have preceded Mark 1:6c. Nonetheless, even if Eisler does not offer a compelling argument concerning the diet of the historical Baptist, he can at least offer a plausible impetus for the transition from Mark 1:6c‖Matt 3:4c to later Christian traditions about John as a 'vegetarian.'

5. *'John within Judaism' as a Wilderness Dweller (Lohmeyer) or an Authoritative Hellenistic Herald (Windisch)*

The aforementioned endeavors to understand John's diet were followed by two different but more substantive attempts in the 1930s, by Ernst Lohmeyer and Hans Windisch. In his classic monograph on the Baptist, Lohmeyer devotes attention to the distinctiveness of John's diet, its function within Mark 1:1–8, the source of this Synoptic tradition, and the place of John's diet within Palestinian Judaism.[71] He notes, for example, that in Mark, "Wir hören . . . daß er seltsam in Tracht und Nahrung war."[72]

Like Dibelius, Lohmeyer is interested in the function of this characterization in Mark. Different from Dibelius, however, Lohmeyer emphasizes not the Baptist's prophetic identity but John's connection with the *desert*: "Der Erzähler scheint ihn darin gefunden zu haben, daß er den Täufer als 'Stimme eines Rufers in der Wüste' legitimiert."[73] The lacuna in Lohmeyer's analysis is the same as that noted above for Dibelius, namely it does not establish how Mark's audience would have made the connection between John's food and clothing and the Baptist's legitimization as the figure in the wilderness men-

---

[70] With R. T. France, *The Gospel of Mark: A Commentary on the Greek Text* (NIGTC; Grand Rapids: Eerdmans/Carlisle, UK: Paternoster, 2002), 69: "There is no basis in Greek usage for the traditional notion (born no doubt of Western squeamishness) that the word [ἀκρίδες] refers here not to locusts but to the carob or 'locust'-bean (hence called 'St. John's bread')." So also C. S. Mann, *Mark*, 1.196.

[71] Ernst Lohmeyer, *Das Urchristentum* (Vol. 1: *Johannes der Täufer*; Göttingen: Vandenhoeck & Ruprecht, 1932), esp. 1.50–2. Lohmeyer (1.50–1 n.4) mentions certain early Christian interpretations of John's diet as well.

[72] Ibid, 1.13. That John's food was 'strange' or 'peculiar' is not developed, however.

[73] Ibid, 1.50. On this point see also idem, "Zur evangelischen Überlieferung von Johannes dem Täufer," *JBL* 51 (1932): 300–19; here, 301–5; idem, *Das Evangelium des Markus* (Meyer I.2; Göttingen: Vandenhoeck & Ruprecht, [17]1967), 16–17. Cf. above on A. McNeile, *Matthew*, 26.

tioned in Isaiah 40.[74] Additionally, the wilderness interpretation must account for the fact that people in various locations *other than* the wilderness ate locusts. Without argument, then, Lohmeyer simply assumes that eating locusts would point an ancient audience to a particular geographic location such as the wilderness. Other scholars who posit a connection between John's diet and the wilderness include John P. Meier,[75] Robert H. Gundry,[76] Douglas R. A. Hare,[77] Eve-Marie Becker[78] and Ulrich B. Müller.[79]

With regard to the origin of this tradition, Lohmeyer notes correctly that the description of John's clothing and diet does not stem from 'Isaiah' and that analogies to Elijah do not account for his diet.[80] Lohmeyer regards Mark 1:4–8 as a commentary on 1:2–3 and all of 1:1–8 as a traditional, pre-Markan unit.[81] Of course, all of these points need to be sustained by arguments (which Lohmeyer does not provide). Perhaps when form criticism was relatively new in NT studies such brief observations seemed sufficient.

Lohmeyer also differs from Dibelius in positing a basic continuity between Mark 1:6c and the life of John:

> Sie mag bis zu einem gewissen Grade mit dem Steppendasein gegeben sein, aber sie scheint auch gegen die Lebensweise in kultivierteren Gegenden zu protestieren. Denn

---

[74] The present study will establish the plausibility of a connection between John's food and location in the wilderness in Mark. On this, see the discussion of Mark 1:2–8 in chapter 4.

[75] Meier, *Marginal Jew*, 2.49: "Clearly, then, both the clothing and the diet of John point first of all simply to his habitation in the desert. Whatever further meaning they may have must be derived from his own stated understanding of his [sc. John's] ministry."

[76] Gundry, *Mark: A Commentary on His Apology for the Cross* (Grand Rapids: Eerdmans, 1993), 37: "A tradition probably contributes also to the description of John's diet as consisting of 'locust[s] and wild honey.' For Mark, this piece of information harks back to John's being 'in the wilderness' and thus reemphasizes correspondence to God's plan as written in Isaiah the prophet."

[77] Hare, *Mark* (Westminster Bible Companion; Louisville: Westminster John Knox, 1996), 15: "The details concerning John's clothing and diet are probably intended to reinforce the reference to his wilderness habitat. . . . 'Wilderness' is stressed because of its symbolic power" concerning God's past and future expressions of grace and judgment.

[78] Becker, "'Kamelhaare... und wilder Honig,'" 20–1.

[79] U. Müller, *Johannes der Täufer: Jüdischer Prophet und Wegbereiter Jesu* (Leipzig: Evangelische Verlagsanstalt, 2002), 24–5. So also William L. Lane, *The Gospel of Mark* (NICNT; Grand Rapids: Eerdmans, 1974), 51; Lamar Williamson, Jr., *Mark* (IBC; Atlanta: John Knox, 1983), 32; C. H. Kraeling, *John the Baptist*, 10–13; Ezra P. Gould, *Critical and Exegetical Commentary on the Gospel according to St. Mark* (ICC; New York: Scribner's/Edinburgh: T. & T. Clark, 1983 [1896]), 8; J. R. Edwards, *Mark*, 32; Étienne Trocmé, *L'Évangile selon Saint Marc* (CNT 2; Geneva: Labor et Fides, 2000), 28; Timothy J. Geddert, *Mark* (Scottdale, PA: Herald, 2001), 32; R. Schnackenburg, *Matthew*, 30.

[80] Lohmeyer, *Johannes*, 1.50.

[81] Ibid. So also Gundry, *Mark*, 37.

wilder Honig oder Milch oder Heuschrecken gelten als reine Speisen, etwa im Gegensatz zu der Fleischnahrung, die erst durch die rituelle Schlachtung des Tieres rein wird.[82]

Offering a then-rare attempt to understand the Baptist in his Palestinian Jewish context, Lohmeyer posits that locusts and wild honey were "als heilige Speise auszusuchen."[83] The paradigm that Lohmeyer seems to presume is that of 'John against Judaism': The Baptist avoids meat stemming from ritual slaughtering in the Jerusalem Temple and eats instead a different type of "holy meal."[84] From this it is not clear if Lohmeyer is flirting with an ascetic interpretation of John's diet, but such could well be a logical implication of the notion that John rejected the food of the priests in Jerusalem.

Unlike Lohmeyer, who discusses John's diet as distinctive within Palestinian Judaism, Hans Windisch explores certain Greco-Roman parallels. Windisch recognizes the emphasis within Mark 1:3a, 4 and 7 on oral proclamation.[85] Windisch is not, however, interested in redaction-critical questions and even downplays the differences between Mark 1:6c and Matt 3:4c.[86]

After noting that the biblical writings offer no analogy to Mark 1:6c, Windisch turns to the following four examples: Pythagoras's clothing and avoiding wine during the day;[87] the Cynic Menedemos (3rd c. C.E.);[88] Josephus's description of Bannus, who "fed on such things as grew of themselves";[89] and the later Christian tradition attributed to Hegesippus concerning James (the Lord's brother), who is said to be noteworthy because of his clothing and diet.[90] For Windisch, these depictions of Pythagoras, Menedemos, Bannus and James clarify that John's diet in Mark highlights the authority of the Baptist's proclamation.

---

[82] Lohmeyer, *Johannes*, 1.50–1. That Lohmeyer is open to a 'vegetarian' interpretation of John's diet is not to be overlooked, as he cites the works of Kieferndorf, Marx, and Eisler (discussed above).

[83] Ibid, 1.52; cf. 1.128, 1.165.

[84] Similarly, and also without argument, J. R. Edwards, *Mark*, 32: "John's rustic dress and diet set him apart from the refined temple cult in Jerusalem and further identify him with 'the desert region' (1:4)." Cf. T. William Manson, "John the Baptist," *BJRL* 36 (1953–54): 395–412; here, 401: "His choice of food and clothing and dwelling-place was a standing visible protest against the moral and spiritual deterioration which he, like many before him in Israel, felt to be the inevitable accompaniment of alien culture and civilization."

[85] Windisch, "Die Notiz," 66.

[86] Ibid, 67: "Jeder der beiden hat die verschieden stilisiert. . . . Die entscheidenden Bezeichnungen sind aber identisch, so daß die Annahme, Matthäus schöpfe die Nachricht aus anderer Überlieferung, nicht nötig ist."

[87] Ibid, 67, on Diogenes Laertius, *Lives* 8.1.19.

[88] Ibid, 67–71, on Diogenes, *Lives* 6.9.102. Windisch concludes, "Johannes ist ein biblischer Menedemos und Menedemos ein hellenistischer Johannes" (71).

[89] Ibid, 72, on Jos., *Vita* 2 §11.

[90] Ibid, 75, on Hegesippus *apud* Euseb., *Hist. eccl.* 2.23.4–6.

The parallels Windisch cites are indeed fascinating, but his use of them to account for John's diet in Mark is wanting for at least two reasons. First, Windisch has not made a compelling case that Mark (or Matthew) has a primary motivation of presenting John as an authoritative teacher/philosopher. Second, and like Dibelius and Lohmeyer, Windisch does not account for the particular mention of "locusts and wild honey," that is, why *these* foods—and not others—receive attention in Mark (and Matthew).[91]

Despite these criticisms, Windisch's study has value for showing how Mark 1:6c and Matt 3:4c could well have been understood by some in the early church. Whatever Mark's rationale may have been for mentioning the Baptist's clothing and diet, subsequent Christian authors could indeed have interpreted Mark 1:6c as Windisch does and may for this reason have sought to minimize or augment (cf. Matt 3:4c) this Markan material.

6. The 'No Significance' Interpretation: Kraeling, Yamasaki and Juel

In contrast to the aforementioned studies, Carl H. Kraeling argues that no particular significance is to be attached to John's food and clothing:

> The importance of these details has been greatly developed and exaggerated, particularly in later Byzantine legend. . . . Except for the fact that it is specific, there is nothing in Mark's statement about John's food that could be construed as involving a special dietary program. . . . What is said about his food is to be taken merely as an attempt to characterize his life in the wilderness.[92]

This negative argument seems to be fuelled equally by a discussion of the Markan passage in light of Q/Luke 7:33 and L/Luke 1:15b and by this scholar's reaction to the significance attributed to John's diet and garb in later Christian literature.[93] Despite his harmonizing approach to Mark 1:6c and lack of affinity for the patristic materials, Kraeling's analysis is nevertheless

---

[91] Additionally, Mark 7:1–23 (cf. Matt 15:1–20) would also seem to call into question Windisch's interpretation. Jesus' pronouncement that foods do not make a person clean or unclean (Mark 7:18–19; cf. Matt 15:17–18) would exclude Windisch's construal of food as something that elevates John's stature, at least in Mark. On this passage, see, e.g., Jesper Svartvik, *Mark and Mission: Mk 7:1–23 in Its Narrative and Historical Contexts* (ConBNT 32; Stockholm: Almqvist & Wiksell, 2000), esp. 375–402. This criticism of Windisch does not at all plead for the 'consistency' of Mark or Matthew, however. Windisch's interpretation of John's diet would not even work for an author like Luke, who has no parallel to Mark 7:1–23, since in Luke there is also not a parallel to Mark 1:6 and Acts 15 (esp. vv. 22–29) makes affirmations similar to Mark 7:18–19.

[92] Kraeling, *John the Baptist*, respectively 10, 10, 13. Cf. the discussion of John Calvin in chapter 5.

[93] Ibid, 10–13, although it is interesting that wild honey in Mark could mean "honey collected by wild bees or the gum exuded by certain types of trees" (Ibid, 195 n.11, referring to p. 11).

valuable for calling attention to the 'vegetarian' depictions of John's diet in the Slavonic edition of Josephus and the Karshuni *Life of John*.

Gary Yamasaki offers a more recent example of the 'no significance' interpretation of John's diet: "[T]he narrator does not hold the information [in Matt 3:4] . . . to be especially important; this information is presented in summary narrative, as opposed to scene narrative, thus indicating that it is to be considered mere background material."[94] Yamasaki's conclusion is informed by his literary approach to the Matthean Baptist and does not stem, for example, from redactional observations concerning Matthew's use of this Markan material.[95] On the following page of his study, moreover, the conclusion cited immediately above seems not to be followed in that Yamasaki acknowledges that the description does have significance for Matthew: "[T]he narrator gives this description to provide the narratee with information that will help him or her to interpret a passage later in the narrative."[96]

Indeed, Yamasaki seems to abandon his initial conclusion in his later discussion of Q/Matt 11:18: In Matthew, Matt 3:4 serves as background for 11:18–19, so that "the naratee realizes that it [11:18–19] is nothing more than a hyperbolic representation of John's ascetic lifestyle."[97] Yamasaki's interpretation of Matt 3:4 in light of Q/Matt 11:18 is likewise problematic in that it still does not account for the "locusts and wild honey," or how the attribution could have been meaningful in *Mark's* narrative, which lacks material like Q/Matt 11:18. Accordingly, if, as Yamasaki asserts, "the story-line of [Matt] ch. 3 would remain intact without" numerous details, including "the description of John's clothing and food (v. 4),"[98] why does Matthew (or Mark!) bother to include them? If nothing else, Yamasaki's work illustrates the inadequacy of employing a solely literary methodology to the questions pertinent to the present study.

A final attempt to dismiss the importance of John's diet is given by Donald H. Juel: "[H]is diet and clothing are unusual. None of these things is explained further. His diet and clothing apparently mark him as peculiar. Some knowledge of the geographic setting . . . and the peculiar clothing adds depth to the story but is not necessary to appreciate what is happening."[99] To this

---

[94] Yamasaki, *John the Baptist in Life and Death: Audience-Oriented Criticism of Matthew's Narrative* (JSNTSup 167; Sheffield: Sheffield Academic, 1998), 83, on Matt 3:4; cf. p. 143.

[95] Additionally, Yamasaki (26, 29, respectively) can justifiably fault others for uncritically assuming the historicity of Mark 1:6 (P. W. Hollenbach, "Social Aspects of John," 853) or of Mark 1:6∥Matt 3:4 (J. E. Taylor, *Immerser*, 34), but his literary approach to Matt 3:4 does not address the problem either.

[96] Ibid, 84.

[97] Ibid, 122–3; here, 123.

[98] Ibid, 148.

[99] Juel, *The Gospel of Mark* (Interpreting Biblical Texts; Nashville: Abingdon, 1999), 55.

one may respond that the deliberate allusion to the clothing of Elijah in Mark 1:6ab is indeed significant for understanding 'what is happening' (cf. 2 Kgs 1:8, LXX). One cannot on such grounds so easily dismiss the importance of John's food.

7. Marxsen's Alternate Reconstruction of Tradition History

Willi Marxsen is best known for applying redaction criticism to the gospel of Mark. It thus comes as no surprise that his programmatic essay on John the Baptist in Mark is largely concerned with distinguishing between pre-Markan and Markan elements in Mark 1:2–8, among other passages in this gospel.[100] Marxsen disagrees with Lohmeyer that Mark 1:4–8 constitutes an expansion of the citation of 'Isaiah' in Mark 1:2–3. Instead, the earlier "formula quotation" of 1:2–3 should be regarded as a commentary on 1:4–8.[101] Marxsen further maintains that the wilderness motif in 1:2–8 was *Mark's* creation and not taken over from a pre-Markan source.[102] The same is true, he maintains, for Mark's detail about the Baptist's diet.[103] Marxsen's argument that the Baptist's diet stems not from a pre-Markan source is tenuous at best, however, in that it is based on the supposed silence about John in the wilderness in the Fourth Gospel [*sic*: John 1:23] and in the (partially preserved) *Gospel of the Ebionites*.[104]

Concerning the gospel of Mark as a whole, Marxsen states plausibly that "Mark composes backward" in that "what follows interprets what precedes. . . . What precedes (the Baptist) takes its shape from what follows (Jesus)."[105] In the case of Mark 1:4–8 and 1:2–3, Marxsen takes this principle "one step further back," to the effect that the Baptist (1:4–8) interprets the preceding OT citation (1:2–3).[106] A deficiency in Marxsen's analysis of 1:2–8 is his inability to relate Mark's detail about John's diet to either Jesus or the OT citation. Indeed, Marxsen is aware that Mark 1:6 does not 'fit' his hypothesis concerning 1:2–8 but nonetheless states without argument: "It is

---

[100] Marxsen, "John the Baptist," in: idem, *Mark the Evangelist: Studies on the Redaction History of the Gospel* (Nashville: Abingdon, 1969 [1956, [2]1959]), 30–53.

[101] Ibid, 31–2.

[102] Ibid, 35, following K. L. Schmidt, *Rahmen*, 21–2. Cf. Rudolf K. Bultmann, *The History of the Synoptic Tradition* (Oxford: Blackwell, [2]1968 [[2]1931]), 245–7.

[103] Marxsen, "John the Baptist," 35–6.

[104] There is no reason to suspect that the authors of Mark, John and *Gos. Eb.* would have reflected their source materials extensively or even with the same redactional principles. Thus, the silence of the Fourth Gospel and *Gos. Eb.* about the Baptist's diet does not offer a compelling reason for regarding Mark 1:6 as a Markan composition. Cf. John 1:23: "He said, 'I am the voice of one crying out in the wilderness, Make straight the way of the Lord,' as the prophet Isaiah said."

[105] Marxsen, "John the Baptist," 32, 33; the parenthetical clarifications are original.

[106] Ibid, 33–4; cf. 42.

best to proceed from vs. 6, which of course cannot be clearly interpreted. Yet this much appears to emerge with relative certainty: the diet points to a vegetarian ascetic. . . ."[107] These shortcomings in Marxsen's analysis warrant in the present study a different approach more in line with Lohmeyer's traditio-critical hypothesis.

8. John and the Cuisine at Qumran: Filson, Davies and Charlesworth

Floyd V. Filson was among the first scholars[108] to connect John's diet with both the wilderness and the Qumran community: "All four Gospels agree that John preached *in the wilderness*, a phrase from Isa. xl. 3; only Matt. adds *of Judea*, which indicates strictly the barren region west of the Dead Sea (including the region of the Qumran sect). . . ."[109] He further notes that the Baptist "ate food available in the wilderness."[110] Filson's comparison emphasizes only how John's location in the wilderness influenced the Baptist's cuisine, as he does not seem to be aware that the Damascus Document from Qumran actually mentions locusts as food. Others who have emphasized John's diet in light of QL include S. L. Davies and James H. Charlesworth.[111]

---

[107] Ibid, 36. Marxsen accounts for the lack of explanation within Mark for the details of 1:4–6 in terms of the purpose for which Mark composed these verses, i.e., to 'prove' the fulfillment of 1:2–3 by John's association with "the wilderness" (37–8). This part of Marxsen's analysis is also problematic in that it does not follow. We are to suppose that "Mark composes backward" and read Mark 1:2–3 in light of what is later said about John in Mark 1:4–6. Yet the brevity in 1:4–6 is explained by the desire to 'prove' John's association with the wilderness. Additionally, when part of the passage (1:6, on John's diet) does not fit Marxsen's redactional hypothesis, he simply ignores it. Given the distinctiveness of Mark 1:6 and the lack of an explanation given within 1:2–8, it makes better sense (following Lohmeyer) to regard this verse as pre-Markan, rather than a Markan composition.

[108] Already John M. Allegro, *The Dead Sea Scrolls* (London: Penguin Books, ²1958 [1956]), 163–5; here, 164: "We are told that besides his wearing of only the simplest garments, he ate only honey and locusts, both of which are mentioned in the food laws at the end of the Damascus Document. This again may indicate that the food he was able to eat was strictly limited owing to his purity vows taken in the Community."

[109] Filson, *A Commentary on the Gospel according to St. Matthew* (HNTC; New York: Harper, 1960), 64, emphases original.

[110] Ibid, 65.

[111] Charlesworth, "John the Baptizer and Qumran Barriers in Light of the *Rule of the Community*," in: *The Provo International Conference on the Dead Sea Scrolls* (STDJ 30; ed. D. W. Parry and E. Ulrich; Leiden: Brill, 1999), 353–75, esp. 353–6, 366–8. S. L. Davies, "John the Baptist and Essene Kashruth," *NTS* 29 (1983): 569–71, maintains that John's eating "locusts and wild honey" did not make him an ascetic; rather, it was concerned with ritual purity. Davies and Charlesworth also call attention to the prescription of the Damascus Document 12:13 that one needs to be careful not to eat the larvae of bees when eating honey. Additionally, the Damascus Document 12:14–15 states that roasted or boiled locusts may also be eaten. These scholars do not, however, explain how the Essenes were concerned about purity in connection with the consumption of bee honey.

Against a direct (or even an indirect) influence of the Qumran community, it may simply be noted that the eating of locusts would not have been regarded as a distinctive activity for either John or certain Essenes. The comparison is not a compelling one, for as is discussed in chapter 2 locusts were a common food in much of the ancient Near East and could hardly be construed as distinctive among Palestinian Jews, much less the Essenes.

9. John's Diet as a Recognized Problem: Andersen, Scobie, Vielhauer, Boismard and Böcher

The studies of five scholars, F. I. Andersen, Charles H. H. Scobie, Philipp Vielhauer, M. É. Boismard and Otto Böcher, reflect that John's diet was recognized as meriting more focused attention between 1961 and 1971 than it had received previously. The first of these to appear is the important article by F. I. Andersen, who begins with a discussion of different terms for "locust" in the HB and the ancient Near East, as well as certain ancient testimonies to locust eaters in Herodotus, Pliny (E), Strabo and Jerome.[112] A significant insight concerns the popularity of locusts among the Babylonians (Assyrians?), who "evidently prized [them] as a delicacy."[113] Since locusts could constitute both a treat at royal banquets and a common food for the poor masses, Mark 1:6c cannot *ipso facto* be assumed to portray John as a poor wilderness dweller or an ascetic.[114]

Also helpful for interpreting John's diet is Josephus's mentioning the abundance of honey produced from bees in the vicinity of Jericho.[115] Andersen does not, however, address the question of historicity of Mark 1:6c‖Matt 3:4c. Instead, he notes simply that "[t]he testimony of ancient geographers and of modern travellers supplies all the confirmation needed" for "the text of the Gospel."[116]

In addition to other patristic testimonies, Andersen may have been the first to mention those of Clement of Alexandria and Theophylactus.[117] Concerning the patristic interpretations of John's diet, Andersen notes plausibly:

---

[112] Andersen, "The Diet of John the Baptist," *AbrN* 3 (1961–62): 60–74; here, 60–1.

[113] Ibid, 60, referring to *CAD* 4.257a.

[114] Likewise, Morna D. Hooker, *The Gospel according to Saint Mark* (BNTC; London: A & C Black/Peabody, MA: Hendrickson, 1991), 37, notes: "Locusts and honey would not be John's entire diet but might well be his greatest delicacies." It does not necessarily follow, however, that since this diet "was permitted in the Torah . . . John stands in the Mosaic tradition" (37).

[115] Andersen, "Diet," 60, referring to Jos., *B.J.* 4.8.3 (§468).

[116] Ibid, 65.

[117] Ibid, 63–4, referring to Clem., *Paed.* 2.1 and Theophylactus of Ochrida, *Commentary on Matthew*.

Western scholars were explaining away a practice which they did not understand because they were una[c]quainted with the eating of locusts, or which they found repulsive because of preconceptions. Just why locusts should not be considered suitable food for a person like John is not clear, but perhaps this prejudice is a genuine survival of the Ebionite outlook.[118]

With an appreciation of the difference between the Synoptic and later patristic materials on John's diet and of the need to explain both, Andersen's article represents the most thorough twentieth-century study of the Baptist's diet.

Given the plethora of explanations for John's diet surveyed thus far in this chapter, sooner or later the need to differentiate between and evaluate the merits of them would be sensed by scholarship. Charles H. H. Scobie offers the first such evaluation of four possible reasons why John may have had such a diet:[119]

1. *Necessity*, because of the difficulties of life in the wilderness. Scobie dismisses this solution as unlikely, because one could easily travel to, e.g., Jericho for supplies. Thus, this diet was John's deliberate choice.
2. John was a *Nazarite* (cf. Num 6:1–21). This option depends on Luke 1:15, which as Scobie correctly notes is "probably legendary to a great extent" and a dubious reference for interpreting Mark 1:6c‖Matt 3:4c.
3. *Essene influence*: Philo, *Hypothetica* 11.8 (*apud* Euseb., *Praep. evang.* 8.11.8), suggests that honey is part of a frugal diet and that some Essenes attended to the swarms of bees. Additionally, the Damascus Document states that as long as the locusts are roasted or boiled, they may be eaten. For Scobie, the problem with this explanation is that at Qumran the diet included also bread and wine, which Mark 1:6c‖Matt 3:4c does not include in John's diet.
4. The analogy of Josephus's *Bannus*: John ate what does not require cultivation or breeding but rather what could be found naturally in the wild.

Concerning the third option, one could add to Scobie's objection that the Damascus Document gives stipulations for eating locusts *and fish* (provided that the blood is drained from the fish beforehand). If John's diet was indeed influenced by the Essenes, why, then, would John, who baptized in the Jordan River (!), not have eaten fish as well?[120]

Scobie himself favors none of the aforementioned interpretations but rather attaches to John's diet a deuteronomistic explanation: John's diet "expressed humiliation before God and symbolized repentance for sin."[121]

---

[118] Ibid, 64, alluding to John's 'vegetarian' diet in *Gos. Eb.*

[119] What follows in the indented section is my paraphrase of, with occasional quotations from, Scobie, *John the Baptist* (Philadelphia: Fortress, 1964), 136–9.

[120] For an affirmation of this solution, see, e.g., É. Trocmé, *Marc*, 29.

[121] Scobie, *John the Baptist*, 139–40; cf. Meier, *Marginal Jew*, 2.49; Martin Luther, *First Lectures on the Psalms* (on Ps 78:46): "And our food should be locusts, so that our place in which we should dwell with God (that is, conscience), the bridegroom with the bride, might be burned and destroyed by the constant anger of remorse (*iram compunctionis*). . . ." (ET:

Although possible, there is no evidence for connecting such a diet with repentance or waiting for God's promised deliverance. Thus, Scobie offers an apt critique of certain studies but does not himself advance the discussion of the historical Baptist's diet.

Despite the title, nearly all of Philipp Vielhauer's essay is devoted to John's clothing rather than his diet.[122] Given the lack of an overt comparison of John with Jesus in Mark 1:6, Vielhauer suggests that it may be accurate historically: "Vor allem in der Notiz v.6 findet sich kein christliches Element; sie dürfte eine historisch zuverlässige Nachricht sein."[123] Concerning the locusts and wild honey, Vielhauer refers to studies by J. J. Hess[124] and Gustaf Dalman[125] and notes simply, "Die Heuschrecken und der wilde Honig, die in der handschriftlichen Überlieferung zu zivilisierteren Speisen umgedeutet wurden, gehören zu der kargen Nahrung der Beduinen."[126] Vielhauer's arguments for the historicity and pre-Markan character of Mark 1:6c are followed by Rudolf Pesch.[127]

For his part, M. É. Boismard accounts for the difference between Mark 1:6c ("locusts [ἀκρίδες] and wild honey") and *Gos. Eb.* ("wild honey, of

---

Luther's Works [gen. eds. Jaroslav Pelikan and Helmut T. Lehmann; Saint Louis, MO: Concordia Publishing House/Philadelphia: Fortress, 1955–86], 11.84; Lat.: *D. Martin Luthers Werke: Kritische Gesamtausgabe* [Weimar: Böhlau, 1883–], 1/3.593).

[122] Vielhauer, "Tracht und Speise Johannes des Täufers," 47–54; pp. 48–53 are concerned with John's clothing.

[123] Ibid, 47; cf. 53–54; U. B. Müller, *Johannes der Täufer*, 23, who also notes correctly the lack of a christological comparison in Mark 1:6.

[124] Hess, "Beduinisches zum Alten und Neuen Testament," *ZAW* 35 (1915): 120–36, esp. 123–4 on locusts; and 131 on Mark 1:6 and similarities to Bedouins' clothing (but not their diet).

[125] Gustaf Dalman, *Orte und Wege Jesu* (Schriften des Deutschen Palästina-Instituts 1; Gütersloh: C. Bertelsmann, ³1924 [1919]), 92; ET: *Sacred Sites and Ways: Studies in the Topography of the Gospels* (London: SPCK/New York: Macmillan, 1935), 84: "Locusts, which the Baptist ate . . . (Mt. iii. 4), are, as a matter of fact, found more frequently in uncultivated districts than in cultivated. . . . But it is clear from the uncertainty of the coming of the locusts [that] they cannot be considered as a regular article of food. . . . The Baptist would naturally have had to depend on other things which the desert offered, besides locusts and honey." Dalman thus casts some doubt upon the claim of Matt 3:4.

[126] Vielhauer, "Tracht und Speise," 53. Given Dalman's word of caution (at least concerning Matt 3:4), it is surprising not to find mention of this difficulty in Vielhauer. Dalman's study is cited selectively also by David E. Garland in the *Zondervan Illustrated Bible Backgrounds Commentary* (Vol. 1: *Matthew, Mark, Luke*; gen. ed. C. E. Arnold; Grand Rapids: Zondervan, 2002), 210.

[127] Pesch, "Anfang des Evangeliums Jesu Christi," 316: "Unzweifelhaft ist auch V. 6 ein von Markus übernommenes Traditionsstück." Following Vielhauer, Pesch (321) also argues for the historicity of Mark 1:6: "Wie die voraufgehenden beiden Verse bildet auch V. 6 eine Verbindung von historischer Überlieferung und kerygmatischer Deutung." To support an ascetic interpretation, Pesch (321–2) refers to Q/Luke 7:31–35‖Matt 11:16–19.

which the taste was that of manna, like cakes [ὡς ἔγκρις] in olive oil") in terms of the independence of these 'gospel' traditions. The argument offers a useful and perennially necessary caution against assuming that *Gos. Eb.* reflects a revision of 'our' Mark or Matthew.[128] Boismard's article does not adequately account for the origin of the two different depictions of John's diet, however. Given Boismard's source-critical reconstruction, there would be no reason for John to have been *transformed into* a locust eater in a later stratum of the Synoptic tradition. On the contrary, this chapter has already noted certain 'vegetarian' tendencies in antiquity that could well explain a shift in the other direction, that is, from 'our' Mark or Matthew (or their prototypes or sources) to the version of John's diet in *Gos. Eb.*[129] At least with regard to John's diet, then, Boismard's arguments for a particular—and in the view of this author unnecessarily complex, if not speculative—explanation of the Synoptic Problem are neither helpful nor compelling.

Otto Böcher's article on Q/Luke 7:33 gives attention also to Mark 1:6c. Although Böcher notes correctly the difference between Mark 1:6c and this Q material, he nonetheless argues that the former Synoptic passage offers an illustration of the latter:

> Wenn also der Täufer Heuschrecken (als feste Nahrung) und Honig (als Getränk) genießt, so bedeutet das unbezweifelbar den Verzicht auf Fleisch und Wein. Johannes reiht sich damit ein in die große Schar der antiken Asketen, die sich wie durch sexuelle Enthaltung so auch durch Fleisch- und Weinverzicht von dämonischer Befleckung freihalten wollen. . . .[130]

Somewhat like Windisch's literary approach, Böcher's socio-historical analysis compares John with various religious ascetics of the ancient world, including Neo-Pythagoreans and Neo-Platonists, to the effect that John's peculiar diet protected him from demonic powers. Böcher's argument that John's diet of locusts and honey-water exemplifies his abstention from meat[131] and wine is guilty of conflating two Synoptic passages (that is, Mark

---

[128] Boismard, "Évangile des Ébionites et problème synoptique (*Mc*, 1, 2–6 et par.)," *RB* 73 (1966): 321–52, esp. 327–8. Cf. Kelhoffer, *Miracle and Mission: The Authentication of Missionaries and Their Message in the Longer Ending of Mark* (WUNT 2.112; Tübingen: Mohr Siebeck, 2000), 123–30.

[129] See further on this point in chapter 5.

[130] Böcher, "Ass Johannes der Täufer kein Brot (Luk. vii. 33)?" *NTS* 18 (1971–72): 90–2; here, 91; cf. 90. Böcher construes μέλι ἄγριον in Mark 1:6c as honey-water, which—he further states with reference to Plato, *Symp.* 203B; Porph., *De antr. nymph.* 16; Luke 24:42; the Essenes, according to Philo (*apud* Euseb., *Praep. evang.* 8.11.8); 1QS 6:4–5; and 1QSa 2:17–21—is feared by the demons and is the 'wine' of the gods.

[131] Böcher's interpretation ("Ass Johannes der Täufer," 92) of ἄρτον as meat in Q/Luke 7:33 posits that ἄρτον misconstrues the Hebrew לֶחֶם in that the latter would include meat. On this point J. P. Meier (*Marginal Jew*, 2.48) is appropriately critical, since ἄρτον is attested only in Luke, and a person who ate locusts would not be 'vegetarian.' Nonetheless,

1:6c‖Matt 3:4c with Luke 1:15b) and, moreover, misconstrues Mark 1:6c as depicting John as a 'vegetarian.' Böcher's arguments are followed by I. Howard Marshall and Michael Tilly.[132] Nonetheless, even if Böcher's interpretations of these two Synoptic passages (individually and collectively) are problematic, his calling attention to the protection from demons afforded by a particular diet is intriguing.

The aforementioned studies by Andersen, Scobie, Vielhauer, Boismard and Böcher that appeared in the 1960s and early 70s are noteworthy for the additional attention they devote to John's diet. Andersen's encyclopedic article calls attention to numerous materials in need of further analysis. Scobie was the first scholar to differentiate between and critique certain explanations for the Baptist's cuisine. Vielhauer at least places "Speise Johannes" in the title of his article, even if he is primarily interested in the Baptist's "Tracht." Boismard brings certain distinctive readings of *Gos. Eb.* into the larger question of the Synoptic Problem. Finally, Böcher construes John's diet of locusts and honey-water as an abstention from meat that offered a safeguard from demons. The preceding analysis has lauded positive contributions in each of these studies but has also noted that the fundamental question, Why John is presented as eating "locusts and wild honey," has yet to be resolved satisfactorily.

10. John's 'Natural' Food: R. H. Smith, E. F. Lupieri and J. E. Taylor

Although reflecting the errors of harmonization and 'vegetarianism,' Robert H. Smith's commentary is innovative for highlighting that John's food occurs naturally in the wild: "John's diet was locusts and wild honey, food provided by the grace of the Creator, not produced by human labor or effort of cultivation. . . . It may further signify John's standing as a Nazir (2:23), a holy man who renounced meat and wine. . . ."[133] Edmondo F. Lupieri also emphasizes John's adherence to "the levitical norms of purity for food" and decision "to eat only what is produced by nature, avoiding food prepared by human hands."[134] Similarly, Joan E. Taylor finds an analogy to John's food in Josephus's Bannus, who, like John, lived in the wilderness and, moreover, was "wearing only clothing that trees provided and eating what grew on its

---

Robert A. Guelich, *Mark 1–8:26* (WBC 34A; Dallas, TX: Word, 1989), 21 follows Böcher's construal of John as a 'vegetarian' and μέλι ἄγριον as non-alcoholic honey-water.

[132] Marshall, *Luke*, 301; Tilly, *Johannes der Täufer*, 38, construes locusts and 'honey-water' (Honigwasser) "als Surrogate für Fleisch und Wein." Tilly continues, "Ein solcher Nahrungsverzicht begegnet nun auch als Kennzeichen verschiedener Propheten" (38).

[133] R. H. Smith, *Matthew* (ACNT; Minneapolis: Augsburg, 1989), 50.

[134] Lupieri, "John the Baptist in New Testament Traditions and History," *ANRW* 2/26/1 (1993): 430–61; here, 439; cf. 440; idem, "'The Law and the Prophets Were until John': John the Baptist between Jewish Halakhot and Christian History of Salvation," *Neot* 35 (2001): 49–56; here, 51.

own accord."[135] The comparison made by Lupieri and Taylor is helpful insofar as locusts and wild honey "were neither subject to human control nor the
result of human labor," and "[i]n Hebrew מִדְבָּר refers to uncultivated land,
as does the equivalent Greek word ἔρημος."[136]

11. Ulrich Luz on the History of Interpretation of Matt 3:4

In his important commentary on Matthew, Ulrich Luz suggests the likeli-
hood that Matt 3:4c was *interpreted* as a model for ascetic practices:

> Naturally the verse describes John also as ascetic. Even if nothing else was originally
> thought of but the food and clothing of Bedouins, the description of John must have been
> seen as ascetic. . . . The description hardly has a paranetic undertone. Nevertheless, the
> passage was *interpreted paranetically* as an explanation of the church and thereby was
> drawn into the maelstrom of church disputes.[137]

In distinguishing between the pre-Matthean (possibly also pre-Markan)
meaning of John's diet, Matthew's (allegedly) ascetic characterization of John
and the hortatory interpretations derived from that diet in later centuries, Luz
appreciates a diversity of meaning *within* the Synoptic tradition, and not simply after Mark and Matthew in the patristic literature. Given his interest in
Matthew's history of interpretation, it comes as no surprise that Luz calls attention to certain understandings of the Baptist's diet through the centuries,
including those of John Chrysostom ("We want to imitate him") and even
John Calvin.[138]

12. John's 'Liberationist' Diet? (M. E. Boring, W. Carter and
E. LaVerdiere)

Yet another interpretation of John's diet is given by M. Eugene Boring,
who combines an identification of John in the wilderness with the Baptist's
testimony against the rich: "The description of John's clothing and food
serves to separate him from elegant society and to identify him with the wil-

---

[135] Taylor, *The Immerser: John the Baptist within Second Temple Judaism* (Studying the
Historical Jesus; Grand Rapids: Eerdmans/London: SPCK, 1997), 34, referring to Jos., *Vita*
2 §11; cf. Trocmé, *Marc*, 29.

[136] Ibid; already William H. Brownlee, "John the Baptist in the New Light of Ancient
Scrolls," in: *The Scrolls and the New Testament* (ed. Krister Stendahl; New York: Harper,
1957), 33–53; here, 33: "this food represents that which grows by itself in nature, without
cultivation or breeding" and "may represent a repudiation of civilization as corrupting."

[137] Luz, *Matthew: A Commentary* (Hermeneia; 2 Vols.; Minneapolis: Augsburg Fortress,
1990–2001 [1985]), 1.168, emphasis original.

[138] Luz concludes (168 n.15): "The connections between" later Christian interpretations of
John "and the ascetic and monastic movements are as clear as day." Viewed in this light,
modern 'vegetarian' construals of John's diet could well be a recent revival of hailing the
Baptist as an ethical model. See further on Chrysostom and Calvin in chapter 5.

derness that was to be the scene of eschatological renewal."[139]   Warren Carter also understands John's diet as a criticism of the rich.[140]   Somewhat analogously, Eugene LaVerdiere draws a connection between John's diet and Jesus' later instructions to the disciples in Mark 6:8–10 "to take no possessions" but rather "to accept whatever local hospitality provided."[141]   The implicit assumption in these quasi-liberationist interpretations of Matt 3:4c is that eating "locusts and wild honey" identifies the Baptist with the poor. As noted above and is to be addressed further in chapter 2, however, such a motivation or social location for an ancient Mediterranean locust eater cannot be assumed.

13. Summation

This survey of scholarship on John's diet reveals that there is not—nor has there ever been—a consensus concerning what ἀκρίδες καὶ μέλι ἄγριον means in Mark 1:6c‖Matt 3:4c. The most prevalent interpretations maintain that "locusts and wild honey," however construed, highlight John as prophet, wilderness dweller, ascetic or 'vegetarian.' Of course, no two of these interpretations are mutually exclusive, and it is not uncommon to find overlapping or complementary explanations given in the secondary literature. A recurrent weakness in interpretations of Mark 1:6c‖Matt 3:4c is that they ignore the possibility that this characterization could have meant different things for the historical John, the author of Mark and the author of Matthew. An additional shortcoming concerns the lack of argument or historical analogy in support of any given interpretation of John's diet.

It is for these reasons that the present study considers Mark 1:6c‖Matt 3:4c in light of actual locust eaters in antiquity (chap. 2), ancient conceptions of "wild honey" (chap. 3), and the interpretations of John's diet in the Synoptic gospels (chap. 4) and in the early church (chap. 5). The topics to be addressed in chapters 2, 3 and 4 have up to this point yet to receive a full investigation. Furthermore, the interpretation of Mark 1:6c‖Matt 3:4c in the early church also merits a comprehensive analysis. It is thus hoped that the reader's appe-

---

[139] Boring, "Matthew," *New Interpreter's Bible* (Vol. VIII; Nashville: Abingdon, 1995), 156.

[140] Carter, *Matthew and the Margins: A Sociopolitical and Religious Reading* (The Bible and Liberation; Maryknoll, NY: Orbis, 2000), 95: "His food denotes poverty, as well as his commitment to trust in God by not being distracted . . . because of concern with daily food (cf. 6:25–34. 11). He is indebted to no one. . . . John's unusual food . . . presents a critique of the economic extravagance of the powerful elite, who maintain their own abundance at the expense of the poor. . . ."

[141] LaVerdiere, *The Beginning of the Gospel: Introducing the Gospel according to Mark* (Collegeville, MN: Liturgical Press, 1999), 31–2. It is not clear, however, if LaVerdiere thinks that the author of Mark presents the Baptist (or Jesus' disciples) as a model of either discipleship or missionary activity.

tite is whetted to learn more about John's diet and that this inquiry will further the understanding of John's place within Second Temple Judaism and legacy in early Christianity.

Chapter 2

Locust/Grasshopper Eating in Ancient Near Eastern and Greco-Roman Antiquity

μὴ μεριμνᾶτε τῇ ψυχῇ ὑμῶν τί φάγητε. (Matt 6:25a)

A. Introduction

Neither Mark nor Matthew specifies why John the Baptist ate ἀκρίδες καὶ μέλι ἄγριον, or how this particular diet contributes to their presentations of the Baptist in Mark 1:2–8 and Matt 3:1–6. As a result, the interpreter must ask what the depiction of an eater of grasshoppers/locusts and unrefined honey could mean to an ancient audience. As indicated in chapter 1, such a study has yet to be done and is the task of this and the following chapter. It is not the assumption of the present study that all people in antiquity would have had the same understanding of what such a diet would mean, or that the historical John, the author of Mark and the author of Matthew would have given the same explanation for its significance. Indeed, in chapter 4 it is argued that different shades of meaning (or lack thereof) are to be noted for the Baptist and these two evangelists.

Although honey remains to this day a common food in many parts of the Western and the Two-Thirds World, the idea of eating locusts, grasshoppers or cicadas has long been regarded as peculiar in many, particularly Western, cultures.[1] Partially for this reason, this chapter on John's lo-

---

[1] As Marston Bates, "Insects in the Diet," 43, among others, observes: "Insects are an important element in human diet in many parts of the world, but they have long been taboo in European civilizations." Bates further notes, "There is one striking exception to the Western refusal of insects as food—honey. To be sure, honey is not an insect, but it is an insect product, and a very intimate product at that, for the bees have to carry the nectar home in their crops to regurgitate it into the honeycomb" (44). Similarly, in a broad and comprehensive survey of Talmudic and other witnesses to the Palestinian 'food basket,' Magen Broshi, "The Diet of Palestine in the Roman Period — Introductory Notes," *Israel Museum Journal* 5 (1986): 41–56, notes that "grasshoppers (locusts)" are "virtually the only food eaten in antiquity that is not consumed today" (51). Cf. Joseph C. Bequaert, "Insects as Food: How They Have Augmented the Food Supply of Mankind in Early and Recent Times," *Natural History* 21 (1921): 191–200; here, 191; Ronald L. Taylor, *Butterflies in My Stomach, Or: Insects in Human Nutrition* (Santa Barbara, CA: Woodbridge, 1975), 15–21.

custs/grasshoppers is longer than the discussion in chapter 3 of his "wild honey." This chapter will evaluate a plethora of ancient sources with reference to understandings of eating such insects in antiquity, in order to provide the background necessary for assessing the historical plausibility of Mark 1:6c and Matt 3:4c.[2] In chapter 4, it will then be possible to assess whether "locusts and wild honey" were important to John, or at least why they were deemed to be significant by the author of Mark or his/her source material. In chapter 4 it will also be asked whether this characterization should be interpreted on a socio-historical or a literary level, with an eye to John's prophetic role.[3]

B. Prolegomena: What is a 'Locust'?

For philologists and anthropologists alike, the task of distinguishing between references to locusts, grasshoppers and cicadas can be exasperating.[4] Depending on whom a person reads, or asks, a word that usually denotes a 'locust' may in a particular context refer to a 'grasshopper,' and vice-versa. Adding to the confusion is the immense variety of species of grasshoppers that exists in our world today. A clarification of terms is thus necessary before the ancient evidence is examined.

In modern scientific taxonomy, locusts and grasshoppers are not two different insects: "All grasshoppers (except the so-called long-horned

---

[2] As is noted in chapter 1, Mark 1:6 claims only that John was in the habit of eating "locusts and wild honey" (ἦν . . . ἐσθίων ἀκρίδας καὶ μέλι ἄγριον), possibly among other items during his time "in the wilderness." Matt 3:4, however, states that John's wilderness food was only "locusts and wild honey" (ἡ δὲ τροφὴ ἦν αὐτοῦ ἀκρίδες καὶ μέλι ἄγριον).

[3] Chapter 4 will also consider the function of Mark 1:6c as a part of 1:2–8 and examine what light these observations shed on this diet for the historical Baptist and the author of Mark. It will be argued that within Mark 1:2–8 Mark 1:6c complements other characterizations of John in ths wilderness. The function of Matt 3:4c within Matt 3:1–6 and the possible reasons for Luke's omission of this Markan material will also be addressed in chapter 4.

[4] Ian C. Beavis, *Insects and Other Invertebrates in Classical Antiquity* (Exeter: University of Exeter, 1988), 62: "Because of their song, the harmless species of *akris* are often closely associated with cicadas, and it is probable that there was some degree of confusion between the two groups of insects" (cf. 91–2). Mark Q. Sutton, *Insects as Food: Aboriginal Entomophagy in the Great Basin* (Ballena Press Anthropological Papers 33; Menlo Park, CA: Ballena, 1988), 11, likewise calls attention to this problem for the contemporary anthropologist: "Grasshoppers and locusts (Orthoptera:Locustidae) are here considered under the same heading due to their general similarity and to the difficulty in separating the different genera in the ethnographic literature (e.g., one native group denied eating grasshoppers, but said they did eat locusts, which may have actually been cicadas)." Cf. Taylor, *Butterflies*, 146.

grasshoppers) belong to the super family *Acridoidea*."[5] Locusts comprise a specific kind, or genus, of grasshoppers. The 'family' name given to most locusts is *acrididae*, who belong to the 'order' *orthoptera* (= "straight-winged").[6] It may be counterintuitive to the non-scientist that successive generations *of the same type of locust* can exhibit remarkable differences in physiology, including body structure and color, as well as social behavior. According to the "phase theory" pioneered by entomologist Boris P. Uvarov in the early-twentieth century, locusts are polymorphic insects that exist, alternatively, in 'solitary,' 'transitional' and 'gregarious' phases.[7] 'Solitary' locusts (*solitaria*) act much like other kinds of grasshoppers and are not a threat to crops or other vegetation. Young 'solitary' locusts can, however, enter a 'transitional' phase (*transiens*) before swarms of 'gregarious' locusts (*gregaria*) appear. What distinguishes the gregarious phase of locusts from the solitary phase is the gregarious locusts' comparatively longer rear legs for jumping, proclivity for migration over long distances, procreation *en masse*, and, of course, ravenous appetite. To the unsuspecting farmer, there is naturally a huge difference between a harmless handful of grasshoppers or 'solitary' locusts and a smothering swarm of devouring, 'gregarious' locusts.[8] It thus comes as no surprise that a plurality of terms in languages ancient and modern came to designate grasshoppers and (different phases of) locusts.

In both the Jewish and the Christian tradition, the most well-known locust in scripture is the Desert Locust (*schistocerca gregaria*). It is this particular kind of locust that the Lord is said to have sent against the Egyptians (Exod 10:3–20) and, later, threatened against the disobedient covenant people (for example, Deut 28:38). For those who read the Christian Bible from a 'ca-

---

[5] Alison Steedman, ed., *Locust Handbook* (Kent, UK: Natural Resources Institute, Overseas Development Administration, [3]1990), 2.

[6] Although the bodies of grasshoppers and cicadas are quite similar, cicadas are differentiated from locusts by their wider (butterfly-like) wings and for this reason belong to a different order, *homoptera*.

[7] See Uvarov, *Grasshoppers and Locusts: A Handbook of General Acridology* (Cambridge: Cambridge University, [2]1966–77 [1928]), 1.332–86, 2.142–219; Jacob C. Faure, *The Phases of Locusts in South Africa* (London: Imperial Institute of Entomology, 1932 [= *Bulletin of Entomological Research* 23 [1932]: 293–405 + Plates]); Lucy W. Clausen, *Insect: Fact and Folklore* (New York: Macmillan, 1954), 172–3; John Ledger, "The Eighth Plague Returneth! The Locusts Are Coming!" *African Wildlife* (Linden, South Africa) 41 (1987): 197–210; here, 198–9; Steedman, *Locust Handbook*, 2–3, 21–32.

[8] Concerning the Desert Locust (*schistocerca gregaria*), Allan S. Gilbert, "The Flora and Fauna of the Ancient Near East," in: *Civilizations of the Ancient Near East* (ed. Jack M. Sasson; New York: Scribner's, 1995), 1.153–74, notes: "Normally existing in a harmless, dispersed 'solitarious' phase, they grow larger and darker in color under conditions of increased population density and ultimately coalesce into the ravenous migrating hordes of their 'gregarious' phase, which may last up to several years bringing with it the inevitable ruin evoked by the Eighth Plague of Exodus 10" (1.172). Cf. Ael., *NA* 10.13.

nonical' perspective (whether intentionally or subconsciously), it might be all too easy to infer that *schistocerca gregaria* is the type of ἀκρίς named in Mark 1:6c‖Matt 3:4c. The translation of ἀκρίς as "locust" can reinforce this interpretation. It must be remembered, however, that the Desert Locust is not the only species of locust/grasshopper indigenous to Palestine. Others include the Moroccan Locust (*Dociostaurus maroccanus*), the Tree Locust (*Anacridium melanorhodon arabafrum*), and the Sudan Plague Locust (*Aiolopus simulatrix*).[9]

It is also noteworthy that neither Mark 1:6 nor Matt 3:4 suggests that the Baptist was grazing upon the remnant of a locust/grasshopper infestation. Nor is there evidence that such an infestation occurred during the Baptist's lifetime. For the following reasons, then, "grasshoppers" is the preferred English translation of ἀκρίδες in Mark 1:6c[10] and Matt 3:4c:

1. In Greek, ἀκρίδες does not designate a particular kind of grasshopper or locust, whether 'solitary,' 'transient' or 'gregarious.'
2. Rendering ἀκρίδες as "locusts" in Mark 1:6c‖Matt 3:4c runs the risk of leading many Western readers to make one, possibly two, unwarranted assumptions. The first is that John dined on a 'plague' of 'gregarious' locusts that had invaded Palestine from Eastern Africa (or elsewhere). The other is that Mark 1:6c‖Matt 3:4c intends some 'intertextuality' with the locusts predicted by the Hebrew prophet Joel.
3. Biologically, the broader English term "grasshopper" includes locusts and corresponds to the more general term given to this family of insects (*acrididae*).

In light of these considerations, the analysis to follow will give full weight to the ambiguity inherent in the term ἀκρίς in Mark 1:6c‖Matt 3:4c and will consider a variety of ancient testimonies to locusts/grasshoppers, regardless of an author's intended or actual referent.

---

[9] Additionally, Frederick S. Bodenheimer, "Note on Invasions of Palestine by Rare Locusts," *IEJ* 1 (1950–51): 146–8; here, 146, notes that, in addition to *schistocerca gregaria*, "The European locust (*Locusta migratoria* L.), is common in all the more humid habitats of Palestine, but generally only in its solitary phase," rather than its notorious 'gregarious' phase. Bodenheimer (147–8) calls attention also to "the Moroccan locust (*Dociostaurus maroccanus* Thnbg.)," which "lives permanently in Palestine without ever causing damage or increasing" in numbers. In its 'gregarious' phase, however, it did infest Palestine 1897–1900 and again in the mid-twentieth century, at the time Bodenheimer wrote this article. See further Steedman, ed., *Locust Handbook*, 104, 110, 113, 117 (with maps).

[10] With Joel Marcus, *Mark 1–8*, p. 149.

C. From Leviticus to Moses Maimonides:
Locust Eating in Jewish Literature and the Ancient Near East

1. Overview: "Locusts" in the Hebrew Bible

Most passages in Hebrew scripture and Second Temple Jewish literature that mention locusts are concerned with the crops these insects devour. For example, the Lord who sent a plague of locusts against the Egyptians[11] could also send them against the covenant people.[12] The prophet Malachi offers a corollary to this affliction by way of the Lord's promise to remove the locust: "I will rebuke the locust for you (וגערתי לכם באכל), so that it will not destroy the produce of your soil; and your vine in the field shall not be barren, says the LORD of hosts."[13]

Numerous other ancient Jewish authors refer to locusts metaphorically, to highlight the size of a crowd,[14] frighteningly rapid movement,[15] or the shortness of life.[16] Likewise, the prophet Nahum bases a threefold metaphor on

---

[11] E.g., Exod 10:3–20; Wis 16:8–9; *Jub.* 48.5; Ezek. Trag. 144–146 (*apud* Cornelius Alexander Polyhistor [*c.* 105 B.C.E.–after 80 B.C.E.], *apud* Euseb., *Praep. evang.* 9.28–29); Artapanus (*apud* Alexander Polyhistor, *apud* Euseb., *Praep. evang.* 9.27.32); Philo, *De vita Mos.* 1.121, 122, 126; cf. 1.145; Jos., *Ant.* 2.14.4 (§306) (on Exodus 10); Ronald Hendel, "The Exodus in Biblical Memory," *JBL* 120 (2001): 601–22, esp. 610 on the 8th c. B.C.E. curse involving hail and locusts in Sefire I.25–28.

[12] Deut 28:38; 1 Kgs 8:37 = 2 Chr 6:28; 2 Chr 7:13; Pss 78:46, 105:34; Joel 1:4, 2:25; Amos 4:9, 7:1; Philo, *Praem.* 128.3 (alluding to Deut 28:38).

[13] Mal 3:11; cf. Hom., *Od.* 4.287–288; Cyranides 3.33.9–12; Diod. Sic., *Hist.* 1.87.6; Aristonicus Alex., *De sig. Od.* 4.285–289; Strabo, *Geog.* 13.1.64.

[14] Judg 6:5: The enemy came with "their tents, as thick as locusts" (cf. 7:12); Jer 46:23, concerning the enemies of Egypt: "They shall cut down her forest, says the LORD, though it is impenetrable, because they are more numerous than locusts; they are without number" (cf. 46:20–22); and against Babylon: "Surely I will fill you with troops like a swarm of locusts, and they shall raise a shout of victory over you" (Jer 51:14; also 51:27: "bring up horses like bristling locusts"). Similarly, Judith 2:20 describes a "mixed crowd like a swarm of locusts." Cf. Din., *Fr.* 6.3 (*apud* Harp., *Lex.* 54.3), Greek texts: Nicos C. Conomis, ed., *Dinarchi, Orationes cum fragmentis* (Teubner; Leipzig: Teubner, 1975), 80–1; Wilhelm Dindorf, ed., *Harpocrationis, Lexicon in decem oratories Atticos* (Oxford: Oxford University, 1853), 54; Menander Protector (Hist.; 6th c. C.E.), *Fr.* 108; Greek: L. A. Dindorf, ed., *Historici Graeci minores* (Teubner; Leipzig: Teubner, 1870–71), 2.108, ll. 19–24.

[15] A horse leaps like a locust (Job 39:20; the context in vv. 19–25 suggests that the horse should thus be feared); Isa 33:4: "Spoil was gathered as the caterpillar gathers; as locusts leap, they leaped upon it." So also Sir 43:17, referring to the snow: "its descent is like locusts alighting." In the NT, moreover, note the eschatological context of Rev 9:1–11, where locusts (ἀκρίδες, Rev 9:3, 7) are sent "not to damage the grass of the earth or any green growth or any tree, but only those people who do not have the seal of God on their foreheads" (9:4). So also Herm. *Vis.* 4.1.6 (ἀκρίδες πύριναι).

[16] In Psalm 109, an individual Psalm of lament, the petitioner complains, "I am gone like a shadow at evening; I am shaken off like a locust" (Ps 109:23). Similarly, 2 Esdr 4:24

the ability of locusts to devour, multiply and shed their 'skin.'[17] Perhaps the only positive reference to locusts in the HB—notably, in their 'gregarious' phase—is the admiration conferred in Proverbs 30 for their ability to organize without a recognizable leader.[18]

With regard to the eating of locusts/grasshoppers, Leviticus 11 allows the Israelites to consume four different kinds of 'leaping' insects:

> [20] All winged insects that walk upon all fours are detestable to you. [21] But among the winged insects that walk on all fours you may eat those that have jointed legs above their feet, with which to leap on the ground. [22] Of them you may eat: the locust (ארבה) according to its kind, the bald locust ([?] Heb: סלעם) according to its kind, the cricket ([?] Heb: חרגל) according to its kind, and the grasshopper (חגב) according to its kind. [23] But all other winged insects that have four feet are detestable to you. (Lev 11:20–23)

For reference in later discussions in this chapter, the terms used for "locust" in the HB and LXX at Lev 11:22 are as follows:

Lev 11:22a	ארבה	βροῦχος
Lev 11:22b	סלעם	ἀττάκης
Lev 11:22c	חרגל	ἀκρίς
Lev 11:22d	חגב	ὀφιομάχης

Attention will be given to Lev 11:20–23 in the following section.

In addition to Leviticus 11, the other part of the HB reflecting different terms for locusts is the prophet Joel, who mentions four: the cutting locust (הגזם), swarming locust (הארבה), hopping locust (הילק) and destroying locust (החסיל, Joel 1:4). When this prophet later uses the same four designations, גזם occurs last rather than first in the list of assailants (הארבה הילק והחסיל והגזם, Joel 2:25). In Joel, these terms could designate distinct species of locusts, or different phases of the Desert Locust (*schistocerca gregaria*). Joel either offers the swarming locusts as a meta

---

observes, "We pass from the world like locusts, and our life is like a mist, and we are not worthy to obtain mercy." Cf. *m. Pesaḥ.* 3:5 ("like the horns of a locust").

[17] Nah 3:15–17: "[15] The fire will devour you, the sword will cut you off. It will devour you like the locust. Multiply yourselves like the locust, multiply like the grasshopper! [16] You increased your merchants more than the stars of the heavens. The locust sheds its skin and flies away. [17] Your guards are like grasshoppers, your scribes like swarms of locusts settling on the fences on a cold day—when the sun rises, they fly away; no one knows where they have gone."

[18] Prov 30:24, 27: "Four things on earth are small, yet they are exceedingly wise: . . . the locusts have no king, yet all of them march in rank." Cf. David Daube, "A Quartet of Beasties in the Book of Proverbs," *JTS* n.s. 36 (1985): 380–6, esp. 383–5.

phor for attacking (human) combatants[19] or, more probably, describes an actual plague of locusts in terms of an invading army.[20]

---

[19] This interpretation is sometimes based on the mistaken assumption that locusts would never enter Palestine *from the north*, i.e., from Assyria. See, e.g., Pablo R. Andiñach, "The Locusts in the Message of Joel," *VT* 42 (1992): 433–41, who argues that the locusts in Joel are not actual locusts, because Joel 2:20 refers to a "northerner," and in Palestine "locusts always come from the desert areas of the south" (433). Andiñach also dismisses the interpretation of the locusts as "the eschatological army of God" (436). Instead, Andiñach regards the locusts as a reference to a foreign army (437–9; cf. Ar., *Ach.* 149–152; Nic., *Ther.* 801–805). Additionally, Harold Brodsky, "'An Enormous Horde Arrayed for Battle': Locusts in the Book of Joel," *Bible Review* 6 (1990): 32–9, states erroneously, "The desert locust migrates back and forth, around North Africa and the Near East, from about 5° to about 35° north of the equator. (Israel is the northernmost extension of the locusts' range.)" (34), although he maintains that Joel refers to actual locusts (33–4). See L. W. Clausen, *Insect: Fact and Folklore*, 57–8, on migrations of 'gregarious' locusts from Africa as far north as England and even across the Atlantic Ocean to North America. It thus follows that locusts could well have entered Assyria first and then subsequently into Palestine.

[20] Victor A. Hurowitz, "Joel's Locust Plague in Light of Sargon II's Hymn to Nanaya," *JBL* 112 (1993): 597–603, cites an 8th c. B.C.E. Sumerian (Assyrian) prayer to the goddess Nanaya asking that "the evil locust which destroys the crop/grain . . . be turned into nothing" (597–8; cf. Joel 2:18–27). Hurowitz notes, "nearly every detail in this passage has either general or quite specific parallels in Joel's description of the locusts afflicting Judah" (599). Moreover, Cornelis van Leeuwen, "The 'Northern One' in the Composition of Joel 2,19–27," in: *The Scriptures and the Scrolls* (ed. F. García Martínez et al.; VTSup 49; Leiden: Brill, 1992), 85–99, disagrees with W. van der Meer and others that the 'northern one' is the Babylonian army (90–1). Following Keil (95), van Leeuwen notes ancient witnesses that locusts could on occasion come from the north. These swarming insects are regarded as the Lord's judgment (96–7), and their destructiveness is compared to an invading army (98). See also Ernst Kutsch, "Heuschreckenplage und Tag Jahwes in Joel 1 und 2," *TZ* 18 (1962): 81–94; John A. Thompson, "Joel's Locusts in the Light of Near Eastern Parallels," *JNES* 14 (1955): 52–5; S. R. Driver, "Excursus on Locusts," in: *The Books of Joel and Amos* (ed. H. C. O. Lanchester; Cambridge: Cambridge University, [2]1915), 84–93; Malcolm Davies and Jeyaraney Kathirithamby, *Greek Insects* (New York: Oxford University Press, 1986), 139–41; I. C. Beavis, *Insects*, 73–5; cf. V. A. Hurowitz, "אַרְבֶּה in Malachi 3:11–Caterpillar," *JBL* 121 (2002): 327–30; H. Gossen, "Heuschrecke," art. PW 8/2.1381–6; here, 1385; Peter Garnsey, *Famine and Food Supply in the Graeco-Roman World: Responses to Risk and Crisis* (Cambridge: Cambridge University, 1988), 3–6, 20–5, 196–7; Steedman, ed., *Locust Handbook*, 3–6. For additional references to locust infestations, see Theoc., *Id.* 5.108; Posidonius (Phil), *Fr.* 66.7 (80.8), in: F. Jacoby, *Die Fragmente der griechischen Historiker* [Berlin: Weidmann, 1923–43], 2A.271); Theoc., *Id.* 5.108–111; PTebt 772.1–3 (236 B.C.E.), in: Bernard P. Grenfell et al., eds., *The Tebtunis Papyri* (London: Oxford University, 1902), 3/1.201–2; Philo, *Praem.* 128.3 (alluding to Deut 28:38); Jos., *Ant.* 2.14.4 (§306); Plin. (E), *HN* 11.35.104–106; Ar., *Av.* 588–589; Pausanias, *Descr. Gr.* 1.24.8 (in Attica); Cyranides 1.15.12–14; Gal., *In Hipp. aph.* 1.9.57 (1.5.240–41), in: Karl Gottlob Kühn, ed., *Claudii Galeni, Opera omnia* (Hildesheim: Olms, 2001 [1821]), 17b.484.15–485.2; Nepualius (Med. et Phil.; 2nd c. C.E.?), 86, in: Wilhelm Gemoll, ed., *Nepualii, fragmentum* περὶ τῶν κατὰ ἀντιπάθειαν καὶ συμπάθειαν *et Democriti, περὶ συμπαθειῶν καὶ ἀντιπαθειῶν* (Striegau: Tschörner, 1884), 3; Ael., *NA* 3.12; 17.19 (cf. 11.27); Heph. (Astr.; 4th c. C.E.)

2. The Prescription in Leviticus 11

As the only part of Hebrew scripture to mention locust/grasshopper eating, the aforementioned passage in Leviticus 11 merits additional consideration. The section devoted to food laws in Lev 11:9–42 offers instructions concerning creatures that inhabit the water (11:9–12), the air (11:13–23) and the land (11:24–42). The second part, Lev 11:13–23, is concerned with birds (vv. 13–19) and four (types of?) insects.[21] Scholars are well aware of the difficulty of ascertaining which four insects Lev 11:22 prescribes.[22] In v. 22a, אַרְבֶּה is a generic term for "locust,"

1.20–21, in: David E. Pingree, ed., *Hephaestionis Thebani, Apotelesmaticorum libri tres* (Teubner; Leipzig: Teubner, 1973), 1.48–62; Arnobius, *Adv. Gentes* 1.3–13; August., *Civ. Dei* 3.31; Basil, *Hom.* 8.7; John Cassian, *Adv. Nest.* 7.5; *Geoponica* 1.8, 1.10, 7.1–2; *m. Taʿan.* 3:5; *m. Soṭah* 9:15; *m. B. Meṣiʿa* 9:6; Michael G. Morony, "Michael the Syrian as a Source for Economic History," *Hugoye: Journal of Syriac Studies* 3/2 (2000), online: http://syrcom.cua.edu/Hugoye/Vol3No2/HV3N2Morony.html (on 8 April 2004); Lyd., *Ost.* 56 (194C–D) = Joannes Laurentius Lydus (490–*c.* 560 C.E.), *De Ostentis et calendaria Graeca omnia* (ed. Curt Wachsmuth; Leipzig: Teubner, 1897), 113; Theophylact Simocatta (*c.* late 580s–after 640 C.E.), *Ep.* 41, in: Joseph Zanetto, ed., *Theophylacti Simocatae, Epistulae* (Teubner; Leipzig: Teubner, 1985), 24–5; R. E. A. Sewter, *The Chronographia of Michael Psellus [1018–after 1078 C.E.]* (New Haven: Yale University, 1953), 296 n.32; Frank Cowan, *Curious Facts in the History of Insects, Including Spiders and Scorpions: A Complete Collection of the Legends, Superstitions, Beliefs, and Ominous Signs Connected with Insects, together with Their Uses in Medicine, Art, and as Food and a Summary of Their Remarkable Injuries and Appearances* (Philadelphia: Lippincott, 1865), 101–19; S. Krauss, "Zur Kenntnis der Heuschrecken in Palästina," *ZDPV* 50 (1927): 244–9, esp. 248–9; John D. Whiting, "Jerusalem's Locust Plague: Being a Description of the Recent Locust Influx into Palestine, and Comparing Same with Ancient Locust Invasions as Narrated in the Old World's History Book, the Bible," *The National Geographic Magazine* 28/6 (1915): 511–50; Ledger, "Eighth Plague," 199–203, 210; F. S. Bodenheimer, "Note on Invasions," 147–8. Cf. the fragmentary PColZen 114m 6 (Greek text: William Linn Westermann et al., eds., *Zenon Papyri: Business Papers of the Third Century B.C. Dealing with Palestine and Egypt* [Columbia Papyri, Greek Series 3–4; New York: Columbia University, 1934–40], 2.145) and the predictions of locust attacks in *Sib. Or.* 5.454 (against Cyprus); *3 Bar.* 16.3; Rev 9:3, 7. Finally, in Jos., *B.J.* 4.9.7 (§536), locusts are used in an allusion to war much like they are in Joel: "Just as a forest may be seen stripped quite bare by the locusts ([ὑπὸ] τῶν ἀκρίδων), so in the rear of Simon's army nothing remained but a desert (ἐρημία)."

[21] Jacob Milgrom, *Leviticus 1–16: A New Translation with Introduction and Commentary* (AB 3; New York: Doubleday, 1991–2001), 1.664, notes the following distinction within Lev 11:13–23: "two-legged winged creatures mostly fly, hence they are called birds (vv 13-19), but four-legged creatures mostly walk and for this reason constitute a discrete group." Cf. the later conception of Plutarch, who compares the flying habits of birds and locusts (τέττιγες, in *De soll. an.* 962D).

[22] Milgrom, *Leviticus*, 665–6; idem, "The Biblical Diet Laws as an Ethical System," in: idem, *Studies in Cultic Theology and Terminology* (SJLA 36; Leiden: Brill, 1983), 104–18; Martin Noth, *Leviticus: A Commentary* (OTL; Philadelphia: Westminster, [2]1977), 94; John E. Hartley, *Leviticus* (WBC 4; Dallas, TX: Word, 1992), 161; Philip J. Budd, *Leviticus: Based*

indeed "the most common term in the HB for this species."[23] In v. 22b–c, סלעם and חרגל are *hapax legomena* in the HB and difficult if not impossible to identify. Finally, חגב (v. 22d) in Num 13:33 and Isa 40:22 signifies a "grasshopper."[24]

Whatever their precise identity in Leviticus 11, one may fairly ask why *only these four* insects are allowed to be eaten. Lev 11:21 states simply that these insects' possession of "hind legs above their feet" and corresponding ability to hop rather than crawl distinguishes them from other 'swarmers,' which are forbidden.[25] Frank Gorman finds a basis for this distinction in the order of creation in Genesis 1: "[W]inged insects that walk on all fours" are

---

on the *New Revised Standard Version* (NCB Commentary; London: M. Pickering/Grand Rapids: Eerdmans, 1996), 172; R. K. Harrison, *Leviticus: An Introduction and Commentary* (Downers Grove, IL: Inter-Varsity, 1980), 129; John A. Thompson, "Translation of the Words for Locust," *Bible Translator* 25 (1974): 405–11; Berel Dov Lerner, "Timid Grasshoppers and Fierce Locusts: An Ironic Pair of Biblical Metaphors," *VT* 49 (1999): 545–8 (on Num 13:31–33); S. R. Driver, "Excursus on Locusts," 84–9; H. Brodsky, "Locusts in the Book of Joel," 36; [UBS Committee on Translations], *Fauna and Flora of the Bible* (Helps for Translators 11; London/New York: United Bible Societies, [2]1980), 53; Aryeh Kaplan, *The Living Torah: The Five Books of Moses, A New Translation Based on Traditional Jewish Sources* (New York/Jerusalem: Maznaim, [2]1981), 319–20; Murray B. Isman and Martin S. Cohen, "Kosher Insects," *American Entomologist* 41 (Summer 1995): 100–2; here, 101; Bates, "Insects in the Diet," 45; Edwin Firmage, "Zoology," art. *ABD*, 6.1109–67, esp. 1150 (s.v. 'locusts'); W. W. Frerichs, "Grasshoppers," art. *IDB*, 2.470; F. S. Bodenheimer, "Fauna," art. *IDB*, 2.246–56; here, 254; Y. Palmoni, "Locust," art. *IDB*, 3.144–8; here, 145.

[23] Hartley, *Leviticus*, 161.

[24] Depending on whether one translates primarily for the 'original meaning' or the understanding of a particular contemporary audience, in the NRSV it may be awkward to translate ארבה as "locust" (11:22a) and חגב as "grasshopper" (v. 22d). As noted above, locusts are a particular kind of grasshopper.

[25] Jean Soler, "The Semiotics of Food in the Bible," in: *Food and Drink in History: Selections from the Annales, Économies, Sociétés, Civilisations, Volume 5* (ed. R. Forster and O. Ranum; Baltimore: Johns Hopkins University, 1979), 126–38; here, 135, argues for this interpretation: "The key expression [in Lev 11:20] is 'go upon' [walk]. The insects that are meant here are those that 'go upon all fours,' like the normal beasts of the earth, the quadrupeds. Their uncleanness comes from the fact that they walk rather than fly, even though they are 'winged.' The exception mentioned in Leviticus (11: 21) only confirms the rule: no uncleanness is imputed to insects that have 'legs above their feet, with which to romp on the earth.' Leaping is a mode of locomotion midway between walking and flying. Leviticus feels that it is closer to flying and therefore absolves these winged grasshoppers." So also L. R. Arrington, "Foods of the Bible," *Journal of the American Dietetic Association* 35 (1959): 816–20; here, 818; Mary Douglas, "The Abominations of Leviticus," in: eadem, *Purity and Danger: An Analysis of Concepts of Pollution and Taboo* (New York: Praeger, 1966), 41–57; here, 56: "Whether we call it teeming, trailing, creeping, crawling or swarming, it is an indeterminate form of movement. Since the main animal categories are defined by their typical movement, 'swarming' . . . cuts across the basic classification. . . . The case of the locusts is interesting and consistent." Compare the observation of Arist., *PA* 4.6 (683A) that locusts bend their hind legs inward and can thus jump higher than many other insects.

prohibited because "[t]he means of locomotion is not appropriate for their bodily appearance. They represent a disruption of the normative order . . . [and] are 'detestable' (vv. 20, 23)."[26] In the case of the four insects specified in Lev 11:22, however, "[w]ings are consistent with leaping as a means of locomotion. Thus, they appropriately reflect their location within the created order."[27] From the standpoint of the final editor of Leviticus, such an explanation may well have been employed to sanction toleration for consuming this quartet of winged insects but not other types of insects.

Writing with an expertise in entomology that the present author cannot claim, Murray Isman and Martin Cohen argue that the permission to eat locusts but not other insects is based upon the locusts' 'vegetarian' (that is, non-flesh eating) diet:

> As both the blood and carrion are strictly taboo according to the dietary laws, so are the animals that thrive on them. All flying insects, other than the orthopterans, may have been viewed as predators (blood-feeding dipterans, stinging hymenopterans), or carrion feeders (dipterans). In contrast, orthopterans, particularly locusts and other acridids, are primarily graminivorous.[28]

However attractive from a contemporary point of view, the explanation suffers from an inability to postulate credibly that the author of Lev 11:20–23 possessed such a 'scientific' understanding or justification. Since the eating of blood is a concern elsewhere in Leviticus (Lev 3:17; 7:26–27; 17:10–14; 19:26a), there is no reason to infer that it could not have been specified as a rationale in Lev 11:20–23 as well. As is discussed below, however, such a motivation is clearly evident for the later Jewish author of the *Letter of Aristeas*.

More persuasively, Erhard Gerstenberger considers the normative eating habits of the common people and asks whether the exception offered in Lev 11:21–22 may have been an "[a]daptation to some prevalent eating custom in Israel's proximity? Experience of the distresses of famine forcing them no longer to disdain 'even' grasshoppers?"[29] Gerstenberger's first question mer-

---

[26] F. H. Gorman, Jr., *Divine Presence and Community: A Commentary on the Book of Leviticus* (International Theological Commentary; Grand Rapids: Eerdmans, 1997), 73. Concerning למינו and למינהו ("according to its kind," Lev 11:22), Gorman (73) also points plausibly to "the language of creation found in Gen. 1 (see, e.g., vv. 11, 12, 24, 25)." Cf. Jacques Trublet, "Alimentation et sainteté: Lévitique 11 Deutéronome 14," *Christus* 29 (1982): 209–17, esp. 214–15; Jirí Moskala, "Categorization and Evaluation of Different Kinds of Interpretation of the Laws of Clean and Unclean Animals in Leviticus 11," *BR* 46 (2001): 5–41.

[27] Gorman, *Divine Presence*, 73.

[28] Isman and Cohen, "Kosher Insects," 102.

[29] Erhard S. Gerstenberger, *Leviticus: A Commentary* (OTL; Louisville, KY: Westminster John Knox, 1996), 140.

its additional attention in light of other witnesses to locust eating in the ancient Near East.

3. Locust Eating in the Ancient Near East

Lev 11:20–23 does not at all point to a distinctively Israelite culinary practice of locust/grasshopper eating. On the contrary, the widespread and well-attested delight in eating such insects in the ancient Near East may well lie behind the partial prescription afforded in this passage.

R. K. Harrison notes that, "[a]s a food, locusts have been eaten in the Near East for millennia. A royal banquet scene from the palace of Ashurbanipal (*c*. 669–627 BC), the last great Assyrian king, depicted servants bringing locusts on sticks for the guests to eat."[30] The Assyrian bas-relief of servants carrying skewered locusts and pomegranates, which Harrison describes, is reproduced immediately below:[31]

---

[30] Harrison, *Leviticus*, 129. See further on the diet of the Australian aborigines in chapter 4.

[31] Reproduced from Y. Palmoni, "Locust," 146; this bas-relief appears also in: Don Brothwell and Patricia Brothwell, *Food in Antiquity: A Survey of the Diet of Early Peoples* (Baltimore: Johns Hopkins University, [2]1998), 70, fig. 24; Jean Bottéro, "The Cuisine of Ancient Mesopotamia," *BA* 48/1 (1985): 36–47; here, 37.

Oded Borowski refers first to another Assyrian relief and then to the afore-mentioned relief:

> The locust was considered a delicacy; and, on one Assyrian bas-relief, servants can be seen carrying, among other foodstuffs, long pins of skewered locusts to a royal feast (Aynard 1972:60). Another relief from the palace of Ashurbanipal shows two servants, one of whom is carrying . . . rows of locusts (Brothwell and Brothwell 1969:fig. 24).[32]

Complementing this pictographic evidence, the *Assyrian Dictionary of the Oriental Institute of the University of Chicago* cites numerous literary testimonies to locust eating, including the following:

> On the steppe its (the enemy's land) animal life is famished, he roasts (it) like crows (var. locusts) (with his fiery, divine brilliance). (Lugale 3.5)
>
> Send me a hundred locusts and (some) food. (YOS 2.15.27 [OB let.])
>
> . . .and the locusts for which I asked you, do not forget the . . . and the locusts! (CT 29.11a.7, 9)
>
> I have forwarded to my lord as many locusts as they were able to catch for me. (ARM 3.62.15)
>
> Send me as many locusts as you have been able to collect and kill. (ABL 910.5)[33]

The first passage points to the eating of locusts during a time of hardship, in this case following military defeat (Lugale 3.5). The other four testimonies, however, corroborate the depictions of the two bas-reliefs in that they point to orders from individuals of some wealth who *desired this particular food.*

This same inference applies to locust eating in Mesopotamia: "In a letter found at Mari the writer addresses the King thus: 'Locusts often come to Terqa and the day they arrived the heat was torrid so they did not alight. But all the locusts that were taken I have sent to my Lord.'"[34] It thus follows that locusts were not just the food of necessity for those who possessed no other means with which to feed themselves. On the contrary, locusts routinely comprised the *chosen* cuisine of the *wealthy.*[35] Understood within this light,

---

[32] Borowski, *Every Living Thing: Daily Use of Animals in Ancient Israel* (Walnut Creek, CA: AltaMira, 1998), 159.

[33] These passages are cited in the entry for *erbu* (cf. Heb. אַרְבֶּה) in *CAD* (Vol. 4, 1958; ed. I. J. Gelb et al.; Chicago: University of Chicago Oriental Institute, 1956–), 4.256–8; here, 257.

[34] J. M. Aynard, "Animals in Mesopotamia," in: *Animals in Archaeology* (ed. A. H. Brodrick; New York: Praeger, 1972), 42–68; here, 60. Aynard continues, "These insects were in fact much esteemed as a foodstuff, and on one Assyrian bas-relief servants are carrying a hare, birds and long pins of skewered locusts to a royal feast" (60; cf. 59–60, 64). Moreover, Bottéro, "Cuisine," 39, notes that the Mesopotamians "prepared a fermented sauce (*šiqqu*), for both kitchen and table use, out of fish, shellfish, or grasshoppers."

[35] Note the overgeneralization of J. Milgrom, "Ethics and Ritual: The Foundations of the Biblical Dietary Laws," in: *Religion and Law: Biblical-Judaic and Islamic Perspectives* (ed. E. B. Firmage et al.; Winona Lake, IN: Eisenbrauns, 1990), 159–91: "Here it would seem an

John's diet does not self-evidently constitute a critique of the rich or point to a wilderness dweller.[36] Both rich and poor people ate locusts in a variety of rural and (comparatively more) urban locations in the ancient Near East.

Furthermore, Elizabeth Douglas Van Buren summarizes the following archeological evidence for the prevalence of locusts in ancient Near Eastern cultures:

> A stamp-seal found at Lagaš was adorned with a design of a grasshopper executed with a drill. A golden dagger found in the grave of Meskalamdug at Ur had an image of a locust incised upon it. A locust appears on a few cylinder seals of the time of the First Dynasty of Babylon as one of the symbols scattered in the field. . . , but on seals of the Kassite period it seems to be a grasshopper which is placed near the deity. Lead figurines of a locust, natural size and rendered with great accuracy of observation, came to light in Room 4 of the Temple of Ašur in Kâr-Tukulti-Ninurta, and on a plaque of glazed fayence a locust is represented in the background of a scene showing an Assyrian, probably the king himself, making his petition to a seated divinity. . . . A wall relief from the palace of Sanherib at Nineveh depicts attendants bringing locusts strung on sticks and other provisions for a banquet, and another relief representing Sanherib and his queen feasting in a garden shows a locust on one of the topmost branches of a palm-tree to the left of the group.[37]

Although the interpretation of some of the items to which Van Buren refers may be disputed or less clear than she suggests, her work is valuable for highlighting the place of locusts not only as food but also in ancient Near Eastern folklore.

Given the copious findings of locust artifacts from other civilizations, Oded Borowski notes correctly about a seal that was found within Palestine and depicts a locust:

> Since, according to the biblical prescription, the locust was edible, it should not be surprising that the insect is depicted on a Judean seal inscribed 'belonging to Azaryahu (of) the locust (family)' with an engraved grasshopper under the inscription (Avigad 1966; Neufeld 1978:fig. 1).[38]

---

exception was made because allowing locusts as food was a hallowed practice stemming back to the wilderness period when, as pastoralists, they lived off their herds and feasted on locusts. . ." (189).

[36] Against M. E. Boring, *Matthew*, 1.168; E. LaVerdiere, *Beginning of the Gospel*, 31–2; W. Carter, *Matthew*, 95. See the discussion of this point in chapter 1.

[37] E. D. Van Buren, *The Fauna of Ancient Mesopotamia as Represented in Art* (AnOr 18; Rome: Pontificium institutum biblicum, 1939), 109–10; cf. Jaromir Malek, "The Locusts on the Daggers of Ahmose," in: *Chief of Seers: Egyptian Studies in Memory of Cyril Aldred* (ed. Elizabeth Goring et al.; Studies in Egyptology; London/New York: Kegan Paul International, 1997), 207–19; J. A. Thompson, "Joel's Locusts," 54–5.

[38] Borowski, *Every Living Thing*, 160; cf. 235. Nahman Avigad, "A Hebrew Seal with a Family Emblem," *IEJ* 16 (1966): 50–3; here, 50–2, offers an argument supporting the translation of the inscription לעזריו הגבה as "Belonging to Azaryaw [son of] HGBH [= locust]."

Nahman Avigad is persuaded that the same Israelite craftsman was responsible for the carved locust and the inscription.[39] Moreover, the *Testament of Solomon* would later account for Solomon's insanity/apostasy in terms of the king's sacrificing locusts to foreign deities.[40]

The preceding observations are valuable to the present inquiry because they demonstrate that Lev 11:20–23 is not a distinctive literary testimony. That locust eating was a common practice is documented by copious materials from the ancient Near East. What is unusual about Lev 11:20–23 is the tolerance granted to the eating of *only certain kinds* of 'clean' grasshoppers/locusts. The reason for this limited indulgence has been touched upon briefly above and may be explored somewhat further in light of the materials discussed in this section. It is the view of the present author that Lev 11:20–23 offers an argument from the order of creation to support a dispensation for eating locusts, which were not merely for the poor or famine-stricken but a prized delicacy in the ancient Near East.[41] In short, locusts were just too popular and delightful to proscribe completely, and a theological rationale was thus found for allowing the eating of at least some of these insects.

4. Are *Locusts Permitted? Lev 11:20–23 and Deut 14:19*

A notable contradiction to the exception given for "jointed legs" in Lev 11:21 is Deut 14:19, which proscribes the eating of any and all insects that have wings: "And all winged insects are unclean for you; they shall not be eaten." Deut 14:19 begins much as Lev 11:20 but does not offer an exception like that in Lev 11:21–22 for certain types of (winged) locusts:

---

[39] N. Avigad, "Hebrew Seal," 52–3.

[40] *T. Sol.* 26.5 [§129], concerning the Shummanite woman whom Solomon wished to marry: "So because I loved the girl—she was in full bloom and I was out of my senses—I accepted as nothing the custom (of sacrificing) the blood of the locusts (τῶν ἀκρίδων τὸ αἷμα). I took them in my hands and sacrificed in the name of Raphan and Molech to idols, and I took the maiden to the palace of my kingdom." Greek text: C. C. McCown, ed., *The Testament of Solomon* (Leipzig: Hinrichs, 1922), 74; ET: *OTP*, 1.986.

[41] With Frederick S. Bodenheimer, *Insects as Human Food: A Chapter of the Ecology of Man* (The Hague: W. Junk, 1951), 40–1: "This permission to eat locusts [Lev 11:21–22] is nothing more than a codification of a habit existing since oldest times among the nomads of the Middle East, which, as we will see, has lasted down to our day." Cf. David Nevo, "The Desert Locust, *Schistocerca gregaria*, and Its Control in the Land of Israel and the Near East in Antiquity, with Some Reflections on Its Appearance in Israel in Modern Times," *Phytoparasitica: Israel Journal of Plant Protection Sciences* 24 (1996): 7–32, esp. 19–22; Gorman, *Divine Presence*, 73.

Lev 11:20	Deut 14:19
כֹּל שֶׁרֶץ הָעוֹף הַהֹלֵךְ עַל־אַרְבַּע שֶׁקֶץ הוּא לָכֶם	וְכֹל שֶׁרֶץ הָעוֹף טָמֵא הוּא לָכֶם לֹא יֵאָכֵלוּ

The similarity in wording between this and other parts of Leviticus 11 and Deuteronomy 14 has suggested to a majority of scholars a direct literary relationship between the two and that one passage reflects a revision of the other:

> The fact of a literary connection between Lv 11,2b–23 and Dt 14,4–20 is evident and challenged by no one; the common topical arrangement of the two texts and their verbatim correspondence in so many places, both in the general norms for the distinction of clean and unclean animals and in the long list of unclean birds, admits of no other explanation.[42]

The question then becomes which tradition is earlier and which passage offers a modification of the other. William L. Moran is persuaded that Deuteronomy 14 is the later tradition, in part because of the mention of an additional "ten quadrupeds in [Deut 14:]4b–5."[43] If correct, this would mean that Deuteronomy came to issue a blanket statement against insect eating as an objection to Lev 11:21–22.

Alternately, if Leviticus 11 reflects a revision of Deuteronomy 14,[44] Lev 11:21–22 could be viewed as an attempt to forge some common ground between a common practice among the people and the absolute prohibition of Deut 14:19. A resolution to this problem is not necessary for the present inquiry. What is important to note is that even within the Pentateuch there is disagreement concerning the propriety of eating locusts. It is thus an oversimplification to characterize John the Baptist as an eater of locusts/grasshoppers *because* one part of the Pentateuch prescribes certain species of them.[45]

---

[42] Moran, "The Literary Connection between Lv 11,13–19 and Dt 14,12–18," *CBQ* 28 (1966): 271–7; here, 271.

[43] Moran, "Literary Connection," 272; so also Bernard J. Bamberger, *The Torah: A Modern Commentary* (Vol. 3: *Leviticus*; New York: Union of American Hebrew Congregations, 1979), 3.90: "The Torah contains a number of repetitions, but none as extended as this one. Since the passage seems typical of P in content and in style, it is probable that a priestly editor inserted the passage into Deuteronomy" (cf. 3.xviii).

[44] So Louis Khalifé, "Étude sur l'histoire rédactionnelle des deux textes parallèles: Lv. 11 et Dt. 14, 1–21," *Melto* 2 (1966): 57–72. J. Trublet, "Alimentation et sainteté," 214–15, does not take a stand on this issue.

[45] See further the discussion in chapter 1 of S. L. Davies, "John the Baptist and Essene Kashruth," 569–71; J. H. Charlesworth, "John the Baptizer and Qumran Barriers," 353–6, 366–8; J. M. Allegro, *Dead Sea Scrolls*, 163–5.

5. The Letter of Aristeas *and Philo of Alexandria: Locusts as a Recognized Food in the Egyptian Jewish Diaspora*

Regardless of the tension resulting from the inclusion of both Lev 11:20–23 and Deut 14:19 in the final form of the Pentateuch, ancient Jewish writings that mention locust eating embrace Lev 11:20–23 consistently and seem to ignore Deut 14:19. The witnesses to locust eating discussed in this and the following sections are: the *Letter of Aristeas*, Philo of Alexandria, the Temple Scroll and Damascus Document from Qumran, the Mishnah and midrashim, and, finally, Moses Maimonides.

If a Hellenistic date for the *Letter of Aristeas* (2nd c. B.C.E.) is correct, then this letter—probably from Alexandria—offers the earliest literary testimony subsequent to Lev 11:20–23 to locust eating by certain Jews.[46] *Aristeas* presents a list of 'vegetarian' "birds," including locusts, which the Jews known to this author eat in accordance with kashrut:

> [144b] These laws have all been solemnly drawn up for the sake of justice, to promote holy contemplation and the perfecting of character. [145] For of the winged creatures of which we make use (οἷς χρώμεθα) all are gentle and distinguished by cleanliness and they feed on (χρώμενα πρὸς τὴν τροφήν) grain and pulse, such as pigeons, doves, 'locusts' (ἀττακοί), partridges, and also geese and all similar fowl. [146] But of the winged creatures which are forbidden you will find that they are wild and carnivorous (σαρκοφάγα). . . .[47]

The inclusion of locusts (ἀττακοί; cf. Lev 11:22b, LXX) in a list of "winged creatures" assumes the context of Lev 11:13–23, which mentions clean creatures who inhabit the air—first birds (11:13–19) and then locusts/grasshoppers (11:20–23). In an apology for the propriety of the Jewish Law, including its dietary requirements (cf. *Let. Aris.* 128–172), the author builds on Leviticus in offering locusts as an example of clean, 'vegetarian' birds that at least some Jews continue to eat. There is clearly no aversion to locust eating, since the author of *Aristeas* assumes that his/her audience will recognize both the validity of the Law and the corresponding dietary practices among diasporic (Alexandrian?) Jews at the time of this letter.

Philo of Alexandria (1st c. C.E.) offers another witness to locust eating in the Jewish Diaspora. In his *Legum Allegoriae*, Philo refers indirectly to locusts as human food, which serve as a referent for his allegorical interpretation of Lev 11:21–22:

---

[46] On the date of *Aristeas*, see the discussion of R. J. H. Shutt in *OTP*, 2.8–9.

[47] *Let. Aris.* 144b–146a; Greek text and ET: Moses Hadas, ed., *Aristeas to Philocrates (Letter of Aristeas)* (Jewish Apocryphal Literature; New York: Dropsie College for Hebrew and Cognate Learning/Harper, 1951), 158–9. On the 'vegetarian' eating habits of locusts, see further Nepualius 31, in: W. Gemoll, *Nepualii, fragmentum*, 2.

Now in Leviticus the sacred word advises (παραινεῖ . . . ὁ ἱερὸς λόγος) them to feed 'on creeping things that go upon all four, which have legs above their feet, so as to leap with them' [11:21]. Such are the locust (ὁ βροῦχος), the wild locust (ὁ ἀττακός), the grasshopper (ἀκρίς), and in the fourth place the snake-fighter.[48] And this is how it should be. For if serpent-like pleasure is an un-nourishing (ἄτροφον) and injurious thing, self-mastery, the nature that is not in conflict with pleasure, must be wholesome and full of nourishment (τροφιμώτατον . . . καὶ σωρήριον). (*Leg.* 2.105; ET: LCL, modified)

Philo's comparison of locusts/grasshoppers with snakes (cf. the citation of Gen 3:1 in *Leg.* 2.106) is predicated upon the assumption that locusts/grasshoppers are indeed a wholesome type of human food. Notably, Philo interprets Leviticus 11, an indulgence allowing the eating of certain locusts/grasshoppers, as God's exhortation (παραινέω) illustrating humanity's moral development.[49] Such advice from heaven only makes sense if Philo's Hellenistic Jewish audience already recognizes locusts as "most nutritious" (τροφιμώτατος, superlative of τροφιμότης) and "granting of safety" (σωρήριος), whether to the body (so Lev 11:21–22) or, in Philo's allegory, to the soul.

6. Conditional Affirmation of Locust Eating in the Dead Sea Scrolls

The assumption of Philo, *Leg.* 2.105 and the statement of *Let. Aris.* 145 that Jews recognized locusts as food are echoed by the Qumran community. In particular, the Temple Scroll more or less repeats the instructions of Lev 11:21–22:

[3] [Of the][50] winged [insects] you can eat: the locust and its species, the bald locust and its species, the cricket [4] and its species, the grasshopper and its species. These you can eat from among winged insects: those which crawl on four paws, which [5] have the hind legs wider than the forelegs in order to leap over the ground with them and to fly with their wings. (11Q19 [11QT*ᵃ*] 48:3–5)

The only detail added to the prescription given in Leviticus 11 concerns the physiology of locusts: Their hind legs are "wider" than their forelegs. This

---

[48] Gk.: ὁ ὀφιομάχης, following the LXX of Lev 11:22d: καὶ τόν ὀφιομάχην καὶ τὰ ὅμοια αὐτῷ. Cf. Arist., *HA* 8(9).6 (612A). In *Leg.* 2.105, the terms that Philo uses for locusts/grasshoppers correspond to Lev 11:22 (LXX), except that Philo has ὁ ἀττακός (cf. ἀττακοί in *Let. Aris.* 145) instead of ὁ ἀττάκης (Lev 11:22b, LXX). In his work *On the Creation*, Philo also mentions the 'snake-fighter,' which "springs from the ground and lifts itself into the air like the grasshopper" (*Opif.* 58 [163]). Similarly to *Leg.* 2.105, Philo offers a figurative interpretation of this allusion to Lev 11:22 in *Opif.* 58 (163), that the snake-fighter "is nothing but a symbolic representation of self-control." See also Alexander of Aphrodisias (Phil.; *fl. c.* 198/209 C.E.), *In Aristotelis metaphysica commentaria* 535.35 for a comparison of the grasshopper (ἀκρίς) with the snake.

[49] Cf. in the LXX: ταῦτα φάγεσθε (Lev 11:21, 22), for תאכלו.

[50] 11Q19 48:1–2 are corrupt. It is plausible that the paraphrase included Lev 11:20 in 11Q19 48:2 or, perhaps, 48:1.

differs only slightly from Lev 11:21b, which mentions the insects' ability to jump from having "jointed legs above their feet." The distinctive detail in the Temple Scroll could well have come from a scribe who had observed locusts' legs, perhaps in connection with the preparation of a meal. Such repetition of Leviticus 11 without comment suggests that allowing locusts/grasshoppers to be eaten could be affirmed without reference to Deut 14:19. Moreover, fragmentary copies of parts of Lev 11:20–23 survive in MasLev[b], 4Q365 and 2Q5 (paleoLev).[51]

In addition, the Damascus Document (sometimes called the Zadokite Fragment) offers specific instructions for preparing fish and locusts:

> [11b] No-one should defile his soul [12] with any living being or one which creeps, by eating them, from the larvae of bees to every living [13] being which creeps in water. And fish: they should not eat them unless they have been opened up [14] alive, and the[ir blood poured] away. And all the locusts (וכל החגבים), according to their kind (במיניהם), shall be put into the fire or into water [15a] while [they are] still alive, as this is the regulation for their species.[52]

The interpretation is notably closer to Lev 11:20–23 than to Deut 14:19 in that locusts are kosher, provided that they be captured alive and roasted or boiled prior to consumption. The process of roasting or boiling the locusts would presumably allow for the easy removal of the insects' wings and legs, which in fact are not easily digestible.[53]

As noted in chapter 1, CD 12:14–15 is a significant literary testimony that locusts were still eaten by at least some Jews around the time of the Baptist. The Damascus Document does not, however, support an Essene influence (whether direct or indirect) on John's eating habits. Since locusts were such a common food in much of the ancient Near East and not distinctive in Jewish literature (cf. above on Philo and *Aristeas*), the comparison is as flimsy as noting that any two Americans like to eat hamburgers or two Germans have a penchant for bratwurst. The eating habits of one such American or German cannot be said to have influenced those of a compatriot without additional corroborating evidence. In the case of the Baptist and the Essenes, then, there is not adequate evidence to support James H. Charlesworth's contention that "[t]he description of what John ate [in Mark 1:6c‖Matt 3:4c] has a decidedly

---

[51] David L. Washburn, *A Catalog of Biblical Passages in the Dead Sea Scrolls* (Text-Critical Studies 2; Atlanta: Society of Biblical Literature, 2002), 40.

[52] CD–A 12:11b–15a. Heb. and ET: Gracía Martinez and Tigchelaar, *Dead Sea Scrolls*, 1.570–1.

[53] This point is discussed in chapter 4 concerning certain recent and contemporary locust-eating peoples.

Qumran or Essene ring to it" in that John intentionally ate like a (current or) former Essene.[54]

7. Locusts in the Mishnah: Like Fish, But Not Quite Fowl

The Mishnah reflects a rather lively discussion on whether, and under what conditions, locusts/grasshoppers—usually referred to as חגבים (cf. Lev 11:22d)—are permitted as food. Three passages in particular point unambiguously to locust/grasshopper eating among certain Jews in late antiquity:

> Unclean locusts (חגבים טמאים) which were pickled with clean locusts (חגבים טהורים) have not invalidated [imparted uncleanness to] the brine [in which they were pickled]. Testified R. Sadoq[55] concerning the brine of unclean locusts, that it is clean. (*m. Ter.* 10:9)

> Over something which does not grow from the earth one says, "For all [was created according to his word]." Over vinegar, unripe fruit, and edible locusts (הגובאי) one says "For all [was created at his word]." (*m. Ber.* 6:3)

> Testified R. Yose b. Yoezer of Seredah about an qamsa locust (איל קמצא), that it is clean [for eating]; . . . And they called him 'Yose the Easy-going.' (*m. ʿEd.* 8:4)

According to *m. ʿEd.* 8:4, Jose b. Joezer of Zereda's reception of the nick-name "Easy-going" (or "Permitter") suggests that not everyone was pleased

---

[54] Charlesworth, "John the Baptizer," 366–8; here, 367, who argues that John adheres to this diet because he was a former Essene who had been excluded from the community but nonetheless still regarded himself bound to an oath corresponding to the instructions of CD 12:14–15 (cf. Jos., *B.J.* 2.8.8 [§143]). On the contrary, neither Mark 1:6c nor Matt 3:4c specifies that John ate in accordance with the additional requirements placed upon the Essenes (roasting or boiling the locusts/grasshoppers beforehand). Moreover, according to Philo, *Hypothetica* 11.8 (*apud* Euseb., *Praep. evang.* 8.11.8, discussed in chapter 3), the Essenes kept bees. If accurate, this would represent a difference, since John is said to eat wild honey (μέλι ἄγριον) rather than honey produced by domesticated bees. In the view of the present author, the larger thesis that the Baptist had ever been an Essene is also dubious. On this last point, see, e.g., Jörg Frey, "Die Bedeutung der Qumranfunde für das Verständnis des Neuen Testaments," in: *Qumran: Die Schriftrollen vom Toten Meer* (ed. M. Fieger et al.; NTOA 47; Freiburg: Freiburg Schweiz/Göttingen: Vandenhoeck & Ruprecht, 2001), 129–208, esp. 168–70; F. I. Andersen, "Diet," 62–3; Scobie, *John the Baptist*, 137–9; Meier, *Marginal Jew*, 2.49.

[55] I.e., in *m. ʿEd.* 7:2: "R. Sadoq gave testimony concerning brine made from unclean locusts that it is clean. For the first Mishnah holds: unclean locusts which were pickled with clean locusts—they have not invalidated their brine." Here and elsewhere, translations of the Mishnah are from Jacob Neusner, *The Mishnah: A New Translation* (New Haven: Yale University, 1988); Heb.: Chanoch Albek, *Shishah Sidrei Mishnah* (Jerusalem/Tel Aviv: Mosad Biyalik, 1952–59). Cf. Strack and Billerbeck, *Kommentar zum NT*, 1.98–100; Elijah Judah Schochet, *Animal Life in Jewish Tradition: Attitudes and Relationships* (New York: Ktav, 1984), 92, 98; M. Broshi, "Diet of Palestine in the Roman Period," 51: "Grasshoppers were a popular food and were regarded as a luxury (Bereshit Raba 67, 2; Tanhuma, Vaere, 14). . . . After the grasshoppers were dewinged and peeled (Tosefta, Okazin 2, 16), they were eaten in a variety of ways. They were also preserved for use in sauce (Mishnah, Teruma 10, 9)."

with his interpretation allowing that a particular type of locust be eaten. Additionally, *m. Šabb.* 9:7 refers to a "living unclean locust" (חגב חי טמא) as something that a child plays with (R. Judah), thus suggesting the common place of the locust in Jewish (and other) homes.

Moreover, two other passages from the Mishnah, like the Damascus Document, append stipulations to Lev 11:20–23:

> Among locusts (ובחגבים) [these are clean]: Any which has (1) four legs, (2) four wings, and (3) jointed legs, and (4) the wings of which cover the greater part of its body. R. Yose says, "And (5) the name of which is locust (ושמו חגב)." (*m. Ḥul.* 3:7)

> These are things which [to begin with] are permitted for [Israelite] consumption: . . . Locusts which come from [the shopkeeper's] basket are forbidden. Those which come from the stock [of his shop] are permitted.[56]

Whether one should consider the physical characteristics or the source of the locusts (*m. Ḥul.* 3:7; *m. ʿAbod. Zar.* 2:7), the practice of eating locusts was seen to need at least some regulation. On this point R. Jose (Yose) again offers a more permissive interpretation of kashrut (*m. Ḥul.* 3:7; cf. above on *m. ʿEd.* 8:4).

Elsewhere in the Mishnah, locusts, along with fish, belong to a special classification of meat:

> Every [kind of] flesh [of cattle, wild beast, and fowl] it is prohibited to cook in milk, except for the flesh of fish and locusts (חוץ מבשר דגים וחגבים). And it is prohibited to serve it up onto the table with cheese, except for the flesh of fish and locusts. He who vows [to abstain] from flesh is permitted [to make use of] the flesh of fish and locusts. (*m. Ḥul.* 8:1)

Additionally, Jews are not allowed to consume the blood of cattle, wild animals or birds, but are not liable because of "the blood of fishes or the blood of locusts" (דם דגים דם חגבים).[57] Thus, locusts and fish may be 'mixed' with dairy, and the blood of these two creatures does not result in impurity as that of other meats does.

These statements from *m. Ḥullin* and *m. Kerithot* would not, however, warrant a 'vegetarian' construal of locusts in the Mishnah or, by implication, of the Baptist's diet.[58] According to *m. Kelim*, contact with locusts can impute uncleanness, but touching fruit cannot: "There are three [kinds of] leather gloves. . . . That of the locust-catchers (של חגבין) is susceptible to corpse

---

[56] *m. ʿAbod. Zar.* 2:7. Herbert Danby, *The Mishnah* (London: Oxford University, 1933), 440 n.3, suggests that the shopkeeper's locusts are forbidden because "[h]e is suspected of sprinkling them with wine."

[57] *m. Ker.* 5:1. Cf. *m. ʿUq.* 3:9; *m. Ḥul.* 3.7 and *m. Ter.* 10:8–9, which mention fish and locusts together.

[58] Against Joel Marcus, *Mark 1–8*, p. 151; cf. A. Pallis, *A Few Notes*, 3–6; P. Kieferndorf, "Seine Speise war Heuschrecken?" pp. 188–9; R. Eisler, "The Baptist's Food and Clothing," 235–40.

uncleanness. And that of the fruit-pickers is clean of all" (*m. Kelim* 24:15). Thus with regard to matters of purity, the Mishnah discusses locusts and fish as something in-between fruits and vegetables, on the one hand, and most other meats, on the other. Locusts are indeed meat, but these insects and fish can be eaten under certain circumstances when other types of meat would be forbidden.

8. Locust Eating in Later Jewish Literature: Midrashim and Maimonides

This study has observed that the *Letter of Aristeas*, the Temple Scroll, the Damascus Document and numerous tractates of the Mishnah do not prohibit the eating of locusts, but rather consistently allow them as human food under certain conditions (with Lev 11:20–23; *pace* Deut 14:19). Such toleration is also attested in the midrashim. For example, concerning Isaac's statement to Esau in Gen 27:33, "I ate from all [of it] (מכל ואכל) before you came,"[59] the Genesis Midrash places into the mouth of Isaac the following answer to Esau concerning what the patriarch had eaten: "'I do not know,' he replied, 'but I tasted in it the taste of bread, the taste of meat, the taste of fish, the taste of locusts and the taste of all the delicacies in the world.'"[60] The commentary assumes that locust eating is permitted and calls attention to the quality of the meal that Rebekah had prepared for Jacob to give to his father Isaac (cf. Gen 27:5–17).

In addition, the Lamentations Midrash acknowledges numerous types of permitted locusts:

> R. Ḥanina b. Abbahu said: There are seven hundred species of clean fish, eight hundred of clean grasshoppers, and birds beyond number; and they all went into exile with Israel to Babylon; and when the people went back, they returned with them. . . .[61]

Here one learns that myriad kinds of locusts permitted as human food traveled into exile with the covenant people and returned with them after the period of captivity in Babylon had ended. A similar statement may also be found in the

---

[59] Gen 27:30–40 reports what transpired upon Esau's arrival, after Isaac had already blessed Jacob, who was impersonating his brother Esau. Gen 27:32–33: "His father Isaac said to [Esau], 'Who are you?' He answered, 'I am your firstborn son, Esau.' [33] Then Isaac trembled violently, and said, 'Who was it then that hunted game and brought it to me, and I ate from all [of it] (מכל ואכל) before you came, and I have blessed him?—yes, and blessed he shall be!'"

[60] Genesis Midrash (Toledoth) 67.2; ET: *Midrash Rabbah* (trans. H. Freedman; ed. H. Freedman and M. Simon; London: Soncino, 1961 [1939]), 2.607–8; cf. S. Krauss, "Heuschrecken," 244.

[61] Lamentations Midrash (Proems) 34, following a citation of Jer 9:10c: "both the birds of the air and the animals have fled and are gone." ET: *Midrash Rabbah* (trans. A. Cohen; ed. H. Freedman and M. Simon; London: Soncino, 1961 [1939]), 7/2.64.

Babylonian Talmud.[62] The implication is that Jews have always had, *and continue to have*, copious varieties of clean fish, grasshoppers and birds to eat.

For whatever reason, the midrashim on Leviticus 11 and Deuteronomy 14 have nothing to say about the directions for eating certain kinds of locusts or grasshoppers (Lev 11:20–23) or about the proscription of all winged insects (Deut 14:19).[63] One may safely infer that the rabbis had more pressing concerns than to comment on such a commonplace activity as locust eating.

In addition to these midrashim, the medieval testimony of Moses Maimonides (1135–1204 C.E.) further affirms the consistency of Jewish interpreters' allowing the eating of certain locusts. His famous Code (*Holiness* 5.2) contains a treatise on forbidden foods, including locusts:

> [5.2.21] The Torah permits eight species of locusts: the grasshopper; another species of grasshopper called *razbaniṭ*; the cricket; another species of cricket called ʿ*arṣubya*; the common locust; another species of locust called 'the vineyard bird'; the bald locust; and another species of bald locust called 'the Jerusalemite *Joḥana*.' [22] He who is an expert in them and in their names may eat of them, and a hunter is to be believed in their case as in the case of birds. But he who is not an expert in them must examine their tokens. They possess three tokens: Whichever has four legs and four wings which overlie most of the length of its body and most of its circumference, and has in addition two legs with which to leap, is deemed a clean species. Even if it has an elongated head and a tail, so long as it is known by the name of locust, it is clean. [23] If at present the locust has no wings or legs, or if its wings do not cover the greater part of the body, but it is known that it will grow them after some time when it has matured, it is deemed permitted immediately.[64]

Apparently following the sequence in Leviticus 11, Maimonides's instructions concerning locusts follow on the heels of his interpretations on clean and unclean birds (*Holiness* 5.2.1.14–20). As in the Mishnah, moreover, locusts appear in the same context as fish (*Holiness* 5.2.1.24; cf. *b. Ḥul.* 66a–67a [V.1–2]).

Maimonides seems to draw from the Babylonian Talmud for his discussion of the "tokens," or characteristics, of locusts (*b. Ḥul.* 65a [IV.1.A]). He also echoes this tradition in allowing that *eight* kinds of locusts/grasshoppers be eaten, rather than the four mentioned in Lev 11:22: "What does it come to

---

[62] See *b. Ḥul.* 63b (II.10.B); ET: Jacob Neusner, *The Talmud of Babylonia: An Academic Commentary* (Vol. 30: *Bavli Tractate Hullin*, 1994; Atlanta: Scholars Press, 1994–99), 30.278.

[63] An ET of the Leviticus Midrash (Shemini) 13 is conveniently available in: *Midrash Rabbah* (trans. J. Israelstam; ed. H. Freedman and M. Simon; London: Soncino, 1961 [1939]), 4.162–76; for the Deuteronomy Midrash (Re'eh) 4: *Midrash Rabbah* (trans. J. Rabbinowitz; ed. H. Freedman and M. Simon; London: Soncino, 1961 [1939]), 7/1.89–101.

[64] Maimonides, *Holiness* 5.2.1.21–23; ET: *The Code of Maimonides (Mišneh Torah)* (Yale Judaica Series 16: *Book Five: The Book of Holiness [Sefer Qᵉdušah]*, 1965; trans. L. I. Rabinowitz and P. Grossman; New Haven: Yale University, 1949), 16.157.

teach by repeating 'according to its kind' four times [in Lev 11:22]? To include [in the rules] the vine-hopper, the Jerusalem *ywhn²*, the *ʿrzwby²*, and the *rzbnyt*" (*b. Ḥul.* 65a [IV.2.B]). In allowing that one trust the intuition of a locust hunter (locust gatherer?), moreover, Maimonides may be seen as comparatively more permissive, when weighed against the rather detailed debates concerning the identification of characteristics of permitted locusts in *b. Ḥul.* 65a–66a (IV.3.C–IV.5.C; cf. above on *m. Ḥul.* 3:7). The important thing to note in the Babylonian Talmud and Maimonides is that these disputes concern *which*—not whether—locusts may be eaten. To these observations may be added the comparatively more recent observation that "Yemenite and North African Jews also ate [eat?] 'clean' grasshoppers in various ways."[65]

Of course, with the eight types of locusts/grasshoppers mentioned by Maimonides and the Babylonian Talmud, the same exegetical problem persists as was noted earlier for Lev 11:22: The modern interpreter does not know which insects are prescribed and, by implication, which others are proscribed. It was perhaps for this reason that certain modern Jewish interpretations of *halakha* have in effect come to embrace Deut 14:19 over Lev 11:20–23.[66] For example, J. H. Hertz observes:

> None of the four kinds of locusts [in Lev 11:22] is certainly known. . . . For this reason also, later Jewish authorities, realizing that it is impossible to avoid errors being made, declare *every species of locust to be forbidden.*[67]

Hertz does not specify which Jewish authorities ultimately came to this conclusion. Whatever the origin of this development, the present study suggests that it occurred not earlier than Maimonides at the turn of the thirteenth century C.E.[68]

---

[65] Broshi, "The Diet of Palestine in the Roman Period," 51, referring to Samuel Krauss, *Talmudische Archäologie* (Grundriss der Gesamtwissenschaft des Judentums; Leipzig, 1910–12 [= Hildesheim: G. Olms, 1966]), 1.112–13; cf. 1.347 n.542; D. Nevo, "Desert Locust," 20; A. Kaplan, *Living Torah*, 320; Moshe Sokol, "Maimonides on Freedom of the Will and Moral Responsibility," *HTR* 91 (1998): 25–39.

[66] Such a difficulty could well have supplied the original impetus for Deut 14:19 in response to Lev 11:20–23.

[67] Hertz, *The Pentateuch and Haftorahs* (London: Soncino Press, ²1960), 451, emphasis added.

[68] Such an inquiry would indeed be interesting but lies beyond the scope of this study and the expertise of the present author. Commenting on Lev 11:20–23, Bernard J. Bamberger states that "Medieval halachists, uncertain about the identity of the kosher species, forbade the eating of any insects" (in: *The Torah: A Modern Commentary* [ed. W. Gunther Plaut; New York: Union of American Hebrew Congregations, 1981], 815). Bamberger's generalization may well be correct for certain Medieval Jewish interpreters (other than Maimonides), but Bamberger, like J. H. Hertz, unfortunately does not specify to which interpreters he (Bamberger) refers.

Excursus: Al-Damīrī on Locust Eating and Islam

Some two centuries after Moses Maimonides recognized the eating of certain kosher locusts by Jews, in the Islamic tradition Muḥammad ibn Mūsā al-Damīrī (1341–1405 C.E.) affirmed the lawfulness of the locust (*Al-Jarād*) as food for Muslims: "All the Muslims are agreed as regards its eating being permitted.[69] Al-Damīrī's work on animals is a compilation from various authors vis-à-vis the Koran, folklore, medicine and food. His entry on locusts cites five different authorities that the prophet Muhammad ate locusts.[70] Indeed, Allah is the one who sends locusts to the people, whether as food or as an affliction.[71] Such prescriptions contrast notably with al-Damīrī's instructions concerning certain red worms (caterpillars: *al-Asārīᶜ*), which may not be eaten, "as they are reckoned among the creeping animals."[72]

The present author does not assume that al-Damīrī's collection of Arabic materials on locusts is representative for all Islamic literature either prior to or at the turn of the fifteenth century. There is no reason, however, to dismiss his remarks as simply anecdotal any more than one would precipitously dispense with Aelian's *De natura animalium*. What is significant for this study is that the complementary testimonies of Maimonides and al-Damīrī highlight the distinctiveness of the Western/European aversion to the eating of locusts and other insects. The origins of this repugnance—which, it is argued below, are to be found not earlier than the Roman period—are taken up in the second half of this chapter.

9. Summation: Locust Eating in Jewish Literature

John the Baptist's eating of locusts/grasshoppers in Mark 1:6c‖Matt 3:4c belongs to a cultural heritage shared for centuries by many Jews and other peoples of the ancient Near East, and continued in Islamic traditions from Muhammed (purportedly) to al-Damīrī and beyond. That certain Jews ate locusts/grasshoppers is attested by not only Lev 11:20–23 but also—and

---

[69] Al-Damīrī, *Ḥayāt al-Ḥayawān*; ET: A. S. G. Jayakar, *Ad-Damīrī's Ḥayāt al-Ḥayawān: (A Zoological Lexicon)* (London/Luzac/Bombay: Taraporevala, 1906–08), 1.413; cf. 1.407; L. Kopf, "al-Damīrī, Muḥammad b. Mūsā b. ᶜĪsā Kamāl al-Dīn," art. *The Encyclopaedia of Islam* (ed. H. A. R. Gibb et al.; Leiden: Brill, [2]1960), 2.107–8; F. S. Bodenheimer, *Insects as Human Food*, 43–4.

[70] E.g.: "Ibn Mājah relates on the authority of Anas, who said that the wives of the Prophet used to have sent to them locusts in trays as presents" (Al-Damīrī, *Ḥayāt al-Ḥayawān*; ET: 1.413).

[71] "I am the Lord of locusts and their sustainer, if I desire I send them as food for a people and if I desire I send them as a trial for a people" (ET: 1.410). Al-Damīrī also calls attention to medicinal uses for locusts (ET: 1.417). Cf. 1.409–12 on locust infestations.

[72] Al-Damīrī, *Ḥayāt al-Ḥayawān*; ET: 1.49–50; here, 1.50. The similarity of this proscription to Lev 11:20‖Deut 14:19 is noteworthy.

closer to the time of the Baptist—the *Letter of Aristeas*, Philo, the Temple Scroll and the Damascus Document.

Although the pitfalls of interpreting the NT gospels in light of later rabbinic materials are well known, one point of contrast is enlightening. Unlike the Damascus Document, the Mishnah and the midrashim, conspicuously absent in Mark 1:2–8 and Matt 3:1–6 is an attempt to show that John the Baptist ate of prescribed locusts/grasshoppers and in a 'proper' way, that is, in accordance with some interpretation of kashrut. This suggests that Mark 1:6c is not intended primarily for an audience that was concerned with the finer details of kashrut.

Especially in light of Mark 7:1–23, which dispenses with such requirements, this observation may come as no surprise. It is nonetheless significant for the argument to be offered in chapter 4 that Mark 1:6c is best interpreted from the perspective of a non-locust eating (Greco-)Roman audience. That John himself ate of grasshoppers/locusts from time to time is entirely plausible (so Mark 1:6c). Many Jews both before and after John—possibly including Jesus himself—ate such insects. What is unusual for Mark 1:6c‖Matt 3:4c as compared with the Jewish testimonia is the absence of some qualification of *which* locusts John ate or *how* he ate them. In order to gain a fuller understanding of Mark 1:6c, then, a survey of the Greco-Roman materials is necessary.

D. *Locustae classicae*: Depictions of Locust Eaters and Locust Eating in Greco-Roman Antiquity

The difficulties of identifying the types or phases of locusts/grasshoppers in the HB and other Jewish writings have already been noted. Hans Gossen calls attention to the same problem in Greco-Roman literature, and especially that different terms for locusts do not correspond to particular species of locusts/grasshoppers: "Wenn uns also auch verschiedene Namen überliefert werden (ἀκρίς, βροῦχος, βρύκος, κόρνωψ, μάσταξ, πάρνοψ; *locusta*), so durften wir dahinter nicht ebensoviel verschiedene Spezies vermuten."[73] The following inquiry will consider these and other terms for such insects (for example, ἀττέλαβος, γραῦς, μάντις, ὄνος, τετραπτερυλλίς, τέττιξ, τρωξαλλίς) in an effort to ascertain what ancient Greek and Latin authors understood about them and especially how they regarded those who ate them.

---

[73] H. Gossen, "Heuschrecke," 1382; cf. idem, PWSup 8.179–81; Christian Hünemörder, art. "Heuschrecke," *DNP*, 5.526–8; Otto Keller, *Die Antike Tierwelt* (Leipzig: W. Engelmann, 1909–13), 2.458–60; M. Davies and J. Kathirithamby, *Greek Insects*, 134–9; I. C. Beavis, *Insects*, 62–9; 93–5.

To this end, the following inquiry will discuss critically the argument of Davies and Kathirithamby that, in contrast to their Near Eastern counterparts, the Greeks actually did not eat locusts during the Classical and Hellenistic periods:

> [S]everal ancient authors mention locusts as eaten by an Ethiopian tribe who were therefore known as *akridofagoi*. . . . The idea that the Greeks (or at least the poor in ancient Greece) ate them is less securely founded.[74]

A definitive finding on this point is not necessary for the present study. What is most important is to demonstrate is how a Greco-Roman audience would have understood ἄκριδες in Mark 1:6c‖Matt 3:4c, regardless of whether that audience would have shared in the Baptist's cuisine. Nonetheless, there is good reason to question the position of Davies and Kathirithamby.[75] It will be argued, on the contrary, that there is ample evidence for the eating of locusts/grasshoppers in various parts of the eastern half of the ancient Mediterranean world, including Macedonia. The contrast to be noted in the present study concerns the absence of testimonies indicating the presence of such a cuisine in the Latin West, and, in particular, the odium expressed toward locust eating expressed by certain authors, beginning in the Roman period.[76]

After surveying Greek and Latin witnesses to and attitudes toward locust eating, it will be possible to comprehend how Mark 1:6c and Matt 3:4c would have been understood and, possibly, how Mark and Matthew themselves interpreted John's ἀκρίδες. The analysis to follow is primarily diachronic, beginning with the earliest witnesses and concluding with a handful of authors later than the NT. At certain points the diachronic portrayal gives way to a more thematic or comparative approach. Other scholars will have to evaluate whether the buffet of assorted narratives offered in what follows does justice to the Greco-Roman sources and offers a savory context for the interpretation of Mark 1:6c‖Matt 3:4c.

---

[74] Davies and Kathirithamby, *Greek Insects*, 142; cf. Nicholas Purcell, "Eating Fish: The Paradoxes of Seafood," in: *Food in Antiquity* (ed. J. Wilkins, F. D. Harvey and M. Dobson; Exeter: University of Exeter, 1995), 132–49, esp. 132.

[75] With Andrew Dalby, *Siren Feasts: A History of Food and Gastronomy in Greece* (London/New York: Routledge, 1997 [1996]), 62; María José García Soler, *El arte de comer en la antigua Grecia* (Madrid: Biblioteca Nueva, 2001), 279–80; I. C. Beavis, *Insects*, 76, 102. Without good reason, Dalby is more cautious concerning the prevalence of locust eating in the ancient Mediterranean world in his *Food in the Ancient World*, 199.

[76] See the analysis offered below of M. Broshi, "Diet of Palestine in the Roman Period," 51 n.4.

1. Early References to Locusts/Grasshoppers

Knowledge of locusts/grasshoppers is attested early in the Classical period.[77] For example, the *Iliad* compares retreating troops to locusts who flee toward a river before the onrush of fire: Both are consumed by water (Hom., *Il.* 21.12; cf. *Od.* 4.287–288). A sixth-century Attic red-figure cylix depicting an insect, "perhaps a grasshopper," points to the knowledge of such (or at least similar) insects early in the classical period.[78] If the later testimony of Aelian can be believed, the ancient Athenians entwined golden grasshoppers/locusts (χρυσοῦς ἐνείροντες . . . τέττιγας) in their hair.[79]

2. Herodotus: Historian and Ethnographer of Locust Eaters

Perhaps the earliest surviving reference to a locust-eating people in Greek literature is from Herodotus (5th c. B.C.E.) concerning the Nasamonians in Cyrene, who cease tending their flocks during the summer and gather from the land a different form of subsistence: "They hunt grasshoppers (ἀττέλαβοι), which when taken they dry in the sun, and after grinding sprinkle them into milk and drink it."[80] The task of relating at some length other peoples' foods would be taken up by later ethnographers, such as Strabo, Diodorus Siculus and the Elder Pliny.

3. Aristophanes: The Humor of Grasshopper Eating

Like Herodotus, the famous comic Aristophanes (*c.* 460/445–*c.* 385 B.C.E.) alludes to locust eating by humans twice in his *Acharnians*. Although the following humorous passages do not necessarily offer a reliable witness to what Greeks commonly ate, it is clear that knowledge of locust eating is presupposed in *Ach.* 870–871 and 1114–1117:

---

[77] In order to avoid unnecessary repetition, a number of Greco-Roman references to locusts/grasshoppers not relevant to the present inquiry have already been mentioned in connection to analogous passages in the HB. Unfortunately, certain other references to locusts/grasshoppers are too poorly preserved to be of use to the present study. Such fragmentary references include Aesch. (525/4–456/5 B.C.E.), *Frr.* 10.D.100 and 36.B.402, in: Hans Joachim Mette, ed., *Die Fragmente der Tragödien des Aischylos* (Schriften der Sektion für Altertumswissenschaft 15; Berlin: Akademie-Verlag, 1959), 34, 150; Soph. (496/5–406 B.C.E.), *Fr.* 716, in: Stefan Radt, ed., *Tragicorum Graecorum fragmenta* (Göttingen: Vandenhoeck & Ruprecht, 1971–77) 4.489; Phylarchus (3rd c. B.C.E.; Hist.), *Fr.* 4b.2 (= *Pap. Ox.* 15.1801), in: Felix Jacoby, ed., *Die Fragmente der griechischen Historiker*, 2A.164.

[78] Davies and Kathirithamby, *Greek Insects*, 33, fig. 5.

[79] Ael., *VH* 4.22.4. Greek text and ET: James G. DeVoto, *Claudius Aelianus, ΠΟΙΚΙΛΗΣ ΙΣΤΟΡΙΑΣ (Varia historia)* (Chicago: Ares, 1995), 137–8.

[80] Herod., *Hist.* 4.172; Herodotus goes on to describe this people's polygamous behavior. Cf. 4.165.

On the selling of four-winged fowl [that is, grasshoppers]: "Buy some of what I am carrying, some of the fowl or of the four-wingers (τῶν τετραπτερυλλίδων)."[81]

"My boy and I have been having an argument for a while now. Do you want to bet . . . whether locusts or thrushes are tastier (πότερον ἀκρίδες ἥδιόν ἐστιν ἢ κίχλαι;)? . . . He's strongly for the locusts (τὰς ἀκρίδας κρίνει πολύ)."[82]

The first passage suggests that (dried?) grasshoppers were sold in the marketplace. In *Ach*. 1114–1117, moreover, Aristophanes assumes that his audience knows what locust eating is. For Aristophanes, 'everyone' (supposedly) knows that a bird makes for a better meal than these insects do. What is funny is that the matter is even raised and, moreover, that the pompous Lamachus is being distracted with the question.

4. Locusts as Bird Food and Fish Bait

Given that people could eat locusts, it is perhaps not surprising that certain Greek authors describe birds who eat locusts as food. The earliest such description that I have found appears in a fragment of the comic Nicophon (*fl.* late-5th–early-4th c. B.C.E.):

ἅπερ ἐσθίει ταυτὶ τὰ πονήρ᾽ ὀρνίθια,
σέρφους ἴσως, σκώληκας, ἀκρίδας, πάρνοπας.
Wicked birds eat these things:
Winged ants, as well as grubs, grasshoppers [and] locusts.[83]

Unlike Nicophon's partially preserved remark, Plutarch's later testimony offers a reason for such hostility toward the locust-eating swallow: "Is the

---

[81] Ar., *Ach*. 870–871; cf. O. Keller, *Die Antike Tierwelt*, 2.455. Davies and Kathirithamby, *Greek Insects*, 142, erroneously suggest that the presence of humor in the comic (!) Aristophanes discredits its plausibility. On the contrary, concerning this important interpretive issue see: Nicola A. Hudson, "Food in Roman Satire," in: *Satire and Society in Ancient Rome* (ed. Susan H. Braund; Exeter Studies in History 23; Exeter: University of Exeter, 1989), 69–87; Dwora Gilula, "Comic Food and Food for Comedy," in: *Food in Antiquity* (ed. Wilkins, Harvey and Dobson, 1995), 386–99, esp. 389–91; Richard Saller, "Martial on Patronage and Literature," *CQ* 33 (1983): 246–57; John Wilkins, *The Boastful Chef: The Discourse of Food in Ancient Greek Comedy* (New York: Oxford University Press, 2000), 4–51.

[82] Ar., *Ach*. 1114–7; Davies and Kathirithamby, *Greek Insects*, 142, note correctly that the choice between locusts and thrushes is "obviously ludicrous." This does not, however, discount the witness of Aristophanes to locust eating in the Classical period.

[83] Nicophon, *Aphr*. 1.2. Greek: Theodor Kock, ed., *Comicorum Atticorum fragmenta* (Leipzig: Teubner, 1880–88), 1.775; the ET is mine. The citation offered above is all that survives of this fragment. See also: Hecataeus of Abdera (*c.* 360–290 B.C.E.), *Fr.* 25.(1427.)87.6, in: Felix Jacoby, *Die fragmente der griechischen historiker*, 3A.58; Aristonicus Alex., *De sig. Il.* 9.324.1; Plut., *Sull.* 7.6; *Quaest. conv.* 8.7.3 (727E); *De soll. an.* 976D; Gal., *De loc. aff.* 6.3.7.512 [6.3.311]), in: K. G. Kühn, ed., *Claudii Galeni, Opera omnia*, 8.397.4–6; Ael., *NA* 3.12; 8.6 (perhaps from Plut., *De soll. an.* 976D). Cf. O. Keller, *Die Antike Tierwelt*, 2.5–6, 81–2, 455–6.

swallow perhaps in bad repute among [the Pythagoreans]. . . ? She is a flesh-
eater (σαρκοφάγος), and is especially prone to kill and feed on cicadas, sacred and musical (ἱεροὺς καὶ μουσικούς) insects."[84] Additionally, the
Geoponica commends locusts as a useful bait for catching fish (*Geoponica*
20.32, 20.44).

5. Locusts as a Food for Poor People: Alexis and Aesop

The comic Alexis (4th–3rd c. B.C.E.) offers locust eating to exemplify the
reason for an old woman's grief at her family's poverty. Poor people can expect a diet that includes acorns, roots, wild pears, as well as an occasional
locust/cicada (τέττιξ).[85] If Alexis points to the existence of a literary *topos*
concerning poor people as locust eaters, such may well be assumed in the
anonymous *Life of Aesop* (1st/2nd c. C.E.?).[86] According to this work, the legendary Aesop pleaded for his life in the court of Croesus. Aesop offers the
following fable, arguing that he should not be killed, just as a locust-catcher
once spared a locust instead of eating it:

Aesop answered, "There was a time when animals spoke the same language as people,
and a poor man who had no food would catch locusts (πένητα ἀπορούμενον τροφῆς
ἐπιλα<μ>β<άν>εσθαι δὲ ἀκρίδας); he would pickle and sell them at a fair price. Once
he caught one (πιάσας δέ τινα ἀκρίδα), called 'sweet-humming cicada,' and was
about to kill it. It saw what was about to happen and said, 'Do not be so quick to kill me. I
have not harmed the wheat or eaten the new shoots; nor have I destroyed the branches,
but by moving my well-adapted wings and feet in harmony, I make a marvelous sound,
and give rest to the traveler.' The man was moved by these words and released it to fly
away. In the same way, I fall at your feet. Have mercy on me. I am not powerful enough
to attack your army, or distinguished enough in my bearing to bring false charges against

---

[84] Plut., *Quaest. conv.* 8.7.3 (727E); cf. 8.7.3 (727A).

[85] Alexis, *Fr.* 167.13 (162.13), in: T. Kock, *Comicorum Atticorum fragmenta*, 2.356.
Note also the similar witness to locust eating in the list of foods given by the comic
Anaxandrides (*fl.* 376–349 B.C.E.), *Fr.* 42.59 (41.59), in: Kock, *Comicorum Atticorum
fragmenta*, 2.153. Cf. Dalby, *Siren Feasts*, 25; Steedman, ed., *Locust Handbook*, 185–6.
Note also Theocritus (Bucol.; *fl.* 270s B.C.E.), *Id.* 1.45–56, where the child (τὸ παιδίον) accompanying the fisherman makes, depending on which MS one follows at *Id.* 1.52, a "cage"
(ἀκριδοθήκα, 1.52) or a "trap" (ἀκριδοθήρα, 1.52) for grasshoppers. It is thus not clear
whether the grasshoppers are being caught as 'pets' for the child's idyllic amusement or if the
child, like the fisherman, is in search of food. See further on this text-critical and interpretive
problem Richard Hunter, *Theocritus, A Selection: Idylls 1, 3, 4, 6, 7, 10, 11 and 13* (Cambridge Greek and Latin Classics; Cambridge: Cambridge University, 1999), 84; Kenneth
James Dover, *Select Poems: Theocritus* (London: Macmillan, 1971), 82; cf. Theoc., *Id.*
5.108–111.

[86] On the date of the *Life of Aesop*, see Grammatiki A. Karla, *Vita Aesopi: Überlieferung,
Sprache und Edition einer frühbyzantinischen Fassung des Äsopromans* (Serta Graeca 13;
Wiesbaden: Reichert, 2001), 8–9; Ben Edwin Perry, *Studies in the Text History of the Life
and Fables of Aesop* (Philological Monographs 7; Haverford, PA: American Philological
Association, 1936), 24–6.

anyone and make them stick. My worthless body is my instrument, by which I utter wise sayings to benefit the lives of mortals."[87]

Croesus can 'consume' Aesop by taking his life, just as the poor man would put together a meal of edible locusts.[88]

6. Aristotle: Philosopher, Acridologist and Locust Eater

Aristotle's (384–322 B.C.E.) assorted writings reflect a fascination with not only the physical characteristics and habits of locusts, grasshoppers and cicadas but also their value as food. Noteworthy is his attempt to distinguish between such insects.[89] Aristotle also comments on the sound that male grasshoppers make by rubbing their legs together.[90] He further observes that locusts have a coiled—that is, a rather complex—stomach.

Aristotle also opines that such insects have no ciscera or fat, as is the case with the other "bloodless animals" (οὐδ' ἄλλο τῶν ἀναίμων οὐδέν, *HA* 4.7 [532B]). Such a classification of locusts as "bloodless" may account for the dispensation later given in the Mishnah for eating locusts (and fish) when other types of meat would be prohibited (*m. Ḥul.* 8:1; *m. Ker.* 5:1). The later reference of Galen (*c.* 129/130–199/216 C.E.) to Aristotle's classification of locusts and crickets (καθάπερ ἀκρίσι τε καὶ πάρνοψι) as "bloodless" strengthens the possibility that an 'Aristotelian' understanding of locusts

---

[87] *Life of Aesop* 99. ET (modified): Lawrence M. Wills, *The Quest of the Historical Gospel: Mark, John, and the Origins of the Gospel Genre* (London/New York: Routledge, 1997), 208; Greek: Manolis Papathomopoulos, *Ho vios tou Aisopou: He parallage G* (Ioannina: Aphoi Phrangoude, 1990), 139; cf. Perry, *Aesopica*, 66.

[88] Gregory Nagy, *Pindar's Homer: The Lyric Possession of an Epic Past* (Baltimore: Johns Hopkins University, 1990), 323–4, notes correctly this comparison between Aesop and the locust: "a poor man, who resorts to eating locusts in order to stay alive, happens to catch a cicada, who pleads for his life on the grounds that he does not harm men by robbing them of their possessions, as locusts do, but instead benefits them through his song. . . ."

[89] Aristotle distinguishes between ἀττέλαβοι, ἀκρίδες and τέττιγες before mentioning other insects that supposedly reproduce spontaneously (*HA* 5.19 [550B]). Here and elsewhere, Greek text and ET: A. L. Peck, ed., *Aristotle, History of Animals* (LCL; Cambridge, MA: Harvard University, 1991–93). Likewise, Theophrastus (*c.* 371–287 B.C.E.) distinguishes between ἀκρίδες, ἀττέλαβοι and βροῦκοι (*Fr.* 174.3–4, in: Friedrich Wimmer, ed., *Theophrasti Eresii opera, quae supersunt* [Frankfurt am Main: Minerva, 1964 <1866>], 459). Aelian also mentions the sounds made by various "birds," including cicadas (τέττιγες), the cricket (ἀκρίς), the locust (πάρνοψ) and the grasshopper (τρωξαλλίς, *NA* 6.19). Cf. *NA* 10.44; O. Keller, *Die Antike Tierwelt*, 2.457–8.

[90] Arist., *HA* 4.9 (535B), 5.30 (556B), *Aud.* 804A; cf. Pl., *Phdr.* 10 (230C; 259A–D; "the myth of the Cicadas"); Timaeus (Hist.; *c.* 350–260 B.C.E.), *Frr.* 43a.5–6, 19, 23; 43b.5, 14, 32 (in: F. Jacoby, *Die Fragmente der griechischen Historiker*, 3B.614); Ps. Arist., *Mir. ausc.* 64; Ar. Byz., *Epit.* 1.139; Theoc., *Id.* 5.34, 7.41; Ath., *Deip.* 4.133B; Ael., *NA* 1.20; 3.38; 5.13; 6.19; 11.26; cf. 3.35; 5.9. See further: Hermann Beckby, ed., *Anthologia Graeca* (Munich: Heimeran: ²1965–68), 2.117–123 (§§7.189–198); 2.213 (§7.364).

influenced Jewish *halakha* on locusts as food in late antiquity.[91] The same is true for the (later Byzantine) epitome of Aristophanes of Byzantium's work, *On the Animals* (*Epit.* 1.20, discussed below).

Of Aristotle's various other remarks about locusts/grasshoppers,[92] the most interesting for the present study are his observations concerning these insects' procreation, to which he adds a few remarks about locusts as food. Aristotle lists locusts among insects that procreate by copulation.[93] Furthermore, he notes a general preference for eating the larvae of the cicadas before they 'hatch' and, among the mature adults, for eating the males unless the females have recently ovulated:

> The larva (ὁ σκώληξ), when it has increased in size in the ground, becomes a 'cicada mother' (τεττιγομήτρα), and that is when they are pleasantest (ἥδιστοι) [to eat], before the integument bursts open. . . . The [adult] males are tastier (καὶ τό μέν πρῶτον ἡδίους οἱ ἄρρενες) [to eat]. But after (μετὰ δέ) copulation, the females are, because they have white eggs. As they fly up[94] after you have startled them, they discharge a liquid like water. The farmers (οἱ γεωργοί) will tell you this is urine—that is, that they have residue, and feed on dew.[95] If you approach them, moving your finger, bending the

---

[91] See Gal., *UP* 3.2. Greek text and ET: Georg Helmreich, ed., ΓΑΛΗΝΟΥ, ΠΕΡΙ ΧΡΕΙΑΣ ΜΟΡΙΩΝ ΙΖ': *Galeni, De usu partium libri XVII* (Teubner; Amsterdam: Hakkert, 1968 [1907–09]), 1.129–30; Margaret Tallmadge May, *Galen, On the Usefulness of the Parts of the Body* (Cornell Publications in the History of Science; Ithaca, NY: Cornell University, 1968), 1.158. See also Jerome, *Adv. Iovin.* 2.15 (discussed below).

[92] E.g., Arist., *HA* 8(9).6 (612A) refers to the testimony of others who have seen the locust fight with the snake and grab its neck.

[93] Arist., *HA* 5.19 (550B), 5.28–30 (555B–556B), *GA* 1.16 (721A), on the copulation habits of ἀττέλαβοι, ἀκρίδες and τέττιγες. He notes that the females are larger than the males and that the females' additional size is advantageous for procreation by copulation. Cf. *HA* 10.6 (637B), summarizing a report about a woman who observed female grasshoppers procreating on their own, i.e., without intercourse.

[94] Preferring, with D. M. Balme, ed., *Aristotle, Historia Animalium* (Cambridge Classical Texts and Commentaries 38; Cambridge: Cambridge University, 2002), 1.260; H. Aubert and F. Wimmer, eds., *Istoriai peri zoon: Kritisch-berichtigter Text Aristoteles, mit deutscher Übersetzung* (Leipzig: W. Engelmann, 1868), 1.534, the feminine ἀναπετόμεναι, which points to the women's eggs. The masculine ἀναπετόμενοι, favored by Pierre Louis, *Aristotle, Histoire des animaux* (Paris: Les Belles Lettres, 1964–69), 2.55; Leonhard Dittmeyer, ed., *Aristotelis, De animalibus historia* (Teubner; Leipzig: Teubner, 1907), 202; F. Cowan, *Curious Facts*, 255; A. L. Peck, *Aristotle, History of Animals*, 2.206; and I. C. Beavis, *Insects*, 102, makes no sense in this context. The originality of ἀναπετόμεναι can account for the mistaken masculine ending (ἀναπετόμενοι), as well as feminine forms attested in other MSS (ἀναπεττόμεναι; ἀναπεπταμέναι).

[95] Concerning the dew allegedly eaten by locusts/cicadas, compare Plut., *Quaest. conv.* 4.1 (660F); Verg., *Ecl.* 5.74–8 and *Aesop's Fables* 184 [183] ("The Ass and the Locusts" [ὄνος καὶ τέττιγες]), which likewise assume that dew is the food of locusts. An ET of the last mentioned passage appears in: Lloyd W. Daly, *Aesop without Morals: The Famous Fables, and a Life of Aesop* (New York: T. Yoseloff, 1961), 171; Greek: B. E. Perry, *Aesopica*, 394. Perry, *Life and Fables of Aesop*, 129, places this fable among the earliest

tip of it back and then stretching it out again, they are more likely to stay than if you simply held it straight out, and they begin to climb on to your finger. The reason is that they are poor in sight, and think they are climbing on to a moving leaf.[96]

Of particular interest is Aristotle's contrasting how common rural people (οἱ γεωργοί) try to catch τέττιγες with his own subtler and more rewarding approach.[97] Presumably, the reason for catching these insects is to eat them, and Aristotle seems to relate from personal experience how not to startle an ovulating female, lest she release her tasty eggs prior to her capture.[98] Since Aristotle counts himself among other Greeks who eat locusts, it does not follow that these insects were the food of only destitute people at the dawn of the Hellenistic period.[99]

7. Ethnographic Depictions of Locust Eaters: Diodorus Siculus, Strabo and the Elder Pliny

At least three different Hellenistic and Roman authors—Diodorus Siculus, Strabo and the Elder Pliny—comment at some length about a particular Ethiopian locust-eating people. It was perhaps not coincidental that such extensive attention to the food of this and other peoples arose during the Hellenistic period, after Alexander's conquests had disseminated Greek language and culture, and fueled curiosity about the plethora of 'other' peoples

---

surviving fables associated with Aesop ('Class I'), which he dates to not later than the 3rd c. C.E. and probably at least a century earlier (pp. 156–60). Cf. Plut., *Amat.* 767D; Ael., *NA* 1.20; Gregory Nazianzen, *Ep.* 26.

[96] Arist., *HA* 5.30 (556B). At *Mirabilium auscultationes*, moreover, Ps.-Aristotle mentions a locust in Argos called the 'scorpion fighter': "They say it is a good thing to eat (ἐπιεσθίω) a locust as a protection against the scorpion's sting" (*Mir. ausc.* 139). Cf. *Mir. ausc.* 176: "Among the Aetolians they say that moles see (ὁρᾶν τοὺς ἀσπάλακας) indistinctly, and do not eat earth but locusts." Also Philo, *Opif.* 58 (163), on the "snake-fighter" (Greek; ὀφιομάχης), which "springs from the ground and lifts itself into the air like the grasshopper." As mentioned above, Philo offers a figurative interpretation of this allusion to Lev 11:22, that the snake-fighter "is nothing but a symbolic representation of self-control."

[97] In *Aesop's Fables* 241 [224] ("The Locust and the Fox" [τέττιξ καὶ ἀλώπηξ]), it is the fox who wishes to eat the locust and confuses a leaf for the locust. ET: Daly, *Aesop*, 194; Greek: Perry, *Aesopica*, 415. Perry, *Life and Fables of Aesop*, 150–1, places this fable also among the earliest surviving fables (3rd c. C.E. or earlier; pp. 156–60, 229).

[98] On the eggs of the τέττιξ, cf. Plut., *Quest. conv.* 2.3 (636E). By contrast, Plut., *Quaest. conv.* 2.3 (637B) suggests that this insect reproduces 'spontaneously' without eggs. Plutarch thus points to a plurality of understandings on this point.

[99] Against H. Gossen, "Heuschrecke," 1386: "Selbst in Griechenland fingen wohl ärmere Leute H[euschrecken] und aßen sie. . . ." Gossen does not refer to Arist., *HA* 5.30 (556B) in his discussion of locusts as human food.

and cultures (un)touched (?) by Greek rule.[100] These authors also reveal much about *attitudes toward* people who eat locusts.

In what follows, it will be argued that although Diodorus finds this Ethiopian tribe's subsisting entirely on locusts to be remarkable, he would presumably not deem occasional locust eating to be extraordinary. In Strabo and Pliny, however, a markedly different presentation of this people emerges, one that reflects surprise that they partake of locusts at all. Such a shift in emphasis in relating the same material is consonant with an aversion to locust eating that surfaces in a number of other writers during the Roman period.[101] *That such a shift in attitude toward locust eating occurred* in the first centuries of the Common Era is to be argued in this and the following sections. The potential significance of this shift for John the Baptist's "locusts" will be assessed in chapters 4 and 5.

a) Diodorus Siculus, Agatharchides and Aristophanes of Byzantium

For the present discussion, it is significant that the earliest quasi-ethnographic descriptions of a locust-eating people—after Herodotus's description of the Nasamonians in Cyrene (*Hist.* 4.172)—predate both the historical Baptist and the gospel of Mark. What is particularly noteworthy in Diodorus Siculus (*fl. c.* 60–30 B.C.E.) and others is an explicit connection between *locust eating and the wilderness* (cf. Mark 1:2–8).

The description by Diodorus Siculus may well stem from Agatharchides of Cnidus (*c.* 215–after 145 B.C.E.), who in turn may have borrowed from Aristophanes of Byzantium (*c.* 257–180 B.C.E.). Aristophanes of Byzantium's work, *On the Animals* (περὶ ζῴων), unfortunately survives only in a later Byzantine epitome.[102] The matter is further complicated in that this part of Agatharchides's text does not survive. In his translation of Agatharchides's *On the Erythraean Sea* (that is, the Red Sea; written shortly after 145 or 132 B.C.E.), Stanley M. Burstein plausibly infers Diodorus's use of Agatharchides

---

[100] Brent D. Shaw, "'Eaters of Fish, Drinkers of Milk': The Ancient Mediterranean Ideology of the Pastoral Nomad," *Ancient Society* (Louvain) 13–14 (1982–83): 5–31; here, 30, argues persuasively that "[w]ithin the ideology concerning the pastoral nomad there are a number of 'fixed' points in the mental structure that are repeated by most ancient ethnographers and historians, and the nature of the barbaric food consumption or diet appears to be one of the more important of these constants." Although Shaw does not seem to be aware of some of the ancient ethnographers to be discussed in this chapter, the present study confirms Shaw's thesis.

[101] For example, Athenaeus, Plutarch, Dioscorides Pedanius and Galen, whose works are discussed below.

[102] The relevant portion is Ar. Byz., *Epit.* 2.57–58; Greek: Spyridōn Paulou Lampros, ed., *Supplementum Aristotelicum* (Vol. 1/1: *Excerptorum Constantini, De natura animalium libri duo; Aristophanis, Historiae animalium epitome, subiunctis Aeliani,* 1885; Berlin: Reimer, 1885–1903), 1/1.50–1.

and fills the lacuna in Agatharchides's work with Diodorus's text.[103] The source-critical question is relevant to the present inquiry only insofar as it is possible that Diodorus's material could have been more widely attested in antiquity, and thus to the audience of the gospel of Mark. Precisely how much Diodorus may have borrowed from Agatharchides, and Agatharchides from Aristophanes of Byzantium, is open to speculation. In what follows, Diodorus Siculus's account of this people will receive primary attention.

Quite possibly following Agatharchides or Aristophanes of Byzantium, Diodorus Siculus describes various Ethiopian peoples in terms of their distinctive habits, including what they eat. He attributes the name, "Locust Eaters" (Ἀκριδοφάγοι), to one such Ethiopian people. Diodorus's description of this people is cited at some length because of its many similarities to Mark 1:6c‖Matt 3:4c:

> A short distance from these people the Locust Eaters inhabit the region that borders on the desert (Ἀκριδοφάγοι κατοικοῦσι τὰ συνορίζοντα πρὸς τὴν ἔρημον). They are smaller than the others, lean of body and extremely black. During the spring in their region, powerful west and southwest winds drive out from the desert an innumerable multitude of locusts,[104] that are unusual for their large size and have wings that are ugly and dirty-looking in color. From this source they have abundant food during their whole life.[105] They catch these creatures in a way unique to them, for adjacent to their territory there extends for many stades a ravine of considerable depth and breadth. They fill this with brushwood, which abounds in the region. Then, when the previously mentioned winds blow and swarms of locusts approach (προσφέρηται τὰ νέφη τῶν ἀκρίδων), they divide up the whole area of the ravine into sectors and set fire to the tinder in it. A great amount of pungent smoke is thus generated, and the locusts flying over the ravine are suffocated by the pungency of the smoke and fall to the ground after flying through it for a short distance.[106] As the destruction of the locusts continues for several days, great heaps of them pile up (μεγάλοι διανίστανται σωροί). Since the region has much salt-endowed soil, all the people bring this to the piles. Having saturated them with the salt to a suitable extent, they give the locusts a pleasant taste and make it possible for them to be stored free of decay for a long period (ποιοῦσι ... τὸν ἀποθησαυρισμὸν ἄσηπτον

---

[103] Burstein, *Agatharchides of Cnidus, On the Erythraean Sea* (Hakluyt Society 2.172; London: Hakluyt Society, 1989), 101–3. Concerning the text-critical problems associated with Agatharchides's work, see Burstein, *Agatharchides*, 36–41; on the date of this work: Burstein, *Agatharchides*, 15–18. Cf. the argument of Kenneth S. Sacks, *Diodorus Siculus and the First Century* (Princeton: Princeton University, 1990), that Diodorus offers not "an arbitrary collection of thoughts derived from whatever source Diodorus happened to be following at the moment," but rather "a document substantially reflecting the intellectual and political attitudes of the late Hellenistic period" (5). Sacks further maintains "that Diodorus had far more control over his work than is generally assumed" (7).

[104] Gk.: ἐκρίπτουσιν ἐκ τῆς ἐρήμου πλῆθος ἀκρίδων ἀμύθητον. The surviving epitome of Aristophanes of Byzantium does not connect locusts with the desert at this point: ἀκρίδων πλῆθος ἀμύθητον (Ar. Byz., *Epit.* 2.57.4; but see *Epit.* 2.58.1–2).

[105] Gk: ἅπαντα τὸν βίον. Cf. Ar. Byz., *Epit.* 2.57.7: πάντα τὸν χρόνον.

[106] Cf. Hom., *Il.* 21.12.

καὶ πολυχρόνιον). Accordingly, their food, for both the short and the long term, is derived from these creatures (ἀπὸ τούτων τῶν ζώων).

For they do not raise stock or live near the sea or have any other resource. They are slight of build and very swift of foot, but they are extremely short-lived (βραχύβιοι παντελῶς) as the oldest among them does not exceed forty years of age.[107]

In addition to the obvious similarity of Diodorus's (and Aristophanes of Byzantium's) witness to a locust-eating people, the following observations are also significant:

1. Diodorus connects this tribe with the desert (πρὸς τὴν ἔρημον), much as Mark 1:2–8 does with John (φωνὴ βοῶντος ἐν τῇ ἐρήμῳ, Mark 1:3a; ἐγένετο Ἰωάννης [ὁ] βαπτίζων ἐν τῇ ἐρήμῳ, Mark 1:4a). Although the Locust Eaters do not live in the desert (so also Ar. Byz., *Epit.* 2.58.1–2), the locusts blown by the wind come from the desert.

2. The Locust Eaters' surviving *exclusively* on dried locusts offers a striking parallel to the heightened claim of Matt 3:4c, that John's food in the wilderness consisted solely of "locusts and wild honey."[108]

3. Diodorus does not suggest that eating locusts *per se* is unusual. Rather, the extraordinarily large quantity of locusts being eaten to the exclusion of other foods and the particular means of catching them[109] are what Diodorus deems to be remarkable. A modern analogy might be a group of Americans who survive entirely on fast-food hamburgers and, as a result, do not enjoy the usual life expectancy of others in the States who adhere to a well-balanced diet.

It thus follows that neither Mark 1:6c nor Matt 3:4c offers a novel type of characterization. In chapter 4 it will be argued that the ethnographic depictions of Diodorus and others are significant for understanding Mark's association of John with the wilderness and Matthew's presentation of the Baptist as a bona fide wilderness survivor. The similar descriptions of Strabo

---

[107] Diod. Sic., *Hist.* 3.29.1–6 (=? Agathar., *De mar. Eryth.* 5.59 [5.58]). Greek: Karl O. Müller, ed., *Geographi graeci minores: E codicibus recognovit prolegomenis annotatione indicibus instruxit* (Paris: Didot, 1855–61), 1.148–9; ET (modified): Burstein, *Agatharchides*, 101–3. The version cited above is listed as section 59b in Burstein's translation and is somewhat longer than another, mostly parallel version that Burstein also translates (59a). Burstein also offers in a footnote a much shorter version (59c). The Greek text and an ET may also be found in C. H. Oldfather, ed., *Diodorus of Sicily* (LCL; Cambridge: Harvard University, 1935), 2.160–5.

[108] S. M. Burstein, *Agatharchides*, 102 n.2, is incorrect to suggest that "Agatharchides, however, was clearly mistaken on one important point. Because locust swarms are cyclical events with periods of several years often intervening between outbreaks. . . , locusts can only serve as a secondary food source. . . ." On the contrary, Diodorus (Agatharchides) does not claim that an unusually large swarm of 'gregarious' locusts offered this people food. Rather, the predictable spring winds bring the grasshoppers/locusts from the desert. Cf. Davies and Kathirithamby, *Greek Insects*, 141–2.

[109] The epitome of Aristophanes of Byzantium's description does not mention overwhelming the locusts by means of smoke.

and the Elder Pliny also merit attention in this regard. The apparent use of Diodorus (or an earlier source) by Strabo and the Elder Pliny further supports the argument that a connection between the Baptist's food and location "in the wilderness" may be safely inferred for Mark's audience.

b) Strabo: Reworking Traditional Ethnographic Material

Albeit briefer than that (those?) of his predecessor(s), Strabo's (c. 64/63–after 21 B.C.E.) description of this Ethiopian people shares many features in common with Diodorus:

> The 'Locust Eaters' (ἀκριδοφάγοι) are blacker than the rest [in Ethiopia] and shorter in stature and the shortest-lived; for they rarely live beyond forty years, since their flesh is infested with parasites. They live on locusts (ζῶσι δ' ἀπὸ ἀκρίδων), which are driven into this region in the spring by strong-blowing southwest and western winds. They cast smoking timber in the ravines, lighting it slightly, (and thus easily catch the locusts), for when they fly above the smoke they are blinded and fall. The people pound them with salt, make them into cakes, and use them for food. Above these people lies a large uninhabited region (ἔρημος . . . μεγάλη), which has pastures in abundance. It was abandoned by reason of the multitude of scorpions and tarantulas, the 'four-jawed,' as they are called; these once prevailed and caused a complete desertion by the inhabitants.[110]

These observations occur in a series of descriptions of non-Roman peoples whom Strabo characterizes in part by what they eat: the Fish Eaters (*Geog.* 16.4.4), the Root Eaters (16.4.9), the Seed Eaters (16.4.9), the Flesh Eaters (16.4.9), the Elephant Eaters (16.4.10), the Bird Eaters (16.4.11), and—after mention of the Locust Eaters (16.4.12)—the Turtle Eaters (16.4.14). Although there is nothing unusual about eating fish, roots, seeds or meat, Strabo's subsequent mentioning of elephants, birds, locusts, and turtles marks foods that would likely have been regarded as more distinctive, at least as a primary source of food, by Strabo and his audience.

Strabo repeats numerous details of his source, whether Aristophanes of Byzantium, Agatharchides or Diodorus. Perhaps most noteworthy for the present study, Strabo echoes his predecessor(s) in describing this people's proximity to a "large wilderness" (ἔρημος . . . μεγάλη). Strabo also makes two noteworthy changes to his source, however. First, the rather short life span of forty years is mentioned before the description of locust eating, rather than afterward in Diodorus (and Agatharchides?), where it begins a separate section. From Strabo's arrangement of the materials, the reader could (should?) easily infer that the parasites (what we could today recognize as harmful bacteria?) *stem from* the locusts that this people eat. If correct,

---

[110] Strabo, *Geog.* 16.4.12. Cf. *Geog.* 17.3.10, where Strabo refers to the testimony of Poseidonius that locusts are prevalent in Ethiopia because of the drought and lakes filled with mud (not water).

Strabo would suggest the inadequacy—indeed, the danger—of locusts as human food. Such editing of his source material represents a change in emphasis on the part of Strabo. As noted above, what is remarkable for Diodorus is not locust eating *per se* but a particular people's living *exclusively* on dried locusts.

An additional point concerns Strabo's elaboration on the desert region adjacent to this people from which the locusts are blown by the wind. Apparently agreeing with his source, Strabo highlights the unsuitability of the desert region for human habitation and, by implication, the desperate circumstances under which this Ethiopian tribe must find food. However subtle, such differences between Strabo and his predecessor(s) suggest that Strabo had to elaborate further upon his source material in order to make it intelligible to a non-locust eating (Roman?) audience why a certain Ethiopian people actually had to resort to eating locusts for sustenance. Sarah Pothecary's argument that Strabo (b. *c.* 64/63 B.C.E.) wrote his *Geography* from 17/18 C.E. until 23 C.E.,[111] if correct, would point to an author writing close in time to, if not contemporary with, the activities of the historical Baptist.

c) Pliny the Elder's Rendition of This Locust-Eating People

If Strabo attests the prevalence of this type of ethnographic activity roughly contemporary with the historical Baptist, the Elder Pliny (23/24 C.E.–79 C.E.) witnesses to the perseverance of such generalizations concerning food and clothing around the time of the author of the gospel of Mark. Pliny is aware that it was not only poor, exotic peoples that ate such insects. He notes, for example, the preference of the wealthy Parthians for eating cicadas.[112] A little later, he notes that even among this somewhat respected people locusts were on the menu: "but among the Parthians even these [locusts] are acceptable as food" (*Parthis et hae in cibo gratae*, 11.35.106).

Of particular interest to this inquiry are Books 3–6 of Pliny's *Natural History*, which describe the geography and peoples of the ancient world. In *HN* 6.35.178–197, Pliny characterizes numerous peoples of Ethiopia, the Nile valley and Meroë. Like Mark 1:6||Matt 3:4 does for John, Pliny often refers to these peoples' physical characteristics, including their clothing, along with their diet (cf. *HN* 7.2). In Pliny's accounts, the transliterated Greek terms (for example, *Gymnetes, Agriophagi, Pamphagi, Anthropophagi*) highlight Pliny's indebtedness to one or more Greek sources. Representative features of the peoples Pliny describes may be paraphrased and quoted as follows:

---

[111] Pothecary, "Strabo, the Tiberian Author: Past, Present and Silence in Strabo's *Geography*," *Mnemosyne* 55 (2002): 387–438. The present author finds Pothecary's arguments compelling.

[112] Plin. (E), *HN* 11.32.92. Lat. and ET: Harris Rackham, ed., *Natural History* (LCL; Cambridge, MA: Harvard University, 1938–63).

Certain Ethiopians are said to have altered their facial features, for example, by removing the nose or upper lip (*HN* 6.35.187–8).

Another group dubbed (doubtless by outsiders) the 'Gymnetes' are said not to wear any clothes at all (*Gymnetes semper nudi*, 6.35.190).

Yet another tribe, the Mesanches, change their skin color by spreading red clay over their bodies (6.35.190).

Pliny describes the foods of these assorted peoples as follows:

A nomadic group of the Megabarri eat elephants (*quae elephantis vescitur*, 6.35.189; likewise the Simbarri, the Palunges and the tribes of Asachae [*vivunt elephantorum venatu*, 6.35.191]).

The Medimni, another nomadic tribe, gain subsistence from the milk of a dog-faced baboon (*Medimni . . . cynocephalorum lacte viventes*, 6.35.190).

Other 'Wild-Beast Eaters' live chiefly from the flesh of panthers and lions (*Agriophagi pantherarum leonumque maxime carnibus viventes*, 6.35.195).

Another group receives the name 'The Omnivores' because they devour everything (*Pamphagi omnia mandentes*, 6.35.195).

Still another tribe, the 'People Eaters,' is said to eat human beings (*Anthropophagi humana carne vescentes*, 6.35.195).

Elsewhere Pliny notes that "One section of the Ethiopians live only on locusts (*locustis tantum vivit*), dried in smoke and salted to keep for a year's supply of food; these people do not live beyond the age of forty" (6.35.195).

Thus, Pliny's attention to foreign or exotic details about assorted other peoples offers an additional ethnographic parallel to the bits of information about the Baptist given in Mark 1:6, namely John's clothing (v. 6ab) and diet (v. 6c). It is thus plausible that Mark 1:6 serves a function analogous to Pliny's descriptions, namely to introduce a non-Palestinian people to John's clothing and food. A corollary to this observation is that John's garb and locusts would have been regarded as foreign by the intended audience of Mark 1:6c (or its pre-Markan source).

Moreover, the Elder Pliny echoes a remarkable parallel to Matt 3:4c when stating that "one section of the Ethiopians lives only on locusts (*locustis tantum vivit*)" (*HN* 6.35.195). The claim to living exclusively on locusts has a striking resemblance to Matt 3:4c, which claims that John ate only "locusts and wild honey." As noted in Strabo's version of this material, in Pliny the short life span of these Ethiopians indicates a prejudice against this type of food, which he can assume without argument for his fellow Romans as well. Eustathius of Thessalonica, moreover, attests an interest in this Ethiopian locust-eating people in the twelfth century C.E.[113]

---

[113] See Eustathius of Thessalonica (*c.* 1115–1195/6 C.E.), *Commentarii ad Homeri Odysseam* 1.293.3.

8. Additional Expressions of Aversion to Locust Eating: Plutarch, Athenaeus, Galen, Dioscorides, Pseudo-Dioscorides, Oribasius, and a Later Fable of Aesop

In addition to Strabo and Pliny, a number of other authors during the Roman period express an aversion to locusts as human food. As already mentioned, this development is potentially significant to the present study's interest in the history of interpretation of John's diet (chapter 5). The writers to be assessed in this section are Plutarch, Dio Chrysostom, Athenaeus, Galen, Dioscorides, Pseudo-Dioscorides, Oribasius, and the *Fables of Aesop*.

a) Plutarch's Aversion and Dio Chrysostom's Apology

In his work *On the Cleverness of Animals*, Plutarch (before 50 C.E.–after 120 C.E.) implicitly suggests that cicadas are not human food but rather bird food:

> For nothing that swims and does not merely stick or cling to rocks is easily taken or captured without trouble by human[s] (ἀνθρώπῳ), as are asses by wolves, bees by bee eaters, cicadas by swallows (χελιδόσι δὲ τέττιγες), and snakes by deer, which easily attract them. (*De soll. an.* 976D)

A vegetarian, Plutarch even dispenses criticism upon such meat-eating birds.[114] In this case the lesser exemplifies the greater: If birds come up for such criticism, how much more would Plutarch have disdained humans' partaking of such food! Dio Chrysostom (c. 40/50 C.E.–after 110 C.E.), a contemporary of Plutarch, even sensed the need to argue that the parts of Homer that merely mention locusts (ἀκρίδες) are not inferior to other portions of Homer that make reference to other creatures (Dio Chrys., *Or.* 55.10–11). Although Dio Chrysostom does not refer to locusts as human food, he points to a general construal of locusts as a subject requiring justification even in the revered canon of the Homeric poems.

b) Athenaeus's Aversion

Athenaeus, *Deipnosophistae* (Δειπνοσοφισταί, "The Learned Banquet," written shortly after 192 C.E.) 4.132F–133F describes a series of delicacies that "the ancients" (οἱ παλαιοί) served as appetizers at banquets. A native of Naucratis (c. 80 km. [50 mi.] SE of Alexandria), Egypt, Athenaeus wrote

---

[114] Plut., *Quaest. conv.* 8.7.3 (727E): "Is the swallow perhaps in bad repute among [the Pythagoreans]. . . ? She is a flesh-eater (σαρκοφάγος), and is especially prone to kill and feed on cicadas, sacred and musical insects (καὶ μάλιστα τοὺς τέττιγας, ἱεροὺς καὶ μουσικοὺς ὄντας)." Bodenheimer's (*Insects*, 40) partial citation of this passage does not reveal the context of Question 7, which refers to the Pythagoreans. Cf. Plut., *Sull.* 7.6.

this work in Rome toward the end of the second century C.E.[115] Athenaeus's explanation following his mention of grasshoppers and cicadas highlights the foreignness of such items to his Roman audience:

> They used to eat even grasshoppers and cicadas as an incentive to appetite (ἤσθιον δὲ καὶ τέττιγας καὶ κερκώπας ἀναστομώσεως χάριν). [Thus] Aristophanes in *Anagyrus*: 'By the gods, how I yearn to eat a grasshopper and a cicada caught on a thin reed.' Now the cicada is an animal like a grasshopper (τέττιγι) or a *titigonion* (τιτιγονίῳ), as Speusippus describes them in the second book of his *Similars*. Epilycus mentions them in *Coraliscus*. Alexis in *Thrason* says, 'Never have I seen such a chatterbox as you, woman, be it cicada (κερκώπην) or magpie, nightingale or swallow, turtle-dove or grasshopper (τέττιγα).'[116]

The last statement attributed to Alexis, which alludes to the sounds made by cicadas rather than their role as food, highlights the efforts which Athenaeus exerts in order to make grasshopper and cicada eating intelligible to his audience. In addition, the imperfect tense of ἤσθιον could denote a practice belonging to the past, and therefore that such insects would not be served at such banquets in Rome in the 190s C.E.

c) The Use of Locusts for Medicinal Purposes (Rather than Regular Human Food): Galen, Dioscorides, Pseudo-Dioscorides and Oribasius

Galen (*c.* 129/130–199/216 C.E.) is among the ancient physicians who attest to the use of locusts in ancient medicine. He notes, for example that some physicians "use dried cicadas/locusts (τέττιξι ξηροῖς) where there is tendency to colic, adding one peppercorn per insect," and that "others bake [cicadas/locusts] and give them as food to those who have pain in the bladder.[117] From his discussions of colic in another work, *On the Affected Parts*, however, it is clear that Galen himself did not treat colic with locusts.[118]

---

[115] See further: Dorothy Thompson, "Athenaeus in His Egyptian Context," in: *Athenaeus and His World: Reading Greek Culture in the Roman Empire* (ed. D. Braund and J. Wilkins; Exeter: Exeter University, 2000), 77–84, esp. 77–9.

[116] Ath., *Deip.* 4.133B. Greek: Luciano Canfora, ed., *Ateneo, I deipnosofisti: i dotti a banchetto* (Rome: Salerno, 2001), 4.152; ET (modified): Charles B. Gulick, *Athenaeus, The Deipnosophists* (LCL; Cambridge, MA: Harvard University, 1927–41). Cf. Athenaeus's descriptions of the παῖδες ἰχθυοφάγοι (e.g., *Deip.* 8.345E) and Antonia Marchiori, "Between Ichthyophagists and Syrians: Features of Fish-Eating in Athenaeus' *Deipnosophistae* Books Seven and Eight," in: *Athenaeus and His World*, 327–38.

[117] Gal., *De simp. med. temp.* 11.13.312 (11.2.149); Greek text: K. G. Kühn, *Claudii Galeni, Opera omnia*, 12.360.3–8; the ET is my own. See further I. C. Beavis, *Insects*, 77, 103.

[118] Gal., *De loc. aff.* 1.4.8.391–392 (1.4.3.254–5); cf. 2.5.8.406 (2.5.3.261–2); 6.2.7.507–509 (6.2.3.309–10); *Geoponica* 17.19. Greek: K. G. Kühn, ed., *Claudii Galeni, Opera omnia*, 8.40–3, 82–5, 384–7; an ET is available in: Rudolph E. Siegel, *Galen, On the Affected Parts: Translation from the Greek Text with Explanatory Notes* (Basel; New York: S. Karger, 1976), 32, 48–9, 170–2.

Elsewhere in his *On the Affected Parts*, moreover, Galen refers to locusts/grasshoppers as the food of a particular kind of bird, rather than of humans.[119] Accordingly, in *De simp. med. temp.* 11.13.312 (11.2.149) Galen simply relates the practice of other "physicians."

Somewhat analogous pharmaceutical uses of grasshoppers/locusts are attested, for example, in Galen's predecessor Dioscorides Pedanius (Med.; *fl.* 41–68 C.E.). The infirmities for which Dioscorides uses locusts are discomfort in the bladder and during urination (= urinary tract infections?) and scorpion stings:

> [51] Roasted cicadas when eaten (τέττιγες ὀπτοί ἐσθιόμενοι) relieve pain in the bladder. [52] Smoked locusts (ἀκρίδες ὑποθυμιώμεναι) help with difficulties of urination, especially in women. But the locust called Troxallis or Onos (τρωξαλλὶς ἢ ὄνος) is without wings and long-legged; a fresh one, once it is thoroughly dried and drank with wine, helps those stung by scorpions. And the Libyans in Leptis eat [this locust] indulgently (χρῶνται δὲ αὐτῇ κατακόρως).[120]

Dioscorides's remedy suggests that his patients would only eat cicadas or grasshoppers under such dire conditions. The diet of Dioscorides's presumed audience may thus plausibly be distinguished from that of certain Libyans, who regularly, and abundantly, made use of Troxallis or Onos locusts/grasshoppers as food.

In addition, the Elder Pliny, whose depiction of the Ethiopian Locust Eaters has already been discussed in this chapter (*HN* 6.35.195; cf. 11.32.92; 11.35.106), also knows of such a remedy:

> To eat thrushes with myrtle berries is good for the urine (*edisse . . . prodest urinae*), [as are] cicadas roasted (*cicadas tostas*) in a shallow pan; to take in drink the millipede *oniscos* is also [good] for pains in the bladder (*bibisse et in vesicae doloribus*), [as is] the broth of lambs' trotters. (*HN* 30.21.68)

Additional medicinal uses for locusts/grasshoppers are also mentioned by Pseudo-Dioscorides and Oribasius (*c.* 320–400 C.E.; Med.).[121] Each of these medical writers of the Roman period—Dioscorides, Galen, Pseudo-

---

[119] Gal., *De loc. aff.* 6.3.7.512 (6.3.3.311): ἀττελάβους . . . ἀπλήστως ἐσθίοντα. Greek: K. G. Kühn, ed., *Claudii Galeni, Opera omnia*, 8.397.4–6; ET: Siegel, *Galen*, 176.

[120] Dioscorides, *De mat. med.* 2.51–52. Greek: Max Wellmann, ed., *Pedanii Dioscuridis Anazarbei, De materia medica libri quinque* (Berlin: Weidmann, 1958 [1907]), 1.137; cf. Otto Mazal, *Der Wiener Dioskurides: Codex medicus Graecus 1 der Österreichischen Nationalbibliothek* (Glanzlichter der Buchkunst 8; Graz: Akademische Druck u. Verlagsanstalt, 1998–99); the ET is mine. A dated and less literal ET is available in: Robert T. Gunther, ed., *The Greek Herbal of Dioscorides* (New York: Hafner, 1968 [Oxford: Oxford University, 1934]), 105 (listed as *De mat. med.* 2.56–57).

[121] Ps. Dioscorides, *De mat. med.* 2.115 (2.109); Oribasius, *Ecl. Med. Fr.* 63.5 (64.5). The Greek texts appear, respectively, in: M. Wellmann, ed., *Pedanii Dioscuridis Anazarbei, De materia medica*, 3.296–7; Johann Raeder, ed., *Oribasii, Collectionum medicarum reliquiae* (CMG 6.2.2; Amsterdam: Hakkart, 1964 [1933]), 227.

Dioscorides and Oribasius—supports the inference that most people in good health in these authors' implied audiences would ordinarily not eat such insects.

d) *A Later Fable from the* Fables of Aesop

Complementing the aforementioned witnesses, a later, possibly medieval, fable associated with Aesop implies the inadequacy of locusts as food:

> A fowler heard a locust and thought he was going to make a big catch, making the mistake of judging the size of his catch by the song. But when he put his art into practice and caught his prey, he got nothing but song and found fault with expectation for leading people to false conclusions.[122]

This testimony contrasts with earlier Aesopic materials that present locusts as human food (*Aesop's Fables* 241 [224]; *Life of Aesop* 99). Along with the testimonies of Strabo, Pliny, Athenaeus, Plutarch, Galen, Dioscorides, Pseudo-Dioscorides and Oribasius, this fable of Aesop highlights a significant shift that began during the Roman period: Locusts are not an adequate source of food for humans and can therefore exemplify the fable's moral teaching against presumptuousness.

9. Tertullian on the Delight of Marcionite Christians in Locusts as Food

The North African church father Tertullian (*c.* 160–240 C.E.) likewise reflects knowledge of locust eating. In his treatise *Against Marcion*, Tertullian presents his Marcionite Christian opponents as extolling the goodness of the creation of humanity as superior even to the divinity's gift of locusts as human food: "Hemmed in by these arguments, they break out and say, 'Sufficient to our god is this one single work, that he has by his great and particular kindness set man free, a kindness of more value than all the preferred [types of] locusts (*omnibus locustis anteponenda*).'"[123] Additionally, a less certain,

---

[122] *Aesop's Fables* 397 ("The Fowler and the Locust" [ἰξευτὴς καὶ τέττιξ]). Greek: Perry, *Aesopica*, 482; ET: Daly, *Aesop*, 221. Perry, *Life and Fables of Aesop*, 82–145, notes that this fable is not extant in the earliest MSS (2nd c. C.E.?) of *Aesop's Fables* and therefore cannot be dated with confidence prior to *c.* 1100 C.E. (cf. 229–30).

[123] Tert., *Adv. Marcionem* 1.17. Lat.: Ernest Evans, ed., *[Tertullian,] Adversus Marcionem* (OECT; Oxford: Clarendon, 1972), 42. The ET is also Evans's, with the exception that Evans's translation of *omnibus locustis anteponenda* ("any number of destructive insects") is corrected above. Evans seems to infer incorrectly that Tertullian's reference to 'locusts' is unfavorable, which is impossible given the positive comparison to the liberation of humanity. On the contrary, Tertullian understands correctly his opponent's favorable reference to 'locusts' as human food.

but nonetheless plausible, reference to locust eating may be found in Tertullian's work *On the Soul*.[124]

10. The Witness of Jerome to a Plurality of Sentiments about Locust Eating

Additional comments by Jerome (*c.* 347–419/20 C.E.) on the Baptist's diet will be examined in chapter 5 (*Epp.* 22.36, 38.3, 107.3, 125.7). Of interest to the discussion at present is his witness to the eating of locusts in certain areas, as well as the aversion to this food elsewhere. In his work *Against Jovinian*, Jerome maintains that, however peculiar, the food of various peoples corresponds to what flourishes in their midst: "But who does not know that no universal law of nature regulates the food of all nations, and that each eats those things of which it has abundance?" Jerome offers the following example to illustrate this point:

> Again, because throughout the glowing wastes of the desert clouds of locusts are found, it is customary with the peoples of the East and of Libya to feed on locusts (*rursum Orientales et Libyae populos . . . locustis vesci moris est*). John the Baptist proves the truth of this. Compel a Phrygian or a native of Pontus to eat a locust, and he will think it scandalous (*nefas*).[125]

What peoples Jerome designates as Eastern/'Oriental' is not entirely clear, since his mention of the non-locust eating peoples in Phrygia and Pontus would exclude, respectively, the south-western and northern parts of Asia Minor. For Jerome, then, the mention of actual locust eaters in the East and Libya provides ammunition in a polemical debate concerning different peoples' habits concerning food.

In addition to those in Phrygia and Pontus, Jerome suggests that, around the turn of the fifth century C.E., Christian monks also eat locusts:

> *Præcursor ejus et præco Joannes locustis alitur, et silvestris melle, non carnibus: habitatioque deserti et incunabula monachorum, talibus inchoantur alimentis.*

---

[124] At *De anima* 15.2, Tertullian writes of removing the heads of locusts and certain other creatures: "Asclepiades rides rough-shod over us with even this argument, that very many animals, after losing those parts of their body in which the soul's principle of vitality and sensation is thought mainly to exist, still retain life in a considerable degree, as well as sensation: as in the case of flies, and wasps, and locusts (*locustae*), when you have cut off their heads; and of she-goats, and tortoises, and eels, when you have pulled out their hearts. (He concludes), therefore, that there is no special principle or power of the soul." Unlike Aristotle or Galen, Tertullian was not a 'scientist' with interests in anatomical observations. Even if Tertullian's main concern in *De anima* is to demonstrate the existence of the soul, the most likely reason for his knowing about the removal of locusts' heads would be from knowledge of people who eat them. Lat.: J. H. Waszink, ed., *Quinti Septimi Florentis Tertulliani, De anima* (Amsterdam: Meulenhoff, 1947), 19; ET: ANF, 3.193.

[125] Jerome, *Adv. Iovin.* 2.7. Lat.: *PL* 23.221–352; here, 23.308; ET: NPNF, II/6.393.

His [Jesus'] forerunner and herald, John, fed on locusts and wild honey, not on flesh—both the habitation of the desert and the initial residence of monks begins with such foods.[126]

The oddity of this food is precisely the reason why Jerome mentions it as an example in this work.[127]

11. Conclusion: Locust Eating during the Classical and Hellenistic Periods, and the Aversion to Locust Eating that Began with the Roman Period

The present study has argued that the eating of locusts, grasshoppers or cicadas was not particularly extraordinary during the Classical and Hellenistic Periods.[128] Much more common in the Roman period, however, are expressions of aversion to locust eating.[129] As noted immediately above, Jerome testifies to both perspectives (*Adv. Iovin.* 2.7, 2.15). In general, the subject of insect eating tends not to receive much attention from classicists or ancient historians, let alone scholars of religion, such as the present author. Even less effort has been devoted to explaining the relative *lack* of witnesses to locust eating in certain sources, beginning in the Roman period.

Two scholars—the only two the present author has found—address this problem, suggesting that, unlike in the Greek East, the culinary tastes of the Latin West did not favor locusts/grasshoppers. Magen Broshi, after noting the habit of locust eating in Palestine in antiquity, suggests that, by contrast, "In Rome grasshoppers were regarded as food fit only for Orientals."[130] For this comparison, Broshi refers to Jacques André, who writes:

La concommation de vers du rouvre, qui'on engraissait même parfois à la farine, est aussi un résidu de l'alimentation primitive. C'est, avec l'escargot, tout ce que les Romains

---

[126] *Adv. Iovin.* 2.15. Lat.: *PL* 23.308; ET (modified): NPNF, II/6.400.

[127] So also the seventh-century Byzantine historian Theophylact Simocatta, *Ep.* 14, with locusts recognized as "meat" (ἀκρίδες τὰ ὄψα); cf. H. Gossen, "Heuschrecke," 1386; Bochart, *Hierozoicon,* 3.330. On the date and activities of Theophylact, see: Michael Whitby and Mary Whitby, *The History of Theophylact Simocatta* (Oxford: Clarendon/New York: Oxford University Press, 1986), xiii–xvii.

[128] Herod., *Hist.* 4.172; Ar., *Ach.* 870–1, 1114–7; Theoc., *Id.* 1.52; Arist., *HA* 5.30 (556B); Alexis, *Fr.* 167.13 (162.13); Anaxandrides, *Fr.* 42.59 (41.59); Diod. Sic., *Hist.* 3.29; *Life of Aesop* 99; Plin. (E), *HN* 11.32.92; 11.35.106; 30.21.68; Tert., *Adv. Marcionem* 1.17; *De anima* 15.2.

[129] Strabo, *Geog.* 16.4.12; Plin. (E), *HN* 6.35.195; Ath., *Deip.* 4.133B; Plut., *De soll. an.* 976D, *Quaest. conv.* 8.7.3 (727E); Dioscorides (Med.), *De mat. med.* 2.51–2; Ps. Dioscorides, *De mat. med.* 2.115 (2.109); Oribasius, *Ecl. Med. Fr.* 63.5 (64.5); Gal., *De simp. med. temp.* 11.13.312 (11.2.149); *Aesop's Fables* 397.

[130] Broshi, "Diet of Palestine in the Roman Period," 51 n.4, referring to Jacques André, *L'alimentation et la cuisine à Rome* (Études et commentaires 38; Paris: C. Klincksieck, 1961), 129 n.201.

doivent au ramassage. Ils ont ignoré les cigales et les sauterelles dont se régalaient les Orientaux.[131]

Of great interest to this study is André's negative generalization (followed by Broshi) that the Romans, unlike Palestinian Jews and other peoples of the ancient Mediterranean world, ignored cicadas and grasshoppers as food, or at least would have disdained the eating of these insects if they had known about them.

Of course, it is exceedingly difficult to prove definitively what inhabitants of the Italian peninsula during the imperial period *did not* eat.[132] Nonetheless, in stating that the Romans were unaware of cicadas and grasshoppers as food, André notes correctly that the Elder Pliny and several other ancient authors mention locust eating, in order to make the practices of such exotic peoples known to a Roman audience. The most likely context for a communication describing peoples somehow 'different' from 'us' is one in which *the author's* (whether Pliny or Mark the evangelist) *own culture or presumed audience does not eat locusts/grasshoppers.*

It does not necessarily follow, however, that a simple East-West distinction best accounts for the divergent views toward locust eating in the ancient sources. Rather than an exclusively *geographic* (the Latin West) or *ethnic* (the Italian peninsula) exception to locusts/grasshoppers as food, the development seems to have occurred over time, perhaps a product of the 'Romanization'—however unintentional or unorganized this may have been—of the ancient Mediterranean diet in late antiquity. Differing somewhat from Broshi and André, then, the present study proposes a *diachronic* account for the more pronounced aversion to humans' eating such insects during the Roman period. This development offers a remarkable parallel to numerous patristic authors, to be discussed in chapter 5, who deprive the Baptist of his locusts and apportion to him instead manna (*Gospel of the Ebionites*), milk (several witnesses to Tatian's *Diatessaron*), or vegetation (Athanasius of Alexandria, Isidore of Pelusium and many others) with his honey. An examination of the Baptist's other wilderness provision, his "wild honey," follows in chapter 3.

---

[131] J. André, *L'alimentation et la cuisine à Rome* (Collection d'études anciennes; Paris: Belles Lettres, [2]1981), 126. In a footnote (126 n.201), André refers to Plin. (E), *HN* 6.195; 11.92; 11.106; and H. Gossen, "Heuschrecke," 1386 (although Gossen himself does not make this claim).

[132] Of potential interest in this regard is the silence of *De re coquinaria* (4th c. C.E.), attributed to M. Gavius Apicius (1st c. C.E.), concerning locusts as human food. Latin text and ET: Barbara Flower and Elisabeth Rosenbaum, *The Roman Cookery Book: A Critical Translation of «The Art of Cooking» by Apicius, for Use in the Study and the Kitchen* (London; Toronto: Harrap, 1958).

Chapter 3

The Baptist's "Wild Honey"

μικρὰ ἐν πετεινοῖς μέλισσα
καὶ ἀρχὴ γλυκασμάτων ὁ καρπὸς αὐτῆς[1]

²אכל דבש הרבות לא־טוב

The previous chapter was devoted to the Baptist's ἀκρίδες. Chapter 3 studies ancient perspectives on apiculture (beekeeping) and various kinds of 'wild honey,' in order to ascertain the referent and significance attached to μέλι ἄγριον in Mark 1:6c‖Matt 3:4c. Chapter 4 will consider the nutritional aspects of these foods, as well as what light the habits of recent and contemporary locust-eating peoples shed on the historical Baptist. The implications of these studies of "locusts and wild honey" for our understanding of the historical Baptist and the presentation of his diet in the Synoptics will also be assessed in the following chapter.

A. Prolegomena:
Defining "Honey"

Unlike locusts/grasshoppers, most Western (and non-Western) people today readily identify honey as a pleasing garnish. A word of caution concerning the possible meaning(s) of the Baptist's "wild honey" is in order, however. By itself, μέλι—like the Hebrew דבש or *mel* in Latin—can refer equally to honey produced by bees or to any number of other sweet substances, including those made from dates, figs, pods, or sap/gum from carob or other trees.[3]

---

[1] Sir 11:3: "The bee is small among flying creatures, but what it produces is the best of sweet things."

[2] Prov 25:27a: "It is not good to eat [too] much honey." Cf. Prov 25:16: "If you have found honey, eat only enough for you, or else, having too much, you will vomit it."

[3] Eva Crane, "History of Honey," in: *Honey: A Comprehensive Survey* (ed. E. Crane; London: Heinemann, 1975), 439–88; here, 453; Samuel Krauss, "Honig in Palästina," *ZDPV* 32 (1909): 151–64; D. Simonsen, "Milch und Honig: (Eine Erwiderung)," *ZDPV* 33 (1910): 44–6; Heinrich Hänsler, "Noch einmal 'Honig im hl. Lande,'" *ZDPV* 35 (1912): 186–99; L. H. Silberman, "Honig," art. *Biblisch-historisches Handwörterbuch: Landeskunde, Geschichte, Religion, Kultur, Literatur* (ed. Bo Reicke and Leonhard Rost; Göttingen: Vandenhoeck & Ruprecht, 1962–79), 2.747; LSJ, s.v. μέλι.

For this reason, Eva Crane warns concerning possible references to bee honey in ancient civilizations: "Unless the context makes clear a connection with hives, bees, or honeycomb, caution is warranted."[4] It is therefore difficult to ascertain which sweet substance is designated as 'honey' in certain ancient writings, including a number of biblical passages.[5] Yet most biblical scholars do not even consider which type of 'honey' the Baptist ate.[6] Numerous others simply assume that John ate bee honey[7] or sweet tree sap (sometimes referred to as honey-water)[8] and do not reflect an awareness of the *inherent ambiguity* in almost any occurrence of μέλι without an accompanying reference either to bees or vegetation (trees).

In Mark 1:6c‖Matt 3:4c, the adjective ἄγριον distinguishes the μέλι that John the Baptist ate from other types of 'honey.'[9] Accordingly, the Baptist is portrayed as eating some kind of 'honey' that humans *did not* cultivate. As is

---

[4] "History of Honey," 453.

[5] E.g., Gen 43:11; Exod 16:31; Jer 41:8; Ezek 3:3; 16:13, 19; Pss 19:10; 119:103; Prov 5:3; 24:13; 25:16; 25:27a; 27:7; Song 4:11; Rev 10:9. Exceptionally, Deut 8:8 ("a land of wheat and barley, of the vine and fig tree and pomegranate, a land of the olive tree and honey") distinguishes between the fig tree (תאנה) and honey (דבש). Cf. unspecified references to "honey" in Ar., *Ach.* 1130; Philo, *Det.* 115, 117, 118; 4Q372 f3:5; 4Q378 (4QapocrJoshua^a) f11:6; 4Q386 (4QpsEzek^b) 2:5; 11Q19 (11QT^a) 60:9; Jos., *Ant.* 2.6.5 (§118), 3.1.6 (§28), 14.7.4 (§124) = *B.J.* 1.9.1 (§184).

[6] On this point, see chapter 1, nn.2–5. Conversely, Mauriz Schuster, "Mel," art. PW 15.364–84, esp. 364–6; Gould, *Mark*, 8; Strack and Billerbeck, *Kommentar zum NT*, 1.100–1; Wilhelm Michaelis, "μέλι," art. TDNT, 4.552–4; A. Loisy, *Marc*, 57; M.-J. Lagrange, *Marc*, 3; A. Plummer, *Mark*, 4; A. E. J. Rawlinson, *Mark*, 9; V. Taylor, *Mark*, 156; and C. H. Kraeling, *John the Baptist*, 10–11, do appreciate this ambiguity.

[7] For example, Alford, *Greek NT*, 1.18: "there is no need to suppose any thing else meant but honey made by wild bees"; H. B. Swete, *Mark*, 6; T. Zahn, *Matthäus*, 133; R. C. H. Lenski, *The Interpretation of St. Mark's Gospel* (Minneapolis: Augsburg, 1964), 38; G. Dalman, *Sacred Sites*, 84; F. I. Andersen, "Diet," 62–4; Davies and Allison, *Matthew*, 1.296; Leon Morris, *The Gospel according to Matthew* (Grand Rapids: Eerdmans, 1992), 55; C. S. Keener, *Matthew*, 119; J. E. Taylor, *Immerser*, 34; U. Müller, *Johannes der Täufer*, 24 ("Wildbienenhonig"); J. H. Charlesworth, "John the Baptizer," 367–8; W. B. Tatum, *John the Baptist and Jesus: A Report of the Jesus Seminar*, 11, 29; E. F. Lupieri, "'The Law and the Prophets Were until John,'" 50–1; A. Dalby, *Food in the Ancient World*, 179–80. Additionally, BDAG discusses different possibilities under the entry for ἄγριος (p. 15), but only bee honey in the entry for μέλι (p. 627). Moreover, although BDAG (p. 627) refers to the aforementioned article by S. Krauss ("Honig in Palästina"), it does not call attention to the multivalence of the term μέλι (cf. the translation given at BDAG, 15: "honey fr[om] wild bees").

[8] This view is notably less common in the secondary literature. For John's honey as sweet tree sap see, e.g., H. A. W. Meyer, *Matthew* (New York/London: Funk & Wagnalls, 1884 [^{6}1876]), 76–7; B. Weiss, *Matthew-Mark*, 13.

[9] So Michaelis, "μέλι," 553–4: "ἄγριον rules out both the honey from beekeeping and fruit honey which comes from human labour"; cf. UBS Committee on Translations, *Fauna and Flora*, 103–4.

discussed below, in antiquity, honey from bees is not the only sweet substance that lends itself to the designation "wild." It is therefore conceivable
that the original, or at least a pre-Markan, form of this characterization of the
Baptist may have been intended to denote honey from bees, which could in
turn have been construed as a different sweet substance by Mark, Matthew or
a later recipient of this gospel material. Of course, the opposite scenario is
equally possible. Due to the ambiguity inherent in eating (ἐσθίων, Mark
1:6c) or designating as a food (τροφή, Matt 3:4c) "wild honey," this chapter
will consider ancient materials pertinent to bee honey, as well as other sweet
substances designated דבשׁ, μέλι or *mel*.

B. "Honey" Produced by Bees

This section considers primarily ancient references to 'wild honey' produced
by bees. A certain amount of overlap with the following section, devoted to
'wild honey' stemming from trees, is unavoidable, however.

1. Introduction: The Late Arrival of Apiculture in Palestine

In the in the ancient Near East, the cultivation of bee honey can be documented as early as the 26th or 25th c. B.C.E.: A scene from the Sun Temple of
Ny-woser-Rē at Abusīr depicts beekeeping in Middle Egypt.[10] Evidence for
the use of bee honey on the Nile River survives also from Thebes (modern
Qena; *c.* 1380–1130 B.C.E.).[11] In Egypt the practice continued through the
Ptolemaic and Roman periods, and beyond.[12] The earliest literary references
to honey from bees stem from Nip(p)ur (100 mi./160 km. SE of Babylon;

---

[10] Hélène Chouliara-Raïos, *L'Abeille et le miel en Égypte d'après les Papyrus Grecs*
(Ioannina: Philosophike Schole Panepistemiou Ioanninon, 1989), 19–31; Edward Neufeld,
"Apiculture in Ancient Palestine (Early and Middle Iron Age) within the Framework of the
Ancient Near East," *UF* 10 (1978): 219–47; here, 232–3; G. Kuény, "Scènes apicoles dans
l'Ancienne Égypte," *JNES* 9 (1950): 84–93; H. Malcolm Fraser, *Beekeeping in Antiquity*
(London: University of London, [2]1951), 2–5.

[11] E. Crane, "History of Honey," 455–6; eadem, *The Archaeology of Beekeeping* (Ithaca,
NY: Cornell University, 1983), 45–51; eadem, *Bees and Beekeeping: Science, Practice and
World Resources* (Ithaca, NY: Comstock, 1990), 17–29; Yannis Tzedakis and Holley
Martlew, *Minoans and Mycenaeans: Flavours of Their Time, National Archaeological Mu-
seum, 12 July–27 November 1999* (Athens: Kapon, 1999), 117–19; here, 117, on "a cooking
jar . . . that contained beeswax, an almost certain indication of honey" (cf. 133, 168–70, 176).
Moreover, Neufeld, "Apiculture," 235, dates a wall painting depicting honeycomb from the
tomb of Rekh-mi-Re at Thebes to the 15th c. B.C.E.

[12] Chouliara-Raïos, *L'Abeille*, 65–95.

c. 2100–2000 B.C.E.).[13] In Mesopotamia, moreover, beekeeping had become a practice by the 8th c. B.C.E.[14]

Centuries later, Aristotle would write at some length about the habits of bees, and his references to the practices and testimonies of beekeepers suggest more than a casual acquaintance with those who practiced this trade.[15] Aristotle and numerous other Greco-Roman authors recognized that the quality of honey was dependent upon the amount of rainfall and types of flowers extant in different regions and seasons.[16] It may come as no surprise, however, that Aristotle and other Greco-Roman writers and writings, such as Varro, Columella, the Elder Pliny, Palladius, and the *Geoponica*, offer copious advice concerning apiculture but have little, if anything, to say about 'wild' honeys.[17]

2. Cultivated Bee Honey in the Hebrew Bible?

In contrast to the aforementioned witnesses to beekeeping, the Jewish scriptures contain no reference to the domestication of bees, and there is no evidence for this practice in Palestine prior to the late Hellenistic period.[18] Scholars have therefore sought to clarify whether the HB's many references to "a land flowing with milk and 'honey'" designate a sweet substance derived from trees (dates, figs or sweet tree sap) or honey produced by bees.[19] It

---

[13] Crane, "History of Honey," 454; cf. 439–53, on the uses of bee honey in prehistoric times; eadem, *Archaeology of Beekeeping*, 19–39; Adrienne Mayor, "Mad Honey! Bees and the Baneful Rhododendron," *Archaeology* 48/6 (Nov.–Dec. 1995): 32–40, esp. 33, 38.

[14] Neufeld, "Apiculture," 238–9.

[15] Arist., *HA* 5.22 (533B), 8(9).40 (623A, 626A–B, 627B); *GA* 3.10 (760A); cf. Ps. Arist., *Mir. ausc.* 16–22 (831B-832A); Fraser, *Beekeeping in Antiquity*, 13–28.

[16] *HA* 5.22 (533B, 554B); 8(9).40 (626B–627A), *GA* 3.10 (760B); Cato (234–149 B.C.E.), *Rust.* 76 (on "good honey" [*mellis boni*] as part of a recipe); Varro, *Rust.* 3.16.13–14, 26–28; Pliny, *HN* 11.32–33; Columella, *Rust.* 9.4.7; Apul., *Met.* 1.5 (on traveling regularly through Thessaly, Aetolia and Boeotia to buy honey and cheese); Ael., *NA* 5.42; Palladius, *De vet. med.* 2.18, 3.27, 7.11, 11.14; *Geoponica* 15.7 (10th c. C.E.?); cf. Dalby, *Siren Feasts*, 65, 136, 208–9, 250.

[17] See Varro (116–27 B.C.E.), *Rust.* 3.16.2–38; Columella (*fl.* 50 B.C.E.), *Rust.* 9.2–16; Pliny, *HN* 11.4.11–11.23.70; Palladius (*c.* 363/4–before 431 C.E.), *De vet. med.* 5.7, 6.8, 7.7, 11.13, 12.8; *Geoponica* 15.2–9. Likewise, Aelian's work on the characteristics of the animals understandably has more to say about bees than their honey (*NA* 1.9–11, 1.59–60, 2.53, 2.57, 5.10–13, 5.42, 11.35, 17.37; cf. the Elder Cato, *Rust.* 76–84).

[18] As Neufeld, "Apiculture," 219–25, 240–7, argues, responding aptly to attempts to demonstrate this practice in the HB. See further: Richard J. Israel, "The Promised Land of Milk and Date Jam: The Problems of Bees and Honey in the Bible and the Talmud," *National Jewish Monthly* (Washington) 87/3 (1972): 26–30; here, 26; Firmage, "Zoology," art. *ABD*, 6.1150 (s.v. "bees").

[19] Exod 3:8, 17; 13:5; 33:3; Lev 20:24; Num 13:27; 14:8; 16:13–14; Deut 6:3; 11:9; 26:9, 15; 31:20; Josh 5:6; Jer 11:5; Ezek 20:6, 15; Sir 46:8; Bar 1:20; 2 Esdr 2:19; *Jub.* 1.7; cf. 2 Kgs 18:32; Job 20:17; *Sib. Or.* 3.622. See, e.g., Israel, "Milk and Date Jam," 27: "In *Ezek*.

is not necessary that the present inquiry adjudicate this debate, which highlights in literature centuries earlier than Mark 1:6c‖Matt 3:4c the potential ambiguity of any unspecified reference to 'honey' in antiquity.

Although the Jewish scriptures do not mention beekeeping, they do offer several references to undomesticated bee honey. Two concern the Lord's sustenance of the covenant people, or at least the desire to sustain them:

> He set him atop the heights of the land, and fed him with produce of the field; he nursed him with honey from the crags (דְּבַשׁ מִסֶּלַע), with oil from flinty rock. (Deut 32:13)

> I would feed you with the finest of the wheat, and with honey from the rock (וּמִצּוּר דְּבַשׁ) I would satisfy you. (Ps 81:16)

Two other passages mention the happenstance discovery of uncultivated bee honey:

> [8] After a while he [Samson] returned to marry her, and he turned aside to see the carcass of the lion, and there was a swarm of bees (עֲדַת דְּבוֹרִים) in the body of the lion, and honey (וּדְבָשׁ). [9] He scraped it out into his hands, and went on, eating as he went. When he came to his father and mother, he gave some to them, and they ate it. But he did not tell them that he had taken the honey from the carcass of the lion. (Judg 14:8–9)

> All the troops came upon a honeycomb (בְּיַעַר); and there was honey on the ground (דְּבַשׁ עַל־פְּנֵי הַשָּׂדֶה). (1 Sam 14:25)

It is unlikely that the earliest followers of John (or Jesus) would have employed Judg 14:8–9 or 1 Sam 14:25 to interpret the Baptist's "wild honey." Nonetheless, it is conceivable that Deut 32:13 or Ps 81:16 could perhaps have suggested to some that the Lord provided for John's needs in the wilderness and that such care validates the Baptist's calling as the Lord's messenger or prophet. This is not to stipulate that such was the 'original meaning' of John's μέλι ἄγριον but rather to acknowledge the possibility that such inferences could have been made by recipients of this gospel material.

3. The Proscription against Bee Eating at Qumran

The last chapter called attention to the Damascus Document[a] (Zadokite Fragment) in connection with the practice of eating roasted or boiled locusts/grasshoppers at Qumran.[20] Charlesworth's argument that the similari-

---

27:17 we have a whole list of fruit syrups—*one* of them is honey. . . . What the land was really flowing with was milk and date jam" (emphases original); Robert Blum, "Imkerei im alten Israel," *Bienenvater* (Vienna) 76/10 (1955): 334–6; Crane, "History of Honey," 457.

[20] CD 12:11b–15a: "[11b] No-one should defile his soul [12] with any living being or one which creeps, by eating them, from the larvae of bees to every living [13] being (מֵעֶגְלֵי הַדְּבוֹרִים עַד כֹּל נֶפֶשׁ הַחַיָּה) which creeps in water. And fish: they should not eat them unless they have been opened up [14] alive, and the[ir blood poured] away. And all

ties to the Baptist's diet illustrate that John ate like a former Essene has been shown to be dubious, for neither locusts/grasshoppers nor 'honey' are distinctive foods. Furthermore, CD 12:12 actually forbids eating the bees' *larvae*, not the honey that bees produce. These objections to Charlesworth's 'parallelomania' notwithstanding, the proscription against consuming the larvae of bees in CD 12:12 presupposes that some members of this community had contact with bees and opportunities to eat them.[21] Those same Jews who according to CD 12:12 should refrain from eating bees would presumably have chances to partake of bee honey, which the Damascus Document does not proscribe.

Moreover, *Hypothetica* 11.8, which Eusebius of Caesarea (d. *c.* 340 C.E.) attributes to Philo of Alexandria (1st c. C.E.), makes explicit such a characterization of the Essenes: "Some of them labor on the land skilled in sowing and planting, some as herdsmen taking charge of every kind of cattle and some superintend the swarms of bees (ἔνιοι δὲ σμήνη μελιττῶν ἐπιτροπεύουσιν)."[22] This would represent a difference between the Baptist and the Essenes, since John is said to eat wild honey (μέλι ἄγριον), not cultivated honey.

4. Philo of Alexandria: Explaining the Uncleanness of Bees

The disparity between the development of apiculture outside of Palestine, on the one hand, and the absence of bee domestication within Palestine before the late Hellenistic period, on the other hand, has been noted above. The absence of beekeeping in Palestine could stem in part from Lev 2:11, which forbids all kinds of honey (כל־דבש) from being mixed with grain offerings.[23] Referring to Lev 2:11, Philo offers the following commentary on the uncleanness of bees:

> [God] adds too a further enactment by which he orders every sacrifice to be offered without honey or leaven. Both these substances [God] considers unfit to be brought to the altar; honey perhaps (ἐπειδήπερ) because the bee which collects it is an unclean animal,

---

the locusts, according to their kind, shall be put into the fire or into water [15a] while [they are] still alive, as this is the regulation for their species." See chapter 2, 53–54.

[21] Cf. Gene R. DeFoliart, "Insects as Food: Why the Western Attitude Is Important," *Annual Review of Entomology* (Palo Alto, CA) 44 (1999): 21–50; here, 37; L. Ozimek et al., "Nutritive Value of Protein Extracted from Honey Bees," *Journal of Food Science* (Chicago) 50 (1985): 1327–9, 1332, on the eating of bees.

[22] Euseb., *Praep. evang.* 8.11.8. Greek text and ET: F. H. Colson et al., *Philo* (LCL; Cambridge, MA: Harvard University/London: Heinemann, 1962 [1929]), 9.440–1. The whole of this fragment (*Hypothetica* 11, one of two that survive; both are in Eusebius's *Preparatio*) describes the habits of the Essenes.

[23] Lev 2:11: "No grain offering that you bring to the LORD shall be made with leaven, for you must not turn any leaven or any honey (וכל־דבש) into smoke as an offering by fire to the LORD."

bread from the putrescence and corruption of dead oxen, we are told, just as wasps are from the carcasses of horses; or else (ἤ) [God] forbids it as a symbol of the utter unholiness of excessive pleasure which tastes sweet as it passes through the throat but afterwards produces bitter and persistent pains, which of necessity shake and agitate the soul and make it unable to stand firmly in its place.[24]

Philo suggests that Lev 11:20–23, which prohibits dining on 'creeping' insects but allows the eating of certain species of locusts/grasshoppers,[25] offers a possible rationale for Lev 2:11. The logic imputed to these two commands in Leviticus seems to be that because bees are not to be eaten, bee honey is unfit for the Lord's altar. However tentative, Philo's linking of Lev 2:11 with Lev 11:20–23 may suggest a stigma against coming into close contact with bees. That Philo's reasoning equivocates between eating bee larvae and offering to the Lord the honey these insects produce is beside the point. What is significant to this inquiry is that the dual prohibitions of bees as human food (Lev 11:20–23) and their honey for grain offerings (Lev 2:11) could have given rise to an aversion to entering into the close contact with bees necessitated by apiary. This inference based upon Philo's reasoning in *Spec.* 1.291–292 could contribute to an explanation for the relative lack of apiculture in Palestine.[26]

At any rate, at the time of John the Baptist almost all bee honey in Palestine would have been uncultivated. For a Palestinian audience, then, calling the Baptist's honey "wild" (ἄγριον) could constitute a tautology. Given the suspicion that Philo associates with honey, moreover, it is unlikely that he would have associated Mark 1:6c‖Matt 3:4c with the diet of an ascetic. For Philo, such earthly honey stands in contrast to the 'bread' tasting like honey with which the Lord wishes to fill the human soul (*Fug.* 138; cf. Exod 16:15). It is thus possible that μέλι ἄγριον in Mark 1:6c‖Matt 3:4c either does not refer to bee honey, or was composed for a non-Palestinian audience or by a non-Palestinian author who would not have known about the paucity of apiculture in Palestine.

---

[24] Philo, *Spec.* 1.291–292. Of the two reasons suggested in *On the Special Laws* 1.291–292 for why honey is prohibited in Lev 2:11, Philo mentions only the latter in *Congr.* 169: "And further it is forbidden by law to bring any leaven or any honey (πᾶν μέλι προσφέρειν) to the altar. For it is a hard matter to consecrate the holy as the sweet flavors of bodily pleasures or the risings of the soul in their leaven-like thinness and sponginess, so profane and unholy are they by their very nature."

[25] See the discussion of Lev 11:20–23 in chapter 2.

[26] This is not to suggest an aversion to contact with bees by all Palestinian Jews, however. According to Eusebius of Caesarea, Philo (*Hypothetica* 11.8) characterizes some Essenes as beekeepers.

5. Honeys in Josephus and the Mishnah

Compared with the HB, the Mishnah offers greater specificity concerning kinds of 'honey,' although the same ambiguity remains in several passages.[27] The Mishnah contains references to honeys from both bees[28] and dates.[29] In *Nedarim* 6, date honey seems to be less precious than both dates and another type of 'honey':

> [8] He who takes a vow not to eat dates (מן התמרים) is permitted to have date honey (בדבש תמרים). [He who takes a vow not to eat] winter grapes is permitted to have the vinegar made from winter grapes. . . . [9] He who takes a vow not to have wine is permitted to have apple wine. [He who takes a vow not to have] oil is permitted to have sesame oil. He who takes a vow not to have honey (מן הדבש) is permitted to have date honey (בדבש תמרים). . . . (*m. Ned.* 6:8–9)

In *Ned.* 6:9, the other honey mentioned apparently stems from bees. If correct, a vow to abstain from bee honey would not be broken by partaking of date honey.

The greater esteem given to bee honey suggested in the Mishnah corresponds to an earlier testimony of Josephus (37/8–after 94 C.E.):

> Of the date-palms watered by it [a nearby spring] there are numerous varieties differing in flavor and in medicinal properties; the richer species of this fruit when pressed under foot emit copious honey, not much inferior to that of bees. And so the region is abundant in honey (μέλι δαψιλές ἀνιᾶσιν οὐ πολλῷ τοῦ λοιποῦ χεῖρον. καὶ μελιττοτρόφος δ᾽ ἡ χώρα).[30]

Josephus describes dates and bees (cf. μελίσσαι [μελίτται]), and thus the honey associated with each, as plentiful near Jericho.[31] These two witnesses thus attest a hierarchy among honeys: Bee honey is more highly esteemed than date honey (Jos., *B.J.* 4.8.3 [§468]; *Ned.* 6:9).

6. The Potential Dangers of Consuming 'Wild Honey'

An advantage to consuming cultivated honey is that the eater can anticipate the relative quality (or lack thereof) of what s/he is about to enjoy. Conversely, partaking of wild honey could be dangerous, if the bees were to

---

[27] Mishnaic references to 'honey' without specification: *m. Maʿas. Š.* 2:1, 5:13; *m. Ḥal.* 1:4; *m. Bik.* 1:10; *m. Šabb.* 8:1, 12:5, 22:1; *m. Qidd.* 2:2; *m. B. Qam.* 10:4; *m. Šebu.* 3:3; *m. Ṭehar.* 3:2; *m. Makš.* 5:9; cf. *m. Soṭah* 9:12 (honey of "supim").

[28] Honey from bees: *m. Šeb.* 10:7; *m. ʿAbod. Zar.* 2:7; *m. Ned.* 6:9; *m. Makš.* 6:4 (honey from bees and honey from hornets); *m. ʿUq.* 3:10.

[29] Honey from dates: *m. Ter.* 11:2–3; *m. Bik.* 1:3, 3:9; *m. Ned.* 6:8–9.

[30] Jos., *B.J.* 4.8.3 (§468); Greek text and ET (modified): Thackeray, LCL. Cf. Varro, *Rust.* 3.16.24.

[31] In addition, *Joseph and Aseneth* 16.8–23 points to the existence of undomesticated bees and 'wild honey' in Palestine. Cf. Kraeling, *John the Baptist*, 10–13; Andersen, "Diet," 60.

make honey with pollen from poisonous flowers.[32] Xenophon, Ps. Aristotle, Strabo and Pliny demonstrate that the dangers of eating such 'maddening honey' were well known in antiquity.

a) Xenophon and Ps. Aristotle: Hapless Honey

Xenophon (b. *c.* 430 B.C.E.) describes the infamous 'Retreat of the Ten Thousand' that followed the death of Cyrus the Younger in 401 B.C.E. In the vicinity of Trebizonde in Asia Minor, the soldiers who ate the local bee honey subsequently displayed symptoms like inebriation and madness, as well as vomiting and diarrhea.[33] The soldiers helped themselves to this honey, and Xenophon does not suggest that the local people, who presumably would have known to avoid it, ate from it. Mercifully, no one died from eating the honey, and the ailments dissipated within three or four days (*An.* 4.8.21).

Moreover, the collection of tidbits attributed to Aristotle in the work, *On Marvelous Things Heard*, likewise mentions such dangerous honey in Asia Minor: "At Trapezus in Pontus honey from boxwood has a strong scent (τὸ ἀπὸ τῆς πύξου μέλι βαρύοσμον); and they say that healthy people go mad (ἐξιστάναι), but that epileptics are cured by it immediately."[34]

b) Strabo: "Maddening Honey"

Writing later than Xenophon and, presumably, Ps. Aristotle, Strabo (*c.* 64–after 21 B.C.E.) relates the *intentional* drugging of foreign troops with 'wild honey.' Strabo's account follows how the Heptacometae (Mosynoeci) once inflicted heavy losses on Pompey's army (67 B.C.E.):

> For they mixed bowls of the crazing honey that the branches [boughs?] of trees yield (κρατῆρας . . . τοῦ μαινομένου μέλιτος, ὃ φέρουσιν οἱ ἀκρεμόνες τῶν δένδρων), and placed them in the roads. Then when the soldiers drank the mixture and lost their senses, they attacked them and easily disposed of them. (*Geog.* 12.3.18; ET [modified]: LCL)

---

[32] Jonathan Ott examines this phenomenon, both in antiquity and among the pre-Columbian Yucatecan Mayans in South America: "The Delphic Bee: Bees and Toxic Honeys as Pointers to Psychoactive and Other Medicinal Plants," *Economic Botany* (New York) 52/3 (1998): 260–6. For a more popular treatment of the subject, see A. Mayor's aforementioned article, "Mad Honey! Bees and the Baneful Rhododendron."

[33] Xen., *An.* 4.8.20: "Now for the most part there was nothing here which they really found strange; but the swarms of bees in the neighborhood were numerous, and the soldiers who ate of the honey all went off their heads (ἄφρονες), and suffered from vomiting and diarrhea, and not one of them could stand up (ὀρθός); but those who had eaten a little were like people exceedingly drunk (σφόδρα μεθύουσιν), while those who had eaten a great deal seemed like crazy (μαινομένοις), or even, in some cases, like dying [men]." ET: Carleton L. Brownson, LCL, 1998.

[34] Ps. Arist., *Mir. ausc.* 18. Greek text and ET (modified): Hett, LCL. Cf. Ael., *NA* 5.42, who seems to paraphrase Ps. Arist., *Mir. ausc.* 18.

In Greek, ἀκρεμόνες could refer to the trees' "branches" or "boughs." An additional, and for this study more significant, point of uncertainty concerns whether this 'honey' is the production of wild bees or is to be identified with the trees' own sap.[35]

c) Pliny and Columella: "Maddening Honey" and Third-Rate 'Wild Honey'

In addition to Xenophon, Ps. Aristotle and Strabo, the Elder Pliny (23/24 C.E.–79 C.E.) discusses such maddening honey in Asia Minor, as well as the drawbacks of eating 'wild honey.' He describes the former kind of honey as follows: "At Heraclia in Pontus the honey turns out in certain years very deadly (*perniciosissima*), and this from the same bees" that are known to produce harmless honey in other years.[36] A different type of bee honey, also from Pontus, is consistently deleterious:

> There is another kind of honey . . . among the people [called] Sanni, which from the madness it produces is called maenomenon (*mellis, quod ab insania quam gignit maenomenon vocant*). This poison is supposed to be extracted from the flowers of the oleanders (*flore rhododendri*), which abound in the woods. Although this people supply the Romans with wax by way of tribute, they do not sell the honey, because it is deadly (*exitiale*).[37]

According to Pliny, poisoned honeycombs exist also in Persis (in Persia; modern Fārs or Fārsistan) and in Gaetulia (of Mauretania Caesariensis, in North Africa). Perhaps from observing the effects of this honey on cattle (*HN* 21.44.77), or on humans, the Greeks themselves apparently called this honey 'maddening' (*melos insanindum* ≈ μέλι μαινόμενον).

Elsewhere in his *Natural History*, Pliny extols bees for bringing honey to humankind and describes at some length the habits and characteristics of different types of bees (*HN* 11.4.11–11.23.70). He mentions only in passing two individuals who wrote about bees:

> Nobody must be surprised that love for bees inspired Aristomachus of Soli to devote himself to nothing else (*nihil aliud egisse*) for fifty-eight years, and Philiscus of Thasos in desert places, winning the name of 'Wilderness-Man' (*in desertis apes colentem Agrium cognominatum*); both of these have written about them [bees].[38]

Mention of a wilderness dweller devoted to bees with the corresponding cognomen *Agrium* (cf. ἄγριον) is of potential interest to the Baptist's diet.

---

[35] There is no such ambiguity, however, when Strabo paraphrases Aristobolus's description of a tree in India whose pods are "full of honey" (πλήρεις μέλιτος, *Geog.* 15.1.21). Cf. *Geog.* 15.1.20, 16.1.14.

[36] *HN* 21.44.74. Pliny further notes concerning this honey: "The signs of poison (*venenati signa*) [in the honey] are that it does not thicken at all, its color is mostly red, its smell is strange, at once causes sneezing, and it is heavier than harmless honey" (21.44.75).

[37] *HN* 21.45.77; cf. Mayor, "Honey," esp. 33–7.

[38] *HN* 11.9.19; ET (modified): LCL.

Unfortunately, Pliny does not reveal more about the nature of Philiscus's activities with bees.[39] Like Aristotle, Philiscus may just have studied the insects in the wild without domesticating them.

In addition, Pliny expresses preferences concerning the quality of assorted types of honey.[40] He classifies different kinds of honey according to the time of year they are produced, whether spring (*HN* 11.14.34–35), summer (11.14.36–37) or fall (11.15.41–45). He considers spring honey the most desirable and, moreover, disparages 'wild honey' produced in the fall:

> A third, very little valued, and 'wild' kind of honey (*tertium genus mellis minime probatum silvestre*), which is called heath honey, is collected after the first autumn rains, when only the heath is in bloom in the woods (*in silvis*), and consequently it resembles sandy honey (*ob id harenoso simile*).[41]

In this context, the adjective *silvestris* can designate either honey found 'in the woods' or 'undomesticated' honey.

Pliny should not, however, be accused of bias against all things grown in the wild. At *HN* 20.36.92, he praises the quality of wild cabbage. Although Jerome would later refer to the Baptist's honey thus (*silvestris melle, Adv. Iovin.* 2.15), Pliny does not provide an exact parallel to the Baptist's wilderness honey, since he mentions also the blooming of the heath *in silvis* ("in the woods"), not the desert.[42]

Moreover, Columella, a contemporary of Pliny, also underscores the dubious value of such honey: "The honey which is considered of the poorest quality is the woodland honey (*ex sordidis deterrimae notae mel habetur nemorense*), which comes from dirty feeding grounds and is produced from

---

[39] The ET by H. Rackham (". . . Philiscus of Thasos *to keep bees* in desert places, winning the name of the Wild Man") is problematic in that it ignores the parallelism denoted by Pliny's offering only one infinitive (*egisse*) to describe the actions of both Aristomachus and Philiscus (*HN* 3.445, emphasis added). So also Fraser, *Beekeeping in Antiquity*, 82: "Philiscus . . . kept bees in uninhabited country." The parallelism in the Latin implies that the activities of Aristomachus and Philiscus were similar, but Rackham's ET renders Aristomachus as devoting himself to bees and Philiscus as a beekeeper in the wilderness. To the present author, it is not clear whether observing bees over many years necessarily involves domesticating them. On the contrary, the nickname *Agrium* given to Philiscus suggests that the bees too were "wild."

[40] *HN* 11.13.32: "It is always of the best quality where it is stored (*ubi . . . conditur*) in the calyces of the best flowers. This takes place at Hymettus and Hybla in the region of Attica and of Sicily . . . and also on the island of Calydna." Cf. *HN* 11.15.38–40; 21.43.73–76.

[41] *HN* 11.15.41; ET (modified): LCL. Arist., *HA* 8(9).40 (626B) describes spring and autumn as the ideal seasons for making honey and likewise states that "the spring honey is sweeter and paler and in general better than the autumn honey."

[42] In *HN* 11.15.42, Pliny also mentions harvesting only one-third of this honey, so the bees can eat the rest during the winter months. Cf. *HN* 11.19.59, on wild and forest bees (*apes sunt et rusticae silvestresque*); Job 30:7, LXX.

broom-trees and strawberry-trees."[43] Pliny and Columella therefore highlight the *un*desirability of eating honey whose taste is limited by (pollen from) only certain species of vegetation. Whatever bee honey may have existed in John's wilderness would probably also have been exposed to fewer types of pollen.

With regard to the historical Baptist, one should not infer that his "wild honey" was drugged, as there is no evidence that such 'honey' existed in Palestine. Xenophon and Strabo relate the ailments of soldiers—especially the inability to travel or fight—that almost anyone would not choose to repeat. Nonetheless, these descriptions of Xenophon, Ps. Aristotle, Strabo, the Elder Pliny, and Columella are valuable for showing how Mark 1:6c‖Matt 3:4c could have been construed by those aware of such accounts. For such an audience, eating "wild honey" could be added to the long list of occupational hazards associated with John's prophetic calling and wilderness habitation.

7. Is Bee Honey a 'Food'?

The preceding examination of wild bee honey in antiquity merits consideration in light of a comment of Andrew Dalby. A Classicist, Dalby writes about bee honey in the diet of the ancient Greeks: "Honey is to humans essentially a relish, a flavouring agent and a preserving agent; it is never common enough to be a dietary staple."[44] As is discussed in chapter 4, consuming too much of any sweet substance, including 'honey,' can make a person sick. If correct, Dalby's characterization could mean the following for Mark 1:6c‖Matt 3:4c:

1. Mark 1:6c (ἦν . . . ἐσθίων) is not primarily about what John ate but *where* he ate his locusts/grasshoppers and 'wild honey.' Mark's claim is plausible historically and further connects John with the desert, where things grow 'in the wild' rather than by human cultivation.
2. Matt 3:4c (ἡ δὲ τροφὴ ἦν αὐτοῦ) is not realistic in that it exaggerates the amount of bee honey that would have existed in the wilderness. The motivation for such a possible exaggeration will be examined in chapter 4.
3. At least in Matt 3:4c, μέλι does not refer to bee honey at all. Moreover, a Greek audience probably would not have associated the Baptist's μέλι with honey from bees, because uncultivated bee honey was not available in such quantities, whether in Palestine or elsewhere in the ancient Mediterranean world.

The present examination of "wild honey" in antiquity will remain in dialogue with these possible implications of Dalby's thesis. If nothing else, Dalby's

---

[43] Columella, *Rust.* 9.4.7. Lat. and ET: E. S. Forster and Edward H. Heffner, eds., *On Agriculture: Lucius Junius Moderatus Columella* (LCL; Cambridge, MA: Harvard University/London: Heinemann, ²1968).

[44] Dalby, *Siren Feasts*, 47, does not refer to Mark 1:6c‖Matt 3:4c.

point highlights the importance of considering what other types of μέλι an ancient audience could have construed as the Baptist's sweet wilderness provision.

C. "Honey" Derived from Trees

The previous section considered 'wild honey' produced by bees. Given the ambiguity of 'honey' in Mark 1 and Matthew 3—since these passages do not also mention bees, tree gum/sap, dates or figs—it is incumbent upon the present study to consider other substances that were also referred to as 'honey' in antiquity.

1. Plentiful "Wild Honey" in a Pleasing Beverage: Diodorus and Pliny

Diodorus of Sicily (*fl. c.* 60–30 B.C.E.) appears first in this section because his account of wild 'honey' collected from trees is the most detailed and offers a striking parallel to Mark 1:6c‖Matt 3:4c. In describing "the customs of the Arabs" (τὰ νόμιμα τῶν Ἀράβων), Diodorus notes the proximity to the wilderness (ἔρημος) of certain Arab peoples (*Hist.* 19.94.1–4), especially the Nabataeans:

> While there are many Arabian tribes who use the desert as pasture (οὐκ ὀλίγων δ᾽ ὄντων Ἀραβικῶν ἐθνῶν τῶν τὴν ἔρημον ἐπινεμόντων), the Nabataeans far surpass the others in wealth. . . . [The Nabataeans] are exceptionally fond of freedom; and, whenever a strong force of enemies comes near, they take refuge in the desert (φεύγουσιν εἰς τὴν ἔρημον), using this as a fortress. (19.94.4, 6)

Diodorus next mentions how the Nabataeans and their flocks survive in the desert with little water (19.94.6–9). He also relates the following detail about their wilderness food (τροφή):

> They themselves use as food (χρῶνται τροφῇ) flesh and milk and those of the plants that grow from the ground which are suitable for this purpose; for among them there grow the pepper and plenty of the so-called wild honey from trees, which they use as a drink mixed with water (φύεται . . . ἀπὸ τῶν δένδρων μέλι πολὺ τὸ καλούμενον ἄγριον ᾧ χρῶνται ποτῷ μεθ᾽ ὕδατος).[45]

The Elder Pliny complements Diodorus's testimony, stating that such a beverage was plentiful in Syria:

> There is an oil that grows of its own accord (*sponte nascitur*) in the coastal parts of Syria called *elaeomeli* [= ἔλαιον + μέλι]. It is a rich oil that trickles from trees (*ex arboribus*), of a substance thicker than honey but thinner than resin, and having a sweet flavor; this is also used by the doctors. (*HN* 15.7.32)

---

[45] Diod. Sic., *Hist.* 19.94.10 (ET modified). Cf. Ps. Arist., *Mir. ausc.* 22 on honey wine among the Illyrians.

Without a doubt, Diodorus offers a close literary parallel to the Baptist's μέλι ἄγριον in the wilderness (ἔρημος). This does not *ipso facto* prove that the referent in Mark 1:6c‖Matt 3:4c is honey-water. To aid in assessing this possibility, other depictions of honey-water receive attention immediately below.

2. Early Witnesses to Designating Tree Sap as 'Honey'

Roland K. Harrison calls attention to the following 9th c. B.C.E. relief "from the palace of Ashurnasirpal II Numrûd" depicting Griffin-demons collecting sap from a palm tree:[46]

The relief attests to an ancient practice (9th c. B.C.E.), although it is not entirely clear that the tree sap it depicts was indeed called "honey."[47]

The earliest unambiguous designation of such a substance as "honey" may be Plato's *Timaeus*. Plato (429–347 B.C.E.) describes assorted kinds of water (ὕδωρ) "strained through earth-grown plants and called 'sap.'"[48] He uses the term μέλι for one kind of sap, which is inclusive of all sweet saps: "And all

---

[46] Harrison, "Palm Tree," art. *ISBE* 3.649. Image provided by and used with the permission of The Brooklyn Museum, Brooklyn, NY.

[47] Harrison, "Palm Tree," 649, notes: "The Babylonians made intoxicating liquor by extracting the syrupy content of the spathe [i.e., bract] surrounding the [palm trees'] flowers. This liquor . . . was also known euphemistically as 'honey.'"

[48] Gk.: διὰ τῶν ἐκ γῆς φυτῶν ἠθημένα, χυμοὶ λεγόμενοι, *Ti.* 59E. Greek text and ET: R. G. Bury, LCL.

that kind which tends to expand the contracted parts of the mouth, so far as their nature allows, and by this property produces sweetness (γλυκύτητα παρεχόμενον), has received as a general designation the name of 'honey' (μέλι)" (*Ti.* 60B). Theophrastus (*c.* 371–287 B.C.E.) follows Plato in naming honey (μέλι) among the saps or juices (ἐν χυμοῖς) given off by plants.[49]

3. Additional References to 'Honey' from Trees: Euripides, Aristeas, Virgil, Sibylline Oracles 3 and 5, Second Enoch, Aelian and Galen

Descriptions of this type of 'wild honey' by Euripides, the *Letter of Aristeas*, Virgil, *Sibylline Oracles* 3 and 5, *Second Enoch*, Aelian and Galen complement the testimonies of Diodorus, Pliny, Plato and Theophrastus. For example, Euripides characterizes the gathering of the Maenads devoted to Dionysus in terms of the abundance of water, wine, milk and honey (*Bacch.* 704–711). Concerning the wands, or staffs (thyrsi), that the Maenads carry, Euripides writes: "From their ivy-covered thyrsi dripped streams of honey (γλυκεῖαι μέλιτος . . . ῥοαί)."[50]

Moreover, the *Letter of Aristeas* (2nd c. B.C.E.) describes this type of honey in the vicinity of Alexandria:

> The zeal of the farmers is indeed remarkable. In fact their land is thickly covered with large numbers of olive trees and corn crops and pulse, and moreover with vines and abundant honey (μέλιτι πολλῷ). As for the *other* fruit trees and date palms among them (τὰ μὲν τῶν ἄλλων ἀκρορύδων καὶ φονίκων παρ᾽ αὐτοῖς), no number can be given.[51]

The translation by R. J. H. Shutt in the *OTP* is incomplete in that it does not translate the adjective ἄλλων ("other," italicized above). Shutt's assumption—or at least the translation's implication—is that μέλιτι πολλῷ refers to bee honey. Since the passage describes assorted agrarian products and ἄλλων refers to trees other than those that produce 'honey,' *Let. Aris.* 112 in fact highlights the abundance of fig honey, date honey, or sweet tree sap, *not* bee honey.[52]

Furthermore, Virgil (70–19 B.C.E.), two of the Jewish *Sibylline Oracles*, and *2 Enoch* associate honey-water with the dawning of a new age. In his famous *Fourth Eclogue*, Virgil shows esteem for such honey when illustrating

---

[49] Theophr., *Sens.* 84. Greek text and ET: George M. Stratton, ed., *Theophrastus* (London: Allen & Unwin, 1917), 142–3.

[50] Eur., *Bacch.* 710–711; Greek text and ET: David Kovacs, LCL (2002).

[51] *Let. Aris.* 112; cf. 109, referring to Alexandria. The above ET is modified from that of R. J. H. Shutt, in *OTP*, 2.20. Shutt translates the last sentence as follows: "As for the fruit trees and date palms which they have, no number can be given."

[52] Understood in this light, *Let. Aris.* 112 may have a precedent in Ezek 27:17 ("Judah and the land of Israel traded with you; they exchanged for your merchandise wheat from Minneth, millet, honey, oil, and balm."). Cf. R. J. Israel, "Milk and Date Jam," 27.

the era ushered in by Octavius, who was by then (*c.* 37 B.C.E.) the undisputed ruler of Italy: "On wild brambles shall hang the purple grape, and the stubborn oak shall distill dewy honey (*roscida mella*)."[53] In addition to Virgil's *vaticanus ex eventu* prophecy concerning the eventual emperor Augustus's accomplishments, *Sibylline Oracles* 3 and 5 associate the appearance of honey-water with the arrival of the day of judgment. The third *Sibylline Oracle* predicts, "When indeed this fated day reaches its consummation . . . the all-bearing earth will give . . . a delightful drink of sweet honey from heaven (ἀπ' οὐρανόθεν μέλιτος γλυκεροῦ ποτὸν ἡδύ)."[54] The fifth *Sibylline Oracle* (*c.* 80–132 C.E.; after Virgil's *Fourth Eclogue*) likewise foretells that the "holy land" will flow with this pleasing beverage: "But the holy land of the pious alone will bear all these things: a honey-sweet stream (νᾶμα μελισταγέος) from rock and spring, and heavenly milk will flow for all the righteous" (*Sib. Or.* 5.281–283). The author of *2 Enoch* (late 1st c. C.E.), moreover, presents Enoch as ascending to Paradise and seeing a river flowing with honey-water.[55] Later in *2 Enoch*, the archangel Michael anoints Enoch with special oil, whose "ointment is like sweet dew."[56]

Of course, it does not necessarily follow that the historical Baptist drank honey-water, let alone as a parabolic act complementing a message of repentance and imminent eschatological fulfillment. Like others in Syro-Palestine, the Baptist may simply have drunk what was plentiful in the wilderness (cf. Diod. Sic., *Hist.* 19.94.10). Nonetheless, given the symbolic

---

[53] Verg., *Ecl.* 4.29–30; Greek text and ET: H. Rushton Fairclough, ed., *Virgil* (LCL; Cambridge, MA: Harvard University, [2]1969–74). Cf. *Georg.* 1.31.

[54] *Sib. Or.* 3.741–746 (*c.* 163–45 B.C.E., before Virgil's *Fourth Eclogue*). Greek text: Johannes Geffcken, *Die Oracula sibyllina* (Leipzig: Hinrichs, 1902), 86; ET: J. J. Collins, *OTP*, 1.378.

[55] In *2 Enoch*, Enoch ascends to the third heaven and beholds the wonders of Paradise (8.1–4). One such wonder is a river that flows periodically with honey-water: "[5] And two streams come forth, one a source of honey and milk, and a source which produces oil and wine. And it is divided into four parts, and they go around with a quiet movement. [6] And they come out into the Paradise of Edem [Eden], between the corruptible and the incorruptible. And from there they pass along and divide into 40 parts. And it proceeds in descent along the earth, and they have a revolution in their cycle, just like the other atmospheric elements" (*2 En.* 8.5–6 [J]). ET of the Old Slavonic: F. I. Andersen, *OTP*, 1.116. At least one other MS of *2 Enoch* (A) does not contain this passage, however (ET: *OTP*, 1.117). Accordingly, *2 En.* 8.5–6 (J) may offer a witness to honey-water later than the 1st c. C.E. On the yet unresolved text-critical problems associated with *2 Enoch*, see F. I. Andersen, in: *OTP*, 1.91–4.

[56] *2 En.* 22.8–9 (J): "[8] And the Lord spoke to Michael, 'Go, and extract Enoch from his earthly clothing. And anoint him with my delightful oil, and put him into the clothes of my glory.' [9] And so Michael did, just as the Lord had said to him. He anointed me and he clothed me. And the appearance of that oil is greater than the greatest light, and its ointment is like sweet dew, and its fragrance myrrh; and it is like the rays of the glittering sun." At *2 En.* 22.8–9, MSS J and A are quite similar; both mention "ointment . . . like sweet dew."

character of John's dress, in apparent imitation of Elijah (cf. 2 Kgs 1:8, LXX), such an understanding—whether for the historical John, John's disciples, or certain early followers of Jesus—cannot be excluded.

Moreover, Aelian's anthology preserves material about a liquid manifestation of 'honey' in India:

> During the springtime in India it rains liquid honey (ὕεται . . . μέλιτι ὑγρῷ) . . . and it falls on the grass and on the leaves of reeds in the marshes, providing wonderful pasturage for cattle and sheep. And the animals feast off this most delightful banquet, for the shepherds make a point of leading them to spots where the sweet dew (ἡ δρόσος ἡ γλυκεῖα) falls more plentifully and settles.[57]

Likewise, Galen describes honey as dew found, sometimes abundantly, on plant leaves (*De alim. fac.* 739–742). Collectively, the assorted witnesses of Plato, Theophrastus, Diodorus, Pliny, Euripides, *Aristeas*, Virgil, *Sibylline Oracles* 3 and 5, *Second Enoch*, Galen and Aelian demonstrate that "wild honey" in Mark 1:6c‖Matt 3:4c could have been intended, or interpreted, as honey-water derived from trees.[58] Even if such 'honey' is not familiar to many Western interpreters today, its prevalence among diverse cultures in the ancient Mediterranean world, and beyond, merits serious consideration.

D. Conclusion:
The Baptist's "Wild Honey"

It is not possible to ascertain with certainty to what type of 'honey' Mark 1:6c or Matt 3:4c refers, since neither author specifies either *bees*, or 'honey' as a sweet product of *trees* (for example, dates, figs, or sap/gum). The findings of this chapter have implications for other ancient references to 'honey,' including those in Jewish and Christian scripture.[59]

Despite the exegetical ambiguity in Mark 1:6c‖Matt 3:4c concerning what sweet substance John consumed, the meaning of his "wild honey" is readily ascertained from descriptions of various types of uncultivated 'honey' in antiquity: The honey that John found in the wilderness was not as pleasing or highly esteemed as other types of honey. The Elder Pliny likens autumn 'wild honey' from the forest to "sandy honey" (*HN* 11.15.41; cf. Jos., *B.J.*

---

[57] Ael., *NA* 15.7. Greet text and ET (modified): A. F. Scholfield, ed., *Aelian, On the Characteristics of Animals* (LCL; Cambridge, MA: Harvard University, 1958–59).

[58] For a later witness to honey-water, see Aëtius of Amida (Med.; *fl.* 530–560 C.E.), *Iatricorum* 3.166.1–8; 8.50.179; 8.76.101. Greek text: Alexander Olivieri, ed., *Aetii Amideni, Libri medicinales* (CMG 8.1–2; Vol. 1: Leipsig: Teubner, 1935; Vol. 2: Berlin: Akademie Verlag, 1950).

[59] This chapter's analysis can also be instructive for recognizing misunderstandings, or even incorrect translations, of any number of ancient texts. See above, e.g., on *Let. Aris.* 112.

4.8.3 [§468]; *m. Ned.* 6:8–9). Xenophon, Ps. Aristotle, Strabo and the Elder Pliny even report that not knowing the source of the honey one eats could be dangerous, if not fatal, if the bees interact (that is, pollinate) with poisonous plants.[60] Thus at least in Mark 1:6c, the reference to John's honey has more to do with *where* John was rather than *what* he ate: The Baptist ate such honey because it was abundant in the desert, even if he perhaps could have enjoyed better 'honey' elsewhere. This conclusion complements the analysis of chapter 2, which found that locusts, especially in their 'gregarious' phase, accentuate John's place in the wilderness. John's food is simply a reflection of what was plentiful in his midst: insects and uncultivated 'honey.' In the next chapter it will be argued that the author of Mark mentions the Baptist's food precisely for this reason, namely to emphasize John as the prophetic herald "crying out in the wilderness" (Mark 1:3, citing Isa 40:3).

Concerning *what kind* of honey is presented as being eaten, the possibility of the Baptist's "wild honey" as honey-water derived from the gum or sap of trees is inviting[61]—but by no means certain—for two reasons. First, apiculture had only come to Palestine in the late Hellenistic period, centuries later than to Egypt, Mesopotamia and classical Greece. Second, a plethora of witnesses to honey-water demonstrate that this beverage was both common and well-known.[62] Even if modern (Western) interpreters may not regard the produce of trees as 'honey,' the ancients certainly did. Indeed, Diodorus's description (*Hist.* 19.94) of a particular Arabian tribe, the Nabataeans, who survive with their flocks in the desert (ἔρημος) on 'honey' (μέλι) from trees mixed with water[63] provides the closest extant literary analogy to μέλι ἄγριον in Mark 1:6c||Matt 3:4c.

With regard to Matt 3:4c, it will be recalled that Matthew presents locusts/grasshoppers and "wild honey" as John's *only* wilderness foods (ἡ δὲ τροφὴ ἦν αὐτοῦ). Andrew Dalby's observation that bee honey "is never common enough to be a dietary staple"[64] favors the interpretation of Matt

---

[60] Xen., *An.* 4.8.21; Ps. Arist., *Mir. ausc.* 18; Strabo, *Geog.* 12.3.18; Plin. (E), *HN* 21.44.74–75, 21.45.77.

[61] However tentatively, with H. A. W. Meyer, *Matthew*, 76–7; B. Weiss, *Matthew-Mark*, 13; O. Böcher, "Ass Johannes der Täufer," 91–2; Guelich, *Mark*, 21; Tilly, *Johannes der Täufer*, 38.

[62] Pl., *Ti.* 59E–60B; Theophr., *Sens.* 84; Plin. (E), *HN* 15.7.32; Verg., *Ecl.* 4.29–30; *Sib. Or.* 3.741–746, 5.281–283; *2 En.* 8.1–4; Ael., *NA* 15.7; Aëtius, *Iatricorum* 3.166.1–8; 8.50.179; 8.76.101.

[63] Gk.: ἀπὸ τῶν δένδρων μέλι πολὺ τὸ καλούμενον ἄγριον ᾧ χρῶνται ποτῷ μεθ᾽ ὕδατος, Diod. Sic., *Hist.* 19.94.10.

[64] Dalby, *Siren Feasts*, 47.

3:4c—more so than of Mark 1:6c[65]—as depicting the Baptist surviving on insects and some type of 'honey' other than that produced by bees. The nutritional aspects of these foods and the habits of recent and contemporary locust-eating peoples remain to be investigated in the following chapter, on the meaning of John's diet for the historical Baptist and the Synoptic evangelists.

---

[65] As noted in chapter 1, the imperfect periphrastic in Mark 1:6c (ἦν . . . ἐσθίων) states that John was in the habit of eating locusts/grasshoppers and 'wild honey,' presumably among other foods in the wilderness.

Chapter 4

"Locusts and Wild Honey" in Synoptic Interpretation:
The Historical Baptist, Mark, Matthew (and Luke)

"Do not forget about wild foods which are available at no cost."[1]

"'Why should we imitate these uncivilized races?'"[2]

πᾶν τὸ παρατιθέμενον ὑμῖν ἐσθίετε (1 Cor 10:27b)

The previous two chapters discussed John the Baptist's ἀκρίδες καὶ μέλι ἄγριον in their ancient contexts. These materials shed much light on John's diet, as it is reflected in the Synoptic gospels and various patristic interpretations. The purpose of this chapter is to clarify what has been learned through these assorted inquiries and how the present study aids in the interpretation of the Baptist's "locusts and wild honey." The most likely meaning(s) of this diet will be considered, in turn, for the historical Baptist, the author of Mark and the author of Matthew. The final section of chapter 4 explores the reason for Luke's omission of Mark 1:6c in light of this evangelist's distinctive uses of Elijah traditions. Chapter 5 will consider the interpretations of John's diet in the early and medieval periods, and beyond.

A. The Historical Baptist's "Locusts and Wild Honey"

The first section of chapter 4 examines the historical Baptist's experience of collecting "locusts and wild honey." To this end, the discussion will relate anthropologists' observations concerning recent and contemporary locust-eating peoples to what the ancients actually understood about eating locusts/grasshoppers. The nutritional value of "locusts and wild honey" with

---

[1] Advice given to South African teachers and health care workers in the "Primary Healthcare Booklet," cited in: G. R. DeFoliart, "Insects as Food: Western Attitude," 29. DeFoliart, an entomologist, argues that "Westerners should become more aware of the fact that their bias against insects as food has an adverse impact" on insect-eating peoples, "resulting in a gradual reduction in the use of insects without replacement of lost nutrition and other benefits" (21).

[2] Hypothetical question posed by Vincent M. Holt, *Why Not Eat Insects?* (Hampton/Middlesex: Classey, 1967 [1885]), 33. Holt's suggestion pertains to locust eating by those of European descent and is discussed in this chapter's excursus.

reference to the different claims of Mark 1:6c and Matt 3:4c will also be addressed. It will be argued that, inasmuch as locusts/grasshoppers are rich in protein and certain types of ancient 'honey' in carbohydrates, Mark 1:6c plausibly characterizes parts of the historical Baptist's diet. This study will also evaluate the benefits and potential drawbacks of the exclusive claim of Matt 3:4c—that the Baptist ate only these foods—in light of empirical data on human nutrition.

1. Introduction: Present-Day Locust Eaters

That locust eaters were known to Greek and Latin authors during the Classical, Hellenistic and Roman periods is supported by numerous witnesses.[3] A number of the materials examined in chapter 2 have clarified certain aspects of John's diet, or at least its presentation in Mark or Matthew. This section seeks to ascertain in what ways the practices of modern and relatively recent eaters of locusts/grasshoppers shed additional light on the historical Baptist. In spite of the difficulties inherent in drawing conclusions about life in the ancient Mediterranean world in light of present-day preindustrial societies, certain aspects of locusts as human food, which the ancient Jewish and Greco-Roman sources reveal less clearly, can be better understood, or further illustrated, through the habits of recent and contemporary peoples.[4] These aspects include how John may have gathered locusts and that he could easily have met his daily needs for protein and calories, albeit not all of his dietary needs, from these insects.

2. Locust Eating in the Great Basin of North America and Elsewhere in Our World Today

Since antiquity, locusts have been a vital and cherished food for numerous peoples of the world. *Acrididae* remain so in many parts of the world today. There is copious evidence to support these points from Africa,[5]

---

[3] See the discussion in chapter 2 of Herod., *Hist.* 4.172; Ar., *Ach.* 870–871; 1114–1117; Theoc., *Id.* 1.52; Arist., *HA* 5.30 (556B); Alexis, *Fr.* 167.13 (162.13); Anaxandrides, *Fr.* 42.59 (41.59); Diod. Sic., *Hist.* 3.29.1–6; Strabo, *Geog.* 16.4.12; *Life of Aesop* 99; Plin. (E), *HN* 6.35.195; 11.32.92; 11.35.106; 30.21.68; Ath., *Deip.* 4.133B; Dioscorides, *De mat. med.* 2.51–52; Gal., *De simp. med. temp.* 11.13.312 (11.2.149); Tert., *Adv. Marc.* 1.17; *De anima* 15.2; Jer., *Adv. Iovin.* 2.7, 15.

[4] The present author has searched for but not found analogous material on people today who eat "wild honey," however construed. As a result, the following comparative exercise focuses on locusts, but not uncultivated honeys.

[5] J. C. Bequaert, "Insects as Food," 194–5; F. S. Bodenheimer, *Insects as Human Food*, 163; R. L. Taylor, *Butterflies in My Stomach, Or: Insects in Human Nutrition*, 156–7; G. R. DeFoliart, "Insects as Food: Western Attitude," 27; idem, "Insects as Human Food," 397; Sandra G. F. Bukkens, "The Nutritional Value of Edible Insects," *Ecology of Food and Nutrition* (New York) 36 (1997): 287–319; here, 290; J. Ledger, "Eighth Plague," 210. Ad-

Australia,[6] Southeast Asia,[7] the Middle East (including Palestine),[8] as well as North, Central and South America.[9] Anthropologist Mark Q. Sutton's observations concerning the relatively recent eating habits of indigenous peoples of Western North America are of particular interest to this study. For example, Sutton notes:

> Grasshoppers and locusts were widely utilized throughout the [Great] Basin, and seem to have been a very important resource. *They may have been vastly underrated in the anthropological literature* of the Basin. They were prepared in a variety of ways, but cooking them . . . seems to have been preferred. In most cases they were ground and stored for winter use.[10]

If chapter 1 demonstrated the proclivity of many biblical scholars to overlook or disregard John's locust eating, there may at least be some comfort that

---

ditionally, the internationally recognized writer Chinua Achebe writes of locust eating in his native Nigeria in chapter 6 of his novel *Things Fall Apart* (1958). The edition I read is: Achebe, *Things Fall Apart; No Longer at Ease; Anthills of the Savannah* (New York: Griot, 1995), esp. 54–6.

[6] Helmut Reim, *Die Insektennahrung der australischen Ureinwohner: Eine Studie zur Frühgeschichte menschlicher Wirtschaft und Ernährung* (Städtisches Museum für Völkerkunde [Leipzig] Veröffentlichungen 13; Berlin: Akademie-Verlag, 1962), esp. 107–12; Taylor, *Butterflies*, 153–4. See further on "the ancestors of those presently called aborigines," who first came to Australia some 38,000 (or more) years ago: Sam D. Gill, *Storytracking: Texts, Stories, and Histories in Central Australia* (New York: Oxford University Press, 1997), 45–6; Reg Morrison, *Australia: The Four Billion Year Journey of a Continent* (New York: Facts on File Publications, 1990 [1988]), 298–321; Timothy F. Flannery, *The Future Eaters: An Ecological History of the Australasian Lands and People* (New York: Braziller, 1995), 144–63. Although one cannot be sure at what point Australia's first human inhabitants began eating locusts, this practice could well predate recorded history.

[7] Taylor, *Butterflies*, 154–6; F. Cowan, *Curious Facts in the History of Insects*, 126–7; DeFoliart, "Insects as Food: Western Attitude," 33–4; Bukkens, "Nutritional Value of Edible Insects," 290.

[8] Bodenheimer, *Insects as Human Food*, 210–17.

[9] Taylor, *Butterflies*, 149–53; Cowan, *Curious Facts*, 99, 127; DeFoliart, "Insects as Food: Western Attitude," 38; Bukkens, "Nutritional Value of Edible Insects," 291.

[10] Sutton, *Insects as Food: Aboriginal Entomophagy in the Great Basin*, 21. The "Great Basin" designates an area of Western North America encompassing the state of Nevada, nearly all of Utah, and parts of California, Arizona, New Mexico, Colorado, Wyoming, Montana, Idaho and Washington. On the prevalence of locusts in nineteenth-century North America, see Howard Ensign Evans, "Year of the Locust," in: idem, *Life on a Little-Known Planet* (Chicago: University of Chicago, 1984 = New York: Lyons & Burford, 1993), 195–226, esp. concerning locust infestations reported in assorted Kansas and Nebraska newspapers in 1874 and 1875. Responding to the sequential tragedies of 1874–75, "the states of Missouri and Minnesota enacted laws awarding bounties for the collection of locust eggs and hatchlings"; in Kansas, moreover, the Grasshopper Army Act "required every able-bodied male between the ages of twelve and sixty-five to assemble for the purpose of fighting locusts . . . whenever so ordered by the town officials" (204).

contemporary anthropologists, as well as archaeologists,[11] can be guilty of the same sin of omission. Likewise, this oversight applies to otherwise important and thorough studies of food in ancient Greece and Rome.[12]

Moreover, Sutton and other modern observers of locust-eating peoples posit a connection between avoiding indigestion and taking off the locusts' legs (and wings):

> The removal of the legs seems to have been a fairly common practice in the processing of grasshoppers. The legs are probably of little food value; they tend to have spurs, be very spiny, and may be uncomfortable to swallow. They might, thus, cause some difficulty in the digestive tract.[13]

The following commentary concerning locust eating in Cambodia in the mid-1990s by Rich Garella, a Western journalist and political activist, complements Sutton's description: "May is locust season! Every spring, kids come around with baskets of these tasty fried locusts. The best way to eat them is to snap off their lower legs (otherwise they scratch up your throat something awful), and saut[é] them again so they're piping hot!"[14] Similarly, John D. Whiting, a witness to the invasion of locusts that struck Palestine in 1915, observed then that the Arabs "dismember the insects, pulling off legs and wings, but not the head, and while [the locusts are] still alive roast them in a pan over

---

[11] Note also the difficulty of Elmer G. Wakefield and Samuel C. Dellinger, "Diet of the Bluff Dwellers of the Ozark Mountains and Its Skeletal Remains," *Annals of Internal Medicine* 9 (1936): 1412–18, esp. 1418, to posit an explanation for the relatively good health of Native Americans in Arkansas and Missouri, whose diet included a number of 'non-Western' items, including insects. See further on this lacuna in scholarship: Bukkens, "Nutritional Value of Edible Insects," 287–8; DeFoliart, "Insects as Food: Western Attitude," 40–4, esp. 41–2.

[12] Peter Garnsey, *Famine and Food Supply in the Graeco-Roman World*, goes into great detail concerning the food supply in ancient Greece (89–164) and Rome (167–268) but never discusses the role that insects played in the diet of numerous peoples under Roman rule. To be sure, the distinguished Roman social historian offers an erudite study of grains that farmers harvested but overlooks insects as another source of food that could be gathered. The same oversight applies to Don R. Brothwell, "Foodstuffs, Cooking, and Drugs," in: *Civilization of the Ancient Mediterranean: Greece and Rome* (ed. M. Grant and R. Kitzinger; New York: Scribner's, 1988), 1.247–75; K. D. White, "Farming and Animal Husbandry," in: *Civilization of the Ancient Mediterranean*, 1.211–45; Robert I. Curtis, *Ancient Food Technology* (Technology and Change in History 5; Leiden: Brill, 2001), esp. 395–417; B. A. Sparkes, "The Greek Kitchen," *JHS* 82 (1962): 121–37; Emily Gowers, *The Loaded Table: Representations of Food in Roman Literature* (Oxford: Clarendon/Oxford: Oxford University, 1993); cf. S. M. Burstein, *Agatharchides*, 102 n.2; Davies and Kathirithamby, *Greek Insects*, 141–2.

[13] Sutton, *Insects*, 22; cf. Ledger, "Eighth Plague," 210.

[14] Commentary by Rich Garella, "Interactions with Our Insect Friends," © 1995. Online (with photos): http://www.garella.com/rich/insect.htm (on 12 April 2004); used with permission.

a hot fire; and after being thoroughly dried in the sun, they can be stored away in sacks."[15] The observations of Sutton, Garella and Whiting offer a plausible explanation for why the Damascus Document from Qumran requires that the locusts first be roasted or boiled and, conversely, why Strabo depicts a short-lived Ethiopian people who eat the locusts whole.[16] Roasting or boiling allows for the easy removal of the legs and wings, and failure to do so can result in physical discomfort, if not more serious complications, for the eater. One cannot be sure that John the Baptist himself thus removed any of the locusts' appendages before eating only the remaining parts, but he probably did, given the empirically verifiable drawbacks of failing to do so.

Mark Sutton further notes that one Native American tribe, the Ute (in Utah), were known as the "Grasshopper Indians," apparently because of this people's proclivity for gathering and eating grasshoppers.[17] Given that Native American peoples were unlikely to refer to themselves by the incorrect (South-Asian!) designation "Indian," the name "Grasshopper Indians" was likely given by European settlers. Presumably non-insect eating outsiders described—as Strabo and the Elder Pliny (*HN* 11.32.92; 11.35.106; 30.21.68) had done centuries earlier—an ethnic group different from themselves in terms of the people's particular eating habits.[18]

3. The Collection and Preservation of Locusts

Also of interest to the diet of the historical Baptist is Sutton's calling attention to the fact that, when grasshoppers land upon water, they cannot swim

---

[15] Whiting, "Jerusalem's Locust Plague," 547.

[16] See the discussions of CD 12:11b–15a and Strabo, *Geog.* 16.4.12 in chapter 2. Unlike those of his predecessor Diodorus (*Hist.* 3.29; cf. Aristophanes, *Epit.* 2.57.1, 4; 2.58.1–2; Agathar., *De mar. Eryth.* 5.59 [5.58]), Strabo's depiction of this tribe supports the inference that this people's short life span stems from the (raw?) locusts they eat. Cf. in chapter 5 the interpretation of Hesychius of Jerusalem (*Hom.* 16.3) that the Baptist ate raw locusts.

[17] Sutton, *Insects*, 17. Additionally, John R. Swanton, *The Indian Tribes of North America* (Smithsonian Institution Bureau of American Ethnology 145; Washington: Smithsonian Institution Press, 1969 [1952]), 373, indicates James O. Pattie (*c.* 1804–1850 C.E.), *The Personal Narrative of James O. Pattie, of Kentucky: During an Expedition from St. Louis through the Vast Regions between that Place and the Pacific Ocean* (Chicago: Donnelly, 1930 [Cincinnati: E. H. Flint, 1833]), as his source for the use of the name "Grasshopper Indians" for the Ute.

[18] J. O. Pattie, *Personal Narrative*, 156, traveled in the West 1824–1830. Pattie's judgment about the inferiority of locusts as food is noteworthy: "[W]e met a band of the Grasshopper Indians, who derive their name from gathering grasshoppers, drying them, and pulverizing them, with the meal of which they make mush and bread; and this is their chief article of food. They are so little improved, as not even to have furnished themselves with the means of killing buffaloes."

and soon drown.[19] Notably, that locusts perish in water is assumed in Exodus 10 and by the Elder Pliny:

> The LORD changed the wind into a very strong west wind, which lifted the locusts and drove them into the Red Sea; not a single locust was left (לֹא נִשְׁאַר אַרְבֶּה אֶחָד) in all the country of Egypt. (Exod 10:19)

> They also have another way of dying: they are carried away in swarms by the wind and fall into the sea or stagnant water (*in maria aut stagna decidunt*). This happens purely by accident and not, as was believed by ancients, owing to their wings' being drenched by the dampness of night.[20]

Additionally, the *Geoponica*, an agricultural manual, attributes to the ancient philosopher Democritus (b. 460/57 B.C.E.) the estimation that a locust or a cicada can swim in pure wine but will drown in wine that has been diluted by water.[21] The North African church father Tertullian likewise names locusts among insects that prefer aridity to moisture.[22]

To these points may be added the observation of S. R. Driver that, "[w]hen conditions are favourable, the migratory instinct is strong in [the locusts]; but they have little power of guidance in flight, and are mainly borne along by the wind."[23] That is to say, in the presence of a stiff wind, locusts and grasshoppers are powerless to prevent themselves from being blown down into a lake or river and, subsequently, perishing in the water.

---

[19] Sutton, *Insects*, 12–13, on the vast numbers of grasshoppers that would periodically wash up on the shore of lakes in the Great Basin and could be caught in great quantities with little effort.

[20] Plin. (E), *HN* 11.35.103, referring to *locustis* in 11.35.101.

[21] *Geoponica* 7.8.1–2: "It is necessary for the master often to trust wine or must to the curators or to the servants; it is also necessary that the buyer should prove if the wine is genuine (καθαρός). Some therefore throw an apple into the vessel, but it is better to throw in wild pears; some throw in a locust (ἀκρίς), and some a cicada (τέττιξ). And if these indeed swim the wine is genuine; but if they sink, it is diluted (ὕδωρ ἔχει)." Cf. Hom., *Il.* 21.12; Cato, *Rust.* 106, 111. The *Geoponica* (10th c. C.E.) is based, supposedly, on Cassianus Bassus's 6th c. C.E. Latin treatise. Greek text: Heinrich Beckh, *Geoponica sive Cassiani Bassi scholastici, De re rustica eclogae* (Teubner; Leipzig: Teubner, 1994 [1895]), 193–4; ET (modified): Thomas Owen (1749–1812), *ΓΕΩΠΟΝΙΚΑ: Agricultural Pursuits* (London: Spilsbury, 1805–06), 1.221; online: http://digital.lib.msu.edu/onlinecolls/display.cfm?TitleNo=257&FT=gif (on 8 April 2004). On Democritus in the *Geoponica*, see Wilhelm Gemoll, *Untersuchungen über die Quellen, den Verfasser und die Abfassungszeit der Geoponica* (Berliner Studien für classische Philologie und Archäologie 1/1; Berlin: S. Calvary, 1883 [= Walluf bei Wiesbaden: M. Sändig, 1972]), 107–27; cf. Eugen Fehrle, *Zur Geschichte der griechischen Geoponica* (Leipzig: Teubner, 1913).

[22] Tert., *De anima* 32.353, 6 (ET: ANF, 3.212): "In like manner, those creatures are opposite to water which are in their nature dry and sapless; indeed, locusts (*locustae*), butterflies, and chameleons rejoice in droughts."

[23] Driver, "Excursus on Locusts," 86; cf. 90; Steedman, *Locust Handbook*, 32–3, 177.

With regard to John the Baptist, then, it was not necessarily obligatory that he 'catch' these insects—for example, with a net, or by overwhelming them with smoke, as Diodorus (*Hist.* 3.29.1–6) and others mention. From time to time one could simply proceed to the side of a river or lake toward which the wind was blowing to find a snack or a meal washed up on shore. Mark Sutton further notes that Native Americans in the Great Basin regularly organized groups to collect grasshoppers, and that for some tribes these insects constituted a main staple of food.[24]

Like Sutton, archaeologist David B. Madsen studies Native Americans of the Great Basin. Madsen summarizes the following corroborations of locust eating in the past at "Lakeside Cave, at the western edge of the Great Salt Lake" in Utah:

> Great Basin hunter-gatherers visited the cave intermittently during the past 5,000 years. . . . Bits of the insects pervaded *every stratum* we uncovered, and . . . we estimated that the cave contained remains from *as many as five million [grass]hoppers.* [That most human feces found in the cave] consisted of grasshopper parts in a heavy matrix of sand . . . told us that people ate the hoppers and suggested that the sand was somehow involved in processing them for consumption.[25]

An analogy to the Ethiopian tribe whom Diodorus (*Hist.* 3.29.1–6) and others describe might suggest that salt in the sand was actually used for preserving, rather than "processing," the grasshoppers. Astonished by the discovery of millions of dried grasshoppers, Madsen proceeded to verify empirically that it is indeed possible to collect large quantities of these insects rather quickly:

> [W]e found that enormous numbers of the insects had flown or been blown into the salt water and had subsequently been washed up, leaving neat rows of salted and sun-dried grasshoppers stretched out for miles along the beach. . . . Up until then we had envisioned grasshopper collecting to be a rather tedious task, but we now realized that the prehistoric hunter-gatherers at Lakeside Cave could simply have scooped up grasshoppers piled along the beaches and consumed the sun-dried product directly.[26]

This parallel is particularly remarkable for grasshoppers collected—whether by John or other Judeans—by the salt-laden Dead Sea. Possibly for this reason CD 12:11b–15a stipulates that only החגבים captured alive may be eaten.

Accordingly, for the Baptist, who ministered in the vicinity of the Jordan River and baptized in water (Mark 1:5, 9 par.; John 1:28; 10:40), the ability to gather locusts/grasshoppers—quite possibly with rather little effort—is entirely plausible (Mark 1:6c). Moreover, John's eating ἀκρίδες does not

---

[24] Sutton, *Insects*, 17–18.

[25] Madsen, "A Grasshopper in Every Pot," *Natural History* (New York) 98/7 (1989): 22–5; here, 22, emphases added.

[26] Ibid. See further below on Madsen's empirical reconstruction of locust gathering by Native Americans in this region. Cf. John Mulvaney and Johan Kamminga, *Prehistory of Australia* (Washington, DC: Smithsonian Institution Press, [2]1999), 3–4, 82.

specify fully-developed adult locusts with functional wings. The recently hatched "nymphs," which cannot fly, are vulnerable to attacks even from other insects, not to mention from insect-eating animals[27] and, of course, humans. All this is to say that, whether in the vicinity of water or in the wilderness, the Baptist would have had easy access to this food.

Excursus: Why Not Eat Locusts Today?

The disparity between the positive attitude toward insect eating in most cultures of the world throughout history, on the one hand, and the aversion to eating locusts in European cultures since the Roman Empire, on the other hand, has led certain Western authors to commend to their Indo-European comrades the nutritional benefits of eating arthropods. With a tone of nineteenth-century cultural superiority that is only slowly working itself out of today's academy, Vincent M. Holt suggests:

> 'Why should we imitate these uncivilized races?' But upon examination it will be found that, though uncivilized, most of these peoples are more particular as to the fitness of their food than we are, and look upon us with far greater horror for using, as food, the unclean pig or the raw oyster, than we do upon them for relishing a properly cooked dish of clean-feeding locusts or palm-grubs.[28]

Happily without the imperialist rhetoric, other more recent authors also seek to assuage the Western aversion to insects as food for humans.[29] Simply put, there is no rational basis for proscribing insect eating (although the present author cannot yet claim to have overcome this disposition).

Ironically, two recent publications on 'Bible foods' overlook locusts, despite the fact that throughout antiquity many Jews, possibly including Jesus,

---

[27] Taylor, *Butterflies*, 126–7; Edward O. Essig, *Insects and Mites of Western North America: A Manual and Textbook* (New York: Macmillan, [2]1958), 72–3; cf. 67–111; Whiting, "Jerusalem's Locust Plague," 540.

[28] Holt, *Why Not Eat Insects?* 33; cf. 32–8; J. C. Bequaert, "Insects as Food," 200. Holt's description of locusts as "clean-feeding" denotes their 'vegetarian' diet; that is, these insects do not feed on meat (cf. the discussion in chapter 2 on *Let. Aris.* 144b–146a).

[29] Peter Menzel and Faith D'Aluisio, *Man Eating Bugs: The Art and Science of Eating Insects* (Berkeley: Ten Speed Press, 1998), with illustrative color photos throughout, as well as a Mexican recipe for grasshopper tacos (p. 110); R. L. Taylor, *Butterflies*, esp. 88–90; R. L. Taylor and Barbara J. Carter, *Entertaining with Insects, Or: The Original Guide to Insect Cookery* (Yorba Linda, CA: Salutek, 1996 [1976]), includes a recipe for "John the Baptist Bread," with crickets substituted for locusts (p. 30), and advice for cleaning and preparing crickets prior to cooking (pp. 142–3); David George Gordon, *The Eat-A-Bug Cookbook: 33 Ways to Cook Grasshoppers, Ants, Water Bugs, Spiders, Centipedes, and Their Kin* (Berkeley: Ten Speed Press, 1998), esp. 15–26; Ledger, "Eighth Plague," 210; DeFoliart, "Insects as Human Food," *Crop Protection* (Guildford, England) 11 (1992): 395–9; see further: Thomas J. Elpel, ed., "The Food Insects Newsletter"; online: http://www.hollowtop.com/finl_html/finl.html (on 8 April 2004); Gene R. DeFoliart, ed., "Food-insects.com"; online: http://www.food-insects.com (on 8 April 2004).

ate them.[30]   However well-intended, such popular books highlight that, for many modern Western interpreters, like the ancient Romans before them, understanding John's diet of locusts/grasshoppers literally is somewhat counterintuitive. Could ἀκρίδες not have meant something else besides actual locusts/grasshoppers?

For the historical John, the present study has answered this question with a definitive "No." In this chapter it remains to offer some observations concerning the nutritional aspects of John's diet as depicted in Matt 3:4c; to consider John's likely response to the characterization of Mark 1:6c‖Matt 3:4c; and to examine the meanings attached to this diet in the Synoptic tradition.

4. The Nutritional Value of "Locusts and Wild Honey"

Whether they are, or were, aware of it, people throughout the centuries have eaten locusts, among other insects, for several good reasons. The obvious incentives are that locusts are plentiful and rather easy to catch. Like the ancient Assyrians who ordered locusts for royal banquets centuries ago, people who eat these (and other) insects also seem to enjoy them.[31]   Less apparent reasons are that these insects are high in protein and certain vitamins and minerals.[32]

a) Approximating What John Needed to Sustain Life in the Wilderness

One goal of the following inquiry is to illustrate the claim of Matt 3:4c, that John's wilderness "food consisted of grasshoppers and wild honey."[33] This inquiry into the nutritional value of "locusts and wild honey" is valuable in its own right and will also inform the discussion later in this chapter of Matthew's editing of Mark 1:6c. Additionally, the following investigation will offer an approximation of John's caloric needs in the wilderness, which will serve as a referent for assessing the amount of "locusts and wild honey" John would have needed to consume to subsist.[34]   Further, it will be asked if Matt 3:4c depicts a healthy, sustainable diet or, conversely, if the lack of vari-

---

[30] Don Colbert, M.D., *What Would Jesus Eat?* (Nashville: Thomas Nelson, 2002); Bernard Ward, *Healing Foods from the Bible* (Boca Raton, FL: Globe Communications, 1996).

[31] As DeFoliart, "Insects as Food: Western Attitude," 23–40, among others, discusses; cf. idem, "Insects as Human Food," 395; Bukkens, "Nutritional Value of Edible Insects," 288.

[32] Bukkens, "Nutritional Value of Edible Insects," 294–5.

[33] Gk.: ἡ δὲ τροφὴ ἦν αὐτοῦ ἀκρίδες καὶ μέλι ἄγριον. As already mentioned, the iterative imperfect of Mark 1:6c (ἦν . . . ἐσθίων, "he was in the habit of eating") does not claim that these were John's only foods in the wilderness.

[34] In the field of biblical studies, this investigation may break new ground methodologically. The attempt here is to pursue a holistic approach to the study of one ancient person, John, with the hope that other scholars will build upon and refine the methods employed herein.

ety would have resulted in a nutritional deficiency for a person seeking to live solely on these foods. Scientific data on human nutrition, to be discussed below, support the conclusions that a person deriving nourishment only from these foods would suffer from a lack of Vitamin C (ascorbic acid) and probably also from an insufficient intake of carbohydrates.

i) Prolegomena

Any attempt to assess John's nutritional needs is complicated by at least three major factors. First, as noted in chapter 2 ancient terms for locusts/grasshoppers do not correspond to modern classification systems for particular species. We therefore cannot ascertain the species of locusts that John ate, or how many different species he may have eaten. Species of locusts vary somewhat in size and chemical make-up, and therefore in their nutritional benefits as food.[35]

Second, chapter 3 demonstrated that we do not know whether the Baptist ate uncultivated honey produced by bees or derived from trees (or both). Even if the type of John's honey could be ascertained, the compositional make-up of bee honeys varies by region. Moreover, bee honey can change in its chemical structure over time.

Third, humans 2,000 years ago tended to be slightly smaller than people today and therefore required somewhat fewer calories. How many calories a Judean wilderness prophet would actually have consumed is obscured also because caloric need, along with definitions of thinness and obesity, are to a certain extent culturally defined. Consequently, peoples living at the same point in time (whether today or in antiquity) may eat different amounts because of how their culture construes portion size, being 'full,' and desirable bodily proportions.

Hence, it will not be possible to determine exactly how many insects or how much 'honey' per day the Baptist would have had to consume, according to Matt 3:4c. This inquiry will have been successful if it can offer an approximate illustration of the exclusive claim of Matt 3:4c, and concomitantly a basis for weighing its historical plausibility.

ii) Estimating John's Nutritional Needs

Some background data concerning human nutrition will aid the assessment of the difficulties outlined in the preceding subsection. With the exception of John's gender (male), each of the following variables that this inquiry poses tentatively for the historical Baptist is uncertain:

Body Type: Since John, like most people in antiquity, was poor and, moreover, lived at least part of his life in the wilderness, he was probably not

---

[35] Boris Uvarov, *Grasshoppers and Locusts*, 1.90–5.

overweight and may have been somewhat thin. Dieticians today define Body Mass Index (BMI) as an estimate of body fat as a factor of weight; it is calculated by a person's weight in kilograms, divided by height in meters squared (kg/m²). The American National Academy of Sciences (NAS) defines a "normal" BMI as between 18.5 and 24.99.[36] The *Dietary Reference Intakes* guide of the NAS lists statistics for only three Body Mass Indices within the "normal" range: 18.5 (low/normal); 22.5 (average/normal); and 24.99 (high/normal). Of course, what is construed as average for Americans tends to be higher (that is, heavier) than the norm defined by many other cultures (both post- and pre-industrial) today. Supposing for John a BMI of 18.5 places him at the low (that is, thin) end of "normal" according to the NAS; this BMI quite possibly could have been regarded as average for a poor Palestinian man when John lived. A Body Mass Index for a rather thin person (18.5) is therefore posited for this study.

Age: The NAS uses thirty years of age as its standard; younger people tend to need more calories, and older people fewer. John's age is unknown.[37] The Baptist probably did not live to see his 50s, and perhaps not his 40s, since he was killed by Herod Antipas, tetrarch of Galilee and Perea 4 B.C.E.–39 C.E. (Mark 6:14–29 par.). The typical correction for adults older or younger than thirty years in terms of daily calories needed is rather small, however (around ± 1% per year). This variable, like the others, is not significant for the present study, because it will be shown below that John could have easily met (and surpassed) his daily need for calories from eating locusts.

Height: People in antiquity tended to be somewhat smaller than people today. The height of any individual is the result of both nature (genes) and nurture (environment).[38] On the basis of the human remains from Qumran

---

[36] NAS, *Dietary Reference Intakes for Energy, Carbohydrate, Fiber, Fat, Fatty Acids, Cholesterol, Protein, and Amino Acids (Macronutrients)* (Washington, DC: National Academy Press, 2002), 164–5; online: http://books.nap.edu/books/0309085373/html/index.html (on 8 April 2004).

[37] Luke 3:23 states that Jesus was "about thirty years old" (ὡσεὶ ἐτῶν τριάκοντα) when he began his public ministry. This evangelist also places John's birth a few months before Jesus' birth (esp. Luke 1:24–26). If accurate, one could infer from the Lukan chronology that John began his public ministry in his (late?) 20s. Above all, however, the uncertainty of John's age must be emphasized.

[38] Anthropologist Susan Guise Sheridan, "Scholars, Soldiers, Craftsmen, Elites?: Analysis of French Collection of Human Remains from Qumran," *Dead Sea Discoveries* 9 (2002): 199–248; here, 235, notes: "Comparisons of immigrant parents and their 'transplanted' children demonstrate that while the genotype (genetic makeup) of the individual sets the limits of terminal height, the environment plays a crucial role in the achievement of genetic potential. Adult height is thereby influenced by the subadult environmental context of growth." See further: J. Lawrence Angel, *The People of Lerna: Analysis of a Prehistoric Aegean Population* (Princeton, NJ: American School of Classical Studies at Athens, 1971), 69–109.

thus far analyzed, a height of 1.65 m (65") is posited, albeit cautiously, for the Baptist.[39]

Level of Activity: Naturally, active people require more calories than sedentary individuals. The 1,416 calories per day posited below for John's basal metabolism denotes energy needed to sustain basic bodily functions, without any additional activity. The National Academy of Sciences (NAS) makes four general distinctions for Physical Activity Level (PAL): sedentary (such an individual would require a total of 2,068 calories per day); low active (2,254 calories per day); active (2,490 calories); and very active (2,880 calories). A "very active" person would engage regularly in a cardiovascular activity, such as running. Postulating this wilderness prophet as "active" strikes the present author as plausible.[40]

According to the NAS, then, a rather thin, thirty-year-old man 65" tall (5' 5"; 1.65 m.) requires 1,416 calories per day to sustain life (basal metabolism).[41] Such an individual with an "active" Physical Activity Level would need a total of 2,490 calories per day. At 1.65 meters, moreover, a person with a Body Mass Index (BMI) of 18.5 would weigh approximately 50.4 kg (111 lbs.).[42] The daily diet of an adult at this weight would need to include 40.3 grams of protein: "The Recommended Dietary Allowance (RDA) for both men and women is 0.80 g of good quality protein/kg body weight/day and is based on previous careful analyses of available nitrogen balance studies."[43] The inferences that John needed some 2,490 calories[44] and forty grams

---

[39] Sheridan, "Human Remains from Qumran," 236, examined the remains of eleven men from the French collection of Qumran skeletal remains; their "stature ranged from 159.0–177.0 cm." Sheridan further summarizes that "[t]he mean male stature in the combined de Vaux collection was 165.7 ± 5.9 cm. . ." (236). She also emphasizes the tentative nature of the data available thus far, since only a fraction of the remains from Qumran has been excavated and analyzed (203–4). The present inquiry's use of this data offers only an approximate referent for the historical Baptist and is not intended to connote that John had been an Essene. See further: S. G. Sheridan, J. Ullinger and J. Ramp, "Anthropological Analysis of the Human Remains from Khirbet Qumran: The French Collection," forthcoming in: *The Archaeology of Qumran II* (ed. Jean-Baptiste Humbert and Jan Gunneweg; Presses Universitaires de Fribourg, Suisse and the École Biblique et Archéologique Française).

[40] Of course, John may have been "low active," or somewhere in-between "low active" and "active," depending on how much time he spent in prayer or meditation (rather sedentary activities), or how itinerant his ministry in the wilderness may have been. If only we knew more about the historical John!

[41] Data for such a man's Total Energy Expenditure (TEE), according to the NAS, *Dietary Reference Intakes*. Cf. Peter Garnsey, *Food and Society in Classical Antiquity* (Cambridge: Cambridge University, 1999), 19-21; Steven J. Friesen, "Poverty in Pauline Studies: Beyond the So-called New Consensus," *JSNT* 26/3 (2004): 323–61; here, 343–5.

[42] As mentioned above, BMI = kg/m^2.

[43] NAS, *Dietary Reference Intakes*, 465. Cf. Colbert, *Jesus*, 79: "How much protein do we need a day? The average adult needs about 0.8 grams of protein per kilogram (2.2

of protein per day are offered only as approximate referents for the nutritional data on "locusts and wild honey" to be offered immediately below.

b) The Caloric and Nutrient Contents of "Locusts and Wild Honey"

i) Locusts and Protein

Although perhaps unknown to the eaters, maybe the most significant benefit of eating locusts (and many other insects) is that they are a rich source of protein, and therefore plentiful in calories as well.[45] Dried locusts comprise "up to 75 per cent protein and about 20 per cent fat; 100 grams of locust, when analyzed, showed the presence of 1.75 mg. of riboflavin and 7.5 mg. of nicotinic acid (vitamin B_2 complex), demonstrating that they are also of value for their vitamins."[46] Such a high protein content, even in uncooked grasshoppers (7.6 grams/ounce), compares favorably with the level of protein in many meats—including blood sausage (4.1 grams/ounce), smoked ham (5.1 grams/ounce), and moose liver (6.9 grams/ounce)—which many poorer peoples cannot afford, or choose not, to consume.[47]

David Madsen's approximation of the caloric and nutritional benefits of locust gathering (locust hunting?) by Native Americans in the Great Basin illustrates that the Baptist could indeed have easily met his needs for protein—and calories in general—by eating locusts. Moreover, as compared with the energy exerted in collecting seeds or in hunting, locust gathering requires a rather small amount of effort in return for a valuable yield in calories and nutrition:

---

pounds). In other words, for the average 154-pound person (70K), 56 grams of protein are needed."

[44] For the purposes of the present study, height/stature, like age, does not significantly alter this figure. At the slightly shorter height of 1.60 meters (63"), such an "active" person would require 2,397 calories per day, or 3.7% fewer; at 1.70 m (67"), 2,586 calories, or 3.9% more; at 1.75 m (69"), 2,683 calories, or 7.8% more.

[45] Even today in developing societies, protein deficiency is among the most common and chronic dietary challenges. On this subject in general, see Bukkens, "Nutritional Value of Edible Insects," 287–319. Additionally, Bruno Comby, *Délicieux insectes: Les protéines du futur...* (Geneva: Éditions Jouvence, 1990), esp. 42, 51–77, argues that protein-rich insects offer an important part of the solution to world hunger.

[46] Brothwell and Brothwell, *Food in Antiquity*, 68–9; cf. Borowski, *Every Living Thing*, 159–60. The figures cited by Uvarov, *Grasshoppers and Locusts*, 1.90–5, note variations among different species of locusts but on the whole support this generalization. Cf. K. S. Brown, "The Chemistry of Aphids and Scale Insects," *Chemical Society Reviews* 4 (1975): 263–88; Bukkens, "Nutritional Value of Edible Insects," 294–5.

[47] [Four Winds Food Specialists], *Ethnic Foods Nutrient Composition Guide: Hard-to-Find Items, Selected Foreign Terms, Scientific Names* (Sunnyvale, CA: Four Winds Food Specialists, [2]2001), 60–70, 79–81; esp. 63, 65, 67, 80; cf. Janette Brand Miller et al., *Tables of Composition of Australian Aboriginal Foods* (Canberra, Australia: Aboriginal Studies Press, 1993), 226; Comby, *Délicieux insectes*, 55–9.

We found that one person could collect an average of 200 pounds of sun-dried [grass]hoppers per hour. . . . Laboratory analyses of the hoppers indicated a yield of just over 1,365 calories per pound. (For comparison, a pound of medium-fat beef produces about 1,240 calories and a pound of wheat flour about 1,590 calories.) We thus came up with an average return of 273,000 calories per hour of effort invested. Even when we took a tenth of this figure, to be conservative, we found this to be the highest rate of return of any local resource. It is far higher than the 300 to 1,000 calories per hour rate produced by collecting most seeds . . . and higher even than the estimated 25,000 calories per hour for large game such as deer or antelope. Put another way, an hour spent collecting twenty pounds of sun-dried grasshoppers provides the equivalent of about twenty-two pounds of meat.[48]

Under the ideal conditions of the multitudes of drowned and sun-dried locusts strewn along the beach that Madsen describes, an hour's work could have sustained the Baptist for a week or more[49] and left the wilderness prophet with ample time for other activities. Gathering grasshoppers in areas devoid of lakes and streams results in a substantially lower, but nonetheless rewarding, yield: "The numbers in our tests thus converted to an average of 2,959 calories per hour for handpicking from ground cover and 23,479 calories per hour from along the lake margin."[50] Accordingly, John could have gleaned forty (or many more) grams of protein and 2,490 calories per day from locusts with as little as an hour of work each day (away from water), or even an hour per week (near water).

ii) 'Wild Honeys' and Carbohydrates

At roughly 1.6 grams of carbohydrates per insect, locusts/grasshoppers are not a significant source of carbohydrates.[51] As a result, if the Baptist were to eat only "locusts and wild honey" (so Matt 3:4c), he would need to glean most of his carbohydrates from the latter. The National Academy of Sciences states that every person, regardless of age or size, requires 130 grams (.286 lbs.) of carbohydrates per day to provide energy to the brain and other organs of the body.[52] The preceding chapter noted the difficulty of ascertaining what

---

[48] Madsen, "Grasshopper," 23. Madsen's figures are illustrative, although they pertain only to the collection of locusts and not to the additional time that would be needed to preserve and store them for future consumption.

[49] Using Madsen's calculations ("Grasshopper," 23): One hour to collect 20 pounds (9.1 kg) of locusts at 1,365 calories per pound would glean for the gatherer 27,300 calories, or enough energy to sustain a person needing 2,490 calories per day for nearly eleven days.

[50] Madsen, "Grasshopper," 24.

[51] [Four Winds Food Specialists], *Ethnic Foods Nutrient Composition Guide*, 80 (1.6 g in carbohydrates per raw grasshopper with an average weight of 28.4 g); cf. Brothwell and Brothwell, *Food in Antiquity*, 68–9.

[52] NAS, *Dietary Reference Intakes*, 207: "The primary role of carbohydrates (sugars and starches) is to provide energy to cells in the body, particularly the brain, which is the only carbohydrate-dependent organ in the body. The Recommended Dietary Allowance for carbo-

kind of 'honey' the Baptist ate. For this reason, this study will examine the content and benefits of honey/syrup from bees, dates, figs and tree sap, insofar as they can be determined, and from these data assess whether John could have met his daily needs for carbohydrates from 'honey.' For reasons to be offered below, eating only "locusts and wild honey" would probably not offer the carbohydrates needed to sustain properly the brain and other organs.

a') Bee Honey

Jonathan W. White, Jr. discusses at some length the variables pertinent to ascertaining the "average composition" of bee honey produced within a particular region.[53] He also notes significant differences in the composition of bee honey produced in different parts of the world.[54] The task of evaluating a particular type of bee honey is even more challenging, because the chemical content of stored bee honey can change over time.[55]

Despite these difficulties, the United States Department of Agriculture (USDA) estimates bee honey's nutritional content as 304 kcal/100 g.[56] The USDA Nutrient Database also states that bee honey consists almost entirely of water (17.1%) and of carbohydrates from sugars (82.4%). Bee honey contains no fat (lipids) and almost no protein (0.3%) or fiber (0.2%); it has only trace (that is, insignificant) amounts of vitamins, proteins and amino acids. To be sure, bee honey is a rich source of energy: If John were to consume a handful—that is, an exceptionally large amount equivalent to around one cup (= 339 grams)—he would glean some 1,031 calories, or around forty percent of the energy he needed for one day.

---

hydrate is set at 130 g/day for adults and children based on the average minimum amount of glucose utilized by the brain."

[53] Jonathan W. White, Jr., "Composition of Honey," in: *Honey: A Comprehensive Survey* (ed. E. Crane), 157–206, esp. 157–80. Cf. Gal., *Nat. fac.* 11.115–118; *De alim. fac.* 470–471.

[54] White, "Composition of Honey," 158: "[N]ectars from different plants vary widely in the identity and concentrations of their constituent sugars; in fact, honey types are ascribed to plant sources by flavour or gross composition alone. Weather or climatic conditions and bee-keeper practices in removing and extracting honey may affect composition to a minor extent."

[55] White, "Composition of Honey," 167: "[S]toring honey for two years at 'room temperature' brings about a 69% increase in 'maltose' at the expense of dextrose plus laevulose, which decreased to 86% of its initial value in this period." Cf. Arist., *HA* 5.22 (554A); Plin. (E), *HN* 11.13.32; J. W. White, Jr. et al., "Composition of Honey IV: The Effect of Storage on Carbohydrates, Acidity, and Disease Content," *Journal of Food Science* (Chicago) 26 (1961): 63–71.

[56] USDA, *National Nutrient Database for Standard Reference, Release 16–1*; online: http://www.nal.usda.gov/fnic/foodcomp (on 17 May 2004). Cf. Eva Crane et al., "Biological Properties of Honey," in: *Honey: A Comprehensive Survey* (ed. E. Crane), 258–66; here, 264–5; White, "Composition of Honey," 171–80.

As is well known, however, calories from sugars are beneficial to the body only in the short term.[57] Even more challenging for the historical Baptist would have been the extraordinarily large quantity of a sweet substance such as bee honey that he would have to consume each day—157.8 grams (.347 lbs.)—in order to meet his daily need for carbohydrates.[58] The idea that John would have eaten so much bee honey on a regular basis is therefore implausible.

b') Date Honey

The same generalization concerning the inadequacy of bee honey as a primary food staple applies also to date honey, since this fruit (*Phoenix dactylifera*) is also mostly water (20.5%) and carbohydrates from sugars (75.0%).[59] Dates (277 kcal/100 g) have slightly fewer calories than bee honey (304 kcal/100 g), although date syrup has slightly more calories (313 kcal/100 g).[60] Thus, to meet his daily need for carbohydrates (130 grams per day), the Baptist would need to eat 173.3 grams (.381 lbs.) of dates converted into honey/syrup per day. Depending on the type and size of the dates, this would be equivalent to eating between seven and twenty-one dates per day.[61] Albeit not impossible, it is unlikely that John would have eaten such a large quantity of date syrup each day.

---

[57] Inexplicably, the article for "Honey" [no author listed] in the *Eerdmans Dictionary of the Bible* (gen. ed. David Noel Freedman; Grand Rapids: Eerdmans, 2000), 499, describes bee honey as 'nutritious': "A sweet, viscid, and nutritional fluid produced by bees from flower nectar. . . ."

[58] This calculation is derived from the approximate concentration of carbohydrates from sugars in bee honey (82.4%). Eating 157.8 grams of bee honey would yield to the eater around 130 grams in carbohydrates.

[59] According to the USDA Nutrient Database for common (i.e., deglet noor) dates; the figures for medjool dates are similar. Medjool dates also contain almost no fat (0.4%) and small amounts of protein (2.4%) and fiber (8.0%). Even allowing for regional and seasonal varieties among dates, the general point concerning the high sugar content in dates is valid. Cf. Irene Jacob and Walter Jacob, "Flora," art. *ABD*, 2.803–17; here, 807 (s.v. date palm): Dates were "a basic food consumed both fresh or dried, made into honey (over 60 percent sugar content)."

[60] The caloric content for dates is according to the USDA Nutrient Database for common (deglet noor) dates. For the caloric content of date syrup, see: Food and Agriculture Organization (FAO) of the United Nations: Food Policy and Nutrition Division, *Food Composition Tables for the Near East* (ed. Z. I. Sabry and R. L. Rizek; FAO Food and Nutrition Paper 26; Rome: FAO, 1982), 78–9.

[61] The USDA Nutrient Database lists 8.3 grams as an average weight for common (deglet noor) dates and 24 grams for medjool dates.

c') Fig Honey

In the case of figs (*Ficus carica*), moreover, the percentages of water (79.1%) and carbohydrates from sugars (19.1%) are nearly the opposite of those in bee honey and dates.[62] Because figs contain much more water than dates and bee honey do, *Ficus carica* offers around one-fourth as many calories (74 kcal/100 g). Concerning John's daily need for carbohydrates, the fig honey he would eat on a daily basis would need to contain the equivalent of 680 grams (1.496 lbs.) of this fruit, or between ten and seventeen figs.[63] The attempt to eat so many distilled dates or figs could result in a stomach ache, if not greater physical discomfort.

d') Honey-Water

The present author has not been able to find any data on the nutrient value of tree sap, whether from date trees or other trees. It nonetheless stands to reason that if the Baptist made use of honey-water in the wilderness, the benefit in carbohydrates and gross calories would be rather small. The primary benefit would instead be hydration—always a good idea in the wilderness!

e') Conclusion: 'Wild Honeys' and Carbohydrates

However much "wild honey" John may have consumed, he would not have needed much to supplement the calories he could have easily derived from eating locusts. From the standpoint of John's daily *caloric* need, whether the Baptist's honey was rich in calories (bee honey or date honey) or had fewer calories (fig honey, honey-water) may be a moot point. He would have made himself sick to his stomach if he ate too much bee honey or date honey, because of these honeys' high sugar contents. Furthermore, he would have needed to consume even more fig honey or honey-water, because they would contain a lower concentration of sugars.

Thus, one difficulty with the characterization of Matt 3:4c concerns whether the Baptist could have consumed enough *carbohydrates* from "locusts and wild honey" to maintain adequate brain function. Equally striking about bee, date and fig honey, moreover, is the relative absence of vitamins, minerals and amino acids. These aspects of the Baptist's diet are addressed immediately below.

---

[62] According to the USDA Nutrient Database. The relative absence of protein (0.8%) and fat (0.3%) and small amount of fiber (3.3%) in figs is again noteworthy. Trace (i.e., insignificantly small) amounts of certain vitamins, minerals and amino acids comprise the remaining 0.7% in figs. See further: Ira J. Condit, *The Fig* (New Series of Plant Science Books 19; Waltham, MA: Chronica Botanica, 1947), 148–55.

[63] Depending on the type and size of the figs. The USDA Nutrient Database classifies figs only according to size, whether small (40 g), medium (50 g), or large (64 g).

iii) The Risk of Scurvy: Vitamins and Minerals in "Locusts and Wild Honey"

That "locusts and wild honey" could have met John's needs for protein and calories, but probably not carbohydrates, has been established in the last two subsections. It remains to consider what these foods would offer John in terms of vitamins, minerals and amino acids. It has already been noted that locusts contain riboflavin and nicotinic acid (vitamin B_2).[64] These insects are also a good source of vitamin B_1, niacin (MG), calcium, iron and amino acids.[65]

Notably absent among the vitamins and minerals John would have needed, however, is Vitamin C (ascorbic acid).[66] If John were to live in the wilderness (or elsewhere) for a month or more without some source of Vitamin C (present in many, but not all, fruits and vegetables), he would be prone to developing scurvy. In contrast to the depiction of John's diet in Matt 3:4c, therefore, it is implausible that John would have eaten only "locusts and wild honey" for an extended period of time. If he had adhered to such a diet, it is unlikely that he would have been in good enough health to gain and maintain popular notoriety[67] and devoted followers (Mark 2:18 par.; Luke 7:24; John 3:25–27; Acts 18:25).

c) Summation: John's Diet in Light of Empirical Data on Human Nutrition

The preceding investigation has sought to illustrate in light of empirical data on human nutrition the claim of Matt 3:4c that the Baptist ate only "locusts and wild honey" in the wilderness. The variables posited for John's body type, age, height, and level of activity and for the food he ate—drawn from the National Academy of Sciences (NAS), the United States Department of Agriculture (USDA) and other scientific studies—are conjectural. Nonetheless, they are sufficient to demonstrate that the historical Baptist could indeed have met his needs for protein and calories from these foods. It is un-

---

[64] Brothwell and Brothwell, *Food in Antiquity*, 68–9.

[65] Bodenheimer, *Insects as Human Food*, 32–4; here, 34: "B_1 and B_2 are the vitamins most commonly found in grasshoppers." See also Sutton, *Insects*, 14–15; Taylor, *Butterflies*, 57, 202–3; [Four Winds Food Specialists], *Ethnic Foods Nutrient Composition Guide*, 80; Bukkens, "Nutritional Value of Edible Insects," 300, 309.

[66] According to L. Kathleen Mahan and Sylvia Escott-Stump, eds., *Krause's Food, Nutrition & Diet Therapy* (Philadelphia: W. B. Saunders, [10]2000), 106, adults require 60 mg of Vitamin C daily. The USDA Nutrient Database states that 100 grams of bee honey contain only 0.5 mg of ascorbic acid. The amounts for dates (0.4 mg/100 g) and figs (2.0 mg/100 g) are also quite low. Had the Baptist tried to glean 60 mg of Vitamin C from bee, date, or fig honey in a single day, he most likely would have made himself sick from the accompanying excess quantity of sugar!

[67] As attested, e.g., by Mark 1:5a (ἐξεπορεύετο πρὸς αὐτὸν πᾶσα ἡ Ἰουδαία χώρα καὶ οἱ Ἰεροσολυμῖται πάντες) and par.; Mark 11:32 par.; Jos., *Ant.* 18.5.2 (§§116–119).

likely, however, that he would have been able to consistently eat the large quantities of "wild honey" necessary to satisfy his needs for carbohydrates. Moreover, John *could not* have met his needs for Vitamin C (ascorbic acid) from eating only these foods.

For these reasons, Matt 3:4c must be dismissed as a historically unreliable characterization of the Baptist's food in the wilderness. Matthew's motivation for thus depicting John's diet will be explored below, after two other inquiries have been satisfied, namely how John himself may have responded to the characterization of Mark 1:6c‖Matt 3:4c, and Mark 1:6c as a part of Mark 1:2–8. There is no reason at all, however, to question the claim of Mark 1:6c, that John would eat ἀκρίδες καὶ μέλι ἄγριον from time to time, or even as a staple of a more variegated diet.[68] Indeed, the locusts would be a rich source of protein and calories for anyone seeking to subsist in the wilderness or, for that matter, anywhere else.

5. The Historical Baptist's Likely Response to His Commemoration in Mark 1:6c‖Matt 3:4c

"What?!?"

John probably would have been surprised to learn that Mark and Matthew would later memorialize him for reasons including his eating grasshoppers and 'honey' of poor quality. This inference is justified because, as noted in the preceding two chapters, the characterization of Mark 1:6c‖Matt 3:4c is far from extraordinary when considered in light of analogous ancient Jewish, ancient Near Eastern and Greco-Roman materials. For example, honeys of various qualities are commonly discussed in Greco-Roman antiquity.[69]

With regard to the Baptist's ἀκρίδες, it is already stated in Leviticus 11 (*pace* Deut 14:19) that eating certain locusts/grasshoppers is permitted.[70] Copious evidence from the ancient Near East demonstrates that Lev 11:20–23 is not an isolated literary testimony and, moreover, that this prescription does not point to a distinctively Jewish culinary practice. Additional evidence for

---

[68] With Becker, "'Kamelhaare... und wilder Honig,'" 22–3.

[69] Arist., *HA* 5.22 (533B, 554B); 8(9).40 (626B–627A); *GA* 3.10 (760B); Cato, *Rust.* 76; Varro, *Rust.* 3.16.2–38; Plin. (E), *HN* 11.4.11–11.23.70; 11.32–33; Columella, *Rust.* 9.2–16; Apul., *Met.* 1.5; Ael., *NA* 5.42; Palladius, *De vet. med.* 2.18; 3.27; 5.7; 6.8; 7.7; 7.11; 11.13–14; 12.8; *Geoponica* 15.2–9.

[70] Lev 11:20–23: "[20] All winged insects that walk upon all fours are detestable to you. [21] But among the winged insects that walk on all fours you may eat those that have jointed legs above their feet, with which to leap on the ground. [22] Of them you may eat: the locust (אַרְבֶּה) according to its kind, the bald locust ([?] Heb: סָלְעָם) according to its kind, the cricket ([?] Heb: חַרְגֹּל) according to its kind, and the grasshopper (חָגָב) according to its kind. [23] But all other winged insects that have four feet are detestable to you." See the discussion in chapter 2 on the difficulty of translating certain terms for "locust" in this passage.

locusts as human food in antiquity includes literary references,[71] as well as Assyrian bas-reliefs, one of which depicts servants bearing skewered locusts and pomegranates.[72] Second Temple Jewish literature and subsequent Jewish writings indicate that certain Jews ate locusts both before and after John the Baptist. These witnesses include the *Letter of Aristeas* (2nd c. B.C.E.),[73] Philo of Alexandria,[74] the Damascus Document,[75] numerous tractates of the Mishnah,[76] later interpretations of Hebrew Scripture,[77] and Moses Maimonides (1135–1204 C.E.).[78] There is thus no reason to infer that either

---

[71] E.g., "I have forwarded to my lord as many locusts as they were able to catch for me" (ARM 3.62.15), cited in the entry for *erbu* (cf. Heb. אַרְבֶּה) in *CAD*, 257.

[72] See the discussion of these materials in chapter 2.

[73] *Aristeas* 144b–146a: "[144b] These laws have all been solemnly drawn up for the sake of justice, to promote holy contemplation and the perfecting of character. [145] For of the winged creatures of which we make use (οἷς χρώμεθα) all are gentle and distinguished by cleanliness and they feed on (χρώμενα πρὸς τὴν τροφήν) grain and pulse, such as pigeons, doves, 'locusts' (ἀττακοί), partridges, and also geese and all similar fowl. [146a] But of the winged creatures which are forbidden you will find that they are wild and carnivorous (σαρκοφάγα)...."

[74] Philo, *Leg.* 2.105: "Now in Leviticus the sacred word advises (παραινεῖ ... ὁ ἱερὸς λόγος) them to feed 'on creeping things that go upon all four, which have legs above their feet, so as to leap with them' [Lev 11:21]. Such are the locust (ὁ βροῦχος), the wild locust (ὁ ἀττακός), the grasshopper (ἀκρίς), and in the fourth place the snake-fighter. And this is how it should be. For if serpent-like pleasure is an unnourishing (ἄτροφον) and injurious thing, self-mastery, the nature that is not in conflict with pleasure, must be wholesome and full of nourishment (τροφιμώτατον ... καὶ σωτήριον)."

[75] CD 12:11b–15a: "[11b] No-one should defile his soul [12] with any living being or one which creeps, by eating them, from the larvae of bees to every living [13] being which creeps in water. And fish: they should not eat them unless they have been opened up [14] alive, and the[ir blood poured] away. And all the locusts (וכל הגבים), according to their kind, shall be put into the fire or into water [15a] while [they are] still alive, as this is the regulation for their species." Cf. 11Q19 (11QTᵃ) 48:3–5.

[76] E.g., *m. Ḥul.* 8:1: "No flesh may be cooked in milk excepting the flesh of fish and locusts; and no flesh may be served up on the table together with cheese excepting the flesh of fish and locusts. If a man vowed to abstain from flesh, he is permitted the flesh of fish and locusts."

[77] For example, the Lamentations Midrash states: "R. Ḥanina b. Abbahu said: There are seven hundred species of clean fish, eight hundred of clean grasshoppers, and birds beyond number; and they all went into exile with Israel to Babylon; and when the people went back, they returned with them...."

[78] Maimonides, *Holiness* 5.2.1.21–23: "[21] The Torah permits eight species of locusts: the grasshopper; another species of grasshopper called *razbaniṭ*; the cricket; another species of cricket called ʿarṣubya; the common locust; another species of locust called 'the vineyard bird;' the bald locust; and another species of bald locust called 'the Jerusalemite *Joḥana*.' [22] He who is an expert in them and in their names may eat of them, and a hunter is to be believed in their case as in the case of birds. But he who is not an expert in them must examine their tokens. They possess three tokens: Whichever has four legs and four wings which overlie most of the length of its body and most of its circumference, and has in addition two

ἀκρίδες or μέλι ἄγριον would have been regarded as extraordinary by John or his followers.

It can indeed be illuminating to consider the ways in which an exceptional figure happens to be remembered. Such is certainly so for the historical Jesus—and even the apostle Paul[79]—in certain parts of the NT and other early Christian literature. In the case of the Baptist, one may ask: Would John himself have listed grasshopper and honey eating in his prophetic *curriculum vitae*? Probably not: Neither these insects nor uncultivated 'honey' would have been distinctive foods for a Palestinian Jew. How many of us today can remember what we ate for breakfast three weeks ago? Which of us, moreover, would choose to be remembered for partaking of what our culture defines as a pedestrian meal?

What this suggests is that Mark 1:6c was written for an audience that would associate *some* meaning with this cuisine, a meaning that John and his followers may not have readily comprehended, let alone affirmed. This conclusion concerning the relative insignificance of "locusts and wild honey" for John himself does not, however, dismiss the possibility that Isaiah 40 had some relevance for the historical Baptist.[80] What is unlikely is that John would have eaten locusts/grasshoppers and 'honey' in order to demonstrate some association with Isaiah's wilderness. As is argued in the following section, this was the inference of Mark or Mark's source.

Did John eat locusts? There is no good reason to suspect that he did not,[81] and the aforementioned passages, from Leviticus 11 through Maimonides, collectively satisfy any reasonable criterion of plausibility for the claim of Mark 1:6c. More than anything, the depiction of the Baptist in Mark 1:6c exemplifies that there is much about this wilderness prophet that the Synoptic evangelists or their sources misunderstood or deemed irrelevant. A great deal of John's prophetic message and activities may have once resonated in the details forsaken or assigned new meanings by these early Christian authors.

---

legs with which to leap, is deemed a clean species. Even if it has an elongated head and a tail, so long as it is known by the name of locust, it is clean. [23] If at present the locust has no wings or legs, or if its wings do not cover the greater part of the body, but it is known that it will grow them after some time when it has matured, it is deemed permitted immediately." Cf. *b. Ḥul.* 65a.

[79] E.g., *1 Clem.* 47:1–6, on Paul's alleged harmony with Peter; *pace* Gal 2:11–14.

[80] Isa 40:3 is taken up in Mal 3:1 (cf. Mal 3:23), where the coming messenger is linked with Elijah, and is also a passage quoted quite frequently in Second Temple Jewish literature (e.g., Bar 5:7; Sir 48:24; *1 En.* 1.6; *As. Mos.* 10.3–4). The possibility that John himself may have thought that he fit the image of Elijah, of a prophet of repentance, is neither dismissed nor confirmed by this investigation. That John saw his function in preaching and baptizing (at the place where Elijah was taken up to heaven) as a fulfillment of Isa 40:3 strikes the present author as entirely plausible, if not likely (with J. Taylor, *Immerser*, 25–9).

[81] Against Dibelius, *Johannes*, 48; Ernst, *Johannes*, 6.

B. John as Wilderness Herald: Mark 1:6c

The passages discussed in chapter 2 that are related, however loosely, to Lev 11:20–23 do not resolve the problem with which this query began, namely what the attribution of Mark 1:6c‖Matt 3:4c meant to the Synoptic evangelists. It has been argued that this characterization would have had little, if any, significance to John himself. It remains to consider the importance that Mark and Matthew (or their sources) ascribe to this attribution. This section does not endeavor to offer a complete exegesis of Mark 1:2–11 but aims instead to illustrate how the findings of this study contribute to the understanding of this passage.

As noted in chapter 1, the description of John's clothing (Mark 1:6ab) already assumes a Greek context (2 Kgs 1:8, LXX); the same may be inferred also for his diet (1:6c), since there is no reason to assign the details concerning John's clothing (1:6ab) and diet (1:6c) to two separate strata of 'gospel' traditions. Accordingly, the earliest recoverable Synoptic tradition is removed from the context of John's Aramaic preaching. Mark thus presents the Baptist's diet and clothing as features that a Greek-speaking audience would have understood.

Certain characteristics of locust eaters, discussed in chapter 2, elucidate that Mark 1:6c offers additional 'proof' that John came in fulfillment of "Isaiah." Chapter 2 demonstrated that eating locusts was well-attested in antiquity.[82] Of particular importance to the present inquiry is Diodorus (*Hist.* 3.29.1–6), who connects an Ethiopian tribe of 'Locust Eaters' and their food with the *desert/wilderness* (πρὸς τὴν ἔρημον). Although Diodorus's Ethiopian 'Locust Eaters' do not live in the desert, the locusts blown by the wind come from the desert. Since the author of Mark does not explain the meaning of "locusts and wild honey," he must assume that his characterization had some meaning for his audience, a meaning lost to most (Western) interpreters of Mark through the centuries. If one can assume for Mark's audience a connection between locusts and the desert, then the characterization of Mark 1:6c within 1:2–8 begins to make sense.

Mark 1:2–8 reveals only a handful of details about John the Baptist. This gospel begins[83] with a title for this work (1:1), and then immediately delves into a citation of "Isaiah" (Isa 40:3 and Mal 3:1, Mark 1:2–3), which is tied directly to the coming of the Baptist (καθὼς γέγραπται . . . ἐγένετο Ἰωάννης, 1:2a–4a). Mark asserts that the "voice shouting in the wilderness"

---

[82] A number of the writings examined in chapter 2 indicate that certain Greeks, like their ancient Near Eastern counterparts, also ate locusts/grasshoppers.

[83] The arguments, e.g., of N. Clayton Croy, *The Mutilation of Mark's Gospel* (Nashville: Abingdon, 2003), 113–36, that the original beginning of Mark is lost, are not compelling in the view of the present author.

(ἐν τῇ ἐρήμῳ, 1:3a) was indeed John's (βαπτίζων ἐν τῇ ἐρήμῳ καὶ κηρύσσων, 1:4a).

Within Mark 1:2–8, verse 6 serves to authenticate John's identity as the wilderness herald foretold in Isaiah 40. As noted in chapter 1, that John is a prophet is confirmed by his "hairy mantle."[84] The leather belt bolsters the eschatological significance of John's coming as the new Elijah.[85] Finally, ἀκρίδες καὶ μέλι ἄγριον (Mark 1:6c) describes a particular diet which, for the author of Mark and his/her audience, designates John as a member of a foreign culture whose *social location is in the wilderness* (ἐν τῇ ἐρήμῳ). Analogous passages discussed in chapter 2—not only Diodorus Siculus (*Hist.* 3.29), but also in Strabo (*Geog.* 16.4.12) and the Elder Pliny (*Nat. Hist.* 6.35.178–197)—demonstrate that the locust-wilderness connection was well-attested by the time of the first century C.E. Thus, in Mark 1:2–8 the most likely referent for the cultural designation by means of food is John's place "in the wilderness" (1:3a, 4a). This is where John partook (ἦν . . . ἐσθίων) of grasshoppers and unrefined 'honey,' since these are among the sparse victuals one is likely to find in the wilderness. Thus, it is only in reference to the desert that Mark makes an *indirect* association between John's diet and the wilderness herald of Isa 40:3.[86]

As argued above, however, there is no reason to infer that John or his followers would have associated a particular context "in the wilderness" with this common food. Such a connection between food and the wilderness would hardly be self-evident within a Near Eastern context, where grasshoppers were commonly eaten not just in wilderness regions but at royal banquets as well. Yet in a different culture or location, where locusts were not on the menu, such an association (or misunderstanding) was entirely possible. *The creativity of Mark the evangelist (or his source)* is thus to be recognized for taking this otherwise unremarkable aspect of the historical Baptist's life and endowing it with theological significance, as a roundabout confirmation of Isa 40:3. John's diet of "locusts and wild honey" (v. 6c), together with his

---

[84] Mark 1:6a; cf. Zech 13:4 and below on *Mart. Ascen. Isa.* 2:7–10.

[85] Mark 1:6b; cf. 2 Kgs 1:8, LXX; Markus Öhler, *Elia im Neuen Testament: Untersuchungen zur Bedeutung des alttestamentlichen Propheten im frühen Christentum* (BZNW 88; Berlin: de Gruyter, 1997), 31–7; Becker, "'Kamelhaare... und wilder Honig,'" 15–20.

[86] Cf. 1 Kgs 19:4, 15. With J. Ernst, *Johannes der Täufer*, 6: "Die Wüste (V. 4) und die absonderliche Kleidung und die Speise (V. 6) erhalten einen symbolischen Sinn. Markus illustriert am Beispiel des Johannes erzählend das Dogma des Elias redivivus"; and J. R. Edwards, *Mark*, 32: "John's rustic dress and diet . . . further identify him with 'the desert region' (1:4). . . . Thus, in dress, setting, and proclamation Mark associates John with Elijah, the thundering prophet who renewed God's covenant with Israel on Mt. Carmel (1 Kgs 18:30–45). The stream of crowds that visit John are thus making a pilgrimage to a figure who is a harbinger of the fulfillment of Israel's destiny." So also Becker, "'Kamelhaare... und wilder Honig,'" 20–1, 24–5.

clothing (v. 6ab, with reference to the Baptist as Elijah),[87] confirm the citation of "Isaiah" in Mark 1:2–3. That is to say, Mark 1:6 ties together Mal 3:1 and Isa 40:3, cited at the beginning of the pericope (Mark 1:2–3).

Viewed as a whole, then, Mark's introductory passage begins with the claim that, just as Second Isaiah described Jesus' forerunner in the wilderness (Mark 1:2–3), John appeared there (1:4). C. S. Keener notes the symbolic importance of Mark's emphasizing John's whereabouts: "The meaning of John's location would not be lost on Syro-Palestinian Jews. Israel's prophets had predicted a new exodus in the wilderness (Hos 2:14–15; Is 40:3; later interpreters properly understood such passages as applicable to the time of Israel's restoration—e.g., Ps. Sol. 11:1)."[88] In light of the importance of linking the Baptist with Isaiah 40, Malachi 3 and the return of Elijah, it is not surprising to find in Mark 1:6 examples of food and clothing demonstrating that John does indeed fit the part.[89]

Accordingly, John's clothing (1:6ab) and diet of a wilderness dweller (1:6c) demonstrate that the Baptist is indeed the new Elijah (*pace* John 1:21), who came in fulfillment of Isa 40:3 and Mal 3:1. Mark 1:2–8 may thus be seen as offering an explanation for why John baptizes Jesus (and not vice-versa) in Mark 1:9–11.[90] Jesus can be baptized by John precisely because John is the new Elijah, who came as the Hebrew prophets said he would. Unlike John, who foraged for what provisions were available in the wilderness, Jesus had angels to wait on him during his time of wilderness temptation (Mark 1:13: οἱ ἄγγελοι διηκόνουν αὐτῷ; cf. 1 Kgs 19:4–8).

The conclusion this study offers concerning the wilderness association denoted by John's "locusts and wild honey" is not new.[91] The contribution of the present study involves a demonstration of why this is the correct interpretation of Mark 1:6c and how the Baptist's diet functions as a part of this evangelist's larger concerns in Mark 1.

---

[87] With P. Lamarche, *Marc*, 39: "En [Malachi] 3,23 ce messager est nommé, c'est Elie. Ici Elie, le messager, c'est Jean. . . ."

[88] *Matthew*, 117.

[89] W. L. Lane, *Mark*, 51, notes correctly that later in Mark 9:9–13 this identification is made explicit.

[90] Cf. the connection that the apostle Paul acknowledges between baptizing and the authority ascribed to the one who baptizes in 1 Cor 1:12–17.

[91] See the discussion in chapter 1 of scholars who have come to this conclusion but not offered adequate support for it, including E. Lohmeyer, *Johannes der Täufer*, 50–2; J. P. Meier, *Marginal Jew*, 2.49; R. H. Gundry, *Mark*, 37; D. R. A. Hare, *Mark*, 15; W. L. Lane, *Mark*, 51; L. Williamson, *Mark*, 32; C. H. Kraeling, *John the Baptist*, 10–13; E. P. Gould, *Mark*, 8; B. M. F. van Iersel, *Mark*, 97; J. R. Edwards, *Mark*, 32; É. Trocmé, *Marc*, 28; T. J. Geddert, *Mark*, 32.

C. John as a Bonafide Wilderness Survivor: Matt 3:4c

1. From Mark's Wilderness Confirmation to Matthew's (and Luke's)
Wilderness Assumption(s)

The previous section concluded that the author of Mark 1:2–6 (or some source used by Mark) offers John's clothing and diet as a proof that the Baptist was the wilderness dweller and the new Elijah foretold in Isa 40:3 and Mal 3:1. Despite the many similarities between Mark 1:2–8 and Matt 3:1–6 and, in particular, between Mark 1:6c and Matt 3:4c, it is not a primary concern in Matthew 3 to offer a connection between the wilderness and John's grasshoppers and 'honey.'[92] In order to understand how the author of Matthew interpreted Mark 1:6c, it is necessary to consider first how this evangelist made use of Mark 1:2–6 and other wilderness materials from this gospel.

Unlike Mark, Matthew places John the Baptist ἐν τῇ ἐρήμῳ τῆς Ἰουδαίας (Matt 3:1b‖Mark 1:4a) *before* citing Isa 40:3 (Matt 3:3‖Mark 1:2). What this indicates is that Matthew *assumes* a point for which Mark argues by means of OT scripture and John's clothing and food. Since Matthew does not need the Baptist's cuisine to demonstrate an association with the wilderness, the mention of ἀκρίδες καὶ μέλι ἄγριον in Matt 3:4c could indeed serve a different function in Matt 3:1–6 than it does in Mark 1:2–8.

Also differing from Mark 1:2–8, the early chapters of Luke offer a treatment of John and the wilderness analogous to that in Matt 3:1–6. For example, Luke describes the young John, prior to the beginning of his (adult) public ministry, as having already spent a considerable period of time in the wilderness: "The child (τὸ . . . παιδίον) grew and became strong in spirit, and he was in the wilderness until the day he appeared publicly to Israel" (Luke 1:80). Moreover, and as in Matt 3:1–3, according to Luke 3:2 "the word of God came to John son of Zechariah in the wilderness," prior to the citation of Isaiah 40 (Luke 3:4, from Mark 1:2).

The distinctiveness of Mark's treatment of the Baptist in the wilderness, in contrast to those in Matthew and Luke, may be summarized as follows:

---

[92] Of course, this is a moot point for Luke, who offers no parallel to Mark 1:6c.

Matthew 3–4	Mark 1	Luke 1–4
		• John spends time in the wilderness prior to the beginning of his public ministry (Luke 1:80).
• John *first* appears "in the wilderness of Judea" (Matt 3:1).	• [Mark 1:4, below]	• John *first* receives a prophetic message from the Lord in the wilderness (3:2).
• The citation of Isaiah 40 follows this assumed point (3:3).	• Isaiah predicted the appearance of a wilderness herald (1:2).	• Luke then augments the Markan citation of Isaiah 40 (3:4–6).
• [3:1, above]	• John *then* appears in the wilderness (1:4).	• [3:2, above]
• Mention of John's clothing and diet follows (3:4).	• John's clothing and food authenticate him as that wilderness herald (1:6).	• [no Lukan parallel]
• Jesus' baptism (3:13–17) and subsequent temptation in the wilderness (4:1–11).	• Jesus' baptism (1:9–11) and subsequent temptation in the wilderness (1:12–13).	• Jesus' baptism (3:21–22) and, later, return to the wilderness to be tempted (4:1–13).

It thus follows that, unlike Mark, Matthew and Luke *assume* a connection between John as a wilderness figure and Isaiah 40. As a result, Matthew and Luke organized their narratives without the need to prove this point. That Matt 3:1–3 and Luke 3:2–6 reverse the order of the citation of Isaiah 40 and John's appearance in the wilderness from that in Mark 1:2, 4 is hardly surprising. Once a detail, like John as a wilderness dweller, becomes part of the esteemed tradition, it can be seen to require less confirmation. Additionally, both the wilderness and *the details used to support John's association with the wilderness* can over time become associated with *new meanings and interpretations*. This and the following section endeavor to ascertain what significance Mark 1:6c had for the authors of Matthew and Luke.

2. Matt 3:4c and Reports of Other Judean Wilderness Survivors

The closest literary analogies to Matt 3:4c pertain to other Judeans who survived *exclusively* on foods found in the wilderness. The following discussion of 2 Maccabees 5, *Martyrdom of Isaiah* 2, and Josephus's description of Bannus (*Vita* 2 §11) will support the argument that Matthew is not concerned primarily with *what* John ate or *where* he ate (details taken over from Mark), but rather that the Baptist subsisted *entirely* on uncultivated foods.

a) The Survival of Judas Maccabeus and Others in the Wilderness

2 Maccabees 5 relates the plundering of the Jerusalem Temple by Antiochus IV (Epiphanes) in 165 B.C.E. A persecution of the Jewish people

as a whole is said to follow this event (2 Macc 5:21–26). In response to this situation, a small group of Jews, including Judas Maccabeus, retreat to the wilderness:

> But Judas Maccabeus, with about nine others, withdrew to the wilderness (ἀναχωρήσας εἰς τὴν ἔρημον), and kept himself and his companions alive in the mountains as wild animals do (θηρίων τρόπον); they continued to live on what grew wild, so that they might not share in the defilement (τὴν χορτώδη τροφὴν σιτούμενοι διετέλουν πρὸς τὸ μὴ μετασχεῖν τοῦ μολυσμοῦ). (2 Macc 5:27)

Second Maccabees presents these Judeans' concern for purity as the motivation for their grazing like "wild animals" only on grasses and other 'vegetarian' foods that grew naturally in the wild.

b) The Survival of "Isaiah" and Other Prophets in the Wilderness

The *Martyrdom of Isaiah* (2nd c. B.C.E.?) states that during the reign of Manasseh (*c.* 687/6–642 B.C.E.; cf. 2 Kgs 21:1–18) Isaiah and other Israelite prophets fled Jerusalem and lived "on a mountain in a desert place."[93] For a period of two years, these prophets are said to subsist on only wild herbs: "And they had nothing to eat except wild herbs (which) they gathered from the mountains, and when they had cooked (them), they ate (them) with Isaiah the prophet. And they dwelt on the mountains and on the hills for two years of days."[94]

First Kings 19:1–8, which relates Elijah's flight "into the wilderness" (במדבר, v. 4) from Ahab and Jezebel, offers an obvious literary precedent for *Mart. Ascen. Isa.* 2:7–11. Unlike the prophets in the *Martyrdom of Isaiah*, however, Elijah had the luxury of being fed by an angel (1 Kgs 19:4–8). Thus, prior to the gospel of Matthew, 2 Maccabees and the *Martyrdom of Isaiah* present Judeans who survived entirely on wilderness foods.

c) Bannus's Natural Wilderness Clothing and Food

The Jewish historian Josephus claims to have been a student of a Judean wilderness dweller named Bannus. According to Josephus, Bannus's clothing and food came only from the wilderness:

---

[93] *Mart. Ascen. Isa.* 2.7–10: "[7] And when Isaiah the son of Amoz saw the great iniquity which was being committed in Jerusalem, and the service of Satan, and his wantonness, he withdrew from Jerusalem and dwelt in Bethlehem of Judah. [8] And there also there was great iniquity; and he withdrew from Bethlehem and dwelt on a mountain in a desert place. [9] And Micah the prophet, and the aged Ananias, and Joel, and Habakkuk, and Josab his son, and many of the faithful who believed in the ascension into heaven, withdrew and dwelt on the mountain. [10] All of them were clothed in sackcloth, and all of them were prophets; they had nothing with them, but were destitute, and they all lamented bitterly over the going astray of Israel." ET of the Ethiopic: M. A. Knibb, *OTP*, 2.158.

[94] *Mart. Ascen. Isa.* 2.11, parenthetical clarifications original to Knibb's translation.

On hearing of one named Bannus, who dwelt in the wilderness (ἐρημία), wearing only such clothing as trees provided, feeding on such things as grew of themselves (τροφὴν δὲ τὴν αὐτομάτως φυομένην προσφερόμενον), and using frequent ablutions of cold water, by day and night, for purity's sake, I became his devoted disciple (ζηλωτής). With him I lived for three years and, having accomplished my purpose, returned to the city. Being now in my nineteenth year I began to govern my life by the rules of the Pharisees. . . . (*Vita* 2 §11)

For Josephus, Bannus was an ascetic, whose concern for purity is evident in his regular ablutions and natural food and clothing, not to mention Bannus's choice to reside in the wilderness. These practices were worthy of Josephus's imitation, at least during the eventual historian's later teenage years.

In stating that he was nineteen years old when he completed three years with Bannus, Josephus (b. 37/38 C.E.) places his time with this wilderness ascetic at 53/54–56/57 C.E. Josephus therefore knew Bannus after the Baptist's death.[95] Still, it is not inconceivable that John and Bannus could have known each other.

3. Conclusion: Why Matthew Thus Edited Mark 1:6c

It has been noted that Matthew and Luke had no need for Mark's argument proving by virtue of John's food and clothing that the Baptist came in fulfillment of "Isaiah" (Mark 1:4, 6). These two evangelists presuppose this point. The question pertinent to interpreting Matt 3:4 then becomes: If Matthew's narrative does not require Mark's argument concerning food and clothing, why does Matthew retain it and, moreover, exaggerate the claim about John's food? The first part of this chapter dismissed Matt 3:4c as implausible for the historical Baptist, because any person eating only "locusts and wild honey" would eventually suffer from a lack of Vitamin C (ascorbic acid) and probably from an insufficient amount of carbohydrates as well.

This section has also noted analogies to the exclusive claim of Matt 3:4c—that John ate only "locusts and wild honey" in the wilderness—in 2 Maccabees 5, *Martyrdom of Isaiah* 2, and Josephus's account of Bannus. The choice to discuss 2 Macc 5:21–27, *Mart. Ascen. Isa.* 2:7–11, and Jos., *Vita* 2 §11 in connection with Matt 3:4c—and not Mark 1:6c or the historical Baptist—is intentional on the part of the present author. The exclusive claims attributed to the wilderness food of Judas Maccabeus, Isaiah and Bannus correspond to Matt 3:4c, not to Mark 1:6c. With regard to the historical Baptist, it would be speculative to infer from 2 Macc 5:21–27 and *Mart. Ascen. Isa.* 2:7–11 that John resided in the wilderness because of (a threat of) persecution, whether real or perceived. Additionally, 2 Macc 5:21–27 and Jos., *Vita* 2 §11 are not sufficient to support the inference that John chose uncultivated

---

[95] According to Mark 6:14–29 par., John was killed by Herod Antipas, tetrarch of Galilee and Perea 4 B.C.E.–39 C.E.

wilderness foods out of a concern for purity.[96] Hypothetically, either of these motivations could have influenced the historical Baptist's choices of where to live (persecution) or what he ate (purity), but such inferences are unnecessary in the case of such common foods eaten on occasion (Mark 1:6c).

Two of these three accounts of wilderness edibles predate the gospel of Matthew (2 Maccabees 5; *Martyrdom of Isaiah* 2). As already mentioned, two mention purity as the reason for choosing such natural foods (2 Maccabees 5; *Vita* 2 §11). *Only Josephus*, whose account is roughly contemporary with Matthew, presents Bannus as *an ascetic*. One therefore cannot ignore 2 Maccabees and the *Martyrdom of Isaiah* and argue only with reference to Josephus's Bannus that Matt 3:4c (let alone Mark 1:6c) presents John as an ascetic.[97]

Furthermore, the editing of Mark 1:6c in Matt 3:4c is most plausibly explained by inferring that the author of Matthew had some knowledge of the tales related in 2 Maccabees 5, *Martyrdom of Isaiah* 2, or both. If Matthew possessed such knowledge, then John's way of life "in the wilderness" as depicted in Mark 1 would appear to be *less rigorous* than those attributed to Judas Maccabeus and Isaiah. The rather minor changes Matthew made to Mark 1:6c in Matt 3:4c dispense with this difficulty and, moreover, bolster the credentials of Jesus' prophetic forerunner. In short, Matthew does not need to prove John's connection to Isaiah 40 but does wish to present John's wilderness provisions as equally demanding as those of earlier esteemed Jewish leaders who had spent time in the wilderness. In thus correcting Mark 1:6c, Matthew may unintentionally open the door to later ascetic interpretations of John's diet[98]—to be discussed in chapter 5. More than anything, Matt 3:4c presents John as a bonafide wilderness survivor like Isaiah or Judas Maccabeus, not as an ascetic.

---

[96] *Pace* Lupieri, "'The Law and the Prophets Were until John,'" 50–1, 54. Given the paucity of evidence available, a concern with purity could only be substantiated by positing that Josephus's Bannus had been a disciple of the historical John and had learned from his teacher to keep kashrut by eating wilderness foods. A connection between Bannus and the historical Baptist is only possible, however. It would be speculative to posit a mentor-disciple relationship between the two. Cf. Steve Mason, ed., *Life of Josephus: Translation and Commentary* (Flavius Josephus: Translation and Commentary 9; Leiden: Brill, 2001), 18 (on Jos., *Vita* 2 §11): "Although Shutt (1961:2) and many others opine that Bannus lived 'probably according to Essene ideals,' this observation appears to enjoy no better warrant—unless 'Essene ideals' refers to a general determination to live simply and in purity—than the posthumous induction of Jesus, John the Baptist, and others as Essenes."

[97] Against, e.g., A. H. McNeile, *Matthew*, 26; B. Weiss, *Matthew–Mark*, 13; Peter Böhlemann, *Jesus und der Täufer: Schlüssel zur Theologie und Ethik des Lukas* (SNTSMS 99; Cambridge: Cambridge University, 1997), 202–3. Cf. the criticisms in chapter 1 of attempts to interpret Mark 1:6c‖Matt 3:4c as an ascetic depiction or in terms of John's 'natural' food.

[98] With Luz, *Matthew*, 1.168.

D. Luke's Omission of Mark 1:6:
The Baptist, Jesus and Elijah

Luke's omission of Mark 1:6 has been noted by interpreters at least since the time of St. Augustine.[99] Because neither Matthew nor Luke needed the proof that Mark 1:6 offers in tying John to Isaiah 40 and the coming Elijah, both of these evangelists could have omitted it for this reason. It will be argued that a utilitarian explanation for Luke's passing over Mark 1:6 in silence, albeit possible, is less compelling than Luke's dissatisfaction with Mark's characterizing the Baptist as Elijah as the reason for this Lukan omission.

1. The Return of Elijah: John or Jesus?

According to Second Kings, Elijah left his mantle behind when he ascended/was translated into heaven (2 Kgs 2:1, 11). Elisha's tearing his own clothes into pieces and picking up the departed prophet's mantle symbolizes his assumption of Elijah's power and authority.[100] Subsequent Jewish writings, perhaps most notably Mal 3:23–24, build upon the ascension of Elijah in anticipation of the prophet's making another earthly appearance (cf. *1 En.* 90.31; *4 Ezra* 6.26; Sir 48:1–10). For early Christian authors who chose to interact with this expectation, the obvious choice was whether to express fulfillment with reference to John, Jesus, or both.[101]

---

[99] August., *De cons. evang.* 2.25, notes the omission but does not offer an explanation for it.

[100] 2 Kgs 2:12–13. When Elisha performs a miracle with this mantle, the company of prophets recognizes Elisha as Elijah's successor (2 Kgs 2:14–15).

[101] The secondary literature on this subject is quite extensive. See, e.g., Joachim Jeremias, "Ἡλ(ε)ίας," art. *TDNT*, 2.928–41; P. Dabeck, "'Siehe, es erschienen Moses und Elias' (Mt 17, 3)," *Bib* 23 (1942): 175–89, esp. 180–9; Georg Molin, "Elijahu: Der Prophet und sein Weiterleben in den Hoffnungen des Judentums und der Christenheit," *Judaica* 8 (1952): 65–94; C. F. Evans, "The Central Section of St. Luke's Gospel," in: *Studies in the Gospels: Essays in Memory of R. H. Lightfoot* (ed. D. E. Nineham; Oxford: Blackwell, 1955), 37–53, esp. 51–2; idem, *Saint Luke*, 237–8; J. A. T. Robinson, "Elijah, John and Jesus: An Essay in Detection," *NTS* 4 (1958): 263–81; Georg Hentschel, *Die Elijaerzählungen: Zum Verhältnis von historischem Geschehen und geschichtlicher Erfahrung* (ETS 33; Leipzig: St. Benno, 1977); Morris M. Faierstein, "Why Do the Scribes Say that Elijah Must Come First?" *JBL* 100 (1981): 75–86; Dale C. Allison, "Elijah Must Come First," *JBL* 103 (1984): 256–8; Robert Macina, "Jean le Baptiste était-il Élie?: Examen de la tradition néotestamentaire," *Proche Orient chrétien* (Jerusalem) 34 (1984): 209–32; Robert J. Miller, "Elijah, John, and Jesus in the Gospel of Luke," *NTS* 34 (1988): 611–22; Jerome T. Walsh, "Elijah (Person)," art. *ABD*, 2.463–6; Öhler, *Elia im Neuen Testament*; C. Houtman, "Elijah," art. *DDD*, 282–5; Brenda J. Shaver, "The Prophet Elijah in the Literature of the Second Temple Period: The Growth of a Tradition," (Diss., University of Chicago, 2001); Lawrence Frizzell, "Elijah the Peacemaker: Jewish and Early Christian Interpretations of Malachi 3:23–24," *SIDIC* 35/2–3 (2002): 24–30; cf. Otto F. A. Meinardus's essay on certain later Christian interpretations: "The Relics

The author of Mark highlights the Baptist as the coming Elijah, a claim the author of the Fourth Gospel explicitly denies.[102] As already mentioned, in Mark 1:6a the Baptist's clothing made from camel's hair builds on 2 Kings 2 and presents John as Elijah. Mark's identification of John as Elijah is further underscored by Jesus' explicit statement in this gospel about the Baptist's death: "But I tell you that Elijah has come (Ἠλίας ἐλήλυθεν), and they did to him whatever they pleased, as it is written about him" (Mark 9:13; cf. 6:14–29). Matthew agrees with Mark on this point.[103] Significant for the present study, however, is *Luke's choice to omit Jesus' identification of John as Elijah* (Mark 9:13‖Matt 17:12).

2. An Explanation for Luke's Omission of Mark 1:6

As compared with the appropriations of Elijah traditions in Mark and Matthew, those in the gospel of Luke are distinctive in at least one respect. Walter Wink exaggerates only slightly Luke's choice to identify *Jesus, not John*, as Elijah:

> Luke has retained nothing of John's role as Elijah. . . . [W]hile Luke deletes five of Mark's nine references to Elijah, he adds three of his own—1:17; 4:25, 26. In each case he rejects the concept of the eschatological return of Elijah already familiar to us from Malachi, Mark and Matthew.[104]

As already noted, Luke offers no characterization of John's clothing and food (Mark 1:6‖Matt 3:4) and omits Jesus' statement that John was the Elijah who was to come (Mark 9:11–13‖Matt 17:10–13).

Luke's omission of Jesus' identifying John as Elijah is informative for understanding three Lukan allusions to, or citations of, Isa 40:3 or Mal 3:1, because Luke *does not* use these passages to identify John as Elijah (L/Luke 1:17; L/Luke 1:76; Q/Luke 7:24–27). It is important to interpret Luke's use of these OT passages in the context of *Luke's* narrative and to guard against a harmonizing approach informed by Mark's or Matthew's uses of the same passages.[105] For example, Luke 1:17 credits to John only Elijah's spirit and

---

of St. John the Baptist and the Prophet Elisha: An Examination of the Claims of Their Recent Invention in Egypt," in: *Coptic Studies* (FS Mirrit Boutros Ghali; ed. Leslie S. B. MacCoull; Cairo: Society for Coptic Archaeology, 1979), 26–63.

[102] John 1:21a: "And they [priests and Levites from Jerusalem] asked him [John], 'What then? Are you Elijah?' He said, 'I am not.'" Cf. John 1:19; Georg Richter, "'Bist du Elias?' (Joh. 1, 21)," *BZ* n.s. 6 (1962): 79–92, 238–56.

[103] Matt 17:12 (from Mark 9:13): Ἠλίας ἤδη ἦλθεν.

[104] Wink, *John the Baptist*, 42.

[105] See further: Clare Komoroske Rothschild, *Luke-Acts and the Rhetoric of History: An Investigation of Early Christian Historiography* (WUNT 2.175; Tübingen: Mohr Siebeck, 2004), 158–66.

power, *not* his identity.[106] Moreover, the prophecy of John's father Zechariah in Luke 1:76 alludes to Isa 40:3 but, again, does not designate John as Elijah.[107] Finally, Q/Luke 7:24–27 cites Isa 40:3, but the pericope never mentions Elijah.[108] It follows that in Luke 1:17, 1:76, and 7:24–27, Luke stands in continuity with Mark and Q in retaining the fulfillment of scripture. Equally significant is Luke's departure from earlier 'gospel' materials that identify John as Elijah.

Luke does, however, repeat from Mark the opinion of others that *Jesus* was Elijah (Mark 6:14–15‖Luke 9:7–8 [Herod Antipas]; Mark 8:27–28‖Matt 16:13–14‖Luke 9:18–19 [Jesus' disciples' answer]). In addition, three characterizations of Jesus peculiar to Luke's gospel reflect an understanding of Jesus (not John) as Elijah. The first is Jesus' rejection in Nazareth (Mark 6:1–6a‖Matt 13:54–58‖Luke 4:16–24), which only Luke complements with a comparison to Elijah.[109] Second, Jesus' raising the widow's only son from the dead (L/Luke 7:11–16) shares many similarities with Elijah's healing of the widow's son at Zarephath (1 Kgs 17:8–24). Perhaps most significantly, Jesus' ascension into heaven—a christological attribution distinctive to Luke–Acts and reflected elsewhere in the NT only in a secondary addition to

---

[106] Luke 1:17: "With the spirit and power of Elijah he will go before him, to turn the hearts of parents to their children, and the disobedient to the wisdom of the righteous, to make ready a people prepared for the Lord." Against Jeremias, "Ἠλ(ε)ίας," 936–7; Öhler, *Elia im NT*, 77–84; Frizzell, "Elijah the Peacemaker," 26; and R. J. Miller, "Elijah, John, and Jesus," 616: "[Luke] 1. 17 draws on Mal 3. 1 and explicitly associates John and Elijah." On the contrary, Luke 1:17 alludes to Malachi, but does so without identifying John as Elijah.

[107] Luke 1:76: "And you, child, will be called the prophet of the Most High; for you will go before the Lord to prepare his ways." Against Robinson, "Elijah, John and Jesus," 264; Miller, "Elijah, John, and Jesus," 617, on Luke 1:76: "Here the reference to Elijah is not explicit, though it must be present to some extent through this verse's relation to 1. 17 and 7. 27." Miller's interpretation of Luke 1:17 is criticized in the preceding note. On Q/Luke 7:27‖Matt 11:10, see immediately below.

[108] Q/Luke 7:27: "This is the one about whom it is written, 'See, I am sending my messenger ahead of you, who will prepare your way before you.'" Against Öhler, *Elia im NT*, 87; Miller, "Elijah, John, and Jesus," 617, on Luke 7:27: "Because it is Jesus himself who identifies John with Elijah, Luke cannot but have approved of it." On the contrary, the Lukan Jesus identifies John only with the fulfillment of Isa 40:3, not with Elijah.

[109] Jesus' rejection in Nazareth is likened to the experiences of both Elijah and Elisha in Luke 4:25–27: "[25] But the truth is, there were many widows in Israel in the time of Elijah, when the heaven was shut up three years and six months, and there was a severe famine over all the land; [26] yet Elijah was sent to none of them except to a widow at Zarephath in Sidon. [27] There were also many lepers in Israel in the time of the prophet Elisha, and none of them was cleansed except Naaman the Syrian."

Mark (Mark 16:19)—has obvious similarities to Elijah's ascension into heaven (2 Kgs 2:11–12).[110]

Given Luke's desire to liken Jesus rather than John to Elijah,[111] if the interpretation of Mark 1:6c for which this study has argued—that John's grasshoppers and wild honey place him in the desert where Elijah, the renowned wilderness prophet, once dwelled—was recognized by the author of Luke, the absence of a parallel to John's clothing (Mark 1:6ab; cf. 2 Kgs 1:8, LXX) and diet (Mark 1:6c) in this gospel may be explained by Luke's particular uses of Elijah materials.[112]

E. Summation:
ΑΚΡΙΔΕΣ ΚΑΙ ΜΕΛΙ ΑΓΡΙΟΝ in Synoptic Interpretation

This chapter has argued for the following interpretations of John's diet with respect to the historical Baptist and the authors of Mark, Matthew, and Luke:

The Historical Baptist: No particular significance. There is no evidence to support the inference that John, his followers, or a Palestinian audience would regard John's partaking of these foods as a parabolic act demonstrating, for example, the fulfillment of Isaiah 40 or the return of Elijah. Conversely, there is no reason to doubt that John did eat "locusts and wild honey" from time to time, according to Mark 1:6c. These were probably not John's only foods, however, since they would not supply John with adequate Vitamin C and would yield rather low levels of carbohydrates. This study of locust gathering as a part of John's wilderness experience, built upon the observations of anthropologists Mark Q. Sutton, David B. Madsen and other scholars concerning recent and present-day locust-eating peoples, could be illuminating for understanding any number of locust eaters in antiquity, including at least some Jews at Qumran (CD 12:11b–15a).

Mark: John's eating foods from the desert (1:6c) associates the Baptist with the prediction of a wilderness herald in Isa 40:3 and, by implication, the occasional place of Elijah in the desert. The literary creativity of Mark (or his source) is responsible for taking this otherwise unremarkable aspect of the

---

[110] Luke 24:51; Acts 1:2, 11, 22; Gerhard Lohfink, *Die Himmelfahrt Jesu: Untersuchungen zu den Himmelfahrts- und Erhöhungstexten bei Lukas* (SANT 26; Munich: Kösel, 1971), esp. 163–210; Kelhoffer, *Miracle and Mission*, 111–14, 228–30.

[111] With C. F. Evans, "Central Section," 51–2; idem, *Luke*, 237–8; Dabeck, "Moses und Elias," 189: "Der Christus des Lk-Ev ist ein neuer Elias, er ist der Offenbarer des Hl. Geistes." Cf. Wink, *John the Baptist*, 42.

[112] If the author of the Fourth Gospel also knew Mark, the Johannine omission of Mark 1:6 could be accounted for by analogy to this study's explanation for the Lukan omission. Cf. John 1:21; *Gos. Nic.* 15:6.

historical Baptist's life and endowing it with theological significance. In Mark 1:2–8, the characterization of John's diet complements the explicit comparison made between John's wearing a leather belt as Elijah did (Mark 1:6b; 2 Kgs 1:8, LXX). Because John came as the new Elijah and in fulfillment of Hebrew scripture, Jesus can be baptized by John (Mark 1:9–11). Mark accentuates Jesus' superiority to John through an angel's providing for Jesus' needs in the wilderness (Mark 1:13), which contrasts with John's having foraged for sustenance there (Mark 1:6c).

Matthew: Matthew assumes John's place in the wilderness and therefore does not need Mark's creative effort to establish this point. Rather, Matthew exaggerates Mark's characterization, in order to bring John's credentials into line with other Judeans who had survived *entirely* on wilderness provisions (*Mart. Ascen. Isa.* 2.11; 2 Macc 5:27; cf. Jos., *Vita* 2 §11). For Matthew, the most important point is not what in particular John ate or even where he ate it but that the Baptist subsisted solely on natural, uncultivated foods.

Luke: Luke recognized correctly that materials in Mark and Q alternately associate *John and Jesus* with Elijah. Aiming to alleviate the possible confusion resulting from the Elijah-John and Elijah-Jesus comparisons in earlier 'gospel' materials, throughout his work Luke highlights only those pertaining to Jesus and accordingly modifies certain traditional materials while omitting others. Therefore, the most likely explanation for Luke's omission of Mark 1:6 is that the Third NT evangelist recognized and objected to the allusions to Elijah in Mark 1:6.

Given that such a diversity of expression is already present within the Synoptic tradition, it is perhaps not surprising that later Christian interpretations of John's diet would reflect novel variations on these, and other, themes. That Matthew's depiction receives much attention in the patristic literature is not surprising given the popularity of this gospel in the early church and the possibility that Matt 3:4c could be interpreted ascetically by those unaware of analogous non-ascetic attributions in Mark 1:6c, *Mart. Ascen. Isa.* 2:11 and 2 Macc 5:27. Although Luke's omission of Mark 1:6c cannot be said to stem from the type of aversion to grasshopper eating discussed in chapter 2, such a culinary predilection could underlie certain later Christian interpretations of Mark 1:6c∥Matt 3:4c. Such are the avenues to be explored in chapter 5.

Chapter 5

John's Diet as 'Vegetarian' and a Model of Asceticism: 'Locusts', Wild Honey and the *imitatio Iohannis* in Patristic and Subsequent Christian Interpretation

"Once the biblical literature became established as an
alternative body of classics, it would soon be seen as the
basis of a new *paideia*."[1]

"Just why locusts should not be considered suitable food for
a person like John is not clear, but perhaps this prejudice is
a genuine survival of the Ebionite outlook."[2]

The final chapter of this investigation examines the history of interpretation of
Mark 1:6c‖Matt 3:4c. This study aims to be comprehensive for the patristic
literature on John's "locusts and wild honey" and will survey numerous sub-
sequent interpretations in the medieval and Byzantine periods, and beyond.[3]
To date no such study exists. Important articles by Sebastian Brock and F. I.
Andersen discuss some of the materials pertinent to this study.[4] Additionally,
Henri Grégoire and Friedrich Cramer examine certain medieval and Byzan-
tine witnesses to John's 'vegetarian' diet.[5]

---

[1] Frances M. Young, *Biblical Exegesis and the Formation of Christian Culture* (Cambridge: Cambridge University, 1997), 76.

[2] F. I. Andersen, "Diet of John the Baptist," 64.

[3] At certain points interpretations of John's clothing (Mark 1:6ab‖Matt 3:4ab) will be
brought into this chapter's discussion, but only insofar as they shed light on the understanding
of the Baptist's food. A comprehensive analysis of the history of interpretation of Mark
1:6ab‖Matt 3:4ab would indeed be interesting but lies outside the scope of the present study.

[4] Brock, "The Baptist's Diet in Syriac Sources," *OrChr* 54 (1970): 113–24 (= idem, *From
Ephrem to Romanos: Interactions between Syriac and Greek in Late Antiquity* [Variorum
Collected Studies 664; Aldershot: Ashgate, 1999], 113–24). On Andersen, "Diet of John the
Baptist," see the discussion in chapter 1. Cf. Manlio Simonetti, ed., *Matthew 1–13* (Ancient
Christian Commentary on Scripture: NT 1A; Downers Grove, IL: InterVarsity, 2001), 40–1;
Thomas C. Oden and Christopher A. Hall, eds., *Mark* (Ancient Christian Commentary on
Scripture: NT 2; Downers Grove, IL: InterVarsity, 1998), 7–8.

[5] Grégoire, "Les Sauterelles de Saint Jean-Baptiste: texte épigraphique d'une épître de
S. Isidore de Péluse," *Byzantion* 5 (1929–30): 109–28; Cramer, *Der heilige Johannes im
Spiegel der französischen Pflanzen- und Tierbezeichnungen: Ein Beitrag zur Kenntnis der
volkstümlichen Namengebung* (Giessener Beiträge zur romanischen Philologie Zusatzheft 8;
Giessen: Selbstverlag des Romanischen Seminars, 1932).

A. Models of Interpretation

1. Overview

As compared with the meanings assigned to John's diet in the Synoptic gospels, three novelties pervade many patristic and later Christian interpretations:

Figurative and Allegorical Interpretations: It may come as no surprise that John's "locusts and wild honey" receive attention in various figurative and allegorical interpretations of Mark 1:6c‖Matt 3:4c. What is striking is that the interpretations of Origen of Alexandria and others are so diverse, giving rise to a number of different meanings.

John as a Model of Asceticism: So many of the faithful through the centuries have assumed that every part of scripture, however construed, is "useful (ὠφέλιμος) for teaching, reproof, correction, and training in righteousness" (2 Tim 3:16). Accordingly, the attempt to glean something "useful" from the Baptist's wilderness provisions would follow naturally, at least for a number of early Christian interpreters of John's diet. But what should one infer or put into practice from Mark 1:6c‖Matt 3:4c?

Ethicists today refer to the hero model of ethical appropriation when an individual seeks to live in imitation of an esteemed person, or exhorts others to do the same. Although such ethical admonitions are not to be found in the 'NT' gospels, the author of 1 Peter, for example, utilizes this model when asking that the faithful follow "in Christ's steps."[6] Thomas à Kempis's (1379/80–1471 C.E.) classic and immensely popular work, *On the Imitation of Christ* (*De imitatione Christi*), offers a more recent application of this hermeneutic.

In the patristic literature, this sentiment toward John is exemplified by Chrysostom's exhortation that we should "emulate" John's humble food and clothing (Τοῦτον . . . ζηλώσωμεν, *In Matthaeum* 10.5). Such an appropriation of the deed that Mark 1:6c ascribes to John, or of the description of John's food in Matt 3:4c, is attested in numerous patristic authors, beginning with Clement of Alexandria (*Paed.* 2.16.1; 2.112.1).

John's 'locusts': The other development in many Greek, Latin and Syriac patristic interpretations concerns the notion that John did not eat actual locusts/grasshoppers. Examples of a 'vegetarian' Baptist appear in the second-century *Gospel of the Ebionites* and several later witnesses to Tatian's gospel harmony, the *Diatessaron*; these witnesses to the *Diatessaron* may ultimately

---

[6] "For to this you have been called, because Christ also suffered for you, leaving you an example, so that you should follow in his steps" (1 Pet 2:21). Cf. 1 Cor 4:16, 7:7–8, 10:33, 11:1; Gal 4:12; 1 Thess 1:6–7, 2:14; Heb 6:12, 12:1–2, 13:12–13; Elizabeth A. Castelli, *Imitating Paul: A Discourse of Power* (Louisville: Westminster John Knox, 1991), esp. 89–117.

stem from Tatian himself in the late-second century. For this reason, in this
chapter 'locusts' is at times placed within single quotes.[7]

2. Complementary Tendencies

When these last two developments in the early Christian interpretation—John as a model and as 'vegetarian'—are considered together, the latter
development can be seen to complement the former: If John ate something
offensive to 'us,' why should 'we' seek to imitate him? For some early
Christians, adopting John as a model necessitated some modification of his
diet. Accordingly, certain interpreters dispense with this potential difficulty
by removing the characterization (allegation?) of John's entomophagy (insect
eating). Still others could accept that John himself ate insects, but did not
deem adhering to this particular diet as the only way to take up John's example. John thereby becomes an example of the *type* of simplicity that others
should imitate. In fact, none of these three interpretations—allegory (broadly
construed), John as an ethical model, and John as 'vegetarian'—precludes either of the other two.

Like this monograph's other inquiries, the following analysis is largely
diachronic. Sections devoted to the three main interpretations of John's
diet—allegory, model, and 'vegetarian'—will allow for a comparative analysis of developments in each. Each of these interpretations could be examined
with profit with detailed attention to an author's overarching theological concerns, the rhetorical context in which each interpretation occurs, and various
history of religions parallels to the assorted interpretations.[8] Such could indeed make for a richer—and a much longer—study. This chapter has a more
specific purpose, namely to analyze comparatively the conclusions that patristic and later authors draw from Mark 1:6c‖Matt 3:4c. Toward the end of
the chapter it will be argued that the two most prevalent interpretations of the
Baptist's diet—John as an ethical model and as 'vegetarian'—find precedents
in Greco-Roman philosophical literature and in the depictions of esteemed
philosophers. John's "locusts and wild honey" became a source of *paideia*
for Christians because St. Mark and St. Matthew were assumed to offer the
same type of ethical teaching as authors, such as Aratus Solensis, Plutarch,
Dio Chrysostom and Philostratus, commended. The chapter's summation will
relate more systematically the assorted interpretations of John's diet through

---

[7] The same holds for many occurrences of the terms 'vegetarian' and 'vegetarianism' in
this chapter. In the previous two chapters, 'honey' was placed in single quotes because of the
exegetical ambiguity of what kind of 'honey' Mark and Matthew designate. In this chapter,
however, these single quotes are usually removed, since no such interpretive ambiguity receives acknowledgement in pre-modern interpretations of the Baptist's μέλι ἄγριον.

[8] For example, John's growing wings on his soul like the grasshoppers have, according to
Cyril of Jerusalem, *Catecheses ad illuminandos* 3.6.

the centuries. Afterward, an epilogue considering the implications of this study as a whole will conclude this inquiry.

B. Early Interpretations of the Baptist's Diet

The interpretations of John's diet in the earliest patristic literature are arguably most remarkable for their scarcity. In addition to the relative lack of any interest in the Baptist in the 'Apostolic Fathers,'[9] the silence concerning John's diet in Irenaeus and Tertullian among the second- and third-century Christian authors who commonly interpret 'gospel' materials is noteworthy.[10] The same can be said concerning the surviving fragments of the 'Gnostic' Heracleon, to whom Origen responded in a *Commentary on John.*[11] Whatever their origin, moreover, the Mandaeans, who claim the Baptist as the founder of their religion, seem also not to have derived significance from the Baptist's diet.[12] After Clement of Alexandria, however, it is unusual to find a patristic author who does not attach some meaning to the Baptist's food. The exceptions to the silence concerning John's diet prior to Clement of Alexandria are Justin Martyr, the *Gospel of the Ebionites*, and, possibly, Tatian's *Diatessaron*.

1. Justin Martyr: A Matthean Characterization of John's Diet

In describing Justin Martyr's characterization of John's diet as Matthean, this study neither affirms nor dismisses the possibility of Justin's direct use of the text of Matthew.[13] Rather, it only affirms that Justin's exclusive claim,

---

[9] The one exception does not concern the present study. Ign., *Smyr.* 1:1: Jesus was "baptized by John in order that all righteousness might be fulfilled by him."

[10] On the subject in general, see Edmondo Lupieri, "John the Baptist: The First Monk. A Contribution to the History of the Figure of John the Baptist in the Early Monastic World," in: *Monasticism: A Historical Overview* (Word and Spirit 6; Still River, MA: St. Bede's, 1984), 11–23; here, 11–14; cf. Tert., *Adv. Marcionem* 1.17; *De anima* 15.2, which are discussed in chapter 2. For recent studies of "gospel" materials in the second century, see, e.g., William L. Petersen, "The Genesis of the Gospels," in: *New Testament Textual Criticism and Exegesis* (FS Joël Delobel; BETL 161; ed. Adelbert Denaux; Leuven: Peeters, 2002), 33–65; Kelhoffer, "'How Soon a Book' Revisited: ΕΥΑΓΓΕΛΙΟΝ as a Reference to 'Gospel' Materials in the First Half of the Second Century," *ZNW* 95 (2004): 1–34.

[11] For an analysis of the primary texts, see: Ansgar Wucherpfennig, *Heracleon Philologus: Gnostische Johannesexegese im zweiten Jahrhundert* (WUNT 142; Tübingen: Mohr Siebeck, 2002).

[12] For a recent study with translations of primary texts, see: Lupieri, *The Mandaeans: The Last Gnostics* (Grand Rapids: Eerdmans, 2002 [1993]), esp. §§151–153, pp. 224–5.

[13] See Helmut Koester, *Ancient Christian Gospels: Their History and Development* (London: SCM/Philadelphia: TPI, 1990), 374–5 for a discussion of Justin's 'gospel' source(s). Koester argues, "Usually . . . Justin does not seem to quote sayings directly from a harmo-

that the Baptist ate *only* locusts and wild honey, corresponds to Matt 3:4c, not Mark 1:6c:

> In the days of John the Baptist people needed proof, that they might discern who the Christ was. For, when John, wearing only a cincture of skins and a cloak of camel's hair, and eating nothing except locusts and wild honey (μηδὲν ἐσθίοντος πλὴν ἀκρίδας καὶ μέλι ἄγριον), sat by the River Jordan and preached the baptism of repentance, people supposed that he was the Christ; but he cried to them: "I am not the Christ, but the voice of one crying; for there will come He that is stronger than I, whose shoes I am not worthy to carry."[14]

Not quite a century later than Justin, Origen would reflect a similar assertion of exclusivity concerning what John ate: πλὴν ἀκρίδων καὶ μέλιτος ἀγρίου μηδενὸς μεταλαμβάνων.[15]

Inasmuch as John's wilderness provisions are only a passing detail in *Dialogue* 88, Justin could perhaps be seen as an early example of the 'no significance' interpretation of John's diet.[16] Here Justin wishes to dismiss the notion, alluded to also in John 1:20, 3:25–30, and Ps.-Cl. *Rec.* 1.60, that the Baptist was the Messiah.[17]

With regard to the 'gospel' material utilized in *Dial.* 88.6–7, Helmut Koester suggests that "[f]or a description of John's dress and nourishment, *either Matthew or Mark* could have been Justin's source; in the use of the verb ἐσθίειν Justin agrees with Mark."[18] Actually, it is more likely that elements of *both Matthew and Mark* (not "either . . . or") underlie whatever 'gospel' material Justin utilized for John's diet. Although the verb ἐσθίειν occurs in Mark 1:6c (but not in Matt 3:4c), only Matthew articulates the exclusive claim that John's diet consisted solely of locusts and wild honey. Notably, the second-century *Gospel of the Ebionites*, discussed immediately below, also reflects elements of both Mark and Matthew, but offers a mark-

---

nized gospel text. . . . [H]e is apparently relying upon collections of sayings which were composed on the basis of harmonized gospel texts. . ." (374).

[14] *Dial.* 88.6–7. Greek text: Georges Archambault, ed., *Justin, Dialogue avec Tryphon* (Textes et documents pour l'étude historique du Christianisme 8, 11; Paris: A. Picard, 1909), 2.76; ET (modified): Thomas B. Falls, *Saint Justin Martyr* (FC 6; New York: Christian Heritage, 1948), 289.

[15] Or., *Philocalia* 26.4 [on Psalm 4]. Greek text: Éric Junod, ed., *[Origen,] Philocalie 21–27* (SC 226; Paris: Cerf, 1976), 248. So also Ambrose, *De helia et ieiunio* 11.40 (547D): *Iohannes in deserto erat, ubi solas locustas aut mel siluestre inueniret.* Lat.: C. Schenkl, ed., *Sancti Ambrosii, Opera* (CSEL 32.2; Vienna: Tempsky, 1897), 435.

[16] Discussed in chapter 1, 24–26.

[17] Ps.-Cl. Rec. 1.60 (*apud* Rufinus of Aquileia; *c.* 345–411 C.E.): "And, behold, one of the disciples of John asserted that John was the Christ, and not Jesus, inasmuch as Jesus Himself declared that John was greater than all men and all prophets. 'If, then,' said he, 'he be greater than all, he must be held to be greater than Moses, and than Jesus himself. But if he be the greatest of all, then must he be the Christ'" (ET: ANF, 8.93).

[18] Koester, *Ancient Christian Gospels*, 390, emphasis added.

edly different depiction of John's diet from those in Mark, Matthew and Justin.

2. The 'Vegetarian' Depiction of John's Diet in the Gospel of the Ebionites

Like the gospel of Matthew, Justin Martyr and Origen, the so-called *Gospel of the Ebionites* makes an exclusive claim about what John ate. Different from these other two writings, this second-century gospel, according to Epiphanius, states that John ate only wild honey:

> It happened that John baptized and the Pharisees went out to him and were baptized and all Jerusalem. And John was dressed in a mantle of camel's hair and a leather belt was around his waist. And his food was, it said, wild honey, of which the taste was that of manna, like cakes in olive oil (καὶ τὸ βρῶμα αὐτοῦ μέλι ἄγριον οὗ ἡ γεῦσις ἦν τοῦ μάννα, ὡς ἐγκρὶς ἐν ἐλαίῳ). They say this to turn the word of truth into a lie and they say honey-cakes (ἐγκρίδι ἐν μέλιτι) instead of locusts (ἀντὶ ἀκρίδων).[19]

Klijn observes correctly that the passage reflects a harmonization of distinctive Markan and Matthean materials.[20] Already in 1793, moreover, Samuel Bochart noted the likely influence of the LXX on the distinctive characterization of John's diet in *Gos. Eb.*[21] In particular, the author of this gospel seems to have taken note of the Septuagint's descriptions of the Israelites' manna in the wilderness:

> καὶ ἐπωνόμασαν οἱ υἱοὶ Ισραηλ τὸ ὄνομα αὐτοῦ Μαν ἦν δὲ ὡς σπέρμα κορίου λευκόν τὸ δὲ γεῦμα αὐτοῦ ὡς ἐγκρὶς ἐν μέλιτι
> And the children of Israel called it manna. It was like coriander seed, white, and its taste was like a cake in honey. (Exod 16:31c [LXX])

> ἡ ἡδονὴ αὐτοῦ ὡσεὶ γεῦμα ἐγκρὶς ἐξ ἐλαίου
> Its flavor was like the taste of a cake [made] from olive oil. (Num 11:8c [LXX])

For Epiphanius, the exchanging of honey-cakes (ἐγκριδ–) for locusts (ἀκριδ–) exemplifies the Ebionites' distortion of the gospel tradition. He

---

[19] *Apud* Epiph., *Panarion* 30.13.4–5. Greek text and ET: Albertus Frederik Johannes Klijn, *Jewish-Christian Gospel Tradition* (VCSup 17; Leiden: Brill, 1992), 67. The Greek text can also be found in Karl Holl, ed., *Epiphanius* (GCS 25; Leipzig: Hinrichs, 1915), 1.350. Another English translation appears in: Philip R. Amidon, *The Panarion of St. Epiphanius, Bishop of Salamis: Selected Passages* (New York: Oxford University Press, 1990), 102.

[20] Klijn, 68: "This passage is . . . a composite of words and phrases that have been taken from the canonical Gospels." The main examples in this passage of *Gos. Eb.* as compared with Mark and Matthew are as follows: ἐγένετο Ἰωάννης βαπτίζων = Mark 1:4a; καὶ ἐξῆλθον πρὸς αὐτὸν Φαρισαῖοι ≈ Matt 3:7a; καὶ πᾶσα Ἱεροσόλυμα ≈ Mark 1:5a∥Matt 3:5a; εἶχεν . . . ἔνδυμα ἀπὸ τριχῶν καμήλου = Matt 3:5a; καὶ ζώνην δερματίνην περὶ τὴν ὀσφὺν αὐτοῦ = Matt 3:5b; καὶ τὸ βρῶμα αὐτοῦ μέλι ἄγριον ≈ Matt 3:5c (Matthew has τροφή, and *Gos. Eb.* βρῶμα).

[21] Bochart, "Iohannem, Baptistam, veras locustas habuisse pro cibo," in: idem, *Hierozoicon*, 3.326, referring to Exod 16:31.

does not dispute whether John ate actual locusts/grasshoppers; rather, his sole dispute lies in the changing of the gospel text.[22] Epiphanius offers no praise for the 'biblical' substitution of the Israelites' manna in *Gos. Eb.* for grass-hoppers/locusts.

Concerning the Ebionite Christians for whom this gospel material came to be named, there may indeed be a connection between their vegetarian diet and the food—*without* locusts—ascribed to John in *Gos. Eb.*[23] An additional indication of the distinctiveness, and perhaps the intentional simplicity, of the Ebionites' diet is their use of unleavened bread and water (not wine) in the Eucharist (Epiph., *Panarion* 30.16.1).

Epiphanius (*Panarion* 30.13.2) cites others who "call" this writing the "Hebrew" gospel (Ἑβραϊκὸν δὲ τοῦτο καλοῦσιν). Irenaeus (*Haer.* 3.11.7), moreover, claims that the Ebionites "use Matthew's Gospel only." Within the *Gospel of the Ebionites*, the meaning of honey tasting like manna or a cake is not clear. Such an opaque characterization of John's wilderness sustenance apparently stems from the substitution of ὡς ἐγκρίς ("like a cake") for ἀκρίδες ("locusts"). The emendation removes the problem of meat eating but does not specify what exactly John ate.

One implication of this emendation is that the authors of Mark and *Gos. Eb.* allude to different parts of the OT in connection with John's diet. Whereas Mark connects John to the voice in the wilderness in Isaiah 40, *Gos. Eb.* employs a different "exodus" tradition, namely the food of the wandering Israelites after their departure from Egypt.[24] Given the obvious parallel between manna found in the wilderness and the placement of John there in the Synoptic gospels, it is somewhat surprising that this (albeit partially pre-

---

[22] Cf. Epiph., *Panarion* 30.19.2–3; *Ancoratus* 115.3.

[23] With Scobie, *John the Baptist*, 135, who notes that the early Christian Ebionites were 'vegetarian,' and that probably for this reason they substituted "for *akris* (locust) the word *egkris*, denoting a cake made with oil and honey." So also J. Ernst, *Johannes der Täufer*, 286–7; R. L. Webb, *John the Baptizer,* 82; J. K. Elliott, *The Apocryphal New Testament: A Collection of Apocryphal Christian Literature in an English Translation* (Oxford: Clarendon/New York: Oxford University Press, 1993), 6; Hans-Josef Klauck, *Apocryphal Gospels: An Introduction* (Edinburgh: T & T Clark, 2003 [2002]), 51–2. Cf. Epiphanius's witness to other 'vegetarian' tendencies in this 'gospel': *Panarion* 30.15.3–4; 30.16.4–5; 30.22.4 ("Surely I have no desire to eat the flesh of this Paschal Lamb with you."). Of related interest is Ps.-Cl. *Hom.* 9.10, which explains demon possession by the spirit's desire to experience meat and sexual pleasure.

[24] Note J. Enoch Powell's errant interpretation of Matt 3:4c, which could nonetheless be applied aptly to *Gos. Eb.*: "Wild honey was kosher but 'locusts' (ἀκρίδες) scarcely would be [*sic*]. In Exod. 16.31 manna was described as tasting like ἐγκρίδες ἐν μέλιτι, 'wheatcakes in honey'. So there may have been intended an allusion to the Israelites being fed on manna in the wilderness" (*The Evolution of the Gospel: A New Translation of the First Gospel with Commentary and Introductory Essay* [New Haven: Yale University, 1994], 62–3). Cf. W. Marxsen, "John the Baptist," 35–6.

served) passage from the *Gospel of the Ebionites* does not call attention to John's location in the wilderness (ἐν τῇ ἐρήμῳ, Mark 1:3a, 4a par.) as the Synoptic gospels do.

C. Tatian's *Diatessaron*: An Additional Second-Century 'Vegetarian' Depiction of the Baptist's Diet?

In addition to that in the *Gospel of the Ebionites*, another 'biblical' substitution for the Baptist's locusts/grasshoppers appears in several witnesses to Tatian's gospel harmony, derived primarily from the four 'NT' gospels and known in Greek as the *Diatessaron*. A word of caution is in order, however, since the witnesses to a diet of *milk* and honey—namely Īšoʿdāḏ of Merv, Bar-Ṣalibi, Bar-Hebraeus, and Ibn aṭ-Ṭayyib—are centuries later than Tatian's gospel harmony (*c.* 172 C.E.). The first three to be discussed here are in the *Diatessaron*'s original language, namely Syriac.[25] That of Ibn aṭ-Ṭayyib is in Arabic.

As is well known, the *Commentary on the Diatessaron* attributed to Ephrem (*c.* 307–373 C.E.) offers an early and valuable witness to the *Diatessaron* but does not quote Tatian's work *en toto*. Ephrem's *Commentary* twice mentions John's garment of camel's hair but never the Baptist's diet.[26] Beginning with Īšoʿdāḏ of Merv, each of the witnesses to John's diet of milk and honey in the *Diatessaron* will receive attention individually before this study assesses their potential value for reconstructing the *Diatessaron*.

1. Īšoʿdāḏ of Merv's Witness to the Diatessaron ("Honey and Milk")

In his *Commentary on the Gospels*, Īšoʿdāḏ of Merv (bishop of Ḥadatha [Mesopotamia, on the Euphrates]; d. after 852 C.E.), mentions various explanations of Matt 3:4 before siding with that of "the Interpreter," namely Theodore of Mopsuestia (d. 428/9 C.E.):[27]

---

[25] On the date and original language of the *Diatessaron*, see W. L. Petersen, "Tatian's Diatessaron," in: Koester, *Ancient Christian Gospels*, 403–30; here, 428–9.

[26] Ephrem, *Commentary on the Diatessaron* 3.17 ("John was dressed in a tunic of camel-hair"); 9.4 ("he was clothed in a rough garment of camel-hair," as an illustration of Matt 11:7). ET: Carmel McCarthy, *Saint Ephrem's Commentary on Tatian's Diatessaron: An English Translation of Chester Beatty Syriac MS 709* (JSSSup 2; Oxford: Oxford University, 1993), 81, 156.

[27] Brock, "Syriac Sources," 122, notes that Īšoʿdāḏ refers to Theodore of Mopsuestia as "the Interpreter."

'And his food was locusts and wild honey.'

(ܘܡܐܟܘܠܬܗ ܗܘܬ ܩܡܨܐ ܘܕܒܫܐ ܕܒܪܐ)

But the *Diatessaron* says his food was honey and milk of the mountains.

(ܡܐܟܘܠܬܗ ܠܡ ܗܘܬ ܕܒܫܐ ܘܚܠܒܐ ܕܛܘܪܐ).

Others say that the locusts are tender roots like parsnips, that is to say, cuttings, and not very sweet. . . . Others say that they are roots called *Qauchē*, that in shape resemble locusts, but in taste are sweet like honey;[28] others, that they are the sprouts of plants; and even this honey, they say, is not this which is sweet, but that which is bitter and hateful, which the bees of the wilderness make. According to the *Interpreter*, the locusts were flying [insects], and the honey natural. . . . By the flight of locusts [John signified] the spirituality and flight of the saints who fly in the clouds to meet the Lord; and by the sweetness of honey the sweetness and beatitudes higher than all trials that the saints receive from our Lord. Again, honey is that which polishes the world from the rust of sin, for honey is a polisher by its nature.[29]

There are three peculiar aspects of this alleged Diatessaronic reading: the origin of John's food "of the mountains (ܕܛܘܪܐ);" the appearance of "honey" first in the list; and John's consuming "milk (ܚܠܒܐ)" rather than locusts/grasshoppers. The *Diatessaron*'s alleged substitution of "milk" for "locusts" will be examined below. Concerning the first distinctive element, J. Rendel Harris explains plausibly "that 'of the mountains' is a translation of ἄγριος."[30] The occurrence of ܕܛܘܪܐ ("of the mountains")—instead of, for example, ܕܒܪܐ ("of the wild[erness]")—after ܚܠܒܐ ("milk") is not surprising, because "wild milk" could give the impression that the Baptist ate spoiled milk. Milk derived "from the mountains" in Īšoʿdāḏ's version of the *Diatessaron* would be intelligible, connoting mountain-dwelling creatures (goats?) that produce milk.[31] Concerning the initial appearance of the honey, Brock notes that "the Persian Diatessaron and the Georgian Opiza Gospels (at Mk i 6) retain the reversed order, with the honey first."[32]

2. Bar-Ṣalibi's Witness to the Diatessaron ("Milk and Honey")

Dionysius Bar-Ṣalibi (Bishop of Amida [Mesopotamia], 1166–71 C.E.) offers an indirect, and possibly additional, witness to the purported "milk" reading in the *Diatessaron*:

---

[28] The similarity to *Gos. Eb.* at this point is noteworthy.

[29] Margaret Dunlop Gibson, *The Commentaries of Isho'dad of Merv, Bishop of Ḥadatha (c. 850 A.D.) in Syriac and English* (HSem V–VI; Cambridge: Cambridge University, 1911–16), 1.23–24 (ET [modified]); 2.39–40 (Syriac).

[30] Harris, *Fragments of the Commentary of Ephrem Syrus upon the Diatessaron* (London: C. J. Clay and Sons, 1895), 17; cf. Marie-Joseph Pierre, "Lait et miel, ou la douceur du verbe," *Apocrypha* 10 (1999): 139–76; here, 155. Accordingly, Brock's characterization of this tradition of the Baptist's diet as "mythical" is unnecessary ("Syriac Sources," 115–16).

[31] Cf. *Mart. Ascen. Isa.* 2.11, discussed in chapter 4.

[32] Brock, "Syriac Sources," 115. Brock further notes "that none of the daughter versions" of the *Diatessaron*, "Eastern or Western, retain the slightest hint of the milk" (115).

Others say: that in the *Diatessaron*, i.e., the Gospel of Four,
it is written that his food was milk and honey of the wild
(ܕܝܠܗ ܗܘܬ ܕܒܪܐ ܕܒܫܐ ܘܚܠܒܐ ܘܬܘܠܥܬܐ ܡܐܟܘܠܬܗ);
since milk was proper to his youth and honey to the manly age.[33]

Bar-Ṣalibi's explanation for John's partaking of milk in the wilderness is
probably informed ultimately by the gospel of Luke, which places the young
John in the wilderness from the days of his youth.[34]

Harris infers that Bar-Ṣalibi's text "of the wilderness (ܕܒܪܐ)"[35] constitutes a "correction" of the Diatessaronic text reflected by Īšoʿdād of Merv.[36]
It is also noteworthy that ܕܒܪܐ is in Īšoʿdād's translation of Matt 3:4c (cited
above). Since ܕܒܪܐ ("of the wilderness") also appears in the Curetonian
Syriac (sy[c]) at Matt 3:4c,[37] the text of the *Diatessaron* referenced by Bar-
Ṣalibi seems to reflect "Vulgatization," or assimilation to another esteemed
textual tradition for this gospel passage. Additionally, the reversing of the
order of the foods—from "honey and milk" *apud* Īšoʿdād, to "milk and
honey" *apud* Bar-Ṣalibi—restores the canonical placement of "honey" second
in the order of John's foods and is probably likewise due to "Vulgatization."
Despite these two corrections of the Diatessaron as cited by Bar-Ṣalibi, the
most distinctive element—namely, John's "milk" (ܚܠܒܐ)—remains.

3. Bar-Hebraeus's and Ibn aṭ-Ṭayyib's Witnesses to the Diatessaron
   ("Milk and Honey")

Another witness to John's diet of milk and honey is Gregory Bar-Hebraeus
(1225/26–1286 C.E.): "His food was locusts and honey of the wild. . . . Some
say that 'locusts' means roots and sweet plants, but in the *Diatessaron* 'milk
and honey' is written."[38] Like Bar-Ṣalibi, Bar-Hebraeus also lists "milk"

---

[33] Cod. Mus. Brit. Add. 12,143, fol. 52, cited in: Harris, *Fragments*, 17.

[34] Luke 1:80: "The child grew (τὸ δὲ παιδίον ηὔξανεν) and became strong in spirit,
and he was in the wilderness until the day he appeared publicly to Israel." Additionally, see
below on the anonymous Karshuni *Life of John*.

[35] Cf. מדבר in Hebrew.

[36] Harris, *Fragments*, 17 n.3, working on the assumption that Īšoʿdād of Merv reflects the
original reading of the *Diatessaron*: "Note the correction of the primitive reading."

[37] F. C. Burkitt, *Evangelion da-Mepharreshe: The Curetonian Version of the Four Gospels* (Cambridge: Cambridge University, 1904), 2.10.

[38] Cited in: Harris, *Fragments*, 18. See further on Bar Hebraeus's life and writings: Assad
Sauma, *Gregory Bar-Hebraeus's Commentary on the Book of Kings from his Storehouse of
Mysteries: A Critical Edition with an English Translation, Introduction and Notes* (Studia
Semitica Upsaliensia 20; Uppsala: Uppsala University, 2003), 49–51; George Lane, "An
Account of Gregory Bar Hebraeus Abu al-Faraj and His Relations with the Mongols of
Persia," *Hugoye: Journal of Syriac Studies* 2/2 (1999): §§24–31; online:
http://syrcom.cua.edu/Hugoye/Vol2No2/HV2N2GLane.html (on 30 April 2004); Peter
Joosse, "Barhebraeus' ܚܟܡܬܐ ܕܚܘܒܐ ܒܘܬܪܐ (*Butyrum Sapientiae*): A Description of
the Extant Manuscripts," *Le Muséon* 112 (1999): 417–58.

prior to "honey." It is possible, therefore, that Bar-Ṣalibi and Bar-Hebraeus are informed by the same Diatessaronic tradition.

Finally, it is worthy of mention that ʾAbūʾl Faraj ʿAbdūʾllāh ibn aṭ-Ṭayyib al-ʿIrāqī (d. *c.* 1043 C.E.) also reflects this "milk" reading. Unlike Īšoʿdāḏ, Bar-Ṣalibi, and Bar-Hebraeus, however, Ibn aṭ-Ṭayyib makes no mention of the *Diatessaron* as his source.[39] Nonetheless, it is safe to infer that Ibn aṭ-Ṭayyib offers an additional witness to this distinctive Diatessaronic reading.

Differing with L. Cheikho and others, Tjitze Baarda argues that Ibn aṭ-Ṭayyib translated the *Diatessaron* into Arabic.[40] Cheikho maintains that the Arabic translation predates, and thus could not have been translated by, Ibn aṭ-Ṭayyib. The important point for the present discussion is that Ibn aṭ-Ṭayyib's silence with regard to the *Diatessaron* does not dismiss his potential witness to Tatian's gospel harmony. Either Ibn aṭ-Ṭayyib translated the *Diatessaron* (so Baarda) or, if it had already been translated (so Cheikho), Ibn aṭ-Ṭayyib, as "a secretary of the Patriarch Elias I of Bagdad (*sic*),"[41] most probably would have had access to the *Diatessaron* in an Arabic translation.

4. Analysis: The Diatessaron and the Baptist's "Milk"

These four witnesses to a diet of milk and honey allow for the posing of two related questions:

1. Is the substitution of "milk" for "locusts" the *type* of emendation that one could plausibly credit to Tatian?
2. Is this diet of "milk and honey" original to Tatian's *Diatessaron*?

---

[39] On this point see Tjitze Baarda, "The Author of the Arabic Diatessaron" (1978), re-printed in: idem, *Early Transmission of Words of Jesus: Thomas, Tatian, and the Text of the New Testament. A Collection of Studies* (Amsterdam: VU Boekhandel/Uitgeverij, 1983), 207–49; here, 226–7, who refers to Matt 3:4 and follows Arthur Hjelt, *Die altsyrische Evangelienübersetzung und Tatians Diatessaron* (Leipzig: Deichert, 1901), 68, and D. S. Margoliouth, review of A.-S. Marmardji, *Diatessaron de Tatien* (Beirut: Imprimerie catholique, 1935), in *JTS* 38 (1937): 76–9; here, 76. Cf. Hope W. Hogg's comment in ANF, 9.49 n.4 (emphases original): "On the original *Diatessaron* reading, *honey and milk of the mountains*, or, *milk and honey of the mountains*, which later Ibn-aṭ-Ṭayyib cites in his Com-mentary (folio 44b, 45a) as a reading, but without any allusion to the *Diatessaron*, see, e.g., now Harris, *Fragments of the Com. of Ephr. Syr. upon the Diat.* (London, 1895), p. 17 f." In fact, Harris, *Fragments*, 17–18 does not refer to Ibn aṭ-Ṭayyib. See further: Julian Faultless, "The Two Recensions of the Prologue to John in Ibn al-Ṭayyib's *Commentary on the Gos-pels*," in: *Christians at the Heart of Islamic Rule: Church Life and Scholarship in ʿAbbasid Iraq* (ed. David Thomas; Leiden: Brill, 2003), 177–98.

[40] See Baarda, "Arabic Diatessaron," esp. 247–9; on Cheikho, 211–12.

[41] Baarda, "Arabic Diatessaron," 209; cf. Georg Graf, *Geschichte der christlichen arabischen Literatur* (Studi e testi 133; Vatican City: Biblioteca apostolica vaticana, 1944–53), 2.160–77; here, 160.

The first question, to be addressed in the following subsection, can clearly be answered in the affirmative in light of Tatian's own strong vegetarian convictions. The second question, to be taken up thereafter, does not allow for such a definitive resolution.

a) Analogous Characterizations of Meat Eating as Evil: Aratus and Tatian

In his *Oration to the Greeks* (λόγος πρὸς "Ελληνας), Tatian reveals his vegetarian inclination when likening killing animals for food to the senseless slaughter of gladiators: "You sacrifice animals in order to eat meat (θύετε ζῷα διὰ τὴν κρεωφαγίαν), and you buy men to produce slaughter for the human soul."[42] The present study will argue that substituting "milk" for "locusts" is the type of change that the vegetarian Tatian could have made.

William L. Petersen, however, is not persuaded that *Or.* 23.2 is unambiguous on this point; he notes correctly, though, that Tatian's main concern in *Oratio* 23 is criticizing the gladiatorial spectacles.[43] An additional criticism by Tatian against the gladiators' obesity satisfies Petersen's call for caution, however: "I saw other men who had trained to become heavyweights, and carried around a weight of superfluous flesh" (φορτίον τῶν ἐν αὐτοῖς κρεῶν περιφέροντας, *Or.* 23.1). The inference that Tatian himself was indeed both an ascetic (as is undisputed) *and* vegetarian explains why Tatian chose to highlight gladiators as obese (*Or.* 23.1) and the multitudes who delight in such spectacles as meat eaters (*Or.* 23.2). In Tatian's polemic against spectacles, these criticisms of obesity and meat eating are unnecessary. Only other vegetarians, who agreed with Tatian's premise that killing animals to eat them is evil, would appreciate the comparison of killing animals for food to the human slaughter of gladiatorial combat in *Or.* 23.2.

The argument that Tatian's vegetarianism underlies the particular criticisms of the gladiatorial games in *Oratio* 23 is strengthened with reference to an analogous condemnation of meat eating in the *Phaenomena*, a well-known work in antiquity by Aratus of Soloi (in Cilicia; *c.* 315–before 240 B.C.E.) devoted primarily to astronomy. Aratus reminisces about a "Golden Age" during which people relied on "oxen and ploughs and Justice herself" to meet their needs for food and did not engage in war.[44] It was during this utopian

---

[42] Tatian, *Or.* 23.2. Greek text and ET: Molly Whittaker, *Oratio ad Graecos and Fragments* (OECT; Oxford: Clarendon, 1982).

[43] W. L. Petersen, *Tatian's Diatessaron: Its Creation, Dissemination, Significance, and History in Scholarship* (VCSup 25; Leiden: Brill, 1994), 79 n.141: "Some have seen a disparagement of eating meat in *Or.* 23.2 ('you sacrifice animals to eat meat'), but this must be linked with the next clause: 'and you buy men to provide human slaughter for the soul.' While one cannot exclude the possibility of an attack on the eating of meat, the passage is best read in context as an attack on Greek animal sacrifices and the spectacles."

[44] Aratus, *Phaen.* 96–136; here, 105–114: "And they called her Justice: gathering together the elders, either in the market-place or on the broad highway, she urged them in prophetic

period once upon a time that the constellation of the Maiden lived on earth as Justice. Aratus exemplifies this past age by humanity's eating only the produce yielded by plowing oxen, that is, 'vegetarian' crops from the earth rather than meat.

In subsequent generations, Aratus continues, the involvement of Justice on earth decreases, and the goddess predicts a devolution in future periods of humanity:

> But when . . . there were born the Bronze Age men, more destructive than their predecessors,[45] who were the first to forge the criminal sword for murder on the highways, and the first to taste the flesh of plowing oxen (πρῶτοι δὲ βοῶν ἐπάσαντ᾽ ἀροτήρων), then Justice, conceiving a hatred (μισήσασα Δίκη) for the generation of these men, flew up to the sky and took up her abode in that place, where she is still visible to men by night as the Maiden (Παρθένος) near conspicuous Bootes. (*Phaen.* 129–136)

Two moral aberrations account for Justice's departure from the world 'below' to the sky 'above': the murder of humans and the eating of animal flesh. Notably, these are the same vices that Tatian criticizes in *Or.* 23.1–2 when objecting to the spectacles: the slaughter of men and the eating of meat.[46]

Four inferences follow from this analysis of Tatian's *Oratio* 23 and the analogous condemnation of murder and meat eating in Aratus's *Phaenomena*:

1. Tatian was indeed vegetarian and regarded the eating of meat to be tantamount to homicide.
2. Other witnesses to Tatian's Encratism and vegetarianism can be used to complement Tatian's statement in *Or.* 23.1–2.[47]

---

tones to judgments for the good of the people. At that time they still had no knowledge of painful strife or quarrelsome conflict or noise of battle, but lived just as they were; the dangerous sea was far from their thoughts, and as yet no ships brought them livelihood from afar, but oxen and ploughs and Justice herself (βόες καὶ ἄροτρα καὶ αὐτὴ . . . Δίκη), queen of the people and giver of civilized life, provided all their countless needs. That was as long as the earth still nurtured the Golden Age (ἔτι γαῖα γένος χρύσειον ἔφερβεν)." Greek text and ET: Douglas Kidd, ed., *[Aratus Solensis,] Phaenomena* (Cambridge Classical Texts and Commentaries 34; Cambridge: Cambridge University, 1997), 80–3. I am grateful to Robert Matthew Calhoun for calling this reference to my attention.

[45] I.e., the immediately preceding Silver Age described in *Phaen.* 115–128.

[46] The notion that humanity had devolved from an earlier Golden Age of vegetarian cuisine and relative peace is, of course, not peculiar to Aratus. Daniel B. Levine, "Acorns and Primitive Life in Greek and Latin Literature," *Classical and Modern Literature* 9 (1989): 87–95; esp. 87–90, discusses this idea in Lucretius, Hesiod, Virgil and other ancient writers. The potential influence of such conceptions of meat eating on debates about food in early Christianity merits further inquiry.

[47] E.g., Irenaeus, *Haer.* 1.28.1; Hippol., *Ref.* 8.9, 10.14; Euseb., *Hist. eccl.* 4.29.1–3; Jer., *Adv. Iovin.* 1.3. Furthermore, R. M. Grant, "The Heresy of Tatian," *JTS* n.s. 5 (1954): 62–8; here, 64, finds additional evidence for Tatian's Encratism in *Oratio* 8.2 (criticizing the goddess Aphrodite, who delights in marriage) and 34.1 (a woman with thirty children is an example of much incontinence). See further Grant, "Tatian and the Bible," *StPatr* 1 (1957):

3. If Tatian had known one or more 'gospel' texts mentioning the Baptist's ἀκρίδες and regarded locusts/grasshoppers as meat, he would have had reason to edit or delete this material in the *Diatessaron*.[48]

4. The characterizations of John's food as milk and honey by Išoʿdād of Merv, Bar-Ṣalibi, Bar-Hebraeus, and Ibn aṭ-Ṭayyib are consistent with Tatian's vegetarian convictions. Indeed, this is the very type of change that the second-century *Gospel of the Ebionites*, which is roughly contemporary to Tatian, reflects.

On these grounds we can therefore answer the first of two questions posed above in the affirmative, namely that the substitution of "milk" for "locusts" indeed constitutes the type of emendation that can plausibly be attributed to Tatian. This conclusion does not, however, address the question to be discussed immediately below, namely whether this reading was in fact original to Tatian's *Diatessaron*.

b) Did the Diatessaron *Originally Attribute to John a Diet of "Honey and Milk"?*

Some seven centuries passed between the writing of Tatian's *Diatessaron* (*c.* 172 C.E.) and the earliest surviving witness to this reading, namely Išoʿdād of Merv (*fl.* 860 C.E.). The other witnesses—Ibn aṭ-Ṭayyib (d. 1043 C.E.), Bar-Ṣalibi (d. 1171 C.E.) and Bar-Hebraeus (d. 1286 C.E.)—are even later. The potential witnesses to the original text of the *Diatessaron* for Mark 1:6c‖Matt 3:4c are open to either of the following explanations:

> *Hypothesis A*: The "milk" reading reflected by Išoʿdād and others is original to the *Diatessaron* and reflects Tatian's own vegetarian convictions. Other Diatessaronic readings should be discounted because they reflect assimilation to the Vulgate or other received editions or translations of the NT ("Vulgatization").[49]

> *Hypothesis B*: This reading is not original to the *Diatessaron*. Rather, Išoʿdād and others reflect a local application of Encratite asceticism that was widespread in the Syrian church. In denying the Baptist his grasshoppers, John's purported wilderness asceticism was made more palatable to Encratite Christians in Syria (and elsewhere).

297–306; esp. 300–1; Bruce M. Metzger, *The Early Versions of the New Testament: Their Origin, Transmission, and Limitations* (Oxford: Clarendon, 1977), 33–6; Arthur Vööbus, *Early Versions of the New Testament: Manuscript Studies* (Papers of the Estonian Theological Society in Exile 6; Stockholm: Estonian Theological Society in Exile, 1954), 15–22, 27–31; Andrew B. McGowan, *Ascetic Eucharists: Food and Drink in Early Christian Ritual Meals* (New York: Oxford University Press, 1999), 155–60.

[48] On Tatian's editing of 'gospel' materials for the *Diatessaron*, see Petersen, *Tatian's Diatessaron*, 79–82; idem, "Tatian's Diatessaron," 405, 430; Grant, "Tatian and the Bible," 313.

[49] On the later Vulgatization of the original text of the *Diatessaron* to conform to received canonical texts, see, e.g., Petersen, *Tatian's Diatessaron*, 127–9, 222, 371, 395–7.

In favor of the latter explanation is Harris's observation of "the hostility of the Eastern Christians to the locusts in the diet of St John the Baptist."[50]   The aversion to eating meat could well have inspired this emendation of the *Diatessaron*.

On the other hand, Petersen stresses correctly that even witnesses to the *Diatessaron* centuries later than those examined in the present inquiry merit serious consideration when they offer a distinctive reading:

> It has already been remarked that the Diatessaron's text can only be fixed with certainty where it deviates from the vast majority of gospel manuscripts; it follows that when evaluating its readings, one must always take Vulgatization into account. If only a few Diatessaronic witnesses give a deviating reading while the majority of Diatessaronic witnesses agree with the standard canonical text, then the *deviating* reading must be presumed the *original* reading (of the Diatessaron) until *disproven*.[51]

At this point the present author must recognize the limitations of his own expertise, and possibly those of the several witnesses to the *Diatessaron* as well. Both of the above hypotheses are plausible, and neither can be excluded on the basis of the surviving evidence. At least for now, therefore, it must remain an open question whether Tatian himself wrote something like ܪܝܐܠܕ ܪܒܠܘܐ ܪܝܕܢ ܠܕ ܡܐܠܩܐܪܢ (≈ ἡ δὲ τροφὴ αὐτοῦ ἦν μέλι καὶ γάλα ἄγριον), perhaps substituting ܪܒܠܘ/γάλα for ܪ ܣ̈ܒܕ/ἀκρίδες. At any rate, it is sufficiently clear that this reading of "milk" (ܪܒܠܘ/γάλα) is consistent with Tatian's strong Encratite aversion to eating meat. What remains uncertain is whether Tatian himself or some later Syrian Christian is to be credited with this 'biblical' emendation of Mark 1:6c||Matt 3:4c.

D. Figurative and Allegorical Interpretations of John's Diet

Starting with Origen of Alexandria, a number of figurative and allegorical interpretations of John's diet begin to flourish. Recent scholarship has called attention to the variety of reading and interpretive strategies that so-called allegorists brought to the scriptures.[52]   When analyzed together, the independence and diversity of these interpretations of John's food are noteworthy. The reason these interpretations are brought together in this section

---

[50] Harris, *Fragments*, 18; so also Brock, "Syriac Sources," 116–22; cf. Sidney H. Griffith, "Asceticism in the Church of Syria: The Hermeneutics of Early Christian Monasticism," in: *Asceticism* (ed. V. L. Wimbush and R. Valantasis; New York: Oxford University Press, 1995), 220–45.

[51] Petersen, *Tatian's Diatessaron*, 371, emphases original.

[52] Elizabeth A. Clark, *Reading Renunciation: Asceticism and Scripture in Early Christianity* (Princeton: Princeton University, 1999), 70–152; Young, *Biblical Exegesis*, 140–62.

is that, for the most part, they do not construe John as an ethical model. Such figurative interpretations contrast with the more numerous ethical appropriations of Mark 1:6c‖Matt 3:4c, discussed in the lion's share of this chapter.

1. Origen: The Distinctiveness of John's Diet and Its Meaning

Origen (*c.* 184/85–254/55 C.E.), like several interpreters after him, at times seems to regard John's diet as unusual rather than common:

> He was nourished in a new way, not according to human customs (*nutriebatur novo et extra humanam consuetudinem modo*). Matthew mentions this: 'But his food was locusts and wild honey.' . . . Ponder this, dearest brethren, he was born in a new fashion and reared in a new fashion (*nove . . . nove et nutritus est*).[53]

> But John always ate locusts, and he always ate wild honey. He was content with simple life and light food, lest his body grow fat on richer, savory dishes and be overpowered by exquisite banquets. This is the nature of our bodies; they are weighted down by excess food and, when the body is weighed down, the soul too is burdened. For the soul is spread throughout the whole body and subject to its passions. . . . So John's life was remarkable (*vita mirabilis*), and quite different than other men's way of living (*et multum ab aliorum hominum conversatione diversa*). (*Luc. Hom.* 25.2 [on Luke 3:15]).

Despite the (mistaken) perception of this diet's distinctiveness, Origen hails John's way of life as an example of how to care for one's soul through a simple diet. He elsewhere makes a similar claim concerning the Baptist's clothing.[54] Origen does not resolve how John's life could at the same time be remarkable (*mirabilis*) and quite different (*multum . . . diversa*), and therefore not readily imitated exactly by those who would follow John's example.[55]

Origen is also not entirely consistent on the distinctiveness of the Baptist's diet. In another writing he offers John's "taking nothing but locusts and wild

---

[53] Or., *Luc. Hom.* 11.5 [on Luke 1:80–2:2]; this despite his recognition of locusts as a clean animal (*parvum . . . mundum*). The editions cited for Jerome's translation of Origen's *Homilies on Luke* are: Hermann-Josef Sieben, ed., *In Lucam homiliae = Homilien zum Lukasevangelium* (Fontes Christiani 4; Freiburg: Herder, 1991–92); ET: Joseph T. Lienhard, *Homilies on Luke; Fragments on Luke* (FC 94; Washington: Catholic University of America, 1996). In addition, a portion of Origen's *Commentary on Luke* surviving in Greek expresses a similar sentiment: Or., *Luc. Cat.* 54 (on Luke 1:80, concerning John's time in the wilderness since he was a child [παιδίον]):

καὶ ἡ τροφὴ ξένη

Greek: Max Rauer, ed., *Origenes Werke* (GCS 9: *Die Homilien zu Lukas in der Übersetzung des Hieronymus und die Griechischen Reste der homilien und des Lukas-Kommentars*; Berlin: Akademie-Verlag, ²1959), 9.249.

[54] On this point, see Clark, *Reading Renunciation*, 311, on Or., *Peri pascha* 1.36–37.

[55] Cf. Or., *Peri Pascha* 1.36, where Origen tentatively offers John's belt as evidence that John "had mortified . . . every genital instinct of his body." Greek: Octave Guéraud and Pierre Nautin, eds., *Origène, Sur la Pâque* (Christianisme antique 2; Paris: Beauchesne, 1979), 224; ET: Robert J. Daly, *Treatise on the Passover; Dialogue of Origen with Heraclides* (ACW 54; New York: Paulist, 1992), 47.

honey" as indicating that John kept the law.[56] In his *Commentary on Matthew*, moreover, Origen does not assume the distinctiveness of John's diet:

> He was in the habit of eating (ἤσθιεν) locusts because the people were being nourished by a word that traveled high aloft in the air and had not yet passed over the earth. [John ate] honey, which is not obtained by people through their own efforts. The honey produced under the law and the prophets was not accessible to those who were inquiring only superficially about their meaning and not searching the scriptures [cf. John 5:39].[57]

For Origen, John's eating locusts signifies the Baptist's mission of preaching an exalted word. Origen further infers that John's 'honey' was beyond the reach of Jews who searched the law and the prophets without reference to these writings' fulfillment in Christ.

In light of the many complexities scholars today recognize in assessing the relationship of the historical Baptist to the historical Jesus, Origen's differentiating between John's 'honey' and that of other Judeans is particularly striking. If the historical John did not, in fact, read the law and the prophets in the way that Origen assumes he did (that is, christologically), then Origen's figurative interpretation falls apart: John's 'honey' would actually have been equally unobtainable for both John and his Judean audience.

2. Other Figurative Interpretations of John's Diet: Cyril of Jerusalem, Hilary of Poitiers, Arnobius the Younger and Peter Chrysologus

Other figurative or allegorical interpretations of John's diet include those of Cyril of Jerusalem, Hilary of Poitiers, Arnobius the Younger and Peter Chrysologus. Even though each of these authors interprets John's locusts and honey differently than Origen did, the desire to glean some greater significance from Mark 1:6c‖Matt 3:4c remains constant.

Cyril of Jerusalem (*fl.* 350–387 C.E.), for example, writes that the locusts' wings point to the ascent of John's soul to heaven:

> Of this grace, do you observe what manner of person God chose to be the inaugurator? One who forsook possessions and loved solitude, but no misanthrope. He fed on locusts and grew wings on his soul (ἀκρίδας ἐσθίοντα καὶ πτεροφυήσαντα τὴν ψυχήν). Sated with honey, the words he spoke were sweeter than honey and of more profit. Clothed in a garment of camel's hair, he exemplified in his own person the ascetic life.[58]

---

[56] Or., *Philocalia* 26.4: πλὴν ἀκρίδων καὶ μέλιτος ἀγρίου μηδενὸς μεταλαμβάνων ... τετηρηκέναι τὸν νόμον. An ET is available in George Lewis, *The Philocalia of Origen: A Compilation of St Gregory of Nazianzus and St Basil of Caesarea* (Edinburgh: T. & T. Clark, 1911), 218.

[57] Or., *Mat. Cat.* 41. This part of Origen's *Commentary on Matthew* happily does survive in Greek: Erich Klostermann, ed., *Origenes Matthäuserklärung* (GCS 41/1; Berlin: Akademie Verlag, ²1959), 32; ET (modified): Simonetti, *Matthew*, 41.

[58] Cyril of Jerusalem, *Catechetical Lectures* (*Catecheses ad illuminandos*) 3.6 [on Baptism]). Greek: Wilhelm K. Reischl and Joseph Rupp, eds., *S. Patris nostri Cyrilli Hierosolymorum, Opera quae supersunt omnia* (Hildesheim: Olms, 1967 [1848–60]), 1.72;

Like Clement of Alexandria (*Paed.* 2.112.1, discussed below), Cyril of Jerusalem finds an ascetic example in John's clothing. Cyril differs from Clement of Alexandria (*Paed.* 2.16.1), however, in not recognizing such an example in John's food, which instead Cyril interprets figuratively.

Three other figurative interpretations highlight the salvific significance of John's wilderness foods. Hilary of Poitiers (315–367/8 C.E.) construes the two items of John's diet as the status of the believer before and after the coming of salvation, respectively:

> For food he chooses grasshoppers, which are apt to flee from people and which fly away (*locustae fugaces hominum . . . euolantes*) every time they sense us arriving: it is us (*nos scilicet*), who were removed (*efferebamur*) from every word and meeting of the prophets by the very leaping of our bodies. With a wandering will, useless works, querulous words, a strange habitation, we are now the nourishment of the saints and the satiation of the prophets, being selected at the same time as wild honey to offer the sweetest food from ourselves, not from the beehives of the Law, but from [our] wild tree trunks.[59]

For his part, Arnobius the Younger (*fl.* 432–after 451 C.E.) understands the "locusts and wild honey" with respect to those who came to John: "'John's food was locusts and wild honey.' The locusts are a figure (*demonstrant figuram*) of the many people who came to John. Honey, on the other hand, signifies (*demonstrat*) the fruit of the sweetness of those whose trust and faith John satisfied."[60]

Finally, Peter Chrysologus (*c.* 400–*c.* 450 C.E.; Imola, Italy) focuses on the locusts' wings. Like John's mobile insects, the Baptist's hearers moved from condemnation to forgiveness and perceived that honey could sweeten the bitterness of repentance:

> 'His food was locusts and wild honey.' Locusts intended for sinners worthy of chastisement (*merito poenitentiae*) are rightly considered to be (*figuratur*) [food] for repentance, so that bounding from the place of sin to the place of repentance the sinner may fly to heaven on the wings of forgiveness. The prophet was aware of this when he said, 'I am gone, like a shadow at evening. I am shaken off like a locust. My knees are weak through fasting; my body has become gaunt. . . . Save me according to your steadfast law' [Ps 108:23–26, LXX]. You have heard how John was shaken off like a locust from sin to re-

---

ET (modified): William Telfer, *Cyril of Jerusalem and Nemesius of Emesa* (LCC 4; Philadelphia: Westminster, 1955), 93.

[59] Hilary, *Commentarius in Matthaeum* 2.2 (925A–B). Lat.: Jean Doignon, ed., *Hilaire de Poitiers, Sur Matthieu* (SC 254, 258; Paris: Cerf, 1978–79), 1.104; ET: mine.

[60] Arn., *Exposit. in Matt.* 3 [*De cibo Iohannis*]. Lat.: Klaus-D. Daur, ed., *Arnobius Ivnioris, Opera omnia* (CCSL 25A: *Arnobius Ivnioris, Opera minora*; Turnholt: Brepols, 1992), 277–8; ET (modified): Charles S. Kraszewski, *The Gospel of Matthew with Patristic Commentaries* (Studies in Bible and Early Christianity 40; Lewiston: Mellon, 1999), 262.

pentance. He bent his knees that he might bear the burden of repentance. His food was mixed with honey, so that tender mercy might temper the bitterness of repentance.[61]

3. *Analysis: Unity and Diversity among Figurative Interpretations*

The interpretations discussed in this section may be summarized as follows:

	Origen of Alexandria	Cyril of Jerusalem	Arnobius the Younger	Hilary of Poitiers	Peter Chrysologus
Locusts	John's exalted preaching.	John's soul grew wings.	Those who came to John.	A person prior to salvation.	Those moved from condemnation to forgiveness.
Honey	The relative inaccessibility of the Christian message.	Made John's words sweet.	The sweetness of the faith and trust that John satisfied.	Sweetness one offers the Lord after receiving salvation.	Sweetens the bitterness of repentance.

Although each of these interpretations is different and none can be said to be derived from one (or more) of the others, two points of commonality may be ascertained. First, the locusts' *locomotion* inspired interpretations concerning the travelling of John's words (Origen) and soul (Cyril of Jerusalem), and of John's hearers, whether to John (Arnobius the Younger), or either to (Peter Chrysologus) or from (Hilary of Poitiers) a place of forgiveness. Īšoʿdāḏ of Merv, moreover, connects locusts as flying insects with the "flight of the saints who fly in the clouds to meet the Lord."[62] Likewise, four of these authors extract from honey's *sweetness* significance pertaining to John's words (Cyril of Jerusalem), trusting John (Arnobius the Younger), what a redeemed person offers the Lord (Hilary of Poitiers), or mitigating the bitterness of repentance (Peter Chrysologus).[63]

Among these points of commonality, however, two points of contrast also merit attention. Origen and Cyril of Jerusalem agree that John's food points to his message, but differ on whether the locusts (Origen) or the honey (Cyril) establishes this point. Moreover, Arnobius the Younger and Peter Chrysologus highlight the renewal John's listeners found, but alternately offer

---

[61] Peter Chrysologus, *Sermons* 167.9. Lat.: Alexandre Olivar, ed., *Sancti Petri Chrysologi, Collectio sermonum* (CCSL 24B; Turnholt: Brepols, 1975), 1029; ET: Simonetti, *Matthew*, 41.

[62] Discussed above in connection with Tatian's *Diatessaron*. On additional allegorical interpretations in Syriac literature, see Brock, "Syriac Sources," 122–4.

[63] One might infer the same for Origen as well, inasmuch as the Christian Gospel has a sweetness unlike that in the OT.

John's locusts (Peter Chrysologus) or honey (Arnobius) as the basis for this interpretation. Finally, there is not agreement on whether the locusts designate humans before (Hilary of Poitiers) or after (Peter Chrysologus) salvation.

E. Eastern Witnesses to John's Diet as a Model for Others

Beginning with Clement of Alexandria, ascetic construals of the Baptist's diet and appropriations of the Baptist's example emerge as the most common interpretations of Mark 1:6c‖Matt 3:4c. As noted in the previous section concerning the assorted figurative interpretations, the variety of ways that John constitutes a model for believers today is again noteworthy. For the sake of convenience, witnesses from the Greek East will be analyzed in this section and those from the Latin West in the next. In addition to Clement of Alexandria, the authors to be discussed in this section are: Methodius of Olympus, Cyril of Alexandria, Gregory Nazianzen, Basil of Caesarea, Gregory of Nyssa, Didymus the Blind, John Chrysostom, various Pseudo-Chrysostom(s), and Hesychius of Jerusalem.

1. Clement of Alexandria: John's Temperance Prepares the Way for Jesus' Followers

Clement of Alexandria (*c*. 150–211/16 C.E.) offers the earliest example of ascetic interpretations of John's clothing and food. In his *Paedagogos* (*c*. 190/92 C.E.), Clement twice refers to John's diet. One passage explicitly names John's austere clothing as an example for others to follow:

> The blessed John disdained sheep's wool because it savored of luxury; he preferred camel's hair and clothed himself in it, giving us an example (ὑποτυπούμενος) of simple, frugal living. He also used to eat honey and locusts (μέλι ἤσθιεν καὶ ἀκρίδας), food that is sweet and with spiritual significance (γλυκεῖαν καὶ πνευματικὴν τροφήν), and so prepared the way (παρασκευάζων) of the Lord [cf. Isa 40:3], [keeping it] humble and chaste.[64]

The imperfect tense ἤσθιεν[65] seems to be based on Mark's imperfect periphrastic (ἦν . . . ἐσθίων). In this passage John's honey is not "wild,"[66] but the food (cf. τροφή, Matt 3:4c) is "spiritual" (πνευματική), although in what way Clement does not specify. John's clothing offers a model to Christians today, but the same is not claimed in *Paed.* 2.112.1 for his diet, which

---

[64] Clem., *Paed.* 2.11(2.112.1). Greek: Miroslav Marcovich, ed., *Clementis Alexandrini, Paedagogus* (VCSup 61; Leiden: Brill, 2002); ET (modified at times to conform more accurately to the Greek): Simon P. Wood, *[Clement,] Christ the Educator* (FC 23; New York: Fathers of the Church, 1954).

[65] Also in *Paed.* 2.16.1, discussed immediately below.

[66] But see below on *Paed.* 2.16.1.

Clement ties instead to John's vocation of preparing the way for Christ (ἤσθιεν . . . παρασκευάζων). The allusion to Isa 40:3 perceptively retains something of Mark's interest in connecting John to the desert by these common wilderness foods.

Elsewhere in the *Paedagogos*, Clement does offer the Baptist's diet—and the food of the apostle Matthew as well—as examples worthy of imitation:

> [15.4] I for one would not hesitate to call that devil, the devil of the belly, the most wicked and deadly of them all. . . . Happiness is the practice of virtue. [16.1] Matthew the apostle used to make his meal on seeds and plants and herbs, without flesh-meat (σπερμάτων καὶ ἀκροδρύων καὶ λαχάνων, ἄνευ κρεῶν); John, maintaining extreme self-restraint (ὑπερτείνας τὴν ἐγκράτειαν), "used to eat (ἤσθιεν) locusts and wild honey"; and Peter abstained from pork. But "he fell into an ecstasy" is written in the Acts of the Apostles. (*Paed.* 2.1 [2.15.4–2.16.1])

That Acts 10, from which Clement goes on to cite, reports Peter's apparent indulgence in meat requires an explanation. One can thus infer for Clement that, unless special circumstances analogous to Peter's calling to meet Cornelius's household should arise, those under Clement's tutelage should follow the more austere examples of Matthew and the Baptist.

Given that the apostle Matthew's clearly 'vegetarian' diet is contrasted with Peter's pork, it is quite possible that Clement views the Baptist's locusts and honey also as "without flesh" (ἄνευ κρεῶν), since, unlike Peter's pork, no argument is needed to justify John's eating 'locusts.' Even if the extreme asceticism of Encratite Christians could irk many an early Christian author,[67] Clement unreservedly hails John as one who abounded (ὑπερτείνω) in self-control (ἐγκράτεια) with regard to food (*Paed.* 2.16.1) and left an example of how to dress simply (*Paed.* 2.112.1).[68]

2. Methodius of Olympus: John's Purity and Distinction "among Those Born of Women"

Prior to Origen's condemnation at the Council of Constantinople in 553 C.E., Methodius of Olympus (d. *c.* 311 C.E.) was remembered as an early opponent of Origen's theology of the bodily resurrection. Their considerable theological differences notwithstanding, Origen and Methodius would nonetheless have agreed on John's example of piety. According to Methodius, John's clothing and food explain why Jesus declared John the greatest of those born to women (cf. Q/Luke 7:28‖Matt 11:11).[69] This combination of

---

[67] E.g., Irenaeus, *Haer.* 1.28; Clem., *Str.* 1.21; Hippol., *Ref.* 8, 13; Euseb., *Hist. eccl.* 4.29, 5.11.

[68] Cf. Euseb., *Demonstr. evang.* 3.5 (118B). Clement thus contrasts with Irenaeus and Tertullian, who like Justin Martyr before them attribute no particular significance to this diet.

[69] *De vita* 8.1. The only surviving part of Methodius's *Life and Rational Activity* is in Old Slavonic; the following German translation appears in G. Nathanael Bonwetsch, *Methodius*

Mark 1:6c‖Matt 3:4c with Q/Luke 7:28‖Matt 11:11 represents an innovation in Christian reflection on John's diet.

Methodius offers a possible reason why he associates these two gospel passages in his *Treatise on the Resurrection of the Body*: "John submitted his body for the sake of chastity (ὁ Ἰωάννης ὑπέταξεν αὐτοῦ τὸ σῶμα εἰς ἁγνείαν)."[70] It is likely that Methodius refers to the austere lifestyle of the Baptist—and not, for example, to the apostle John. Accordingly, it stands to reason that Methodius took the Baptist's food and clothing as evidence of purity, which elucidates why John merits the distinction Jesus accords to him in Q/Luke 7:28‖Matt 11:11.

3. Cyril of Alexandria: John as Prophet Calling Others to Repentance

Commenting on Q/Matt 11:17, Cyril of Alexandria (375–444 C.E.) draws a connection between John's time in the wilderness and call to repentance:

> It was fitting for John as a lowly servant to deaden the passions of the body through very hard training (δι' ἀσκητικοῦ βίου), and for Christ by the power of his Godhead freely to mortify the sensations of the body and the innate practice of the flesh, and to do so without reliance on strenuous ascetic labors. Nevertheless John, 'while he was preaching the baptism of repentance' [Mark 1:4‖Luke 3:3], offered himself as a model for those who were obliged to lament. . . .[71]

For Cyril, John offers an example to those called to lament and repent.

In his work, *On the Incarnation of the Lord*, moreover, Cyril hails John as an example that "the life of people is satisfied (συγκορτεῖται) not only with bread (ἄρτοις), but the word of God is sufficient to nourish (ἀρκεῖ . . . διαθρέψαι) every kind of people."[72] Examples of the Israelites wandering in the wilderness for forty years, and of Elijah and Elisha, then follow. Cyril's last example concerns the Baptist:

> This John, who more recently was baptizing in the Jordan and lived all his life in the wilderness, was nourished by locusts and the fruit of wild bees (ἀκρίσι τρέφεται καὶ

(GCS 27; Leipzig: Hinrichs, 1917), 216: "Schaue mir jenen heiligen Mann, den Verkündiger des Kommens des Heiligen, welcher für kurze Zeit in die Welt gesandt, auch kaum in ihr verweilend, alles hier Seiende kaum beachtend; denn von 'Heuschrecken und wildem Honig' nährte er sich und hüllte sich in 'Kamelshaare.' Daher erweis er sich under allen 'Geborenen' als der 'Größere,' wegen der Einfachheit der Kleidung und der Ungekünsteltheit der Speise und der Spärlichkeit des Tisches." Apparently Methodius was impressed that John's food was natural (ungekünstelt) rather than cultivated.

[70] Methodius, *De resurrectione* 1.59.6. Greek: Bonwetsch, *Methodius*, 323; ET: mine. The noun ἁγνεία could also denote cultic purity or moral purity.

[71] Cyril Alex., *Fragment* 143. Greek: Joseph Reuss, ed., *Matthäus-Kommentare aus der griechischen Kirche* (TUGAL 61; Berlin: Akademie-Verlag, 1957), 198. ET: Simonetti, *Matthew*, 225. Cf. above on Peter Chrysologus, *Sermons* 167.9.

[72] Cyril Alex., *De incarnatione Domini* 821B. Greek: *PG* 75.1441; translations from this work are my own.

μελιττῶν ἀγρίων καρπῷ), . . . in order for us to be treated to a banquet of strange food from God, and not to be in need of bread. (*De incarnatione Domini* 821B)

Cyril of Alexandria is among the first interpreters to attempt to specify which kind of 'honey' John ate, inferring "the fruit of wild bees" as the correct referent for "wild honey."[73] Cyril's interpretation of John's food corresponds closely to that argued in the last chapter for Matt 3:4c, emphasizing God's sustenance of John in the wilderness.

Additionally, a catena attributed to Cyril of Alexandria may build upon Cyril's identification of bees in *De incarnatione Domini*. At many points Cyril's indebtedness to Origen (*Mat. Cat.* 41, discussed above) is evident:

Ἡ δὲ τροφὴ αὐτοῦ, ὡς ἡγοῦμαι, σύμβολον ἦν τῆς λογικῆς τοῦ λαοῦ πότε τροφῆς, οὐκ ἐσθίοντός τι τῶν καθαρῶν πετεινῶν τοῦ οὐρανοῦ, τρεφομένου δὲ τῷ μὲν δοκοῦντι λόγῳ μετεωροπόρῳ, ἀλλ' οὐ βεβηκότι ὑπὲρ τῶν πτερύγων, οὐδὲ δυναμένῳ ὑπεραναβῆναι τῆς γῆς, καὶ ἐπί τὰ ὑψηλὰ φθάναι αὐτῆς. Ὥσπερ ἦν καὶ μέλι ἄγριον γενόμενον μὲν ὑπὸ τῶν νοητῶν μελισσῶν τῶν προφητῶν, μὴ γεωργούμενον δὲ καὶ ἡμερούμενον διὰ τῆς ἐμμελοῦς[74] νοήσεως καὶ ζητήσεως.

I believe his food was a symbol of the esteemed food of the people then. He did not eat any of the clean birds of the sky but was nourished by the exalted word, which had not arrived by wings. Nor was it able to go beyond the earth, or transcend its heights. Likewise, the wild honey was [a symbol] of the perceptive bees of the prophets, not farmed but cultivated through careful perception and searching.[75]

In contrasting the locusts John ate with birds that can fly, Cyril seems to assume that John ate younger "nymph" locusts, which in fact cannot fly without the wings that adult locusts develop. The contrast could also suggest ignorance of Leviticus 11, which discusses birds (11:13–19) and locusts (11:20–23) together as creatures that inhabit the sky.[76] Concerning the Baptist's uncultivated bee honey, Cyril refers favorably to the understanding of the OT prophets, which parallels John's exalted message. In this last regard, Cyril differs with Origen, who instead highlights the distinctiveness of John's Christian message vis-à-vis the OT (Or., *Mat. Cat.* 41). For Cyril of Alexandria, then, John's diet highlights the work of the Baptist as a prophet.[77]

---

[73] So also Chrysostom, *Homilies on Matthew* 68.5. See also above on Īšoʿdāḏ of Merv's (later) interpretation of Matt 3:4.

[74] Note the play on words: μέλι . . . ἐμμελοῦς.

[75] Greek: John A. Cramer, ed., *Catenae Graecorum Patrum in Novum Testamentum* (Hildesheim: Olms, 1967 [1840]), 1.269; the ET is my own.

[76] Such unawareness of Lev 11:20–23 is evident also in Origen (discussed above) and Augustine (discussed below).

[77] On this interpretation in recent scholarship, see the discussion in chapter 1, 16–17.

4. Gregory Nazianzen: Following Elijah and John into the Wilderness

In his *Orations*, Gregory Nazianzen (329–389 C.E.) writes of the time that he and Basil of Caesarea had, individually, spent in the wilderness. Gregory connects both his and Basil's wilderness experiences with the example of John. Concerning his own time in the wilderness he writes in *Oration* 33:

> What also lured me was the wilderness of John (ἡ ἔρημος Ἰωάννου), which had "the greatest among those born to women," with his food (μετὰ τῆς τροφῆς ἐκείνης) and belt and clothing. I dare to say something beyond this: I found God to be in agreement with my rusticity (θεὸν εὗρον τῆς ἀγροικίας συνήγορον).[78]

Gregory's description in *Oration* 39 of John as "ill-fed in the wilderness (ὁ τῆς ἐρημίας ἄτροφος)," which assumes the insufficiency of locusts and honey as a person's only foods,[79] complements his statement in *Oration* 33. A logical inference from these statements in *Orations* 33 and 39 is that Gregory was drawn to seek God in a place that the Cappadocian perceived as inadequate to sustain human life indefinitely. In yet another *Oration* Gregory describes what "John's wilderness teaches" him (Gregory).[80] Perhaps it was for these reasons, then, that Gregory senses in *Or.* 33.10 God's pleasure with Gregory's decision to seek the divine in a place devoid of even basic amenities.[81]

In his funeral oration for St. Basil, moreover, Gregory Nazianzen twice commemorates Basil's having followed the examples of Elijah and John in pursuing a period of wilderness habitation:

> He embraced solitude along with (μετά) Elias and John, those perfect philosophers, deeming this more advantageous for him . . . than to lose in the tempest the control which in time of calm he exercised over his reason. Although his departure was so philosophical and worthy of admiration, we shall find that his return was even more admirable. For so it was.[82]

> For it is no little credit to the good that they are imitators of the greatest of human beings, even in a small way. For was not Basil a visible image (εἰκών) of the philosophy

---

[78] *Or.* 33.10 (228A). Greek: Claudio Moreschini, ed., *Grégoire de Nazianze, Discours 32–37* (SC 318; Paris: Cerf, 1985), 178; ET: mine.

[79] *Or.* 39.15 (353A). Greek: C. Moreschini, ed., *Grégoire de Nazianze, Discours 38–41* (SC 358; Paris: Cerf, 1990), 184; ET: mine. On "locusts and honey" and human nutrition, see chapter 4, 108–118.

[80] *Or.* 14.4: διδάσκει με . . . ἔρημος Ἰωάννου. Greek: *PG* 35.861.

[81] Cf. additional comments of Gregory Nazianzen on the Baptist's food (*Carmina moralia* 2.10 [Greek: *PG* 37.593]) and clothing (*Carmina historica* 1.88 [Greek: *PG* 37.1439]; *Carmina theologica* 2.2 [Greek: *PG* 37.719]).

[82] *Or.* 43.29 (536B). Greek text for this *Oration*: Jean Bernardi, ed., *Grégoire de Nazianze, Discours 42–43* (SC 384; Paris: Cerf, 1992), 190–2, 292; ET (modified): Leo P. McCauley et al., *Funeral Orations by Saint Gregory Nazianzen and Saint Ambrose* (FC 22; New York: Fathers of the Church, 1953), 52–3, 93–4.

of John? He also dwelt in the desert and wore at night a garment of hair,[83] concealing it [from sight] and avoiding display. He also loved the same kind of food (τὴν ἴσην τροφὴν ἠγάπησε), purifying himself for God by abstinence (καθαίρων ... ἐγκρατείας). He was also deemed worthy to be a herald, if not a forerunner, of Christ. And there went out to him not only all the country round about but also that beyond its boundaries. (*Or.* 43.75 [597A])

According to Gregory Nazianzen, then, the Baptist's wilderness habitation served as a model to both himself and Basil. John's way of life in the wilderness delineates not simply the type of provisions one should seek but offers a blueprint that these two Cappadocian fathers followed.

5. Basil of Caesarea: Summoning a Plethora of Biblical and Early Christian Precedents for Wilderness Habitation

The preceding section noted Gregory Nazianzen's commemoration of Basil of Caesarea (*c.* 330–379 C.E.) for having followed the examples of Elijah's and John's wilderness habitation. A somewhat different construal of the wilderness appears in Basil's writings, which nevertheless confirms Gregory Nazianzen's claim concerning Basil's imitation of John. In a letter to Chilo, Basil claims to have followed the examples of numerous biblical figures, not just Elijah and John. In addition to Elijah and John, Basil cites as precedents for wilderness habitation Abraham, Jacob, the Israelites after the Exodus, and Christ.[84] In this letter Basil finds prior instances of wilderness dwelling in

---

[83] On John's clothing as a model for others, see also: Gregory, *Or.* 22.5, 45.18; and especially Sulpicius Severus (*c.* 360–*c.* 420 C.E.), concerning monks who dressed like John: "Here, then, he [St. Martin] possessed a cell constructed of wood. Many also of the brethren had, in the same manner, fashioned retreats for themselves, but most of them had formed these out of the rock of the overhanging mountain, hollowed into caves. There were altogether eighty disciples, who were being disciplined after the example of the saintly master. . . . It was not allowed either to buy or to sell anything, as is the custom among most monks. . . . Most of them were clothed in garments of camels' hair. Any dress approaching to softness was there deemed criminal, and this must be thought the more remarkable, because many among them were such as are deemed of noble rank" (*On the Life of St. Martin* 10; ET: NPNF, II/11.9). See also Hyperechius (d. *c.* 425/450 C.E.), *Adhortatio ad monachos* 48; Greek: James V. Smith, "Resurrecting the Blessed Hyperechius," (Diss., Loyola University Chicago, 2003), 218.

[84] Basil, *Ep.* 42.5 [To Chilo]: "What profit, then, is there in all this for me—or is it manifestly harmful to my soul? 'Therefore I migrate to the mountains like a sparrow; for like a sparrow I have been delivered out of the snare of the fowlers.' For I am living, O evil thought, in the wilderness wherein the Lord dwelt. Here is the oak of Mamre [Gen 13:18, 18:1]; here is the ladder which leads to heaven, and the encampments of the angels, which Jacob saw; here is the wilderness where the people, purified, received the law, and then going into the land of promise beheld God. Here is Mount Carmel, where Elias abode and pleased God. Here is the plain whither Esdras withdrew, and at God's bidding poured forth from his mouth all his divinely inspired books. Here is the wilderness where the blessed John ate locusts and preached repentance to people (ἡ ἔρημος ἐν ᾗ ὁ μακάριος Ἰωάννης

unnamed—and presumably numerous, in Basil's understanding—Christian teachers, prophets, apostles, evangelists and monks.

The variety of support Basil cites for wilderness habitation could, on the one hand, suggest that, unlike Gregory Nazianzen, Basil did not regard his time in the desert as inspired particularly by Elijah or John. On the other hand, there are some indications that Basil, like Gregory Nazianzen, did attribute particular significance to John's wilderness habitation, clothing and food.[85] One similarity between Basil and Gregory Nazianzen (*Or.* 39.15) concerns the perceived inadequacy of John's wilderness foods:

> Ἰωάννου δὲ ὁ βίος μία νηστεία ἦν· ὅς οὐ κλίνην εἶχεν, οὐ τράπεζαν, οὐ γῆν ἀροσίμην, οὐκ ἀροτῆρα βοῦν, οὐ σῖτον, οὐ σιτοποιόν, οὐκ ἄλλο τι τῶν κατὰ τὸν βίον.
>
> John's life was one [long] fast. He did not have a bed, a table, arable land, an ox for plowing, grain, means to bake bread, or anything else for sustaining life.[86]

For Basil, then, John's way of life in the wilderness serves as an example of fasting precisely because the Baptist's "locusts and wild honey" are assumed to be deficient forms of sustenance.

Returning to Basil's letter to Chilo (*Ep.* 42.5), it is likely that Basil was informed by an interpretive tradition concerning the Baptist like that reflected by Gregory Nazianzen (*Or.* 33.10) and chose to augment such a tradition with examples of additional people in scripture and the early church who found themselves in the wilderness. A remarkable parallel with Mark 1:6c is Basil's assumption that locust eating *ipso facto* associates John with the wilderness (*Ep.* 42.5: ἡ ἔρημος ἐν ᾗ ὁ μακάριος Ἰωάννης ἀκριδοφαγῶν). Moreover, Basil's comment in this letter that he is "living . . . in the wilderness wherein the Lord dwelt" confirms Gregory Nazianzen's testimony (*Or.* 43.29, 43.75) to Basil's period in the wilderness. As is discussed in the following section, the other Cappadocian, Gregory of Nyssa, apparently was not

---

ἀκριδοφαγῶν μετάνοιαν τοῖς ἀνθρώποις ἐκήρυξεν). Here is the Mount of Olives, which Christ ascended and there prayed, teaching us how to pray. Here is Christ who loved solitude; for he says, 'Where there are two or three gathered in my name, there am I in the midst of them.' Here is the narrow and strait way that leads to life. Here are teachers and prophets, 'wandering in deserts, in mountains, and in dens, and in caves of the earth' [Heb 11:38]. Here are apostles and evangelists and the life of monks, citizens of the desert (ὁ τῶν μοναχῶν ἐρημοπολίτης βίος). . . . I know that Abraham, beloved of God, obeyed [God's] voice and went to dwell in the wilderness. . . ." Greek: Yves Courtonne, *Saint Basile, Lettres* (Paris: Les Belles Lettres, 1957–66), 1.106–7; ET (checked against Courtonne's more recent critical edition of the Greek): Roy J. Defarrari, *Saint Basil, the Letters* (LCL; London: Heinemann, 1926–34), 1.259–63.

[85] Elsewhere, for example, Basil refers to the clothing of Elijah and John (*Asceticon magnum* 1.22, 1.23; Greek: *PG* 31.977C, 981A–B]), as well as their place of habitation (*Asceticon paruum* 11.32–33; Lat.: Klaus Zelzer, ed., *Basili, Regula a Rufino latine uersa* [CSEL 86; Vienna: Hoelder-Pichler-Tempsky, 1986], 56).

[86] Basil, *De ieiunio* 1.9; Greek: *PG* 31.177C; ET: mine.

as daring as Gregory Nazianzen and Basil. Gregory of Nyssa does, however, accord with Basil's desire to relate additional biblical material to John's diet.

It is conceivable, moreover, that these appropriations of John's wilderness habitation and food as a model for pious believers today preserve an echo of the historical Baptist's message. John entered the wilderness and, of necessity because of his surroundings, adopted an austere lifestyle in preparation *for something*, whether eschatological fulfillment (in this author's view, so the historical John) or Jesus (so the NT gospels). Over the centuries, believers wishing to be closer to Jesus have laid the groundwork by approaching John and his ascetically construed life in the wilderness. The uninitiated usually cannot guess beforehand just how a 'locust' will taste, or precisely how one will encounter the divine "in the wilderness."

6. Gregory of Nyssa: Following the Example of "Paul's" Hermeneutics

In his work *On Virginity*, Gregory of Nyssa (*c.* 330–395 C.E.) argues "that Elijah and John [the Baptist] were concerned with the rigid discipline of this life."[87] Like the gospels of Mark and Matthew (but not Luke), then, Gregory finds significance in the similarities between Elijah and John. Gregory notes, additionally, concerning the two prophets' food and place in the wilderness:

> Both of them, right from their youth, alienated themselves from human life and placed themselves beyond human nature by their disdain of the usual food and drink (τῇ τε περὶ τὴν βρῶσιν καὶ πόσιν ὑπεροψίᾳ) and by living in the desert. . . . (*De virginitate* 6.1.1)

Gregory also applies to the Baptist the apostle Paul's words in 1 Cor 10:11 (ἐγράφη δὲ πρὸς νουθεσίαν ἡμῶν) concerning the OT as a source of moral instruction to Christians today:

> These facts "are recorded" for us, not for their own sake (οὐχ ἁπλῶς), but, as the apostle says, "for our correction" (εἰς νουθεσίαν ἡμῶν ἀναγέγραπται), in order that we may direct our lives in accordance with theirs. (*De virginitate* 6.1.1)

Gregory of Nyssa's appeal to Paul's reference to the OT in 1 Corinthians 10 underlies a significant development in the interpretation of John's diet, namely the claim to following Paul's hermeneutics in the use of scripture for moral instruction.

In 1 Cor 10:9–10, Paul refers to the Lord's judgment against the Israelites in Numbers 21. For the Corinthian Christians whom Paul addresses, the

---

[87] Gregory of Nyssa, *De virginitate* 6.1.Pref. The editions cited for this work are: Michel Aubineau, ed., *Traité de la virginité* (SC 119; Paris: Cerf, 1966), 338–42; ET: Virginia Woods Callahan, *Saint Gregory of Nyssa, Ascetical Works* (FC 58; Washington: Catholic University of America, 1967), 28–30. On Elijah and John as examples of virginity, see also Athanasius, *Ep. virg.* 1.7–8 and the discussion in: David Brakke, *Athanasius and the Politics of Asceticism* (Oxford: Clarendon/New York: Oxford University Press, 1995), 55.

Israelites' rebellion in the wilderness should "serve as an example" for those who may not embrace the apostle's teaching on meat sacrificed to idols. Gregory of Nyssa's application of 1 Cor 10:11 to Elijah and the Baptist takes Paul's *negative* example of what *not* to do (that is, rebelling against authoritative teaching, whether from Moses or Paul) and turns it into a *positive* example of *what to do*, namely imitating Elijah's and John's simplicity. New in Gregory of Nyssa's interpretation of John's diet is the claim to finding a precedent for this type of interpretation in NT literature other than the gospels.

Presumably, Gregory of Nyssa would have known about Basil of Caesarea's and Gregory Nazianzen's following the example of John's time in the wilderness. Even if Gregory of Nyssa did not partake in a period of wilderness habitation, he serves his fellow Cappadocians' cause by claiming to find a precedent for imitating John in Paul's interpretation of scripture. Moreover, Gregory of Nyssa offers John as an example even for those who do not enter the wilderness. According to Gregory of Nyssa, then, the scriptures record Elijah's and John's wilderness habitation and simple diet, "in order that we may direct our lives in accordance with theirs," even if we do not follow them into the wilderness, eating and dressing precisely as they did.

7. Didymus the Blind: Identifying the Baptist in Psalm 28 (LXX)

The previous two sections noted how Basil of Caesarea and Gregory of Nyssa associate additional parts of scripture with John's diet. A contemporary of these Cappadocian Fathers, Didymus the Blind (*c.* 313–*c.* 398 C.E.), connects yet another biblical passage with John's diet. In his *Commentary on the Psalms*, Didymus writes concerning Ps 28:7–8a (LXX):[88]

Ἔτι μὴν εὔτονον καὶ αὐστηρὸν βίον ἀναλαβὼν ὁ Ἰωάννης, διοδεύσιμον τὸν φλογμὸν τῶν ἡδονῶν τοῦ βίου ποιήσας, Φωνή ἐστιν κυρίου διακόπτοντος φλόγα πυρός.

John truly adopted a strenuous and austere life by causing the flame of the pleasures of life to pass away. "He is the voice of the Lord cutting through flames of fire."[89]

Part of what inspired Didymus's 'Johannine' interpretation of this Psalm are similarities between Psalm 28 (LXX) and the depictions of the Baptist in Mark (and Matthew):

---

[88] Ps 28:7–8a (LXX; = Ps 29:7–8a): "[7] The voice (φωνή) of the Lord cuts through flames of fire. [8a] The voice of the Lord shakes the wilderness (συσσείοντος ἔρημον)."

[89] Didymus, *Commentary on the Psalms* 256, on Ps 28:7 (LXX), according to the collection of Didymus's interpretations of the Psalms (i.e., the catena) by his contemporary Apollinaris of Laodicea (*c.* 315–before 392 C.E.). Greek: Ekkehard Mühlenberg, ed., *Psalmenkommentare aus der Katenenüberlieferung* (Patristische Texte und Studien 15, 16, 19; Berlin: de Gruyter, 1975–77), 1.260; ET: mine.

- The mention of "waters" in Ps 28:3[90] (cf. Mark 1:5 par.);
- The "voice" in Ps 28:7a, 8a (cf. Mark 1:3a, 4a par.);
- The "wilderness" in Ps 28:8 (cf. Mark 1:3a, 4a par.).

To an ascetic like Didymus,[91] the inference that the Psalmist wrote about the Baptist must have been self-evident. For Didymus, then, the "voice" in this Psalm belongs not to the Lord (or even to Christ) but to John the Baptist, who speaks about Christ the Lord.[92] John's model of piety in the wilderness underlies Didymus's understanding of John's austere way of life and moral excellence.

8. John Chrysostom: Linking the Baptist's Diet to Eschatology and Virginity

The previous sections noted how Basil of Caesarea, Gregory of Nyssa and Didymus the Blind exemplify that after John's diet became accepted as a model for others, any number of additional biblical passages could be mustered to augment this received interpretation. John Chrysostom (*c.* 354–407 C.E.) highlights that John's ascetically construed diet could also be linked with other theological concepts, such as eschatology and virginity. In a homily on Matthew, for example, Chrysostom interprets the Baptist's food and clothing eschatologically:

> It was necessary (ἔδει) that the precursor of the One who was to undo the age-long burdens, such as toil, malediction, pain and sweat, should in his own person be symbolic (σύμβολα) of the coming gift, so as to stand above these tribulations. And so it was that he neither tilled the earth nor plowed the furrow, nor did he eat bread (τὸν ἄρτον ἔφαγεν) of his own sweat, but his table was easily prepared (ἀλλ᾽ ἦν ἐσχεδιασμένη αὐτῷ ἡ τράπεζα), and his clothing more easily than his table. For he had need (ἐδήθη) neither of roof, nor bed, nor table, nor any such thing. But even while still within this flesh of ours he lived almost an angelic life. His clothing was put together from the hair of camels, so that even from his garments he might teach [us] to free ourselves of human needs (ἵνα ... παιδεύσῃ τῶν ἀνθρωπίνων ἀφίστασθαι), and not be bound to this earth, but that we may return to the pristine dignity (ἐπὶ τὴν προτέραν ἐπανατρέχειν εὐγένειαν) in which Adam first lived, before he had need of garments or clothing. Thus John's clothing itself was symbolic (σύμβολα) of nothing less than the coming kingdom and of repentance.[93]

---

[90] Didymus interprets the "waters" as a reference to John's baptism (Didymus, *Commentary on the Psalms* 255, on Ps 28:3a [LXX]; Greek: Mühlenberg, *Psalmenkommentare*, 1.260).

[91] Cf. Quasten, 3.86, who writes concerning Didymus: "His asceticism had won him no less renown [than his learning]. St. Anthony, the father of monasticism, saw him several times in his cell and Palladius paid him four visits there over a period of ten years (*Hist. Lausiac.* 4)."

[92] Thus the translation above construing the Baptist, not the Lord, as the subject of ἐστίν.

[93] Chrysostom, *In Matthaeum* 10.4. Greek: *PG* 57.188; ET (modified): M. F. Toal, ed., *The Sunday Sermons of the Great Fathers* (Chicago: Regnery, 1957–63), 1.86.

The Baptist's clothing and food have eschatological significance because they signify a time when humanity will again live like Adam (and Eve) once did in the Garden of Eden.[94] Notably different from Gregory Nazianzen and Gregory of Nyssa (and others), Chrysostom assumes that John's diet was not a hardship but rather symbolic of what redeemed humanity will someday enjoy again.

Prior to the eschatological realization of this "pristine dignity," moreover, John's way of life teaches (παιδεύω) us in the present to put away (ἀφίστημι) those things on which humans have relied since the fall of humanity. For this reason, Chrysostom urges later in the same sermon on Matthew: "Let us emulate him (Τοῦτον ... ζηλώσωμεν): Getting rid of luxuries and drunkenness, let us pursue the simplified life (ἐπί τὸν κατεσταλμένον μεταθώμεθα βίον)."[95] For Chrysostom, the Baptist offers a source of instruction on how to live simply in the present while anticipating the reversal of the effects of the fall of humanity.

Whereas in a homily on Matthew Chrysostom connects the Baptist's diet with eschatology, in his work *On Virginity* he highlights the power of moderation in food vis-à-vis sexual renunciation. In the latter work Chrysostom describes Elijah, Elisha and John as "genuine lovers of virginity," who differed from (presumably asexual) angels only "in so far as they had been bound to mortal nature."[96] The celibacy of these individuals gave them strength also concerning food. The Baptist illustrates these points as follows:

> And John, who was more than a prophet—no one born of woman has been greater—required no human nourishment (οὐδὲ ἀνθρωπίνης ἐδεήθη τροφῆς). Neither food (σῖτος) nor wine nor olive oil sustained his physical being, but grasshoppers and wild honey did. Do you behold the angels upon earth? Do you comprehend the power of virginity (παρθενίας ἰσχύν)? It has prepared (οὕτως ... παρεσκεύαζεν) in this way those enmeshed in flesh and blood, who walk along the earth and are subject to the necessity of human nature, to approach everything as if they were incorporeal, as if they had already obtained heaven, and were partaking in immortality. (*De virginitate* 79.2)

---

[94] Cf. Chrysostom, *In Joannem* 16.1, also highlighting the Baptist's simplicity: "Now, it was obvious that John had much to recommend him; . . . then, his way of life and austerity (ἡ δίαιτα καὶ ἡ σκληραγωγία), his disdain of all human things (ἡ τῶν ἀνθρωπίνων ὑπεροψία πάντων), for, despising clothing and table and dwelling and food itself, he had spent the time before this in the desert." Greek: Cecilia Tirone, ed., *Le omelie su S. Giovanni Evangelista* (Torino: Società editrice internazionale, 1942–48), 1.327–8; ET: Aquinas Goggin, *Saint John Chrysostom, Commentary on Saint John the Apostle and Evangelist: Homilies 1–47* (FC 33; New York: Fathers of the Church, 1957), 152. An ET can also be found in: NPNF, I/14.55.

[95] Chrysostom, *Homilies on Matthew* 10.5. Greek: *PG* 57.190; ET: mine.

[96] Chrysostom, *De virginitate* 79.1. Greek: Herbert Musurillo, ed., *Jean Chrysostome, La Virginité* (SC 125; Paris: Cerf, 1966), 376–8; ET: Sally Rieger Shore, *John Chrysostom, On Virginity; Against Remarriage* (Studies in Women and Religion 9; Lewiston, NY: Mellen, 1983), 119–21.

Whereas numerous earlier authors had *argued* John's diet is exemplary, in *De virginitate* 79.1–2 and *In Matthaeum* 10.4–5 Chrysostom *assumes* this point and builds upon it, respectively, with regard to virginity and eschatology. In *De virginitate*, he can thus state without elaboration that John's diet offers an example of how to live 'incorporeally' with regard to food.[97] Because Chrysostom regards this interpretation as *already* part of the received tradition, he can use it to support a different ethical admonition concerning chastity. Chastity gives the power to imitate the exemplary piety that the Baptist and certain other biblical figures demonstrated with regard to food.[98]

9. The Variety of Interpretations Attributed to Pseudo-Chrysostom(s)

The numerous spurious works attributed to John Chrysostom also contain various interpretations of John's diet. These works of Pseudo-Chrysostom were composed by any number of authors and are notoriously difficult to date. It comes as no surprise that many of these writings reflect the three main lines of interpretation discussed in this chapter, namely 'allegory,'[99] John as an ethical model,[100] and John as 'vegetarian.'[101] Moreover, two other spurious works of Chrysostom simply mention John's "locusts and wild honey" without attaching any particular significance to this diet.[102]

---

[97] So also in Chrysostom, *Homilies on Matthew* 10.4, concerning eschatological fulfillment.

[98] Elsewhere Chrysostom (*De laudibus sancti Pauli* 1.14 [136]) writes that the apostle Paul's "table" was "even more frugal" (εὐτελεστέραν ... τράπεζαν) than the Baptist's. Yet one can only wonder how the more austere example of Paul, who claimed the right to have a wife, which apparently was the practice of other apostles (1 Cor 9:5), would accord with Chrysostom's exhortation to chastity. Greek: Auguste Piédagnel, ed., *Jean Chrysostome, Panégyriques de S. Paul* (SC 300; Paris: Cerf, 1982), 136; ET: Margaret M. Mitchell, *The Heavenly Trumpet: John Chrysostom and the Art of Pauline Interpretation* (HUT 40; Tübingen: Mohr Siebeck, 2000), 447.

[99] 'Allegory' in Ps.-Chrysostom: *In praecursorem Domini* 1 (Greek: *PG* 59.491).

[100] John as an ethical model in Ps.-Chrysostom: *De eleemosyna* 791 (*PG* 60.709); *De ieiunio* 1 (Greek: *PG* 60.712). See also Ps.-Chrysostom, *Ecloga de virtute et vitio* 26, which draws a connection between John's diet and quasi-angelic existence (Greek: *PG* 63.760).

[101] John as 'vegetarian' in Ps.-Chrysostom: *De poenitentia* 1.3 (ἀκρίδας ἐκ βοτανῶν, *PG* 59.762); *In laudem conceptionis S. Ioannis Baptistæ* 1 (ἀκρίδας βοτανῶν, *PG* 50.787); *Ecloga de virtute et vitio* 26 (ἀκρίδας ἐκ βοτανῶν, *PG* 63.762).

[102] Ps.-Chrysostom, *On the Birth of John the Baptist* 6 (Greek and ET: Cornelis Datema, "Another Unedited Homily of Ps. Chrysostom on the Birth of John the Baptist [BHG 847i]," *Byzantion* 53 [1983]: 478–93). Additionally, in Ps.-Chrysostom, *In saltationem Herodiadis* (κρέα αἱ ἀκρίδες, καὶ πλακοῦς τὸ μέλι τὸ ἄγριον, *PG* 59.523), the description of John's wild honey as "cakes" (πλακοῦς) could ultimately be influenced by the *Gospel of the Ebionites*. Conversely, *Gos. Eb.* uses the term ἔγκρις for cake and, of course, does not concede that John ate meat (κρέας).

10. Hesychius of Jerusalem: The Simplicity of Eating Raw Locusts

Like Chrysostom, Hesychius of Jerusalem (d. after 451 C.E.) highlights the simplicity of John's diet:

> When the age had advanced and the time was progressing, there comes a guest of a table that has not a chef, nor a hired cook. His honey was wild and completely unseasoned. The grasshoppers were meat (ὄψα), whose sacrifice was accomplished without a sword (ἀσίδηρος); the sword-less (ἀμάχαιρος) slaughter did not need cauldrons or require coals. There was no need for a sauce from the outside, but it had the sauce which it derived from itself (ἐξ ἑαυτοῦ).[103]

After describing John's clothing and belt, Hesychius continues:

> He had thus perfected the philosophical life by becoming a true ascetic (τὴν φιλοσοφίαν ἀσκηθεὶς ἀσκητὴς ἀληθινὸς ἀπήρτιστο), a runner without defect, a soldier without reproach, a just leader of the bride (νυμφαγωγός), a pious herald, a mediator (μεσίτης) and a precursor (πρόδρομος), "abstaining from each and every evil deed."[104]

In emphasizing the simplicity of John's food—that its preparation required neither cook nor knife, pot nor seasoning—Hesychius seems to draw upon knowledge of those who eat uncooked, or raw, locusts. Such consumption would, of course, differ from the Damascus Document's instructions for frying or boiling the locusts, as well as Diodorus Siculus's (and others') observation that an Ethiopian tribe added salt, thus flavoring and preserving the dried locusts.[105] Such awareness of locust eating in the fifth century is hardly surprising for someone in Jerusalem like Hesychius and goes beyond the interest in John's natural food reflected early in the fourth century by Methodius of Olympus (*De vita* 8.1).

F. Western Witnesses to John's Diet as a Model for Others

Having surveyed a plethora of eastern Christian interpretations of John's diet from Clement of Alexandria through Hesychius of Jerusalem, the discussion

---

[103] Hesychius, *Hom.* 16.3. Greek: Michel Aubineau, ed., *Les homélies festales d'Hésychius de Jérusalem* (Subsidia hagiographica 59; Brussels: Société des bollandistes, 1978–80), 2.682; ET: mine.

[104] *Hom.* 16.3; Gk.: παντὸς οὑτινοσοῦν πονηροῦ πράγματος ἀπεχόμενος. Cf. Job 1:1, 8; 2:3 (LXX): ἀπεχόμενος ἀπὸ παντὸς πονηροῦ πράγματος.

[105] See the discussions of the Damascus Document 12:11b–15a; Diodorus, *Hist.* 3.29; and Strabo, *Geog.* 16.4.12 in chapter 2. Cf. Bentley Layton, "Social Structure and Food Consumption in an Early Christian Monastery: The Evidence of Shenoute's *Canons* and the White Monastery Federation A.D. 385–465," *Le Muséon* 115 (2002): 25–55, on the detailed regulations governing the simple food of certain monks in Egypt.

now turns to the Latin Fathers of the fourth and fifth centuries. This section will illustrate that ethical appropriations of John's wilderness habitation, clothing and food were not limited to eastern Christianity but flourished in the Latin West as well among Ambrose, Chromatius, Augustine and Jerome.

1. Ambrose of Milan and Chromatius of Aquileia

In one of his letters, Ambrose of Milan (*c.* 340–397 C.E.) refers to John as "the teacher of abstinence (*abstinentiae magister*) and, as it were, a new angel on earth."[106] He elsewhere states that John's "locusts and wild honey" exemplify that John practiced fasting in the wilderness.[107] Additionally, in the preface to his *Commentary on Luke*, Ambrose notes that Mark 1:2, 1:3 and 1:6 illustrate how John

> moves us to admiration and wonder; and teaches us that a person ought to make him/herself pleasing to God by humility, abstinence and faith (*humilitate hominem atque abstinentia et fide placere debere*)—as did Saint John the Baptist (*sicut ille sanctus Iohannes Baptista*). For he ascended the steps to immortality by his manner of dress, by his diet, and by his message (*uestimento cibo nuntio*).[108]

Similarly, Chromatius of Aquileia (d. *c.* 407/8 C.E.) hails John's humility in food and clothing:

> First, the heavenly life and glorious humility of John are demonstrated in his way of living. He who held the world in low regard did not seek costly attire. He who had no use for worldly delights did not have any desire for succulent foods (*opulentas escas*). . . . What dainty foods of the earth could he desire who fed on divine discourses and whose true food was the law of Christ? . . . [John] gave himself completely to his heavenly God and had contempt for the things of this world.[109]

---

[106] Ambrose, *Ep.* 39(14).29 [To the church at Vercelli, 396 C.E.]; cf. *Gos. Bart.* 2.15. Lat.: Otto Faller, ed., *[Ambrosii,] Epistulae et acta* (CSEL 82.3; Vienna: Hoelder-Pinchler-Temsky, 1968–96), 251; ET: Mary M. Beyenka, *Saint Ambrose, Letters* (FC 26; Washington: Catholic University of America, ²1967), 331.

[107] Ambrose, *De helia et ieiunio* 3.4 (537B): *denique in deserto et ille uacabat ieiuniis; esca autem eius erat locustae et mel siluestre.* Lat.: Schenkl, *Sancti Ambrosii, Opera*, 414. Cf. Ambrose, *De helia et ieiunio* 11.40 (547D). An ET of this work is available in: Mary Joseph Aloysius Buck, *S. Ambrosii, De helia et ieiunio* (Patristic Studies 19; Washington: Catholic University of America, 1929).

[108] Ambrose, *Expositio Euangelii secundum Lucam* Prol.3; cf. 1.36, 2.69–70. Lat.: M. Adriaen, ed., *Sancti Ambrosii Mediolanensis, Opera* (CCSL 14; Turnholt: Brepols, 1957), 3; ET (modified): Íde M. Ní Riain, *Commentary of Saint Ambrose on the Gospel according to Saint Luke* (Dublin: Halcyon/Elo, 2001), 2.

[109] Chromatius, *Tractatus in Matthaeum* 9.1. Lat.: R. Étaix and Joseph Lemarié, eds., *Chromatii Aquileiensis, Opera* (CCSL 9A; Turnholt: Brepols, 1974), 231; ET: Simonetti, *Matthew*, 40.

These statements of Ambrose and Chromatius concerning John's diet suggest that the more developed sentiments of Augustine and Jerome could stem at least in part from earlier precedents in the Latin West.

2. Augustine: The Potential Temptation of Yearning to Eat Meat

Like Origen and Ambrose before him,[110] Augustine (354–430 C.E.) twice appears to be unaware of locust eating in Jewish tradition and, not coincidentally, purports the distinctiveness of John's food. In his *Confessions* (c. 397–400 C.E.), for example, Augustine seems not to know the prescription for eating certain kinds of locusts in Lev 11:20–23. Instead, he argues in *Conf.* 10.46 that this food did not make the Baptist unclean.[111]

Seeking to suppress his own uncontrolled desire (*concupiscentia*), Augustine naturally looks to scripture for guidance and consolation. One presupposition informing Augustine's interaction with the scriptures is that a passage mentioning food could shed light on his experience of temptation. When it comes to John's diet, Augustine makes three observations in the *Confessions*. First, John's eating locusts points to the virtue of abstinence (*abstinentia*) from other foods. Second, in characterizing the Baptist's abstinence as remarkable (*mirabilis*), Augustine hails John as a model for those like Augustine who struggle with temptations stemming from food.[112]

---

[110] Cf. above on Or., *Luc. Hom.* 11.5; 25.2; *Mat. Cat.* 41; Ambrose, *De helia et ieiunio* 11.40 (547D).

[111] August., *Conf.* 10.46–47: "[46] Good Father, you have taught me 'All things are pure to the pure,' but it is 'evil for the person who eats and is offended.' And 'all your creation is good, and nothing to be rejected which is received with thanksgiving.' And 'meat (*esca*) does not commend us to God.' And 'Let no one judge us in the matter of meat (*in cibo*) or in drink.' And 'one who eats is not to despise one who does not eat, and one who does not eat shall not judge one who does.' I learned this, thanks to you, praise to you, my God, my teacher. Your words strike my ears, and illuminate my heart. Deliver me from all temptation. It is not the impurity of food (*immunditiam obsonii*) I fear, but that of uncontrolled desire (*immunditiam cupiditatis*). I know Noah was allowed to eat every kind of meat (*omne carnis genus*) used for food; that Elijah was restored by eating meat (*cibo carnis refectum*); that John, practicing admirable abstinence, was undefiled by the animals, that is, the locusts granted him for food (*Iohannem mirabili abstinentia praeditum animalibus, hoc est lucustis in escam cedentibus, non fuisse pollutum*); and I know how Esau was deceived by his greed for lentiles, and David rebuked himself for wanting water. And our King was tempted to eat not meat (*non de carne*) but bread. That explains why the people in the wilderness deserved reproof, not because they wanted meat (*carnes*) but because their desire for food (*escae desiderio*) led them to murmur against the Lord. [47] Placed among these temptations, then, I struggle every day against uncontrolled desire (*adversus concupiscentiam*) in eating and drinking." Lat.: James J. O'Donnell, ed., *Augustine, Confessions* (Oxford: Clarendon/Oxford: Oxford University, 1992), 1.137; ET: Henry Chadwick, *Saint Augustine, Confessions* (Oxford: Oxford University, 1991), 206–7.

[112] See the discussion above on Or., *Luc. Hom.* 25.2 (*vita mirabilis*).

A third observation in *Conf.* 10.46 concerns the potential defilement from uncontrolled desire for meat, from which John, who ate so many grasshoppers, could have suffered.[113] Augustine dismisses the problem as soon as he raises it: John who practiced such admirable abstinence was of course not defiled by what he ate. Teresa M. Shaw notes the parallel that the physician Galen makes between the pleasure derived from eating meat and from sex.[114] Such a connection would go a long way toward explaining why Augustine senses the need to dismiss grasshoppers as a possible source of temptation and defilement.

Augustine's apparent lack of familiarity with Lev 11:20–23, predicated by the defense of John in *Conf.* 10.46, underlies another of his writings: "He did not live without food, but 'his food was locusts and wild honey.' When Christ says that John did not eat or drink, He means that he did not use the food which the Jews used (*quo Iudaei utebantur, ille non utebatur*)."[115] In this response to the Manichaean Faustus, Augustine dismisses a literal interpretation of Q/Matt 11:16–19—that John did not eat or drink anything—with recourse to Matt 3:4c. The unnecessary detail in the *Contra Faustum* that John avoided customary foods of first-century Judeans dovetails nicely with the abstinence Augustine ascribes to the Baptist in *Conf.* 10.46: Rather than being a common meal, locusts as meat are deemed to be for John a source of temptation in the wilderness. Since Augustine assumes that the Baptist did not succumb to food-lust, John becomes in the *Confessions*, along with Elijah and David, a model worthy of imitation.

3. Jerome's Witness to Those Who Imitated John and Instructions to Others Who Should

It has already been noted that Augustine was not the only western interpreter to embrace John as a model of asceticism. Augustine's contemporary Jerome (*c.* 347–419/20 C.E.) ascribes such an appropriation of John's life in the wilderness to monks of an earlier generation. Jerome's comments on the Baptist's diet in his work *Against Jovinian* have already been touched upon in chapter 2. John's eating actual locusts exemplifies that each nation eats what

---

[113] Cf. above on Clem., *Paed.* 2.16.1.

[114] Shaw, *The Burden of the Flesh: Fasting and Sexuality in Early Christianity* (Minneapolis: Fortress, 1998), 53–64; cf. Böcher, "Ass Johannes der Täufer," 91.

[115] Augustine, *Contra Faustum Manichaeum* 16.31 (397–398 C.E.). The Encratite Manicheans apparently found significance in John's abstinence from food and drink, and Augustine's opposition to Encratism seems to inform his presentation of John's diet in contrast to that of the Manicheans. The translation in NPNF, I/4.232, albeit not ideal, suffices for the present discussion; Lat.: Joseph Zycha, ed., *Sancti Aureli Augustini, De utilitate credendi; De duabus animabus; Contra Fortunatum; Contra Adimantum; Contra epistulam fundamenti; Contra Faustum* (CSEL 25/1; Vienna: Tempsky, 1891), 478.

it has in abundance, even insects.[116] Later in this same work, Jerome intimates that John's diet and life in the wilderness had become a model for the
early 'Desert Fathers': *Præcursor ejus et præco Joannes locustis alitur, et
silvestris melle, non carnibus: habitatioque deserti et incunabula
monachorum, talibus inchoantur alimentis.*[117] Jerome may have received this
information directly from such monks in the wilderness, with whom he had
spent some time (375–377 C.E.) prior to his ordination to the priesthood.[118]
Perhaps Jerome himself dined on grasshoppers with them.

Even if some monks of Jerome's day did not still eat the same things that
the Baptist ate (so *Adv. Iovin.* 2.15), Jerome does not miss an opportunity in
his letters to offer the *type* of food John ate as a model for other believers. As
is well known, Jerome advocates asceticism with regard to food, even
referring in one of his letters to such arguments in response to the anti-ascetic
arguments of the monk Jovinian.[119] Given this general predilection toward

---

[116] Jerome, *Adv. Iovin.* 2.7: "Again, because throughout the glowing wastes of the desert
clouds of locusts are found, it is customary with the peoples of the East and of Libya to feed
on locusts. John the Baptist proves the truth of this (*hoc verum esse Joannes quoque Baptista
probat*). Compel a Phrygian or a native of Pontus to eat a locust, and he will think it scandal-
ous." Lat.: *PL* 23.308; ET: NPNF, II/6.393.

[117] *Adv. Iovin.* 2.15: "His [Jesus'] forerunner and herald, John, fed on locusts and wild
honey, not on flesh—both the habitation of the desert and the initial residence of monks began with such foods." Lat.: *PL* 23.308; ET (modified): NPNF, II/6.400; cf. the discussion of
this passage in chapter 2. U. Luz, *Matthew*, 1.168, may not be aware of the potential significance of Jerome's testimony when he writes (on Matt 3:4) that "monasticism in its food and
clothing was not influenced by John and . . . monasticism did not base poverty and celibacy
on John. . . ."

[118] Quaesten, 4.214. Cf. Jerome, *Life of Paul, the First Hermit* 1; Ephrem, *On Hermits
and Desert Dwellers* 37–52; translations are available in: Vincent L. Wimbush, ed., *Ascetic
Behavior in Greco-Roman Antiquity* (Studies in Antiquity and Christianity; Minneapolis:
Fortress, 1990), 359–60 (Jerome) and 69 (Ephrem). See further: Vööbus, *History of Asceticism in the Syrian Orient: A Contribution to the History of Culture in the Near East* (CSCO
184, 197, 500; Louvain: Secrétariat du Corpus SCO, 1958–88), 1.147, 2.262–4; Maria
Roumbalou, "Hermits: Eastern Christian," art. *Encyclopedia of Monasticism*, 1.579–83; here,
580; Mary Lee Nolan, "Pilgrimages, Christian: Western Europe," art. *Encyclopedia of Monasticism*, 2.1024–8; here, 1025; Lupieri, "John the Baptist: The First Monk," esp. 14–21;
here, 16: "The choice of John the Baptist was a very logical one: [I]n the New Testament he
is the only figure who can be considered a model for ascetic life. As a chaste, fasting, total
abstainer who dressed in camel-hair clothing, he—even more than Jesus!—offered a positive
example to people who wanted to follow an ascetic way of life."

[119] E.g., *Ep.* 58.6.1–2 (To Paulinus): "Let your food be coarse—say cabbage and
pulse—and do not take it until evening. Sometimes as a great delicacy you may have some
small fish. He who longs for Christ and feeds upon the true bread cares little for dainties,
which must be transmuted into ordure. Food that you cannot taste when once it has passed
your gullet might as well be—so far as you are concerned—bread and pulse. You have my
books against Jovinian, which speak yet more largely of despising the appetite and the palate
(*de contemptu ventris et gutturis*). Let some holy volume be ever in your hand. Pray

food, it comes as no surprise that Jerome lifts up John's diet as a confirmation of the Baptist's Nazarite identity (*Ep*. 107.3), pursuit of virtue (*Epp*. 125.7; 121.1), and a compulsory model for grieving widows (*Ep*. 38.3).

First, in offering Laeta advice on how to bring up her daughter Paula, Jerome makes a comparison between Samson and John:

> The first as a Nazarite wore his hair long, drank neither wine nor strong drink, and even in his childhood talked with God. The second shunned cities, wore a leather girdle, and ate locusts and wild honey (*lucustis alitur et melle silvestri*). Moreover, to typify that penitence which he was to preach, he was clothed in the spoils of the hump-backed camel. (*Ep*.107.3.3, To Laeta)

In another letter Jerome offers that John's diet was for the purpose of his own "virtue and continence."[120] Elsewhere Jerome remarks similarly:

> *nulli posse adulationi succumbere; et qui locustis vescitur ac melle silvestri, nec opes neque alias terrenas delicias quærere, rigidamque et austeram vitam, aulas vitare palatii, quas quærunt qui purpura et bysso et serico et mollibus vestiuntur.*
> [John] cannot succumb to flattery; and he who eats locusts and wild honey cannot seek wealth or other worldly delights, but rather a strict and harsh life, to shun the courts of the Palatine, which those who are clothed in purple and linen and silk and soft things seek.[121]

In addition to benefiting the Baptist's own moral development, such a challenging lifestyle offers a model to widows, who should find comfort in the difficulties the Baptist experienced:

> A widow who is "freed from the marital bond" has, for her one duty, to continue as a widow. But, you will reply that a somber dress scandalizes the world. In that case, John the Baptist would scandalize it, too; and yet, among those that are born of women, there has not been [one] greater than he. He was called an angel (*angelus*); he baptized the Lord Himself, and yet he was clothed in raiment of camel's hair, and girded with a leather girdle. Is [the world] displeased because a widow's food is coarse (*viliores*)? Nothing can be coarser than locusts (*nihil vilius locustis*). (*Ep*. 38.3 [To Marcella])

---

constantly, and bowing down your body lift up your mind to the Lord. Keep frequent vigils and sleep often on an empty stomach." Unless otherwise noted, the Latin text and ET cited for Jerome's letters are: Isidor Hilberg, ed., *Sancti Eusebii Hieronymi, Epistulae* (CSEL 54–56; Vienna: Verlag der Österreichischen Akademie der Wissenschaften, ²1996 [1910–18]); ET (modified): NPNF, II/6. Cf. Jerome, *Life of S. Hilarion* 3–4, 11 (here, 4): "His [Hilarion's] food was only fifteen dried figs after sunset."

[120] *Ep*. 125.7.2 (To Rustics): "John the Baptist had a religious mother and was the son of a priest. Yet neither his mother's affection nor his father's wealth could induce him to live in his parents' house at the risk of his chastity. He lived in the desert, and seeking Christ with his eyes refused to look at anything else. His rough garb, his girdle made of skins [and] his diet of locusts and wild honey (*cibus locustae melque silvestre*) were all designed to encourage virtue and continence (*virtuti et continentiae praeparata*)." Cf. *Ep*. 22.36.1–3.

[121] Jer., *Ep*. 121.1.6 (To Algasia). For whatever reason, an ET of this letter has yet to be published; this ET is my own. Note how the verbs *vescitur . . . vestiuntur* emphasize Jerome's contrast between John the Baptist's way of life and that of the wealthy at Rome.

In the same letter Jerome defends the asceticism of a certain woman, Blesilla, with reference to the Baptist's locusts.[122] Albeit only with reference to John's clothing (and not his food as well), Jerome offers in another letter an analogous exhortation to Demetrias, a Christian woman who had committed herself to celibacy.[123] John's ascetic lifestyle thus commends an example not simply to the willing, as according to *Adv. Iovin.* 2.15 it had been to certain monks. In Jerome's estimation it offers an imperative even to the widow, who has no right to complain about the strict lifestyle to which she is called by her husband's departure.

G. 'Vegetarian' Interpretations of John's 'Locusts'

Earlier parts of this chapter examined the removal of John's 'locusts' from his diet in the *Gospel of the Ebionites* (honey tasting like cakes) and several witnesses to Tatian's *Diatessaron* (milk and honey). Numerous other interpreters retain ἀκρίδες in Mark 1:6c‖Matt 3:4c but (re)define this term as vegetation. Perhaps not coincidentally, the first explicit argument for this interpretation comes from Athanasius of Alexandria, whose thirty-ninth Paschal letter (367 C.E.) is the earliest writing to acknowledge a closed NT canon comprising twenty-seven writings.[124] As both the text and the canon of the NT were becoming more fixed, the proclivity to alter that text became appreciably less. Rather than changing the text of scripture, it becomes necessary to (re)interpret it.

---

[122] *Ep.* 38.3 [To Marcella]; cf. Barbara Conring, *Hieronymus als Briefschreiber: Ein Beitrag zur spätantiken Epistolographie* (Studien und Texte zu Antike und Christentum 8; Tübingen: Mohr Siebeck, 2001), 146; Shaw, *Burden of the Flesh*, 106–7.

[123] *Ep.* 130.4.1–2 (To Demetrias): "I should rather have commended our virgin for having rejected all these, and for having determined to regard herself not as a wealthy or a high born lady, but simply as a woman like other women. Her strength of mind almost passes belief. Though she had silks and jewels freely at her disposal, and though she was surrounded by crowds of eunuchs and serving-women, a bustling household of flattering and attentive domestics, and though the daintiest feasts that the abundance of a large house could supply were daily set before her; she preferred to all these severe fasting, rough clothing, and frugal living. For she had read the words of the Lord: 'they that wear soft clothing are in kings' houses.' She was filled with admiration for the manner of life followed by Elijah and by John the Baptist; both of them confined and mortified their loins with girdles of skin, while the second of them is said to have come in the spirit and power of Elijah as the forerunner of the Lord." See further: Barbara Feichtinger, *Apostolae apostolorum: Frauenaskese als Befreiung und Zwang bei Hieronymus* (Studien zur klassischen Philologie 94; Frankfurt am Main: Lang, 1995), 222–5.

[124] See further: Brakke, "Canon Formation and Social Conflict in Fourth-Century Egypt: Athanasius of Alexandria's Thirty-Ninth *Festal Letter*," *HTR* 87 (1994): 395–419.

1. Athanasius of Alexandria: A Prooftext for (Re)interpreting ΑΚΡΙΣ

A fragment of Athanasius of Alexandria's (*c*. 295–373 C.E.) commentary on Matthew offers the earliest surviving argument that John's 'locusts' were vegetable rather than meat. Athanasius finds a justification for this interpretation of ἀκρίς in Ecclesiastes. What follows is all that survives of Athanasius's remarks on Matt 3:4c:

> "His food was locusts and wild honey." Solomon teaches us that some kind of plant is translated as "locust" (Ὅτι δὲ καὶ ἡ βοτάνη τίς ἐστιν ἀκρὶς λεγομένη): "The almond tree will blossom, and the locust will become thick" (ἀνθήσει τὸ ἀμύγδαλον καὶ παχυνθήσεται ἡ ἀκρίς, Eccl 12:5b). Yet the wild honey was not some kind of herb (πόα τίς), but the honey was truly wild, extremely bitter and hostile in all its taste (πικρότατον ὄν καὶ πάσῃ γεύσῃ πολέμιον).[125]

For Athanasius, the Baptist's eating honey *and vegetation* rests on the precedent in Ecclesiastes.

Since the witness of Athanasius is fragmentary,[126] one cannot exclude the possibility that Athanasius viewed John's meatless diet as a model for others. Such is clearly the interpretation of Isidore of Pelusium, whose discussion of the Baptist's diet appears immediately below. Isidore's description of John's honey builds upon some earlier source, possibly Athanasius himself. With regard to the bitterness of John's honey, Brock suggests plausibly that, like meat from locusts/grasshoppers, "the wild honey also sounded suspiciously like a delicacy," with the corresponding emphasis "on its bitter character."[127] As noted in chapter 3, Philo of Alexandria offers a precedent for such a concern.[128]

One should also be cautious concerning a possible exegetical origin for this 'vegetarian' interpretation of the Baptist's diet on the basis of Athanasius's partially preserved statement. Given the need for a prooftext, Athanasius seems to correct the notion that John ate actual locusts/grasshoppers. Taking out of context a small part of Ecclesiastes mentioning a tree and a 'locust,'[129] Athanasius maintains that the 'locust,' like

---

[125] Athanasius, *Fragmenta in Matthæum* 8A [on Matt 3:4]. Greek: *PG* 27.1365D; ET: mine.

[126] The preceding fragment from Athanasius's commentary concerns Matt 2:20a (*Fragmenta in Matthæum* 7), and what follows interprets Matt 3:11d (*Fragmenta in Matthæum* 8B).

[127] "Syriac Sources," 118.

[128] Philo, *Spec.* 1.291–292, concerning bee honey: "[God] forbids it as a symbol of the utter unholiness of excessive pleasure which tastes sweet as it passes through the throat but afterwards produces bitter and persistent pains, which of necessity shake and agitate the soul and make it unable to stand firmly in its place."

[129] Athanasius's recognition of synonymous parallelism in Eccl 12:5 is indeed correct: "When one is afraid of heights, and terrors are in the road; the almond tree blossoms, the grasshopper becomes fat (LXX: ἀνθήσῃ τὸ ἀμύγδαλον καὶ παχυνθῇ ἡ ἀκρίς) and

the almond tree, is some kind of (or part of a) plant: Just as the tree blossoms (ἀνθέω), the 'locust' grows thick (παχύνω).[130] The inference could perhaps be logical for an author reading this verse of Ecclesiastes in Greek without the myriad of references to ἀκρίς as an insect in the LXX. No later interpreter of John's 'locusts' as vegetation would try to support this position with recourse to Athanasius's appeal to Eccl 12:5b, however.

2. Isidore of Pelusium: Imitating the 'Vegetarian' John

Possibly following Athanasius, Isidore of Pelusium (c. 360–c. 435 C.E.) construes the Baptist's 'locusts' as vegetable rather than meat. Like many other interpreters, moreover, Isidore affirms that John's 'vegetarian' diet offers an ethical model:

> What are the locusts (αἱ ἀκρίδες), and [what is] the wild honey on which the Baptist fed? The locusts on which John fed are not creatures (ζῷα) like dung-beetles, as some ignorantly (ἀμαθῶς) suppose. Certainly not (μὴ γένοιτο)! Rather, they are twigs of herbs or plants (ἀκρέμονες[131] βοτανῶν ἢ φυτῶν). Nor, again, is the wild honey some kind of grass (πόα τίς). Rather, it is honey of the mountains (μέλι ὄρειον) produced by wild bees. It is extremely bitter and hostile in all its taste (πικρότατον ὂν καὶ πάσῃ γεύσῃ πολέμιον).[132] Through these things John demonstrated exceeding suffering, not in poverty only, but also in ruggedness, by embittering every yearning of the body.[133]

This chapter has called attention to Jerome's observation that monks had previously imitated John's diet of "locusts and wild honey" and habitation in the wilderness (Jer., *Adv. Iovin.* 2.15). Isidore's short letter to Nilus "concerning the food of the Forerunner and concerning asceticism"[134] reflects a similar conviction concerning the "twigs" (ἀκρέμονες) that the Baptist ate:

---

desire fails; because all must go to their eternal home, and the mourners will go about the streets." Brock also calls attention to the recognition of parallelism in this "exceedingly obscure verse" in Ecclesiastes ("Syriac Sources," 114 n.6).

[130] Recognizing ἀκρίς as a locust/grasshopper Eccl 12:5b (LXX) would support the more straightforward translation of παχυνθήσεται ἡ ἀκρίς as "the locust will grow fat," i.e., from consuming the leaves and produce of the blossoming almond tree.

[131] Note the similarity in spelling of ἀκρίδες to ἀκρέμονες. The happenstance similarity between the beginnings of these two words accounts for the creative (and speculative) lexicography attested to (developed?) by Isidore.

[132] Note the identical verbal correspondence between Athanasius and Isidore concerning the Baptist's honey: πόα τίς . . . πικρότατον ὂν καὶ πάσῃ γεύσῃ πολέμιον. It is thus possible that Isidore is indebted to an earlier source (Athanasius?) for other parts of his remarks on the Baptist's diet as well.

[133] Isidore, *Ep.* 1.132. Greek: *PG* 78.269C; ET: mine. Cf. Eisler, "Baptist's Food and Clothing," 614.

[134] Isidore, *Ep.* 5 [To Nilus]; Gk: Περὶ τῆς τροφῆς τοῦ Προδρόμου, καὶ περὶ ἀσκήσεως. Greek text: *PG* 78.181B–184A; translations of this letter are my own. This Nilus is probably to be identified as Nilus Ancyranus (d. c. 430 C.E.); cf. Nilus, *Ep.* 3.153 (Greek: *PG* 79.457A).

> Since the divine oracles reveal with precision, the careful search is extraordinary for those who read them with understanding. Therefore, if we are trained (ἐπαιδεύθημεν) by John the Baptist concerning the food and clothing in the perfect asceticism toward God, we will be content (ἀρκεσθησόμεθα) with hair—or anything else—for a covering, and with twigs of herbs and plants (ἀκρέμοσι βοτανῶν καὶ φύλλων)[135] for a little food and power and simplicity. Since these greater things (ταῦτα ... μείζονα) came to pass on account of [human] weakness (δι' ἀσθένειαν), let them be an example to us (τύπος ἡμῖν ἔστω)[136] of all poverty, of a way of living, of perfection, and of the Lord's[137] scrutiny and calling.

Accordingly, even though Jerome and Isidore differ on whether John ate actual locusts/grasshoppers, they agree that John's diet, however construed, offers a model for others to follow. For Isidore, John's meatless diet thus becomes part of the *paideia*, or training, for would-be ascetics.

Isidore's call to follow John's example was heard by at least one monk in the Byzantine period, and quite possibly by others as well. A ninth-century inscription on the wall of a cave near Miletus demonstrates that John's 'vegetarian' diet as related by Isidore did in fact become a model for ascetic devotion. An anchorite monk recorded Isidore's words about John's diet on the wall of the cave in which he lived, thus suggesting that the monk imitated the food of the 'vegetarian' John.[138]

3. The Baptist's 'Vegetarian' Diet in Syriac Christianity

The present study need not repeat Brock's erudite article on John's 'locusts' in Syriac Christian literature, where 'vegetarian' depictions of the Baptist's diet abounded and were in the majority.[139] It will suffice to note certain representative witnesses.

The earliest such depiction in Syriac Christianity Brock cites is a homily of Jacob of Serugh (Yaʾkub al-Saruji; c. 451–521 C.E.): John "lived off herbs and plants and flowers (ܡܢ ܥܣܒܐ ܘܡܢ ܙܪ̈ܥܘܢܐ ܘܡܢ ܗܒ̈ܒܐ) in the desert of Judah, just like the wild animals."[140] Brock highlights the complementary influences of 2 Macc 5:27 (discussed in chapter 4), as well as the

---

[135] Isidore's expression in *Ep.* 5 (ἀκρέμοσι βοτανῶν καὶ φύλλων) is quite similar to that in *Ep.* 1.132 (ἀκρέμονες βοτανῶν ἢ φυτῶν).

[136] Or: ". . . on account of [*John's*] weakness, let *him* be an example to us. . . ." The subject of ἔστω could be either John or ταῦτα ... μείζονα.

[137] Lit. "the Leader's"; Gk.: τοῦ προεστῶτος. It is not clear if Isidore refers to John or Jesus.

[138] See Grégoire's aforementioned article, "Les Sauterelles de Saint Jean-Baptiste."

[139] "Syriac Sources," 116–22. Exceptions to this tendency in Syriac Christian literature include Ĭšoʿdāḏ of Merv (discussed above) and Aphrahat "the Persian Sage" (*fl.* 337–345 C.E.). The latter writes: "Birds nourished Elijah, whereas John ate flying locusts" (Aphrahat, *Demonstration* 6.13; ET: Kuriakose A. Valavanolickal, *Aphrahat, Demonstrations I* [Changanassery, India: HIRS Publications, 1999–], 1.124.

[140] Cited in Brock, "Syriac Sources," 117.

flight of Jesus' family (to Egypt; cf. Matt 2:13–18) and the presumed corresponding flight of John's family to the wilderness (cf. *Prot. Jas.* 22:3; 23:1–24:4), on Jacob of Serugh and other Syriac authors.[141]

Brock's latter inference is indeed plausible, since such a flight to the wilderness is in fact narrated in the earlier (late-fourth c. C.E.) *Life of John the Baptist*, written in Karshuni (= Arabic in Syriac script).[142] John and his mother escape from Herod to the wilderness, but John's father Zacharias remains behind and is murdered in the Temple by Herod's men.[143] At one point this writing seems to suggest that out of concern for purity John ate actual locusts/grasshoppers: "As to the blessed John he wandered in the desert with his mother, and God prepared for him locusts and wild honey as food, in accordance with what his mother was told about him not to let any unclean food enter his mouth."[144] Later, however, this *Life of John* highlights the Baptist's 'vegetarianism' and asceticism: "And John dwelt in the desert, and God and His angels were with him. He lived in great asceticism and devotion. His only food was grass and wild honey. He prayed constantly, fasted much and was in expectation of the salvation of Israel" (ET: 245). The Karshuni *Life of John* also makes an explicit connection between how Elizabeth clothed John and monks who would later dress like John.[145]

What remains unclear to the present author is whether the notion of John as an eater of vegetation and honey originated in Greek or Syriac Christian circles, or elsewhere. Mingana infers plausibly concerning the *Life of John* that this "author seems to identify the 'locusts' used in the gospel in connection with the food of John, with a kind of grass."[146] Such an identification of "locusts" with vegetation roughly contemporary with Athanasius of Alexandria (d. 373 C.E.) suggests the possibility that the understanding of John's diet as comprising honey and vegetation predated both Athanasius and this

---

[141] "Syriac Sources," 117.

[142] Alphonse Mingana, "A New Life of John the Baptist," in: *Woodbrooke Studies: Christian Documents in Syriac, Arabic, and Garshuni* (ed. J. Rendel Harris; Cambridge: W. Heffer & Sons, 1927), 1.234–87. Mingana (p. 234) dates this writing to *c.* 385–395 C.E. See further: Hugh J. Schonfield, *The Lost "Book of the Nativity of John"* (Edinburgh: T. & T. Clark, 1929), 14–36; Klauck, *Apocryphal Gospels*, 81.

[143] ET: Mingana, "Life of John," 239–42.

[144] ET: Mingana, "Life of John," 242. This *Life of John* does not, however, specify what Elizabeth ate in the wilderness while watching over John. See, however, *Prot. Jas.* 8:1, on Jesus' mother Mary; cf. F.-A. von Metzsch, *Johannes der Täufer: Seine Geschichte und seine Darstellung in der Kunst*, 102, fig. 93.

[145] "And Elizabeth added: 'I went and put on my son a raiment of camel's hair and a leathern girdle in order that the mountain of the holy wilderness may (in future) be inhabited, and in order that monasteries and congregations of monks may increase in it and that sacrifice may be offered in it in the name of the Lord Jesus Christ'" (ET: Mingana, "Life of John," 241).

[146] Mingana, "Life of John," 245 n.4.

anonymous *Life of John* in the late-fourth century. Indeed, this chapter has suggested this as a plausible interpretation of Clement of Alexandria (*Paed.* 2.16.1) in the early-third century. It is thus possible that Pantaleon (*Orationes* 1), a deacon in Constantinople (8ᵗʰ/9ᵗʰ c. C.E.?), was influenced by Syriac, rather than Greek, precedents for his description of John as "the one who from infancy (ἐκ βρέφους) fed himself in the wilderness with the produce of bees and the tips of plants (τοῖς τῶν βοτανῶν . . . ἀκρίσμασι)."[147]

One distinctive aspect of certain Syriac interpretations is the notion that John ate "roots" rather than plants, since the term ܩ̈ܠܐ can be translated as either "roots" or "plants."[148] The *Life of Peter the Iberian* (5ᵗʰ c. C.E.) offers an example of this ambiguity, placing into the mouth of John the Baptist the following explanation of his 'locusts': "They were the tops of wild plants/roots (ܕܒܪܐ ܩ̈ܠܐ ܪ̈ܝܫܝ)."[149] The use of direct speech in this account represents a form-critical novelty, different from the descriptions of John's eating (Mark 1:6c) or food (Matt 3:4c) in the Synoptics, as well as patristic interpretations prior to the *Life of Peter the Iberian*.

4. The Possible Syriac Roots of "Roots" in Slavonic Josephus

The distinctive characterization of John as eating "roots" rather than plants in Syriac Christianity is attested also in the Slavonic additions to Josephus (*c.* 11ᵗʰ c. C.E.). These secondary Christian interpolations into Josephus's *Jewish War* include John's description in the first person of his own food. When John was (supposedly) brought before Archelaus (Ethnarch of Judea 4 B.C.E.–6 C.E.), he explains to Archelaus: "Pure am I, for God's spirit has entered into me, and I nourish my body on reeds and roots and wood-shavings."[150]

---

[147] Greek: *PG* 98.1245C; ET: mine.

[148] Brock, "Syriac Sources," 120, in reference to Išoʿdād of Merv: "The introduction of 'roots' into the discussion will be a purely inner Syriac development, due to the ambiguity of ܩ̈ܠܐ, which can mean either 'plant' or 'root': it is in fact the word used to translate χορτώδης in II Mac. v 27." Išoʿdād's remarks on Matt 3:4c are discussed in this chapter's earlier section on the *Diatessaron*.

[149] In the *Vita Petri Iberi*, Abba Isaiah has a vision of the Baptist and receives this explanation directly from him. Syriac: Richard Raabe, ed., *Petrus der Iberer: Ein Charakterbild zur Kirchen und Sittengeschichte des fünften Jahrhunderts. Syrische Übersetzung einer um das Jahr 500 verfassten griechischen Biographie* (Leipzig: Hinrichs, 1895), 126; ET: Brock, "Syriac Sources," 120.

[150] ET of the Slavonic: F. J. Foakes Jackson and Kirsopp Lake, *The Beginnings of Christianity* (London: Macmillan, 1920), 1.434. An ET also appears in: Thackeray, *Josephus* (LCL), 3.645. According to Thackeray, *Josephus*, 3.644, this secondary insertion occurs in-between Jos., *B.J.* 2.7.2 (§110) and 2.7.3 (§111). On the authenticity of this material, see Solomon Zeitlin, "The Hoax of the 'Slavonic Josephus,'" *JQR* 39 (1948): 171–80; Webb, *John the Baptizer*, 43–4; Jackson and Lake, *Beginnings*, 1.101. Concerning the date of Slavonic Josephus, see H. Leeming and K. Leeming, eds., *Josephus' Jewish War and Its Sla-*

Similar to Chrysostom's argument (*De virginitate* 79.1–2) that John's diet demonstrates the power of celibacy, the Slavonic material likewise assumes the extraordinary nature of John's diet and uses it to demonstrate a different point, namely John's purity. It is possible, moreover, that an understanding of John as an eater of "wild herbs" in certain Muslim circles stems ultimately from Syriac Christianity.[151]

5. Disparate Interpretations in Theophylactus of Ochrida's Commentaries on Matthew and Mark

Theophylactus of Ochrida (*c.* 1050–1107/08 or 1125/26 C.E.) offers remarkably different discussions of John's diet in his commentaries on Matthew and Mark. In the former work he characterizes John as a plant-eating 'vegetarian,' but in the latter he offers a figurative interpretation based on John's consuming actual locusts/grasshoppers.

Following a citation of Matt 3:4c, Theophylactus writes:

> Some say that the 'locusts' are plants, which they also call *Melagra* (βοτάνας εἶναι τὰς ἀκρίδας, ἃς καὶ μέλαγρα καλοῦσι). Others [say that they] are surely growths of wild fruit (τὰ ἀκρόδρυα ἤτοι ὀπώρας ἀγρίας). [The] wild honey is that which is produced by wild bees and found in trees and rocks.[152]

Theophylactus offers the earliest explicit witness to disagreement concerning John's 'locusts.' The first option seems to infer synthetic parallelism between the two parts of John's diet (ἀκρίδες and μέλι ἄγριον). Consequently, a crasis of μέλι and ἄγριον becomes a technical designation for John's 'locusts' (= μέλαγρα). Notably, the disagreement concerns two 'vegetarian' options. Theophylactus does not even entertain whether John ate actual locusts/grasshoppers, an option that Theophylactus's contemporary, Euthymius Zigabenus (discussed immediately below), explicitly sets aside.

In contrast to his *Commentary on Matthew*, in his *Commentary on Mark* Theophylactus seems to presume that John's 'locusts' were flying creatures. In his remarks on Mark 1:6c, Theophylactus initially affirms what he wrote

---

vonic Version: A Synoptic Comparison (Arbeiten zur Geschichte des antiken Judentums und des Urchristentums 46; Leiden: Brill, 2003), 60–73.

[151] See John C. L. Gibson, "John the Baptist in Muslim Writings," *Muslim World* (Hartford, CT) 45 (1955): 334–45; here, 339 n.33. Gibson refers to logion §182 in: Miguel Asín Palacios, ed., *Logia et agrapha Domini Jesu: apud Moslemicos scriptores, Asceticos praesertim, Usitata* (PO 19/4; Paris: Firmin-Didot, 1916–29 [= Turnhout: Brepols, 1974]), 578. Palacios's Latin translation of the Arabic for logion §182 renders John's "food" (*cibus*) as "wild herbs" (*herbae silvestres*). Cf. Gibson, "Muslim Writings," 338, on an ascetic interpretation of John's hairy clothing (Mark 1:6a‖Matt 3:4a) extant in Muslim circles; W. M. Thackston, Jr., ed., *The Tales of the Prophets of al-Kisaʾi* (Library of Classical Arabic Literature 2; Boston: Twayne, 1978), 67, describing John as "a hermit."

[152] Theophylactus of Ochrida, *Enarratio en Evangelium Matthæi* 16. Greek text: *PG* 123.173B–C; ET: mine. Cf. Bochart, *Hierozoicon*, 3.327.

concerning the parallel passage in Matthew and states that John's diet offers an exception to the claim of Q/Matt 11:18 ("John came neither eating nor drinking. . . ."). He further states that "John's food obviously and clearly shows self-control."[153] These last two remarks are absent in Theophylactus's commentary on Matt 3:4c. More cautiously, Theophylactus acknowledges what Cyril of Alexandria had affirmed without reservation: "Yet perhaps (Τάχα δὲ) it was a symbol of the esteemed food of the people then. He did not eat any of the clean birds of the sky[154] or apprehend anything exalted." Moreover, Theophylactus's description of locusts that "leap" and comparison of John's honey with that produced by the OT prophets builds upon material like that in Origen's figurative interpretation (*Mat. Cat.* 41).

Accordingly, in connection with Matt 3:4c Theophylactus mentions two 'vegetarian' interpretations of John's 'locusts,' but his commentary on Mark 1:6c incorporates an earlier figurative interpretation that assumes actual locusts/grasshoppers. More than anything, Theophylactus's contradictory remarks on Mark 1:6c‖Matt 3:4c illustrate that the art of writing a Byzantine biblical commentary (ἑρμηνεία) involved a dynamic interaction with earlier interpretations, even without adjudicating between (or perhaps realizing the) disparate points of view.[155]

6. *Euthymius Zigabenus: A Debate Decided in Favor of a 'Vegetarian' Interpretation of John's 'Locusts'*

Like Theophylactus of Ochrida, the Byzantine monk Euthymius Zigabenus (Zigadenus; d. after 1118 C.E.) acknowledges a debate about John's 'locusts.' Regardless of which option one embraces, it does not seem to affect Euthymius's initial affirmation of John as a model of simplicity:

> [Matthew] calls to mind his robe and his food, showing their plainness and commonness, and teaching [us] to think little about the body and to condemn extravagance (καταφρονεῖν δὲ τῆς πολυτελείας). . . . Some say that the "locusts" are shoots of plants (ἀκρέμονας . . . βοτανῶν); some that the "locust" is called a plant (βοτάνην ἀκρίδα καλουμένην); and others that it is an animal (ἄλλοι δὲ τὸ ζῷον αὐτό). For

---

[153] Gk.: πάντως μὲν καὶ τὴν ἐγκράτειαν αὐτόθεν δηλοῖ. Theophylactus, *Enarratio en Evangelium Marci* 175. Greek: *PG* 123.496C–497A; ET: mine.

[154] This option corresponds exactly to a catena attributed to Cyril of Alexandria (discussed above). Theophylactus offers no acknowledgement for his interaction with earlier interpretations. The discussion above noted the indebtedness of this catena to Origen's partially preserved *Commentary on Matthew* (Or., *Mat. Cat.* 41). Theophylactus's ultimate source for this material may thus be Origen. By implication, Theophylactus could thus be of use in reconstructing Origen's *Commentary on Matthew*. This possibility merits investigation.

[155] Cf. Kelhoffer, "The Witness of Eusebius' *ad Marinum* and Other Christian Writings to Text-Critical Debates concerning the Original Conclusion to Mark's Gospel," *ZNW* 92 (2001): 78–112; here, 106–7.

[the latter] say that even today in those regions many people eat it salted.[156] For with the [other] clean animals this too the lawgiver [Moses] prescribes. [They also say] that it has a foul odor and a taste like fish (ἔχειν δὲ δυσώδη καὶ νηρὰν γεῦσιν). The best option is the first (Κρεῖττον δὲ τὸ πρῶτον). And the wild honey, which is cultivated by the wild bees in the clefts of the rocks, is bitter and disgusting (πικρὸν καὶ ἀηδὲς ὄν).[157]

Without argument Euthymius opts for the first of the two 'vegetarian' options. Victor Hehn and especially Friedrich Cramer have attempted to ascertain the species of plants identified as John's food.[158] Like earlier authors who advocate a 'vegetarian' John (Athanasius; Isidore; Theophylactus?), Euthymius emphasizes the bitterness of John's honey.

The lack of polemic suggests that for Euthymius sincere people can disagree on whether John's 'locusts' were animal or vegetable. He maintains his own position despite the observations (arguments?) of others that inhabitants of the regions where the Baptist lived still eat locusts and that the law of Moses permits them as food (Lev 11:20–23). The idea that John would eat something distasteful to "us" apparently commends to Euthymius the dismissing of actual grasshoppers from the Baptist's cuisine. Such an aversion to locust eating did not, however, dissuade some from affirming that John ate actual locusts/grasshoppers. In fact, the negative qualities given to John's locusts/grasshoppers may have been an extension of the tendency to impute bitterness to his honey: Even if John ate meat regularly, it was neither luxurious nor palatable.

Excursus: From Elijah's Angelic Visitor to John's Eucharistic Provision: The Vision of Mechtild of Magdeburg

Scripture records that an angel fed the prophet Elijah in the desert (1 Kgs 19:4–8). This chapter has discussed earlier Christian interpretations highlighting the parallelism between the wilderness habitation and provisions of Elijah and John.[159] Caroline Walker Bynum notes that Mechtild of Magdeburg (*c.* 1207–1282/94 C.E.) "received a vision in which John the

---

[156] Greek: αὐτό τεταριχευμένον, denoting food preserved, e.g., by salt.

[157] Euthymius, *Comm. in Matthæum* 3. Greek: *PG* 129.160A–B; ET: mine. Cf. Bochart, *Hierozoicon*, 3.327.

[158] Hehn, *Cultivated Plants*, 340–2 [in the German original, "Der Johannisbrotbaum," 456–60], on the carob-tree (*Ceratonia siliqua*); Cramer, *Der heilige Johannes im Spiegel der französischen Pflanzen- und Tierbezeichnungen* (identifying St. John's bread with the carob [κεράτιον] in the Middle Ages). Cf. Theophrastus (372/1 or 371/70–288/7 or 287/6 B.C.E.), *Enquiry into Plants* 1.11.2, concerning the various edible portions of plants and trees, including the carob-tree (κερωνία); Greek text and ET: LCL 1.78–9.

[159] See the discussions above of Aphrahat the Persian, Cyril of Alexandria, Gregory Nazianzen, Gregory of Nyssa, Chrysostom and Augustine.

Baptist celebrated mass for her."[160] Although a direct connection with John's diet cannot indisputably be inferred, the notion of John as miraculous provider by virtue of the extraordinary sustenance that he (and Elijah) had received in the wilderness is probable. One might say that Saint John the Baptist actually becomes a providing "angel" to Mechtild in her vision (cf. ἄγγελος, Mark 1:2 par.) and brings Jesus the Lamb of God to her in the Eucharist (cf. John 1:29, 36).

Mechtild's vision receives attention in this part of the chapter because of her chronological proximity to other medieval/Byzantine witnesses. Her inclusion here does not suggest that Mechtild reflects a 'vegetarian' understanding of the Baptist. On the contrary, since the Baptist brings to her Christ's body and blood, the opposite inference is more plausible. This raises the question of a possible negative correlation between vegetarianism and a Eucharistic theology of the "real presence." Does one preclude the other? Such could make for an interesting study.

7. Meletios Pigas: The Wilderness Habitation and 'Vegetarian' Diet of Silvestros, a Sixteenth-Century Patriarch of Alexandria

The correspondence of Theodore Beza (1519–1605 c.e.), after whom Codex Bezae (D) is named, includes a letter from the Greek humanist, monk, and, later, Patriarch of Alexandria Meletios Pigas (1549–1601 c.e.). Pigas's letter to Beza includes an argument that John's 'locusts' were not insects. Intriguingly, Pigas also interacts with potential Latin translations of ἀκρίδες in Matt 3:4||Mark 1:6c:

> The "locusts" that John the Baptist ate (Τὰς ἀκρίδας ἃς ἤσθιεν Ἰωάννης) I would not have translated with *locustas*: Indeed, the *locustae* [are] the growths of trees (τὰ ἀκρόδρυα τῶν δένδρων). We know them as "locusts" (ἀκρίδες), which are in branches of the vine *pampinus*. I found its species on banks of the Jordan in Palestine, which my blessed master and father Silvestros, the current [Patriarch] of Alexandria, wanting to imitate the way of life of the Baptist, used to pluck in the wilderness (ζηλώσας[161] ποτὲ τὴν δίαιταν τοῦ βαπτιστοῦ ἐν ἐρήμῳ ἐδρέψατο), and from that [food] procured his subsistence (ἐκεῖθεν ποριζόμενος τὸ ἀποζῆν).[162]

As Euthymius Zigabenus did, Pigas seems to respond to an interpretation (of Beza?)[163] that John ate actual locusts/grasshoppers. Also like Euthymius and

---

[160] Walker Bynum, *Holy Feast and Holy Fast: The Religious Significance of Food to Medieval Women* (Berkeley: University of California, 1987), 133.

[161] Cf. Chrysostom, *In Matthaeum* 10.5: Τοῦτον . . . ζηλώσωμεν, discussed above.

[162] The letter was written from Alexandria on 19 July 1581. Greek: Fernand Aubert and Henri Meylan, eds., *Correspondance de Théodore de Bèze* (Geneva: Droz, 1960–), 24.385–99; here, 390; the ET is my own. I am grateful to François Bovon for calling this letter to my attention.

[163] As it happens, Meletios's letter is the last source contained in the most recently published volume of the correspondence of Theodore Beza (2002). I thus do not know if, or

Theophylactus of Ochrida, Pigas knows two different 'vegetarian' under-standings of John's 'locusts': One renders them as *locustae*,[164] but the other, he argues, corresponds more accurately to "branches of the vine *pampinus*."

In addition to characterizing the Baptist's 'locusts' as growths of a par-ticular vine, Pigas draws on the opinion and experience of his mentor Silvestros.[165] Silvestros's wilderness habitation and food in imitation of John indicates that ascetic practices like those of Gregory Nazianzen, Basil of Cae-sarea and others (attested in the Karshuni *Life of John* and Jerome, *Adv. Iovin.* 2.15) continued to be followed in the late-sixteenth century. What in much of Western Europe was known as the period of the Reformations[166] remained for Silvestros, Pigas and many others in the Greek East a time of continued de-light in patristic approaches to scripture and asceticism.

8. Alexis, Origen and J.-P. Migne: Emendations of Classical and Patristic Texts Mentioning "Locusts"

However remarkable, the two (different) depictions of John's diet devoid of locusts in the *Gospel of the Ebionites* and several witnesses to Tatian's *Diatessaron*, as well as the plethora of authors rendering John's ἀκρίδες as plants, do not represent an isolated phenomenon in Christian literature. An analogous treatment of locust eating may be found in a Byzantine interpreta-tion of a poem of the comic Alexis (4/3 c. B.C.E.). As noted in chapter 2, Alexis offers the locust/cicada (τέττιξ) as an example of what poor people eat (*Fr.* 167.13). W. Geoffrey Arnott observes that Eustathius of Thessalo-nike (*c.* 1115–1195/6 C.E.) construes the poor woman's locust/cicada not as an insect but, more vaguely, as "some edible thing":

> [A]t first sight the cicada . . . seems an odd entry in a list otherwise restricted to plants and their produce, and Eustath. 948.41ff. (after citing vv. 12–13 (ὦχρος – ἀχράς)) presuma-bly felt qualms over its interpretation when he defined τέττιξ simply as βρώσιμόν τι.[167]

That is to say, rather than depict the poor woman eating a "locust/cicada" (τέττιξ), Eustathius provides her instead with "some edible thing" (βρώσιμόν τι). Perhaps for Eustathius it would be counterintuitive to find someone poor eating meat. The change that Eustathius makes to the poor

how, Theodore responded to Meletios's assertions about the Baptist's diet. See below, how-ever, on Alexander Ross, who seems to know of such a response.

[164] This interpretation of John's ἀκρίδες/*locustae* could be indebted to Athanasius's 'lexicography' (discussed above).

[165] Silvestros was Patriarch of Alexandria until the time of his death (1569–1590 C.E.) and, incidentally, was succeeded by Meletios (I).

[166] E.g., Martin Luther's posting of his ninety-five theses is dated to 31 October 1517.

[167] Arnott, *Alexis: The Fragments*, 488–9. Arnott (489: "It is absurd therefore to suspect corruption") criticizes the attempt by August Meineke, *Critica ad Athenaei Deipnosophistas* (Leipzig: Teubner, 1867), 4.28, to 'correct' Alexis's original text from τέττιξ to πέξιξ.

woman's diet in a text devoid of any particular theological significance offers a remarkable parallel to the many 'vegetarian' renderings of John's diet in writings before and contemporary with Eustathius in the late-twelfth century.

The same type of emendation made to the comic Alexis came to be associated with certain interpretations of John's diet of locusts, namely in Origen and Pseudo-Chrysostom (both discussed above). Two witnesses to Origen's *Commentary on Matthew* (*Mat. Cat.* 41: "He was in the habit of eating locusts. . . ."), call attention to a debate about the meaning of John's 'locusts':

> καὶ οἱ μέν φασι τὰ τῶν ἀκροδρύων ἀκρίσματα . . . τινὲς δὲ ἀκρίδας τὰ ζῷά φασιν.
>
> And some say that the [locusts] are the tips of plants, . . . but others that [the] locusts are living creatures.[168]

Erich Klostermann identifies these witnesses as an eleventh-century MS (Paris. 230 [C^lb 4]) and the catenae on Matthew attributed to Petrus of Laodicea (= *Π*; 7th c. C.E.?).[169] Even if Origen himself had interpreted the grasshoppers' wings figuratively—and thus had no objection to John's eating flying insects—the remarks of a later copyist of Origen's commentary (preserved in two witnesses) undoubtedly did have such reservations.

A more explicit 'lexicographical' explanation for interpreting John's 'locusts' as plants appears in Jacques-Paul Migne's *Patrologia graeca*. The passage in question is Pseudo-Chrysostom's *De poenitentia* 1.3, which, as mentioned above, depicts the Baptist's 'locusts' as ἀκρίδας ἐκ βοτανῶν ("'locusts' from plants").[170] The Latin translation given in the parallel column of Migne is *summitatibus plantarum* ("[the] tips of plants"). Pseudo-Chrysostom may well not have been the only church Father to confuse the noun ἀκρίς (–ίδος "locust/grasshopper") with the adjective ἄκρις (–ιος "hill-top, mountain peak"). These two words are in fact distinguished by the placement of the accent, as well as the presence of the Delta ("δ") in forms other than nominative singular and dative plural. Thus, Mark 1:6c (ἀκρίδας) and Matt 3:4c (ἀκρίδες) must refer to locusts/grasshoppers and not, for example, to "tips" of plants.

The following footnote justifies this (mis)construal of the Greek in Pseudo-Chrysostom:

> In Vulgata legitur, Joannem Baptistam in cibum sumpsisse mel sylvestre et *locustas;* quæ postrema vox est interpretatio vocis Græcæ ἀκρίδας, cum *locustas* tum *summitates plantarum* significantis.

---

[168] Klostermann, *Origenes*, 32 n.1; ET: mine.

[169] *Origenes*, 12. See further: Joseph Sickenberger, "Über die dem Petrus von Laodicea zugeschriebenen Evangelienkommentare," *TQ* 86 (1904): 10–19; C. F. Georg Heinrici, *Des Petrus von Laodicea Erklärung des Matthäusevangeliums* (Leipzig: Dürr, 1908); Berthold Altaner, *Patrology* (New York: Herder and Herder, 1960 [1931]), 626.

[170] *PG* 59.762.

In the Vulgate it says that John the Baptist took as food wild honey and *'locusts,'* which the earlier Greek language interprets as ἀκρίδας. *'Locusts'* then signifies *tips of plants.*[171]

The aforementioned examples interpreting occurrences of 'locusts' in Alexis, Origen and Pseudo-Chrysostom witness that even ostensibly objective philological or lexicographal analyses can be biased or mistaken.

H. Why a 'Vegetarian' Baptist, a Model of Asceticism, or Both? ΠΑΙΔΕΙΑ and Early Christian Biblical Interpretation

Earlier parts of this chapter have noted that the second-century *Gospel of the Ebionites*, several witnesses to Tatian's second-century gospel harmony, and numerous other interpretations of John's food deprive the Baptist of his locusts/grasshoppers. Instead, John eats honey that tasted like manna (*Gos. Eb.*), milk with his honey (Tatian himself?), or 'locusts' construed as vegetation. This section explores why these and other 'vegetarian' emendations of Mark 1:6c‖Matt 3:4c developed, as well as why John's diet became a model for others to follow.

Chapters 2 and 4 note several reasons why, beginning in the second century, John may not have been embraced as an eater of insects:

1. Neither Matthew nor Luke needed Mark's argument that John's food places the Baptist in the wilderness. In Mark 1:2–8, the "locusts and wild honey" connect Jesus' forerunner with Isa 40:3 ("a voice shouting in the wilderness"). Matthew and Luke assume the point for which Mark argues with reference to John's food.
2. Matthew was not particularly interested in *what* John ate. Rather, his editing of Mark 1:6c reflects the concern that John gleaned *all* his sustenance from the wilderness.[172] The same could also be said for Justin Martyr's 'gospel' material on John's diet (*Dial.* 88.6–7; cf. Or., *Philocalia* 26.4).
3. Only the Roman period (but not the Classical or Hellenistic periods) attests widespread aversion to locust eating.[173] This prejudice could have affected certain Christian interpretations of John's 'locusts.'

---

[171] *PG* 59.762 footnote "(a)" in the Latin column, emphases original; ET: mine. Footnote "(a)" could have been written much earlier than Migne's *Patrologica graeca* (pub. 1857–66), given Migne's proclivity for incorporating earlier critical editions produced by other scholars. On this point see R. Howard Bloch, *God's Plagiarist: Being an Account of the Fabulous Industry and Irregular Commerce of the Abbé Migne* (Chicago: University of Chicago, 1994), esp. 58–77.

[172] On these first two points, see the arguments in chapter 4 and the discussion of Matt 3:4c in connection with 2 Macc 5:21–27; *Mart. Ascen. Isa.* 2.7–11; and Jos., *Vita* 2 §11.

[173] See the discussion in chapter 2 of Strabo, *Geog.* 16.4.12; Plin. (E), *HN* 6.35.195; Ath., *Deip.* 4.133B; Plut., *De soll. an.* 976D, *Quaest. conv.* 8.7.3 (727E); Dioscorides, *De mat.*

This chapter introduces two additional reasons for 'vegetarian' understandings of John's 'locusts':

4. Recent studies of asceticism in early Christianity have highlighted in numerous patristic authors the importance of moderation in regard to food.[174] If Christians should dine on simple foods, how is it that John could enjoy the tempting luxury of meat so regularly?[175]
5. The second-century 'vegetarian' depiction of John's diet in the *Gospel of the Ebionites*, which apparently substitutes "honey tasting like cakes in olive oil" for "locusts and wild honey," could have influenced later Christian authors. It is also possible that Tatian's *Diatessaron* originally related John's diet in 'vegetarian' terms as well, exchanging "milk" for "locusts."

Oftentimes it has not been possible to ascertain which, if any, of the above reasons was, or were, responsible for a particular author's omitting actual locusts/grasshoppers from the Baptist's wilderness cuisine. In the case of the *Gospel of the Ebionites* and Tatian's *Diatessaron*, the 'vegetarian' convictions of the Ebionite Christians with whom this 'gospel' material is sometimes associated, as well as of Tatian (or some later Syrian Christian), most plausibly explain the different non-locust eating traditions in these two writings.

Plutarch (before 50 C.E.–after 120 C.E.), who himself was vegetarian, specifically addresses the aversion to eating the flesh of locusts. Plutarch highlights the Pythagoreans' scorn of swallows—birds that eat such insects:

---

med. 2.51–52; Ps. Dioscorides, *De mat. med.* 2.115 (2.109); Oribasius, *Ecl. Med. Fr.* 63.5 (64.5); Gal., *De simp. med. temp.* 11.13.312 (11.2.149); *Aesop's Fables* 397.

[174] E.g., Wimbush and Valantasis, eds., *Asceticism*; Wimbush, ed., *Ascetic Behavior*; McGowan, *Ascetic Eucharists*; Vööbus, *History of Asceticism*; Brakke, *Athanasius*; Clark, *Reading Renunciation*; Shaw, *Burden of the Flesh*; Conrad Leyser, *Authority and Asceticism from Augustine to Gregory the Great* (Oxford Historical Monographs; Oxford: Clarendon/Oxford: Oxford University, 2000); John Behr, *Asceticism and Anthropology in Irenaeus and Clement* (Oxford Early Christian Studies; New York: Oxford University Press, 2000); cf. Hermut Löhr, "Speisenfrage und Tora im Judentum des Zweiten Tempels und im entstehenden Christentum," *ZNW* 94 (2003): 17–37; Rudolph Arbesmann, "Fasting and Prophecy in Pagan and Christian Antiquity," *Traditio* 7 (1949–51): 1–71. An excellent study of vegetarianism through the centuries, especially in South Asia, is Frederick J. Simoons, *Eat Not This Flesh: Food Avoidances from Prehistory to the Present* (Madison: University of Wisconsin, ²1994); see further: Dario Sabbatucci, "Dieta Carnea e Vegetarianesimo," in: *Homo edens: Regimi, miti e pratiche dell'alimentazione nella civiltà del Mediterraneo* (ed. Oddone Longo and Paolo Scarpi; Milan: Diapress/Documenti, 1989), 243–4; Catherine Osborne, "Ancient Vegetarianism," in: *Food in Antiquity* (ed. J. Wilkins, D. Harvey and M. Dobson; Exeter: University of Exeter, 1995), 214–24; Cora Diamond, "Eating Meat and Eating People" (1976), in: eadem, *The Realistic Spirit: Wittgenstein, Philosophy, and the Mind* (Representation and Mind; Cambridge, MA: MIT Press, 1991), 319–34.

[175] So Brock, "Syriac Sources," 117–18.

Is the swallow perhaps in bad repute among them[176]. . . ? She is a flesh-eater (σαρκοφάγος), and is especially prone to kill and feed on cicadas, sacred and musical insects (καὶ μάλιστα τοὺς τέττιγας, ἱεροὺς καὶ μουσικοὺς ὄντας).[177]

This is not to suggest a direct influence from Plutarch to *Gos. Eb.*, witnesses to the *Diatessaron*, or other 'vegetarian' depictions of John's diet. It does, however, illustrate how a 'flesh-eating' person would likely be viewed by 'vegetarian' Christian readers of Mark 1:6c‖Matt 3:4c. If Plutarch thus disdains such birds, how much more difficulty would 'vegetarian' Christians have with such a presentation of Jesus' predecessor? The important contrast, to be noted in the following paragraphs, is that Greco-Roman writings acclaim 'vegetarian' and other simple diets of esteemed philosophers, but Jewish writings of the Hellenistic and Roman periods do not.

With regard to avoiding meat in general, several Jewish writings mention Jews who adopted vegetarian diets *out of necessity* in a time of crisis. The second century B.C.E. author of Daniel depicts Daniel and his companions' concern about purity in Babylonian exile (Dan 1:8–21; so also Jos., *Ant.* 10.10.2 [§190]). Similarly, the *Lives of the Prophets* presents Daniel's diet as without bread, meat or wine (*Liv. Pro.* 4:14). In 2 Macc 5:21–27, a small group of Jews, including Judas Maccabeus, withdraw to the wilderness after Antiochus IV (Epiphanes) plunders Jerusalem. Bannus offers a possible exception to the aforementioned Jews depicted as adopting a meatless diet in a time of crisis. According to Josephus, Bannus's regular ablutions and natural food and clothing stemmed from a concern for purity but not necessarily from a particular crisis or persecution (Jos., *Vita* 2 §11).

In contrast to these Jewish writings, several Greco-Roman philosophic writings applaud the *choice* to renounce meat altogether. One of these, Aratus, *Phaen.* 96–136, has already been discussed above in connection with Tatian's vegetarian convictions. In addition, Philostratus (d. 244/9 C.E.) offers the following account of Apollonius of Tyana's (1st c. C.E.) decision to renounce meat:

He declined to live upon animate foods (ἐμψύχους βρώσεις), on the ground that such were unclean (ὡς οὔτε καθαράς), and also that it made the mind gross; so he partook

---

[176] Gk.: παρ' αὐτοῖς, referring to the Pythagoreans. Question 7 is concerned with why the Pythagoreans "do not receive a swallow as guest in the house" (*Quaest. conv.* 727A). Bodenheimer's (*Insects*, 40) partial citation of this passage does not reveal the context referring to the Pythagoreans.

[177] Plut., *Quaest. conv.* 8.7.3 (727E). Cf. Plut., *Sull.* 7.6, where a sparrow with grasshopper in mouth is taken as a bad omen. According to Cato (234–149 B.C.E.), moreover, the ostensibly 'vegetarian' Pythagoras even had a type of cabbage named after him (*Rust.* 157: *de brassica Pythagorea*).

only of fried fruits and vegetables, for he said that all the fruits of the earth were clean (καθαρά).[178]

Dio Chrysostom (*c.* 40/50 C.E.–after 110 C.E.), moreover, highlights the virtue of Diogenes the Cynic's (*c.* 412/03–*c.* 324/1 B.C.E.) simplicity with regard to food:

> And so he used to partake of a barley cake (μᾶζαν) with greater pleasure than others did of the costliest of foods, and enjoyed a drink from a stream of running water more than others did their Thrasian wine.[179]

Dio Chrysostom also highlights the virtue of simple clothing (*Disc.* 1.61–62; 4.70; 13.10–11; 60.7–8; cf. Mark 1:6ab‖Matt 3:4ab).

These judgments concerning food by Aratus, Philostratus, and Dio Chrysostom demonstrate that *the two most popular interpretations of the Baptist's diet*—John as 'vegetarian' and an ethical model—*have precedents in Greco-Roman philosophical literature.* The earliest examples of John as 'vegetarian' (*Gos. Eb.*) and as an ethical model (Clem., *Paed.* 2.16.1, 2.112.1) are predated, respectively, by Aratus and Dio Chrysostom. It is worth repeating that these two interpretive models were not mutually exclusive. Indeed, John's 'vegetarianism' would be exemplary for such Christians.

Therefore, it follows that numerous patristic authors interpreted Mark 1:6c‖Matt 3:4c in ways unforeseen by the authors of Mark or Matthew (let alone the historical Baptist!), yet in ways strikingly similar to these depictions of esteemed philosophers. This is not to say that every such interpretation of John's diet is indebted to the philosophical literature. Yet for the many patristic authors who were trained in the classics, the similarities can hardly be ignored. These early Christian interpretations of John as 'vegetarian' or an ethical model (or both) thus offer an example of what Frances M. Young aptly describes as scripture interpreted "as the basis of a new *paideia*."[180]

I. Later Reactions and Protests to Construing John as 'Vegetarian' or an Exemplar

Whether or not John ate actual locusts/grasshoppers, the dominant interpretation for twelve centuries since Clement of Alexandria was that John's food, clothing and wilderness habitation somehow offer a model for believers to

---

[178] Philostr., *VA* 1.8. Greek text and ET (modified): F. C. Conybeare (LCL), 1.18–21. Philostratus refers to meat as food that is "living" or "ensouled" (ἔμψυχος).

[179] Dio Chrys., *Or.* 6.12. Greek text and ET: J. W. Cohoon (LCL), 1.256–9.

[180] Cited at the beginning of this chapter: "Once the biblical literature became established as an alternative body of classics, it would soon be seen as the basis of a new *paideia*" (*Biblical Exegesis*, 76; cf. 203–4).

emulate. Sooner or later, this interpretation, along with the Baptist as a plant-eating 'vegetarian,' was likely to be disputed. John Calvin, Sir Thomas Browne and Samuel Bochart exemplify challenges to these long-embraced convictions concerning John's "locusts and wild honey." The following section notes that Alexander Ross's reply to Browne, as well as Ellen Gould Harmon White's nineteenth-century affirmation of John as 'vegetarian,' illustrate that such challenges would not be left unanswered.

1. John Calvin: The Baptist's Natural, Non-ascetic Food

In light of the continuing discussions through the medieval/Byzantine periods of what John ate and the significance attached to his diet, it is hardly coincidental that the Protestant reformer John Calvin (1509–1564 C.E.) has an opinion on the matter as well. Along with Meletios Pigas's letter to Theodore Beza (1581 C.E.), Calvin's commentary on the Synoptics (1513 C.E.) highlights the extent to which John's food remained a living issue in the sixteenth century.

Dismissing earlier interpretations, Calvin explicitly opposes construing the Baptist's lifestyle as a model for Christian piety. His commentary includes polemic against "superstitious persons," who are too concerned with "outward appearances" and suppose "him [John] to be a man who lived in solitude, and who disdained the ordinary way of living; as the only superiority of hermits and monks is (*quemadmodum eremitae et monachi hoc uno excellunt*) that they differ from other people."[181] Dispensing with an ascetic interpretation, Calvin explains that John ate "only what was fit to be used in its natural state (*nativis cibis*)."[182]

John Calvin's remarks highlight that for the historical John a diet of "locusts and wild honey" was nothing special. Like the author of Matthew, Methodius of Olympus, Hesychius of Jerusalem, and others, Calvin calls attention to John's eating what grew naturally. Yet Calvin explains neither why such a diet *would not* be ascetic nor the meaning of eating such natural foods. For Calvin, the task at hand is primarily polemical and negative, to take John's diet away from the ascetically inclined, without reflecting on what meaning that diet could have had or might continue to have today.

---

[181] Lat.: John Calvin, *Commentarius in harmoniam evangelicam* (Corpus reformatorum 73; ed. K. G. Bretschneider; Bad Feilnbach, Germany: Schmidt Periodicals GMBH, 1990 [1891]), 114; ET: William Pringle, *[John Calvin,] Commentary on a Harmony of the Evangelists: Matthew, Mark, and Luke* (Grand Rapids: Eerdmans, 1949), 1.183–4; cf. Luz, *Matthew*, 1.168.

[182] Cf. Jerome, *Adv. Iovin.* 2.7. Calvin does not, however, consider what other foods in their "natural state" John could have eaten in addition to "locusts and wild honey."

2. Affirming that John Ate Actual Locusts/Grasshoppers: Bochart and Browne

The corollary to Calvin's negative argument that the Baptist does not offer an ascetic model is Samuel Bochart's insistence in 1793 that John did in fact eat actual locusts/grasshoppers, not plants.[183] Over a century before Bochart, moreover, in the mid-seventeenth century Sir Thomas Browne argued the same point at some length:

> CONCERNING the food of John Baptist in the wildernesse, Locusts and wilde hony, lest popular opiniatrity should arise, we will deliver the chiefe opinions; the first conceiveth the Locusts here mentioned to be that fruit the Greeks name κερατιον, mentioned by Luke in the dyet of the Prodigall sonne, the Latins *Siliqua,* and some, *Panis Sancti Iohannis,* included in a broad Cod, and indeed of a taste almost as pleasant as honey. But this opinion doth not so truly impugne that of the Locusts; and might rather call into controversie the meaning of wilde honey.
>
> The second affirmeth they were the tops of tender crops of trees; for so *Locusta* also signifieth: which conceit is plausible in Latin, but will not hold in Greek, wherein the word is ακρις, except for ακριδες, we read ακροδρυα, or ακρεμονες, which signifie the extremities of trees; of which belief have divers been; more confidently Isidore Pelusiota, who in his Epistles plainly affirmeth they thinke unlearnedly who are of another beliefe; and this so wrought upon Baronius that he concludeth in newtrality, *Hæc cum scribat Isidorus definiendum nobis non est, et totum relinquimus lectoris arbitrio; nam constat Græcam dictionem* ακριδες, *et Locustam insecti genus, et arborum summitates significare. Sed fallitur,* saith *Montacutius, name constant contrarium,* Ακριδα *apud nullum authorem classicum* Ακροδρυα *significare.* But above all Paracelsus with most animosity promoteth this opinion, and in his book *de melle,* spareth not his friend Erasmus. *Hoc a nonnullis ita explicatur ut dicant Locustas aut cicadas Iohanni po cibo fuisse; sed hi stultiam dissimulare non possunt, veluti Ieronymus, Erasmus, et alii prophetæ Neoterici in Latinitate immortui.*
>
> A third affirmeth that they were properly Locusts, that is a sheath-winged and six-footed insect, such as is our Grashopper; and this opinion seems more probable then the other: for beside the authority of Origen, Jerome, Chrysostome, Hillary, and Ambrose to confirme it, this is the proper signification of the word, thus used in Scripture by the Septuagint, Greeke vocabularies thus expound it; Suidas on the word Ακρις observes it to be that animall whereon the Baptist fed in the desert; in this sense the word is used by Aristotle, Dioscorides, Galen, and severall humane Authors. And lastly, there is no absurdity in this interpretation, or any solid reason why we should decline it; it being a food permitted unto the Jewes, whereof foure kindes are reckoned up among cleane meats. Beside, not onely the Jewes, but many other Nations long before and since, have made an usuall food thereof. That the Æthiopians, Mauritanians, and Arabians, did commonly eat them is testified by Diodorus, Strabo, Solinus, Ælian, and Plinie; that they still feed on them is confirmed by Leo, Cadamustus and others. John therefore as our Saviour saith, came neither eating nor drinking, that is farre from the dyet of Jerusalem and other riotous places; but fared coursely and poorely according unto the apparell he

---

[183] Bochart, "Iohannem, Baptistam, veras locustas habuisse pro cibo," 326–33.

wore, that is of Camells haire; the place of his abode, the wildernesse; and the doctrine he preached, humiliation and repentance.[184]

As noted above, the position of Browne and Bochart finds a precedent in Syriac Christianity with Išoʿdād of Merv, who in the ninth century attributes John's eating of actual grasshoppers/locusts to Theodore of Mopsuestia (*c.* 350–428/9 C.E.).[185]

J. The Tenacity of 'Vegetarian' Interpretations: Alexander Ross and Ellen Gould Harmon White

Brock notes aptly that "the urge to get rid of the offending locusts dies hard."[186] Whereas in late antiquity many Christians took offense at John's eating *meat*, in the modern period the Scottish poet Alexander Ross (1699–1784) rejected the idea that John would have consumed *insects*. In a pointed response to Sir Thomas Browne, Ross dismisses the allegation that John ate like a bug-eating savage:

> Conversely: that John could not have been like the Akridofagi:
>
> II. That in *Ethiopia* there is a people whose sole food are locusts, is witnessed by *Diodorus* and *Strabo,* [l. 4. c. 16.] these from their food are called *Acridophagi;* they are a lean people, shorter and blacker then others; they are short lived, for the longest life among them exceedeth not 40 years: their countrey affordeth neither fish nor flesh, but God provides them locusts every Spring, which in multituds are carried to them from the Desart by the West and South-west winds: these they take and salt for their use. These wretched people die all of one disease, much like our louse sicknesse: A little before their death, their bodies grow scabby and itchy, so that with scratching, bloody matter and ugly lice of divers shapes, with wings, swarm out of their belly first, then from other parts, so that they pine away and die in great pain. This disease doubtlesse proceeds partly from the corruption of the aire, and partly from the unwholesomenesse of their diet, which turns to putrid humours in their bodies, whence the disease is Epidemical. This vermin breeds most in those who are given to sweat, to nastinesse, and abound with putrified humours, between the flesh and skin, whose constitutions are hot & moist, as children; and according as either of the four humours are predominant, so is the colour of lice, some being red, some white, some brown, some black; sometimes they burst out of all parts of the body, as in *Herod,* and in that *Portugal,* of whom *Forestus* speaks [l. 4. *de*

---

[184] Sir Thomas Browne, "Of the food of John Baptist, Locusts and wilde Honey," in: idem, *Pseudodoxia Epidemica* ([6]1672 [1646]), VII:ix. Online: http://penelope.uchicago.edu/pseudodoxia/pseudo79.html (on 23 Jan. 2003). This page is maintained at the University of Chicago by James Eason and cited in this study with his permission.

[185] "According to the *Interpreter*, the locusts were flying [insects], and the honey natural." As mentioned above, Brock, "Syriac Sources," 122, notes that in Išoʿdād's writings "the Interpreter" is Theodore of Mopsuestia.

[186] "Syriac Sources," 113, referring to Bochart's aforementioned study.

vitiis capitis] out of whose body they swarmed so fast, that his two men did nothing else but sweep them of, so that they carried out whole baskets full. Sometimes they breed but in some parts onely, as in the head or arm-pits *Zacuta* mentioneth one who was troubled nowhere but in his eie-lids, out of which they swarmed in great numbers. Some have voided them by boils and imposthumes. *Forestus* speaks of one who had them only in his back, whom he advised to hold his naked back so close to the fire, till it blistered, out of which blisters they came, and so he was cured. Salt is an enemy to them, yet they are bred in those *Æthiopians* by the frequent eating of the salt locusts: But perhaps it is not the eating of the salt meat so much, as the nastinesse, and sweat, and unwholesom waters, and corrrupted air that breeds them. And it is certain, that wild and savage people are most given to them, because of their carelesse uncleanlinesse, using no other remedy against them, but shirts died with Saffron, which some wilde *Irish* doe wear six months together without shifting. But sometimes this disease is inflicted by the immediate hand of god, as a punishment of sinne and tyranny. Examples we have in *Sylla, Pherecides, Herod, Philip* the second of *Spain,* and others who died of this malady. Now because Locusts are such an unwholesome food, I cannot think that *John Baptist* did feed on them; and therefore it is no vulgar error, to hold, that *akrides* in *Matth.* 3. doth signifie the tops of hearbs rather than locusts, both because these were an unwholesome food, and unpleasant to the palat and nose, used rather for Physick then diet, as *Dioscorides* and *Galen* shew, that Locusts are good against the Cholick and Stone, and may be more safely given then Cantharides to provoke urine. And although the *Æthiopians* did eat them for food, yet this is no argument to prove, that *John* did eat them; which is all the reason that *Beza* and *Casaubon* bring to prove their assertion: neither can it be proved, that Locusts were a food ever used in *Judæa:* For *Pelusiota,* who lived an Eremite many years in those Desarts, never knew any such food used there. But whereas they alledge, that in *Levit.* [c. 11. v. 22.] Locusts are set down for clean food: I answer with *Munster* [*on Levit.* 11. 22], who though an excellent Hebrician, yet confesseth, that neither he, nor the *Rabbins* themselves, doe know the true meaning or signification of the proper tearms there used. Therefore the Hebrew word *Harbe,* which we translate *Locust,* the Septuagints call *Bruchus,* which is another kind of Insect. And the *French* in their Bibles have left the Hebrew word untranslated. And so did *Luther* before, as not knowing what that word meant, nor the other three Hebrew words. Dr. *Brown* then had done well rather to have reckoned the Baptists eating of Locusts among the Vulgar Errors, then his feeding upon hearbs in the Desart.[187]

Indeed, the fact that John's exemplary and 'vegetarian' diet continued to have a life of its own after the dawn of critical scholarship is attested also among the Seventh Day Adventists, an originally American Protestant group founded in the nineteenth century. An early leader of this denomination, Ellen Gould Harmon White (1827–1915), wrote in 1872:

> John separated himself from friends and from the luxuries of life. The simplicity of his dress, a garment woven of camel's hair, was a standing rebuke to the extravagance and display of the Jewish priests, and of the people generally. His diet, purely vegetable, of

---

[187] Alexander Ross, *Arcana Microcosmi* ([2]1652). James Eason notes that this work "is intended mostly as an extended footnote to Sir Thomas Browne's *Pseudodoxia Epidemica.*" Online: http://penelope.uchicago.edu/ross/ross21.html (on 23 Jan. 2003); used with permission.

locusts and wild honey, was a rebuke to the indulgence of appetite and the gluttony that everywhere prevailed. . . . Temperance in all things is to be connected with the message, to turn the people of God from their idolatry, their gluttony, and their extravagance in dress and other things.[188]

As one can see, this study has superceded the point at which the history of scholarship began in chapter 1 (Erasmus). Naturally, drawing a sharp distinction between a passage's history of interpretation and the beginning of serious scholarship can be difficult, as the sometimes insightful observations of both Sir Thomas Browne and Alexander Ross show. Such interest during the modern period in emulating the vegetarian Baptist who ate legumes with his wild honey has been acknowledged in chapter 1 concerning twentieth-century German vegetarians' interest in John's diet.[189]

K. Summation: The Baptist's "Locusts and Wild Honey" in Patristic and Later Interpretation

This monograph's final chapter analyzes the assorted meanings attached to John the Baptist's diet of "locusts and wild honey" in patristic and subsequent Christian interpretation. None of the three main interpretations of John's diet—'allegory,' John as model and John as 'vegetarian'—precludes either of the other two. A diachronic analysis of each of these interpretations has allowed for a comparative analysis of developments in each. For example, the variety among figurative interpretations of Origen, Cyril of Jerusalem, Arnobius the Younger, Peter Chrysologus, Īšoʿdād of Merv and others suggests the popularity of such exegesis but not of any particular figurative interpretation of John's diet.

Unlike the relative lack of attention given to Mark 1:6c‖Matt 3:4c in the second and early-third centuries, beginning with Clement of Alexandria, construing the Baptist as a model for later Christians by his simple food, clothing and wilderness habitation became the dominant interpretation. This understanding of John as a model for others would be unquestioned for some twelve centuries until John Calvin objected to it (1513 C.E.). In many respects Calvin can be seen as setting the agenda in scholarship for the next five centuries, namely highlighting what John's diet *does not* mean without elucidating what it does (or did) mean.[190]

In contrast to the concord among those embracing John as a model, numerous writers dispute whether John ate actual locusts/grasshoppers.

---

[188] White, *Testimonies for the Church* (Mountain View, CA: Pacific Press, [4]1948), 3.62 (= eadem, *Counsels on Diet & Foods* [Washington: Review and Herald, 1938], 71; cf. 225).

[189] See the discussion in chapter 1, 19–21.

[190] On this point see chapter 1, esp. 1–4, 24–26.

Interpreters who seem to accept that John ate insects include: Clement of Al-exandria (?), Origen, Cyril of Jerusalem, Hilary of Poitiers, Peter Chrysologus, Arnobius the Younger (?), Methodius of Olympus, Epiphanius, Cyril of Alexandria, Gregory Nazianzen, Basil of Caesarea, Gregory of Nyssa, Theodore of Mopsuestia (*apud* Īšoʿdād of Merv), Didymus the Blind, John Chrysostom, Hesychius of Jerusalem, Ambrose of Milan, Chromatius of Aquileia, Augustine, Jerome (?), and Theophylactus of Ochrida (on Mark 1:6c). To a certain extent, the inference that a particular author affirms John's entomophagy is an *argumentum e silentio*, except, for example, where the figurative interpretations of Origen and others assume that the Baptist ate flying insects. These inferences are nonetheless probable, since chapter 2 demonstrated the commonness of grasshoppers as food for humans and an item that could routinely be passed over in silence without objection. In the seventeenth and eighteenth centuries, respectively, Sir Thomas Browne and Samuel Bochart would argue that John did, in fact, consume actual grasshop-pers. Prior to Browne and Bochart, only Īšoʿdād of Merv's ninth-century Syriac *Commentary on the Gospels*, asserting the authority of "the Inter-preter" Theodore of Mopsuestia (d. 428/9 C.E.), protests 'vegetarian' interpretations of John's diet.

Rejecting the position of the aforementioned authors, numerous witnesses reconfigure John's diet, deleting the insects. These writings and interpreters include: the *Gospel of the Ebionites*, several witnesses to Tatian's *Diatessa-ron* (Īšoʿdād, Bar-Ṣalibi, Bar-Hebraeus and Ibn aṭ-Ṭayyib), Athanasius of Alexandria, Isidore of Pelusium, Pseudo-Chrysostom, numerous Syriac wit-nesses (for example, Jacob of Serugh; cf. the *Life of Peter the Iberian* and the Karshuni *Life of John the Baptist*), the Slavonic additions to Josephus, Pantaleon, Theophylactus of Ochrida (on Matt 3:4c), Euthymius Zigabenus, and in the late-sixteenth century Meletios Pigas. Even after the objections of Browne and Bochart, Alexander Ross and Ellen Gould Harmon White in the eighteenth and nineteenth centuries, respectively, attest to the tenacity of 'vegetarian' interpretations of John's 'locusts.'

The reasons for removing grasshoppers from John's diet could, hypotheti-cally, be as numerous as the many authors who thus portrayed the Baptist's food. That said, two explanations for depicting the 'locusts' in an herbivo-rous fashion are particularly compelling: opposition specifically to eating meat, general opposition to eating to luxurious foods, or both. Chapter 4 noted that neither of these concerns can be attributed to the historical Baptist or the authors of Mark or Matthew. By contrast, it is Greco-Roman authors, such as Aratus, Plutarch, Dio Chrysostom and Philostratus, who extol these very virtues.

It thus stands to reason that John's wilderness diet of "locusts and wild honey," however construed, offered to patristic commentators and believers in later centuries a source of *paideia* concerning moderation in food. This *paideia* could be emulated literally with wilderness habitation and eating 'locusts,' as Gregory Nazianzen, Basil of Caesarea, the Karshuni *Life of John*, Jerome, Isidore of Pelusium, a ninth-century inscription of Isidore's statement on the wall of a monk's cave, and Meletios Pigas attest. The *paideia* could also teach about the *type* of moderation and simplicity to which all believers are called, as Clement of Alexandria, Gregory of Nyssa, Chrysostom, Jerome and numerous others maintain. The *paideia* derived from Mark 1:6c||Matt 3:4c will be discussed further in the epilogue following this chapter.

If for no other reason than the weariness of the author, at this point this chapter must conclude. Especially with the medieval and more recent sources, no claim has been made at an exhaustive analysis. Such is left to specialists in these historical periods. It is hoped that this chapter has illustrated the rich history of interpretation given to Mark 1:6c||Matt 3:4c in patristic and later periods. The following epilogue reflects on the accomplishments and implications of this study as a whole.

Epilogue

"Locusts and Wild Honey" in Retrospect:
ΠΑΙΔΕΙΑ and Early Christian Biblical Interpretation

longum iter est per praecepta, breue et efficax per exempla.[1]

This investigation began with the simple query, Why Mark and Matthew, but not Luke, mention the Baptist's food of "locusts and wild honey." My initial research happened upon the equally fascinating question, How John's food came to constitute an ethical model in numerous Christian writings of the patristic, Byzantine, medieval and even later periods. I did not begin this inquiry intending to write a book on the subject; I just wanted to resolve these questions. The investigation uncovered more primary source material—and additional questions—than I ever could have hoped initially. The purpose of this epilogue is threefold: to summarize the main conclusions of chapters 1–5; to consider the implications of the methods employed in this study for early Christian studies in general; and to suggest avenues of inquiry that the present investigation could only touch upon.

A. Summation of Chapters 1–5

Chapter 1 notes that numerous commentaries on Mark and Matthew, as well as studies of the Baptist, ignore John's "locusts and wild honey." Among scholars who do address Mark 1:6c or Matt 3:4c, there is no consensus concerning the meaning of John's diet. The most common positions are that this diet highlights John as prophet, wilderness dweller, ascetic or 'vegetarian.'

Certain *desiderata* pervade much of the secondary literature. One is the failure to distinguish between the different meanings that this diet had for the historical Baptist, Mark and Matthew—not to mention Luke, who omits it. A second shortcoming concerns the lack of *argument* for why a particular interpretation is compelling to the exclusion of other possibilities. Third, scholars who interact with extra-biblical evidence (for example, Greco-Roman references to locust eaters) too often fail to specify why these witnesses

---

[1] Sen. (Y), *Ep.* 6.5: "The journey by way of moral maxims is long, but short and efficacious through examples." Lat.: Henri Noblot, ed., *Lettres a Lucilius* (Paris: Les Belles Lettres, 1957–64), 1.17–18; ET: mine.

commend a particular interpretation. Many commentators present their conclusions as self-evident. Indeed, they are not. Thus the need for the present
inquiry.

The primary purpose of chapters 2 and 3 is to offer the requisite background information to answer the question, How would a person in antiquity
understand the attribution of locust eating and consuming 'honey' that was
"wild." The insufficiency of the secondary literature on these subjects, including articles in important reference works, necessitated these inquiries.

Chapter 2 demonstrates the commonness of locusts as a food for humans
in an ancient Near Eastern context. These insects are not simply the food of
necessity for Bedouins and other poor people; locusts were also requested, for
example, for Assyrian royal banquets. Jewish writers and works, including
Leviticus 11, the *Letter of Aristeas*, Philo of Alexandria, the Damascus
Document and other writings from Qumran, the Mishnah, certain midrashim,
and even Moses Maimonides (1135–1204 C.E.), attest the acceptance of locusts as food in at least certain Jewish communities over many centuries.
With the exception of Deut 14:19, none of these Jewish authors (nor any other
Jewish author through the medieval period) ever questions whether locusts
are kosher.[2] Instead, the questions, if any are raised at all, address *which* species of locusts are permitted or *how* they must be prepared. No Jewish author
intimates that eating locusts *per se* is extraordinary or to be associated with
poverty, asceticism or any particular theological affirmation. Nonetheless,
what may have been curious to a Jewish audience is the absence of any atten-
tion to the Baptist's keeping of kashrut in Mark 1:2–8||Matt 3:1–5.

In a Greco-Roman context, a number of different reactions to John's locusts would have been possible. For some like Aristotle, who ate locusts, the
meaning of Mark 1:6c||Matt 3:4c may not have been perspicuous. Beginning
with the Roman period, however, a number of authors attest to an aversion toward locusts as a customary food for humans (for example, Plutarch,
Athenaeus, Dioscorides, Oribasius, Jerome). To an audience that did not eat
grasshoppers, John's food may have come across as foreign (for example,
non-Roman) or barbaric. In addition, the ethnographic descriptions of
Diodorus, Strabo and the Elder Pliny of an Ethiopian locust-eating people
living in proximity to the desert demonstrates a connection between *a diet of
grasshoppers and wilderness topography* prior to the gospel of Mark.

Chapter 3 notes the ambiguity of "honey" in any ancient text, including
Mark 1:6c||Matt 3:4c, without an accompanying reference to the activity of
bees or to the produce of trees (for example, dates, figs, or sap/gum). We
simply do not know what type of "honey" John ate or what kind, if any, Mark

---

[2] The same point is valid concerning the witness of Muḥammad ibn Mūsā al-Damīrī
(1341–1405 C.E.) to locust eating and Islam.

or Mathew wish to present him as eating. In patristic and later interpretations, it is interesting to note which authors fill in this "gap," specifying that John consumed bee honey.[3]

Since an ancient audience could have made any number of associations with different kinds of 'honey,' chapter 3 considers the possible connotations of various honeys that were "wild." Despite the exegetical ambiguity concerning John's honey, the description of it as "wild" indicates that whatever sweet substance John consumed was not as pleasing or highly esteemed as cultivated bee honey. Moreover, the well attested notion that eating bee honey of unknown origin could be harmful and, in some cases, fatal could have suggested to some the danger John faced in the wilderness.[4]

The closest literary analogy to μέλι ἄγριον in Mark 1:6c‖Matt 3:4c pertains to a type of 'honey' other than bee honey, namely honey-water. Diodorus's description of the Nabataeans, an Arabian tribe who survive with their flocks in the desert on 'honey' from trees mixed with water,[5] cannot be excluded as a possible referent for Mark 1:6c, Matt 3:4c or whatever gospel material Mark utilized.

The NT gospels locate the Baptist "in the desert" (Matt 3:3‖Mark 1:2‖Luke 3:4‖John 1:23; Mark 1:4 par.; etc.). Mark 1:6c‖Matt 3:4c invites us to surmise that John's wilderness was flowing with "grasshoppers and wild honey." Chapter 4 argues that a diet including such common foods probably had no particular theological significance to John himself. Rather, the literary creativity of Mark (or his source) merits recognition for using particular foods to associate the Baptist with Isa 40:3 (the "voice" in the desert) and, by implication, the wilderness prophet Elijah. The author of Luke omits Mark 1:6 precisely because of how it characterizes the Baptist. Throughout this gospel, Luke consistently retains (and augments) materials from Mark and Q that associate *Jesus* with Elijah,[6] and deletes those presenting *the Baptist* as Elijah (for example, Mark 1:6b).[7]

For his part, Matthew changes Mark's periphrastic imperfect ("He was in the habit of eating" [ἦν . . . ἐσθίων]) into an exclusive claim ("His food con-

---

[3] See the discussions in chapter 5 of Cyril of Alexandria, *De incarnatione Domini* 821B; Isidore of Pelusium, *Ep.* 1.132; Hilary of Poitiers, *Commentarius in Matthaeum* 2.2 (925A–B); Pantaleon, *Orationes* 1; Īšoʿdād of Merv, *Commentary on the Gospels*; Theophylactus of Ochrida, *Enarratio en Evangelium Matthæi* 16; and Euthymius, *Comm. in Matthæum* 3.

[4] Xen., *An.* 4.8.21; Ps. Arist., *Mir. ausc.* 18; Strabo, *Geog.* 12.3.18; Plin. (E), *HN* 21.44.74–75; 21.45.77.

[5] Diod. Sic., *Hist.* 19.94.

[6] Mark 6:14–15‖Luke 9:7–8; Mark 8:27–28‖Matt 16:13–14‖Luke 9:18–19; Mark 9:13‖Matt 17:12; Luke 4:25–27; 7:11–16; 24:51; Acts 1:2, 11, 22.

[7] Mark 1:6; 9:11–13; cf. Luke 1:17; 1:76; 7:24–27.

sisted of" [ἦν]) about John's wilderness provisions. The best explanation for why Matthew thus edited Mark 1:6c is Matthew's wish to bring the Baptist's credentials into line with those of other Judeans who had survived entirely on wilderness foods (*Mart. Ascen. Isa.* 2:11; 2 Macc 5:27; cf. Jos., *Vita* 2 §11). An important shift in meaning is therefore to be noted from Mark to Matthew: *What* and *where* the Baptist ate are most important for Mark's associating John with the desert, but Matthew's editing emphasizes *how much* John derived from what occurs naturally in the wilderness (that is, *all* of his food).

An analysis of the nutritional contents of locusts/grasshoppers and various kinds of 'honey' reveals that the Matthean claim is exaggerated. These two foods alone could not have sustained an adult indefinitely. Although locusts are rich in protein and therefore calories, a combination of locusts and any ancient type of 'honey' would yield rather low levels of carbohydrates and not supply enough Vitamin C. An outbreak of scurvy would have put a damper on the Baptist's public ministry if he had attempted to live exclusively on these resources (so Matt 3:4c). This conclusion does not, however, set aside the claim of Mark 1:6c, that the historical Baptist did eat "locusts and wild honey" in the wilderness from time to time, if not with some regularity, along with other foods.

Chapter 5 notes that the diversity of opinion about John's diet already present within the Synoptic tradition is complemented by an even greater variety of interpretations in the patristic and later periods. The most prevalent interpretation, from Clement of Alexandria (*c.* 150–211/16 C.E.) through Meletios Pigas (1549–1601 C.E.), asserts that John's simple wilderness provisions (and clothing) offer a model for believers to emulate. In thus imitating John, some ascetics actually journeyed into the wilderness to live and eat like John did. Such imitation of John is attested by Gregory Nazianzen, Basil of Caesarea, the Karshuni *Life of John*, Jerome (*Adv. Iovin.* 2.15), Isidore of Pelusium, a ninth-century inscription of Isidore's statement on the wall of a monk's cave, and Meletios Pigas. Others state that John models the *type* of simplicity to which all believers are called (for example, Clement of Alexandria, Gregory of Nyssa, Chrysostom, Jerome in his letters).

Certain interpreters assign to John's diet a variety of figurative or allegorical meanings (Origen; Cyril of Jerusalem; Arnobius the Younger; Hilary of Poitiers; Peter Chrysologus; Īšoʿdād of Merv). Many others embrace John as an ethical model but deny that John ate actual locusts/grasshoppers.[8] Analogous depictions of Greco-Roman philosophers' simple or 'vegetarian' diets and the 'vegetarian' practices of certain early Christians offer the most

---

[8] E.g., Athanasius of Alexandria, Isidore of Pelusium, Jacob of Serugh and Theophylactus of Ochrida. Cf. the absence of "locusts" among John's food(s) in the *Gospel of the Ebionites* and several witnesses to Tatian's *Diatessaron*.

compelling reasons for why Mark 1:6c‖Matt 3:4c gave rise to so many ethical appropriations in patristic and subsequent Christian interpretation.

B. Methodological Observations: Implications of the Present Inquiry for New Testament and Early Christian Studies

The ultimate validation of any method of study is the fruit that it bears in the elucidation of a particular question, part of scripture, or aspect of early Christianity. Methodologies do not exist in a vacuum; all those employed in the service of biblical studies and Patristics are ancillary to both disciplines.[9] In addition, methods of study are constantly in a state of flux and refinement, based on developments within a particular discipline and in the academy as a whole. A few reflections on the methods employed in the present study are therefore appropriate. The following remarks naturally reflect my own biases on the current state of affairs in New Testament and early Christian studies. I offer them for whatever they may be worth to the academy's ongoing responsibility to critique what it does, and why.

1. The Ongoing Need for Philological Refinement

Despite the innumerable contributions of resources such as the *Theologisches Wörterbuch zum Neuen Testament* and the Pauly-Wissowa *Real-Encyclopädie der classischen Altertumswissenschaft* (along with *Der Neue Pauly*), the simple reliance upon handbooks, Bible dictionaries and encyclopedias can all too easily contribute to a distortion of the presentation of "NT backgrounds." Likewise, the definitions given in standard lexicons (for example, LSJ, BDAG, Lampe) cannot always be taken as definitive. However indispensable, such resources offer the beginning (not the end) of an exegetical inquiry.

Electronic resources, including the Thesaurus Linguae Graecae, can indeed facilitate such inquiries, at times offering the opportunity to surpass previous investigations. Students of early Christianity need not only be the beneficiaries of philologists', classicists' and ancient historians' hard work. We too can advance these (and other) areas. Indeed, we should make such contributions, lest our scholarship be considered derivative rather than equal in stature to the highest standards of these and other Humanities disciplines. Furthermore, at times we can (and should) bring our work into conversation with the social, and even the natural, sciences.

---

[9] On this point, see David E. Aune, "What Bible Dictionaries Tell Us about Our Discipline," *Proceedings: Eastern Great Lakes and Midwest Biblical Societies* 22 (2002): 17–33, esp. 18–22.

2. Argument and Elucidation

Almost every writing leaves certain "gaps" for the audience to fill in, in order to make a coherent whole out of a text's implied or stated narrative. Without such "gaps," exegetes and expositors would be unnecessary, and thus in search of a different vocation. The hypothetical absence of "gaps" in literature would entail that writers (whether ancient or modern) had adhered to the arcane standards of logical positivism and written exclusively in simple propositional statements. Narrative would disappear, interpretation would be unnecessary, and life would be boring.

That people can, and do, interpret texts differently is empirically verifiable. Historically oriented exegesis maintains that, when bringing to a text an inference not specified in that passage or work, it is desirable, if possible, to supply some ancient analogy to support one's elucidation. The present study notes numerous scholarly works that do not supply arguments for their interpretations of John's diet. The more one knows about life, religion and literary expressions in antiquity, the more likely one is to understand an early Christian writing as an ancient audience would have construed it. It is always important to bear in mind this often acknowledged yet under appreciated buffer against pre-critical eisegesis. When diverse interpretations abound, who, if anyone, has the better part of the argument?

3. Method and Eclecticism

The last three decades or so have brought to our guild an assortment of new methodologies and hermeneutical approaches which, when fully brought into conversation with historical-critical methods, can shed new light on early Christian literature. In chapter 1, I criticize certain literary and ideological interpretations of John's diet.[10] This is not because there is anything wrong with such inquiries *per se*, but because they have so far consistently misconstrued Mark 1:6c‖Matt 3:4c. Literary approaches to this passage, especially when divorced from historically oriented methods of study, are particularly myopic, because such inquiries claim to unearth an explanation for John's diet within Mark's or Matthew's narrative, where none is specified.

Socio-historical questions are of particular importance to chapter 4. I wanted to know about the daily experience of an ancient Mediterranean locust gatherer—whether the Baptist or certain Jews at Qumran (CD 12:11b–15a)—and found especially helpful analogies in anthropological studies of Native Americans. I also wished to examine the claim of Matt 3:4c (echoed in Justin, *Dial.* 88.6–7; Origen, *Luc. Hom.* 25.2, *Philocalia* 26.4; Ambrose, *De helia et ieiunio* 11.40) that John's food consisted entirely of "locusts and wild honey." Can this diet actually sustain an adult indefinitely?

---

[10] For example, on pp. 19–21, 24–26, 33–34.

Unfortunately, certain scholars tout that newer methodologies have somehow superceded traditio-historical analyses or "the historical-critical method,"
however construed.[11]   The future of early Christian studies lies not in
antipathy between older and newer approaches but in dynamic interaction
between them. Historians of religion have acknowledged as much for decades. It is time that the over-balkanized discipline of biblical studies move
beyond such a short-sighted and unnecessary dichotomy.

C. Avenues for Future Inquiry

In the course of investigating John's diet in Synoptic and patristic interpretation, I noted several items meriting additional attention—indeed, more than
any individual scholar could pursue during a lifetime of work in these areas.

1. The Historical Baptist and the Historical Jesus

Mark 1:6c reflects an ordinary aspect of the Baptist's life, his eating. For
whatever reasons, previous works on John have focused on certain deeds attributed to John[12] but for whatever reason neglected this one. The present
study argues that "locusts and wild honey" were part of John's regular—although not necessarily his daily—sustenance. The author of Mark (or
his source) endowed these particular foods with theological significance. It is
precisely because of Mark's theological viewpoint concerning John's clothing
and food that Luke chose to omit Mark 1:6. The author of Matthew picks up
on Mark's cue but takes John's diet in a different direction (Matt 3:4c).

Accordingly, Mark 1:6‖Matt 3:4, along with Luke's omission, offers an
additional example that there is much about the historical Baptist that the
Synoptic evangelists or their sources theologized, exaggerated, misunderstood
or deemed irrelevant.[13]   What was the relationship between the historical
Baptist and the historical Jesus? Some aspects of this question may perhaps

---

[11] E.g., Richard A. Horsley, *Hearing the Whole Story: The Politics of Plot in Mark's Gos-*
pel (Louisville: Westminster John Knox, 2001), p. ix; David M. Rhoads, "Narrative
Criticism: Practices and Prospects," in: *Characterization in the Gospels: Reconceiving Nar-*
rative Criticism (ed. D. Rhoads and K. Syreeni; Sheffield: Sheffield Academic, 1999),
264–85, esp. 265–6. Young, *Biblical Exegesis*, 1–5, offers a more balanced discussion.

[12] E.g., John's baptizing in the Jordan River, preaching a message of repentance, having
disciples, and wearing clothing made of camel's hair.

[13] On the general problem, see, e.g., Meier, *Marginal Jew*, 2.46–9; Koester, *Introduction*
to the New Testament (Philadelphia: Fortress/Berlin: de Gruyter, [2]1995), 2.75–8.

never be answered because of inadequate source materials, but there still remains more work to be done in this area.[14]

2. John the Baptist in Patristic Interpretation

Form criticism posits that the sundry materials incorporated into the NT
gospels survived because they were somehow useful to the primitive church.
Much later, with the eventual emergence of a Christian canon of scripture,
this sequence of utility leading to preservation would oftentimes run in the
opposite direction. *Mutatis mutandis*, the abiding interpretive problem became for many—including many of us today—in what way(s) the NT gospels
(among other esteemed writings) could be useful *to us* as scripture. My study
commends the benefits of studying the initial reason(s) for (even part
of) a passage's preservation, as well as the various meanings attached to that
passage in later centuries.[15]

In the case of John the Baptist, chapter 5 mentions only occasionally
John's clothing in patristic interpretation (Mark 1:6ab‖Matt 3:4ab). From
having read many such passages on John's mantle and belt, my sense is that
the patristic authors devoted even more attention to John's clothing than they
did to his diet. Somebody should write an article on the subject. Perhaps
there is enough material to justify a monograph like this one. It would cer-
tainly be interesting to know how often monks wore hairy garments like John,
as well as how many early Christian interpreters exhorted the faithful to dress
simply because of John's purported example.[16]

More broadly, there is certainly enough material to warrant a handful of
monographs on the Baptist in patristic interpretation. Given the copious gospel materials on John and the need to explain the Baptist's relation to Jesus, a
study of a single author, such as Clement of Alexandria or Origen, let alone
Augustine or Chrysostom, could easily fill a volume.[17] To what extent did

---

[14] On this point I would call attention to the work in progress, to be published before long
in the same series as the present volume, on John the Baptist and Q by Clare Komoroske
Rothschild.

[15] Thus studying a passage form-critically *and* in light of its history of interpretation
might also offer a fitting epitaph for "canonical criticism," which myopically employs the
(Protestant?) canon of scripture as a (the?) context for interpreting scripture without
acknowledging either these writings' pre-canonical forms or the various patristic
understandings of scripture that contributed to the emergence of that very canon.

[16] Edmondo Lupieri, "John the Baptist: The First Monk," 16–17, touches upon this point.
Cf. Knut Backhaus, "Johannes der Täufer in den Apokryphen." (Unpublished essay:
Theologische Fakultät Paderborn, 1985); Christoph G. Müller, "Kleidung als Element der
Charakterzeichnung im Neuen Testament und seiner Umwelt: Ein Streifzug durch das
lukanische Erzählwerk," *SNTSU* 28 (2003): 187–214.

[17] Shorter studies by Meinardus, "The Relics of St. John the Baptist and the Prophet Elisha"; and Lupieri, "John the Baptist: The First Monk"; idem, "John the Gnostic: The Figure

these authors recognize the tension between the presentations of Jesus and his "forerunner" in the NT gospels? Do patristic authors associate the Baptist with the Old Covenant, the New Covenant, or both epochs of salvation history? In what ways do reinventions of John's *persona* serve the theological concerns of later centuries?

3. Scripture Construed as a Source of Early Christian ΠΑΙΔΕΙΑ

After several months of studying numerous early Christian interpretations of John's food, I remained at a loss concerning how to explain the phenomenon of construing John as an ethical model. Why so much attention to this rather unremarkable (and non-ascetic) Synoptic passage? Something clicked when I read Frances M. Young's statement about scripture and early Christian *paideia*.[18] After studying explicit acclamations of philosophers' 'vegetarian' or simple diets in Greco-Roman writings,[19] I became persuaded that such formulations, which for the most part predate the patristic interpretations of Mark 1:6c‖Matt 3:4c, offered the necessary lens through which John's diet could be construed as exemplary. Such a connection between philosophers' virtues and John's purported example should not come as a surprise, given Gregory Nazianzen's characterization of Elijah and John as "perfect philosophers" (*Or.* 43.29 [536B], discussed in chapter 5).

Young does not develop the aforementioned point on *paideia* and early Christian biblical interpretation, and my suggestions concerning the larger phenomenon of early Christian *paideia* are, of course, tentative. I would nonetheless suggest that future studies test, and perhaps modify, two aspects of Young's assertion. First, Young's statement that the *paideia* patristic authors derived from scripture was "new" potentially misses the mark.[20] Chapter 5 argues that, in the case of John's diet, the *paideia* is not new but corresponds to that in non-Christian Greco-Roman literature. Benjamin Fiore has argued a similar point concerning the moral example of "Paul" in the Pastoral Epistles vis-à-vis the Socratic literature.[21]

Second, it is not clear to me how Christian scripture constituted, in Young's words, "an alternative" to the classics.[22] At least at the beginning of

---

of the Baptist in Origen and Heterodox Gnosticism," *StPatr* 19 (1989): 322–7, offer fine examples of such inquiries. Cf. E. R. L. Tinambunan, "Elijah according to the Fathers of the Church," *Carmelus* (Rome) 49 (2002): 85–116.

[18] Young, *Biblical Exegesis*, 76: "Once the biblical literature became established as an alternative body of classics, it would soon be seen as the basis of a new *paideia*."

[19] Chapter 5 offers only representative examples in Greco-Roman literature. More material of this sort remains to be digested.

[20] See further her discussion in: eadem, *Biblical Exegesis*, 49–116.

[21] Fiore, *The Function of Personal Example in the Socratic and Pastoral Epistles* (AnBib 105; Rome: Biblical Institute Press, 1986).

[22] The point would have to be examined in the case of each early Christian author.

this development in early Christian biblical interpretation, the necessary pre-requisites to finding *paideia* in scripture are twofold, namely the knowledge and the acceptance of that *paideia* in the Greco-Roman literature. It is there-fore important to guard against imposing a false dichotomy on patristic biblical interpretation as informed by classical *paideia*, unless it should be warranted by the patristic authors themselves. Jerusalem need not be at war with Athens, especially if both parties laud the same types of moral excel-lence for emulation.

Indeed, to understand the various presuppositions that early Christian authors brought to scripture, one must have a firm grasp of the classical edu-cation and *paideia* that so many of them had received and embraced. Nonetheless, in some Christian circles scripture could indeed have functioned as an alternative source for the *paideia* that others derived from classical lit-erature. The question in what ways Christian and classical *paideia* may have differed is beyond the present inquiry. Much work remains to be done in this area.

4. Food, Culture and Theology

It is perhaps axiomatic that attitudes toward food are largely defined by culture and environment. Jerome recognizes as much when noting that whereas people in certain regions regularly eat locusts, others would revile such insects as food.[23] Likewise, today it is common to associate American over-consumption with meat eating, and in particular with a penchant for hamburgers. Thus it comes as little surprise that protesters of "globalization" by America and other developed nations occasionally target McDonalds res-taurants.[24] The food on which a particular chain restaurant built its reputation becomes the focal point for protest against the nation identified with that food.

Complementing the excellent progress made during the last quarter cen-tury in understanding early Christian asceticism, broader examinations of

---

[23] Jerome, *Adv. Iovin.* 2.7, discussed in chapters 2 and 5.

[24] As occurred, e.g., in Gothenburg (Göteborg), Sweden on 15 June 2001 (reported by the BBC: "Three Shot in EU Summit Riots," online: http://news.bbc.co.uk/1/hi/world/europe/1391007.stm [on 8 April 2004]). One Anarchist Web site (Infoshop.org) lists October 16 as the annual date for protesting this restaurant in relation to one such demonstration in Italy in 1999 ("Italian Anarchists Protest McDonalds in Bergamo"; online: http://www.infoshop.org/news4/mcd_italy.html [on 8 April 2004]). See further: BM McSpotlight, "McLibel, McDonald's, Multinations: Judge for Yourself," online: http://www.mcspotlight.org/ (on 8 April 2004); Eric Schlosser, *Fast Food Nation: The Dark Side of the All-American Meal* (Boston: Houghton Mifflin, 2001), esp. 243–52. In the inter-est of full disclosure, the author acknowledges that he is not vegetarian. He does enjoy an occasional hamburger, although perhaps not as frequently as the average American, and cer-tainly not as often as he did in previous years.

food, ethnicity and culture in early Christianity could indeed be fruitful. The present study takes just a small bite out of what will surely prove to be a large apple (or grasshopper). One question meriting attention in this regard is whether the privileging of one culture's preferences (biases?) concerning food necessarily marginalizes Christians of other cultures or ethnicities. According to the apostle Paul, this was an issue for the church in Antioch already in the 40s C.E. (Gal 2:11–14).

As noted in chapter 1, moreover, the Synoptic gospels offer various, and sometimes contradictory, anecdotes about the Baptist's food.[25] What each of the Synoptic evangelists, their sources, the apostle Paul, and numerous patristic interpretations of John's diet assume is that food constitutes a palatable cuisine for theological reflection. My study focuses on one such passage (Mark 1:6c‖Matt 3:4c) and its history of interpretation. Many other morsels in the HB, the NT and the patristic and matristic literature await attention. Part of the discussion should focus on Christian 'vegetarians,' whether Tatian, Ebionite Christians or others. Another inquiry could consider a possible relation between eating meat and a Eucharistic theology of the "real presence." Indeed, some inquiries can be both timely and ideally suited for scholarly analysis. I hope that this study has helped to illustrate that, regardless of whether one embraces every part of scripture as somehow "useful" (2 Tim 3:16), each passage merits elucidation both in its historical context and for the various interpretations it inspired. At times such creative improvisations on scripture can be inspirational to us today, even more so than the original text.

---

[25] John ate "locusts and wild honey" (Mark 1:6c). His food consisted exclusively of "locusts and wild honey" (Matt 3:4c). John's disciples—and presumably John himself—sometimes fasted (Mark 2:18 par.). John was not supposed to imbibe alcoholic beverages (L/Luke 1:15b). John's diet was unlike that of most Palestinian Jews (Q/Luke 7:33); Matthew's version of this Q material claims that John survived without eating or drinking anything at all (Q/Matt 11:18).

Bibliography

Texts and Translations

Adriaen, M., ed. *Sancti Ambrosii Mediolanensis, Opera.* CCSL 14. Turnholt: Brepols, 1957.

Albek, Chanoch. *Shishah Sidrei Mishnah.* Jerusalem/Tel Aviv: Mosad Biyalik, 1952–59.

Amidon, Philip R. *The Panarion of St. Epiphanius, Bishop of Salamis: Selected Passages.* New York: Oxford University Press, 1990.

Archambault, Georges, ed. *Justin, Dialogue avec Tryphon.* Textes et documents pour l'étude historique du Christianisme 8, 11. Paris: A. Picard, 1909.

Aubert, Fernand and Henri Meylan, eds. *Correspondance de Théodore de Bèze.* Geneva: Droz, 1960–.

Aubineau, Michel, ed. *Les homélies festales d'Hésychius de Jérusalem.* Subsidia hagiographica 59. Brussels: Société des bollandistes, 1978–80.

—. *[Gregory of Nyssa,] Traité de la virginité.* SC 119. Paris: Cerf, 1966.

Aubert, H. and F. Wimmer, eds. *Istorai peri zoon: Kritisch-berichtigter Text Aristoteles, mit deutscher Übersetzung.* Leipzig: W. Engelmann, 1868.

Balme, D. M., ed. *Aristotle, Historia Animalium.* Cambridge Classical Texts and Commentaries 38. Cambridge: Cambridge University, 2002.

Beckby, Hermann, ed. *Anthologia graeca.* Munich: Heimeran, [2]1965–68.

Beckh, Heinrich. *Geoponica sive Cassiani Bassi scholastici, De re rustica eclogae.* Teubner. Leipzig: Teubner, 1994 (1895).

Bernardi, Jean, ed. *Grégoire de Nazianze, Discours 42–43.* SC 384. Paris: Cerf, 1992.

Beyenka, Mary M. *Saint Ambrose, Letters.* FC 26. Washington: Catholic University of America, [2]1967.

Bonwetsch, G. Nathanael. *Methodius.* GCS 27. Leipzig: Hinrichs, 1917.

Brownson, Carleton L. and John Dillery. *Xenophon, Anabasis.* LCL. Cambridge, MA: Harvard University, [2]1998.

Buck, Mary Joseph Aloysius. *S. Ambrosii, De helia et ieiunio.* Patristic Studies 19. Washington: Catholic University of America, 1929.

Bury, R. G. *[Plato,] Timaeus; Critias; Cleitophon; Menexenus; Epistles.* LCL. London: Heinemann/New York: Putnam, 1929.

Callahan, Virginia Woods. *Saint Gregory of Nyssa, Ascetical Works.* FC 58. Washington: Catholic University of America, 1967.

Canfora, Luciano, ed. *Ateneo, I deipnosofisti: i dotti a banchetto.* Rome: Salerno, 2001.

Carnuth, Otto, ed. *Aristonici, ΠΕΡΙ ΣΗΜΕΙΩΝ ΟΔΥΣΣΕΙΑΣ: Reliquiae emendatiores.* Leipzig: Hirzel, 1869.

Chadwick, Henry. *Saint Augustine, Confessions.* Oxford: Oxford University, 1991.

Charlesworth, James H., ed. *The Old Testament Pseudepigrapha.* 2 Vols. New York: Doubleday/London: Darton, Longman & Todd, 1983.

Cohoon, J. W. and H. L. Crosby. *Dio Chrysostom.* LCL. Cambridge, MA: Harvard University, 1951 (1932).

Colson, F. H., G. H. Whitaker and Ralph Marcus. *Philo: In Ten Volumes (and Two Supplementary Volumes).* LCL. Cambridge, MA: Harvard University/London: Heinemann, 1962 (1929).

Conomis, Nicos C., ed. *Dinarchi, Orationes cum fragmentis.* Teubner. Leipzig: Teubner, 1975.

Conybeare, F. C. *[Philostratus,] The Life of Apollonius of Tyana, The Epistles of Apollonius and the Treatise of Eusebius.* LCL. Cambridge, MA: Harvard University/London: Heinemann, 1969 (1912).

Courtonne, Yves. *Saint Basile, Lettres.* Paris: Les Belles Lettres, 1957–66.

Cramer, John A., ed. *Catenae Graecorum Patrum in Novum Testamentum.* Hildesheim: Olms, 1967 (1840).

Daly, Robert J. *Treatise on the Passover; Dialogue of Origen with Heraclides.* ACW 54. New York: Paulist, 1992.

Datema, Cornelis. "Another Unedited Homily of Ps. Chrysostom on the Birth of John the Baptist [BHG 847i]." *Byzantion* 53 (1983): 478–93.

Daur, Klaus-D., ed. *Arnobius Ivnioris, Opera omnia.* CCSL 25A: *Arnobius Ivnioris, Opera minora.* Turnholt: Brepols, 1992.

Defarrari, Roy J. *Saint Basil, the Letters.* LCL. London: Heinemann, 1926–34.

DeVoto, James G. *Claudius Aelianus, ΠΟΙΚΙΛΗΣ ΙΣΤΟΡΙΑΣ (Varia historia).* Chicago: Ares, 1995.

Dindorf, Wilhelm, ed. *Harpocrationis, Lexicon in decem oratories Atticos.* Oxford: Oxford University, 1853.

—. *Historici Graeci minores.* Teubner. Leipzig: Teubner, 1870–71.

Dittmeyer, Leonhard, ed. *Aristotelis, De animalibus historia.* Teubner. Leipzig: Teubner, 1907.

Doignon, Jean, ed. *Hilaire de Poitiers, Sur Matthieu.* SC 254, 258. Paris: Cerf, 1978–79.

Dover, Kenneth James. *Select Poems: Theocritus.* London: Macmillan, 1971.

Eason, James, ed. [Sir Thomas Browne,] "Of the food of John Baptist, Locusts and wilde Honey." In: *Pseudodoxia Epidemica.* [6]1672 (1646), VII:ix. Online: http://penelope.uchicago.edu/pseudodoxia/pseudo79.html (on 23 Jan. 2003).

—. [Alexander Ross,] *Arcana Microcosmi.* [2]1652. Online: http://penelope.uchicago.edu/ross/ross21.html (on 23 Jan. 2003).

Ebbell, Bendix, ed. *The Papyrus Ebers: The Greatest Egyptian Medical Document.* Copenhagen: Levin & Munksgaard/London: H. Milford, Oxford University, 1937.

Edmonds, John M. *The Fragments of Attic Comedy after Meineke, Bergk, and Kock.* Leiden: Brill, 1957–61.

Elliott, J. K. *The Apocryphal New Testament: A Collection of Apocryphal Christian Literature in an English Translation.* Oxford: Clarendon/New York: Oxford University Press, 1993.

Étaix, R. and Joseph Lemarié, eds. *Chromatii Aquileiensis, Opera.* CCSL 9A. Turnholt: Brepols, 1974.

Evans, Ernest, ed. *[Tertullian,] Adversus Marcionem.* OECT. Oxford: Clarendon, 1972.

Fairclough, H. Rushton, ed. *Virgil.* LCL. Cambridge, MA: Harvard University, [2]1969–74.

Faller, Otto, ed. *[Ambrosii,] Epistulae et acta.* CSEL 82.3. Vienna: Hoelder-Pinchler-Temsky, 1968–96.

Falls, Thomas B. *Saint Justin Martyr.* FC 6. New York: Christian Heritage, 1948.

Flower, Barbara and Elisabeth Rosenbaum. *The Roman Cookery Book: A Critical Translation of «The Art of Cooking» by Apicius, for Use in the Study and the Kitchen.* London/Toronto: Harrap, 1958.

Forster, E. S. and Edward H. Heffner, eds. *On Agriculture: Lucius Junius Moderatus Columella.* LCL. Cambridge, MA: Harvard University/London: Heinemann, ²1968.

Freedman, H. and M. Simon. *Midrash Rabbah.* London: Soncino, 1961 (1939).

Friedlaender, Ludwig, ed. *Aristonici, ΠΕΡΙ ΣΗΜΕΙΩΝ ΙΛΙΑΔΟΣ: Reliquiae emendatiores.* Amsterdam: Hakkert, 1965 (1853).

García Martínez, Florentino and Eibert J. C. Tigchelaar, eds. *The Dead Sea Scrolls: Study Edition.* Leiden: Brill/Grand Rapids: Eerdmans, 2000.

Geffcken, Johannes, ed. *Die Oracula sibyllina.* Leipzig: Hinrichs, 1902.

Gemoll, Wilhelm, ed. *Nepualii, fragmentum περὶ τῶν κατὰ ἀντιπάθειαν καὶ συμπάθειαν et Democriti, περὶ συμπαθειῶν καὶ ἀντιπαθειῶν.* Striegau: Tschörner, 1884.

Gibson, Margaret Dunlop. *The Commentaries of Isho'dad of Merv, Bishop of Ḥadatha (c. 850 A.D.) in Syriac and English.* HSem V–VI. Cambridge: Cambridge University, 1911–16.

Goggin, Aquinas. *Saint John Chrysostom, Commentary on Saint John the Apostle and Evangelist: Homilies 1–47.* FC 33. New York: Fathers of the Church, 1957.

Grant, Mark. *Dieting for an Emperor: A Translation of Books 1 and 4 of Oribasius' Medical Compilations.* Studies in Ancient Medicine 15. Leiden: Brill, 1997.

—. *Galen, On Food and Diet.* London/New York: Routledge, 2000.

Grenfell, Bernard P. et al., eds. *The Tebtunis Papyri.* London: Oxford University, 1902.

Guéraud, Octave and Pierre Nautin, eds. *Origène, Sur la Pâque.* Christianisme antique 2. Paris: Beauchesne, 1979.

Gulick, Charles B. *Athenaeus, The Deipnosophists.* LCL. Cambridge, MA: Harvard University, 1927–41.

Gunther, Robert T., ed. *The Greek Herbal of Dioscorides.* Oxford: Oxford University, 1934 = New York: Hafner, 1968.

Hadas, Moses, ed. *Aristeas to Philocrates (Letter of Aristeas).* Jewish Apocryphal Literature. New York: Dropsie College for Hebrew and Cognate Learning/Harper, 1951.

Harris, J. Rendel. *Fragments of the Commentary of Ephrem Syrus upon the Diatessaron.* London: C. J. Clay and Sons, 1895.

Helmreich, Georg, ed. *ΓΑΛΗΝΟΥ, ΠΕΡΙ ΧΡΕΙΑΣ ΜΟΡΙΩΝ ΙΖ': Galeni, De usu partium libri XVII.* Teubner. Amsterdam: Hakkert, 1968 (1907–09).

Hett, W. S. *[Aristotle/Ps. Aristotle,] Minor Works.* LCL. Cambridge, MA: Harvard University/London: Heinemann, 1963 (1936).

Hilberg, Isidor, ed. *Sancti Eusebii Hieronymi, Epistulae.* CSEL 54–56. Vienna: Verlag der Österreichischen Akademie der Wissenschaften, ²1996 (1910–18).

Holl, Karl, ed. *Epiphanius.* GCS 25. Leipzig: Hinrichs, 1915.

Hort, Arthur. *[Theophrastus,] Enquiry into Plants and Minor Works on Odours and Weather Signs.* LCL. Cambridge, MA: Harvard University, 1968 (1916).

Hunter, Richard. *Theocritus, A Selection: Idylls 1, 3, 4, 6, 7, 10, 11 and 13.* Cambridge Greek and Latin Classics. Cambridge: Cambridge University, 1999.

Jacoby, Felix, ed. *Die Fragmente der griechischen Historiker.* Berlin: Weidmann, 1923–43.

Jayakar, A. S. G. *Ad-Damīrī's Ḥayāt al-Ḥayawān: (A Zoological Lexicon).* London/Luzac/ Bombay: Taraporevala, 1906–08.

Jones, Horace L. *The Geography of Strabo.* LCL. Cambridge, MA: Harvard University, 1982 (1917).

Junod, Éric, ed. *[Origen,] Philocalie 21–27.* SC 226. Paris: Cerf, 1976.

Karla, Grammatiki A. *Vita Aesopi: Überlieferung, Sprache und Edition einer früh-byzantinischen Fassung des Äsopromans.* Serta Graeca 13. Wiesbaden: Reichert, 2001.

Kidd, Douglas, ed. *[Aratus Solensis,] Phaenomena.* Cambridge Classical Texts and Commentaries 34. Cambridge: Cambridge University, 1997.

Klostermann, Erich, ed. *Origenes Matthäuserklärung.* GCS 41/1. Berlin: Akademie Verlag, ²1959.

Kock, Theodor, ed. *Comicorum Atticorum fragmenta.* Leipzig: Teubner, 1880–88.

Kovacs, David, ed. *[Euripides,] Bacchae; Iphigenia at Aulis; Rhesus.* LCL. Cambridge, MA: Harvard University, 2002.

Kraszewski, Charles S. *The Gospel of Matthew with Patristic Commentaries.* Studies in Bible and Early Christianity 40. Lewiston: Mellon, 1999.

Kühn, Karl Gottlob, ed. *Claudii Galeni, Opera omnia.* Hildesheim: Olms, 2001 (1821).

Lampros, Spyridōn Paulou, ed. *Supplementum Aristotelicum.* Vol. 1/1: *Excerptorum Constantini, De natura animalium libri duo; Aristophanis, Historiae animalium epitome, subiunctis Aeliani,* 1885. Berlin: Reimer, 1885–1903.

Lewis, George. *The Philocalia of Origen: A Compilation of St Gregory of Nazianzus and St Basil of Caesarea.* Edinburgh: T. & T. Clark, 1911.

Liddell, Mark H., ed. *Palladius, On Husbondrie.* London: N. Trübner & Co., 1896.

Lienhard, Joseph T. *[Origen,] Homilies on Luke; Fragments on Luke.* FC 94. Washington: Catholic University of America, 1996.

Louis, Pierre. *Aristotle, Histoire des animaux.* Paris: Les Belles Lettres, 1964–69.

Luther, Martin. *D. Martin Luthers Werke: Kritische Gesamtausgabe.* Weimar: Böhlau, 1883–.

—. *Luther's Works.* Jaroslav Pelikan and Helmut T. Lehmann, gen. eds. Saint Louis, MO: Concordia Publishing House/Philadelphia: Fortress, 1955–86.

Marcovich, Miroslav, ed. *Clementis Alexandrini, Paedagogus.* VCSup 61. Leiden: Brill, 2002.

Mason, Steve, ed. *Life of Josephus: Translation and Commentary.* Flavius Josephus: Translation and Commentary 9. Leiden: Brill, 2001.

May, Margaret Tallmadge. *Galen, On the Usefulness of the Parts of the Body.* Cornell Publications in the History of Science. Ithaca, NY: Cornell University, 1968.

Mazal, Otto. *Der Wiener Dioskurides: Codex medicus Graecus 1 der Österreichischen Nationalbibliothek.* Glanzlichter der Buchkunst 8. Graz: Akademische Druck- u. Verlagsanstalt, 1998–99.

McCarthy, Carmel. *Saint Ephrem's Commentary on Tatian's Diatessaron: An English Translation of Chester Beatty Syriac MS 709.* JSSSup 2. Oxford: Oxford University, 1993.

McCauley, Leo P. et al. *Funeral Orations by Saint Gregory Nazianzen and Saint Ambrose.* FC 22. New York: Fathers of the Church, 1953.

McCown, C. C., ed. *The Testament of Solomon.* Leipzig: Hinrichs, 1922.

Meineke, August. *Critica ad Athenaei Deipnosophistas.* Leipzig: Teubner, 1867.

Mette, Hans Joachim, ed. *Die Fragmente der Tragödien des Aischylos.* Schriften der Sektion für Altertumswissenschaft 15. Berlin: Akademie-Verlag, 1959.

Migne, Jacques-Paul, ed. *Patrologiae cursus completus . . . Series Graeca . . . (Patrologia graeca).* 161 Vols. Paris: 1857–66 = Turnholt: Brepols, 1960.

—. *Patrologiae cursus completus . . . Series Latina, . . . (Patrologia latina).* 221 Vols. Paris: 1844–64.

Mingana, Alphonse. "A New Life of John the Baptist." In: *Woodbrooke Studies: Christian Documents in Syriac, Arabic, and Garshuni.* J. Rendel Harris, ed. Cambridge: W. Heffer & Sons, 1927. 1.234–87.

Moreschini, Claudio, ed. *Grégoire de Nazianze, Discours 32–37.* SC 318. Paris: Cerf, 1985.

—. *Grégoire de Nazianze, Discours 38–41.* SC 358. Paris: Cerf, 1990.

Mühlenberg, Ekkehard, ed. *Psalmenkommentare aus der Katenenüberlieferung.* Patristische Texte und Studien 15, 16, 19. Berlin: de Gruyter, 1975–77.

Müller, Karl O., ed. *Geographi graeci minores: E codicibus recognovit prolegomenis annotatione indicibus instruxit.* Paris: Didot, 1855–61.

Musurillo, Herbert, ed. *Jean Chrysostome, La Virginité.* SC 125. Paris: Cerf, 1966.

Nauck, August. *Aristophanis Byzantii: Grammatici Alexandrini fragmenta.* Hildesheim: Olms, 1963 ([2]1848).

Neusner, Jacob. *The Mishnah: A New Translation.* New Haven: Yale University, 1988.

—. *The Talmud of Babylonia: An Academic Commentary.* Vol. 30: *Bavli Tractate Hullin,* 1994. Atlanta: Scholars Press, 1994–99.

Noblot, Henri, ed. *[Seneca (Y),] Lettres à Lucilius.* Paris: Les Belles Lettres, 1957–64.

O'Donnell, James J., ed. *Augustine, Confessions.* Oxford: Clarendon/Oxford: Oxford University, 1992.

Oden, Thomas C. and Christopher A. Hall, eds. *Mark.* Ancient Christian Commentary on Scripture: NT 2. Downers Grove, IL: InterVarsity, 1998.

Oldfather, C. H., ed. *Diodorus of Sicily.* LCL. Cambridge, MA: Harvard University, 1935.

Olivar, Alexandre, ed. *Sancti Petri Chrysologi, Collectio sermonum.* CCSL 24B. Turnholt: Brepols, 1975.

Olivieri, Alexander, ed. *Aetii Amideni, Libri medicinales.* CMG 8.1–2. Vol. 1: Leipsig: Teubner, 1935. Vol. 2: Berlin: Akademie Verlag, 1950.

Owen, Thomas (1749–1812). *ΓΕΩΠΟΝΙΚΑ: Agricultural Pursuits.* London: Spilsbury, 1805–06). Online: http://digital.lib.msu.edu/onlinecolls/display.cfm?TitleNo=257&FT=gif (on 8 April 2004).

Palacios, Miguel Asín, ed. *Logia et agrapha Domini Jesu: apud Moslemicos scriptores, Asceticos praesertim, Usitata.* PO 19/4. Paris: Firmin-Didot, 1916–29 = Turnhout: Brepols, 1974.

Papathomopoulos, Manolis. *Ho vios tou Aisopou: He parallage G.* Ioannina: Aphoi Phrangoude, 1990.

Parisot, Jean, ed. *[Aphrahat the Syrian,] Demonstrationes.* 2 Vols. Patrologia syriaca 1–2A. Paris: Firmin-Didot, 1894.

Peck, A. L., ed. *Aristotle, History of Animals.* LCL. Cambridge, MA: Harvard University, 1991–93.

Piédagnel, Auguste, ed. *Jean Chrysostome, Panégyriques de S. Paul.* SC 300. Paris: Cerf, 1982.

Pingree, David E., ed. *Hephaestionis Thebani, Apotelesmaticorum libri tres.* Teubner. Leipzig: Teubner, 1973.

Powell, Owen W. *Galen, On the Properties of Foodstuffs = De alimentorum facultatibus.* Cambridge: Cambridge University, 2003.

Raabe, Richard, ed. *Petrus der Iberer: Ein Charakterbild zur Kirchen und Sittengeschichte des fünften Jahrhunderts. Syrische Übersetzung einer um das Jahr 500 verfassten griechischen Biographie.* Leipzig: Hinrichs, 1895.

Rabinowitz, L. I. and P. Grossman. *The Code of Maimonides (Mišneh Torah).* Yale Judaica Series 16: *Book Five: The Book of Holiness [Sefer Q'dušah],* 1965. New Haven: Yale University, 1949.

Rackham, Harris, ed. *[Plin. (E),] Natural History.* LCL. Cambridge, MA: Harvard University, 1938–63.

Radt, Stefan, ed. *Tragicorum Graecorum fragmenta.* Göttingen: Vandenhoeck & Ruprecht, 1971–77.

Raeder, Johann, ed. *Oribasii, Collectionum medicarum reliquiae.* CMG 6.2.2. Amsterdam: Hakkart, 1964 (1933).

Rauer, Max, ed. *Origenes Werke.* GCS 9: *Die Homilien zu Lukas in der Übersetzung des Hieronymus und die Griechischen Reste der homilien und des Lukas-Kommentars.* Berlin: Akademie-Verlag, [2]1959.

Reischl, Wilhelm K. and Joseph Rupp, eds. *S. Patris nostri Cyrilli Hierosolymorum, Opera quae supersunt omnia.* Hildesheim: Olms, 1967 (1848–60).

Reuss, Joseph, ed. *Matthäus-Kommentare aus der griechischen Kirche.* TUGAL 61. Berlin: Akademie-Verlag, 1957.

Riain, Íde M. Ní. *Commentary of Saint Ambrose on the Gospel according to Saint Luke.* Dublin: Halcyon/Elo, 2001.

Rieger Shore, Sally. *John Chrysostom, On Virginity; Against Remarriage.* Studies in Women and Religion 9. Lewiston, NY: Mellen, 1983.

Riese, Alexander, ed. *Anthologia latina.* Teubner. Leipzig: Teubner, 1868–1930.

Roberts, Alexander and James Donaldson, eds. *Ante-Nicene Fathers: The Writings of the Fathers Down to A.D. 325.* Buffalo: Christian Literature Publishing Company, 1885–1896 = Peabody, MA: Hendrickson, 1994.

—. *Nicene and Post-Nicene Fathers of the Christian Church.* First Series. 14 vols. New York: Christian Literature Publishing Company, 1886–90 = Peabody, MA: Hendrickson, 1994.

—. *Nicene and Post-Nicene Fathers of the Christian Church.* Second Series. 14 vols. New York: Christian Literature Publishing Company, 1890–1900 = Peabody, MA: Hendrickson, 1994.

Rodgers, Robert H., ed. *Palladii Rutilii Tauri Aemiliani viri inlustris: Opus agriculturae, De veterinaria medicina de insitione.* Teubner. Leipzig: Teubner, 1975.

Sauma, Assad. *Gregory Bar-Hebraeus's Commentary on the Book of Kings from his Storehouse of Mysteries: A Critical Edition with an English Translation, Introduction and Notes.* Studia Semitica Upsaliensia 20. Uppsala: Uppsala University, 2003.

Schenkl, C., ed. *Sancti Ambrosii, Opera.* CSEL 32.2. Vienna: Tempsky, 1897.

Scholfield, A. F., ed. *Aelian, On the Characteristics of Animals.* LCL. Cambridge, MA: Harvard University, 1958–59.

Sewter, E. R. A. *The Chronographia of Michael Psellus [1018–after 1078 C.E.].* New Haven: Yale University, 1953.

Sieben, Hermann-Josef, ed. *[Origen,] In Lucam homiliae = Homilien zum Lukasevangelium.* Fontes Christiani 4. Freiburg: Herder, 1991–92.

Simonetti, Manlio, ed. *Matthew 1–13.* Ancient Christian Commentary on Scripture: NT 1A. Downers Grove, IL: InterVarsity, 2001.

Stratton, George M., ed. *Theophrastus.* London: Allen & Unwin, 1917.

Telfer, William. *Cyril of Jerusalem and Nemesius of Emesa.* LCC 4. Philadelphia: Westminster, 1955.

Thackeray, H. S. J. *Josephus, The Jewish War.* LCL. Cambridge, MA: Harvard University, 1997 (1926).

Thackeray, H. S. J. and Ralph Marcus. *Josephus, Jewish Antiquities.* LCL. Cambridge, MA: Harvard University, 1998 (1926).

Thackston, Jr., W. M., ed. *The Tales of the Prophets of al-Kisaʾi.* Library of Classical Arabic Literature 2. Boston: Twayne, 1978.

Tirone, Cecilia, ed. *Le omelie su S. Giovanni Evangelista.* Torino: Società editrice internazionale, 1942–48.

Toal, M. F., ed. *The Sunday Sermons of the Great Fathers.* Chicago: Regnery, 1957–63.

Valavanolickal, Kuriakose A. *Aphrahat, Demonstrations I.* Changanassery, India: HIRS Publications, 1999–.

Wachsmuth, Curt, ed. *[Lydus,] De Ostentis et calendaria Graeca omnia.* Leipzig: Teubner, 1897.

Waszink, J. H., ed. *Quinti Septimi Florentis Tertulliani, De anima.* Amsterdam: Meulenhoff, 1947.

Wellmann, Max, ed. *Pedanii Dioscuridis Anazarbei, De materia medica libri quinque.* Berlin: Weidmann, 1958 (1907).

Westermann, William Linn et al., eds. *Zenon Papyri: Business Papers of the Third Century B.C. Dealing with Palestine and Egypt.* Columbia Papyri, Greek Series 3–4. New York: Columbia University, 1934–40.

Whitby, Michael and Mary Whitby. *The History of Theophylact Simocatta.* Oxford: Clarendon/New York: Oxford University Press, 1986.

Wimmer, Friedrich, ed. *Theophrasti Eresii opera, quae supersunt.* Frankfurt am Main: Minerva, 1964 (1866).

Wood, Simon P. *[Clement,] Christ the Educator.* FC 23. New York: Fathers of the Church, 1954.

Zanetto, Joseph, ed. *Theophylacti Simocatae, Epistulae.* Teubner. Leipzig: Teubner, 1985.

Zelzer, Klaus, ed. *Basili, Regula a Rufino latine uersa.* CSEL 86. Vienna: Hoelder-Pichler-Tempsky, 1986.

Zycha, Joseph, ed. *Sancti Aureli Augustini, De utilitate credendi; De duabus animabus; Contra Fortunatum; Contra Adimantum; Contra epistulam fundamenti; Contra Faustum.* CSEL 25/1. Vienna: Tempsky, 1891.

Secondary Literature

Achebe, Chinua. *Things Fall Apart; No Longer at Ease; Anthills of the Savannah.* New York: Griot, 1995.

Achtemeier, Paul J. *Invitation to Mark: A Commentary.* Doubleday NT Commentary Series. Garden City, NY: Image Books, 1978.

—. *Mark.* Proclamation Commentaries. Philadelphia: Fortress, ²1986.

Albright, W. F. and C. S. Mann. *Matthew: Introduction, Translation, and Notes.* AB 26. Garden City, NY: Doubleday, 1971.

Alford, Henry. *The Greek New Testament.* Vol. 1: *The Four Gospels,* ⁴1859 (1849). London: Rivingtons, Waterloo Place/Cambridge: Deighton, Bell and Co., ⁴1859–66.

Allegro, John M. *The Dead Sea Scrolls.* London: Penguin Books, ²1958 (1956).

Allison, Dale C. "Elijah Must Come First." *JBL* 103 (1984): 256–8.

Andersen, F. I. "The Diet of John the Baptist." *AbrN* 3 (1961–62): 60–74.

Anderson, Hugh. *The Gospel of Mark.* New Century Bible. Greenwood, SC: Attic, 1976 = Grand Rapids: Eerdmans, 1981.

Andiñach, Pablo R. "The Locusts in the Message of Joel." *VT* 42 (1992): 433–41.

André, Jacques. *L'alimentation et la cuisine à Rome.* Collection d'études anciennes. Paris: Belles Lettres, ²1981 (1961).

Angel, J. Lawrence. *The People of Lerna: Analysis of a Prehistoric Aegean Population.* Princeton, NJ: American School of Classical Studies at Athens, 1971.

Arbesmann Rudolph. "Fasting and Prophecy in Pagan and Christian Antiquity." *Traditio* 7 (1949–51): 1–71.

Arrington, L. R. "Foods of the Bible." *Journal of the American Dietetic Association* 35 (1959): 816–20.

Aune, David E. "What Bible Dictionaries Tell Us about Our Discipline." *Proceedings: Eastern Great Lakes and Midwest Biblical Societies* 22 (2002): 17–33.

Avigad, Nahman. "A Hebrew Seal with a Family Emblem." *IEJ* 16 (1966): 50–3.

Aynard, J. M. "Animals in Mesopotamia." In: *Animals in Archaeology.* A. H. Brodrick, ed. New York: Praeger, 1972. 42–68.

Baarda, Tjitze. "The Author of the Arabic Diatessaron." In: idem, *Early Transmission of Words of Jesus: Thomas, Tatian, and the Text of the New Testament. A Collection of Studies.* Amsterdam: VU Boekhandel/Uitgeverij, 1983. 207–49.

—. *The Gospel Quotations of Aphrahat the Persian Sage: Aphrahat's Text of the Fourth Gospel.* 2 Vols. Amsterdam: Vrije Universiteit, 1975.

Backhaus, Knut. *Die "Jüngerkreise" des Täufers Johannes: Eine Studie zu den religions-geschichtlichen Ursprüngen des Christentums.* Paderborner Theologische Studien 19. Paderborn: F. Schöningh, 1991.

—. "Johannes der Täufer in den Apokryphen." Unpublished essay: Theologische Fakultät Paderborn, 1985.

Badke, William B. "Was Jesus a Disciple of John?" *EvQ* 62 (1990): 195–204.

Bamberger, Bernard Jacob. *The Torah: A Modern Commentary.* Vol. 3: *Leviticus.* New York: Union of American Hebrew Congregations, 1979.

—. *The Torah: A Modern Commentary.* W. Gunther Plaut, ed. New York: Union of American Hebrew Congregations, 1981.

Bammel, Ernst. "'John Did No Miracle': John 10. 41." In: *Miracles: Cambridge Studies in Their Philosophy and History.* C. F. D. Moule, ed. London: A. R. Mowbray, 1965. 179–202.

—. "John the Baptist in Early Christian Tradition." *NTS* 18 (1971–72): 95–128.

Bates, Marston. "Insects in the Diet." *American Scholar* 29 (1959–60): 43–52.

Beavis, Ian C. *Insects and Other Invertebrates in Classical Antiquity.* Exeter: University of Exeter, 1988.

Becker, Eve-Marie. "'Kamelhaare... und wilder Honig': Der historische Wert und die theologische Bedeutung der biographischen Täufer-Notiz (Mk 1,6)." In: *Die bleibende Gegenwart des Evangeliums.* FS Otto Merk. R. Gebauer and M. Meiser, eds. Marburger Theologische Studien 76. Marburg: Elwert, 2003. 13–28.

Behr, John. *Asceticism and Anthropology in Irenaeus and Clement.* Oxford Early Christian Studies. New York: Oxford University Press, 2000.

Bequaert, Joseph C. "Insects as Food: How They Have Augmented the Food Supply of Mankind in Early and Recent Times." *Natural History* 21 (1921): 191–200.

Bloch, R. Howard. *God's Plagiarist: Being an Account of the Fabulous Industry and Irregular Commerce of the Abbé Migne.* Chicago: University of Chicago, 1994.

Blomberg, Craig L. *Matthew.* NAC 22. Nashville: Broadman, 1992.

Blum, Robert. "Imkerei im alten Israel." *Bienenvater* (Vienna) 76/10 (1955): 334–6.

BM McSpotlight. "McLibel, McDonald's, Multinations: Judge for Yourself." Online: http://www.mcspotlight.org/ (on 8 April 2004).

Bochart, Samuel. "Iohannem, Baptistam, veras locustas habuisse pro cibo." In: idem, *Hierozoicon, sive De animalibus Sanctae Scripturae.* E. F. C. Rosenmüller, ed. Leipzig: In Libraria Weidmannia, 1793. 3.326–33.

Böcher, Otto. "Ass Johannes der Täufer kein Brot (Luk. vii. 33)?" *NTS* 18 (1971–72): 90–2.

Bodenheimer, Frederick S. "Fauna." Art. *IDB,* 2.246–56.

—. *Insects as Human Food: A Chapter of the Ecology of Man.* The Hague: W. Junk, 1951.

—. "Note on Invasions of Palestine by Rare Locusts." *IEJ* 1 (1950–51): 146–8.

Böhlemann, Peter. *Jesus und der Täufer: Schlüssel zur Theologie und Ethik des Lukas.* SNTSMS 99. Cambridge: Cambridge University, 1997.

Boice, James Montgomery. *The Gospel of Matthew.* Vol. 1: *The King and His Kingdom: Matthew 1–17.* Grand Rapids: Baker, 2001.

Boismard, M. É. "Évangile des Ébionites et problème synoptique (*Mc,* 1, 2–6 et par.)." *RB* 73 (1966): 321–52.

Boring, M. Eugene. "Matthew." *New Interpreter's Bible.* Vol. 8. Nashville: Abingdon, 1995.

Borowski, Oded. *Every Living Thing: Daily Use of Animals in Ancient Israel.* Walnut Creek, CA: AltaMira, 1998.

Bottéro, Jean. "The Cuisine of Ancient Mesopotamia." *BA* 48/1 (1985): 36–47.

Bovon, François. *Luke 1: A Commentary on the Gospel of Luke 1:1–9:50.* Hermeneia. Minneapolis: Fortress, 2002 (1989).

Brakke, David. *Athanasius and the Politics of Asceticism.* Oxford: Clarendon/New York: Oxford University Press, 1995.

—. "Canon Formation and Social Conflict in Fourth-Century Egypt: Athanasius of Alexandria's Thirty-Ninth *Festal Letter.*" *HTR* 87 (1994): 395–419.

British Broadcasting Corporation. "Three Shot in EU Summit Riots." Online: http://news.bbc.co.uk/1/hi/world/europe/1391007.stm (on 8 April 2004).

Broadhead, Edwin K. *Mark.* Readings: A New Biblical Commentary. Sheffield: Sheffield Academic, 2001.

Brock, Sebastian. "The Baptist's Diet in Syriac Sources." *OrChr* 54 (1970): 113–24 = idem, *From Ephrem to Romanos: Interactions between Syriac and Greek in Late Antiquity.* Variorum Collected Studies 664. Aldershot: Ashgate, 1999. 113–24.

Brodsky, Harold. "'An Enormous Horde Arrayed for Battle': Locusts in the Book of Joel." *Bible Review* 6 (1990): 32–9.

Broshi, Magen. "The Diet of Palestine in the Roman Period — Introductory Notes." *Israel Museum Journal* 5 (1986): 41–56.

Brothwell, Don R. "Foodstuffs, Cooking, and Drugs." In: *Civilization of the Ancient Mediterranean: Greece and Rome.* M. Grant and R. Kitzinger, eds. New York: Scribner's, 1988. 1.247–75.

Brothwell, Don and Patricia Brothwell. *Food in Antiquity: A Survey of the Diet of Early Peoples.* Baltimore: Johns Hopkins University, [2]1998.

Brown, Colin. "What Was John the Baptist Doing?" *BBR* 7 (1997): 37–50.

Brown, K. S. "The Chemistry of Aphids and Scale Insects." *Chemical Society Reviews* 4 (1975): 263–88.

Brown, Raymond E. *The Birth of the Messiah: A Commentary on the Infancy Narratives in the Gospels of Matthew and Luke.* New York: Doubleday, [2]1993.

Brownlee, William H. "John the Baptist in the New Light of Ancient Scrolls." In: *The Scrolls and the New Testament.* Krister Stendahl, ed. New York: Harper, 1957. 33–53.

Bruce, W. G. "Bible References to Insects and Other Arthropods." *Bulletin of the Entomological Society of America* 4 (1958): 75–8.

Budd, Philip J. *Leviticus: Based on the New Revised Standard Version.* NCB Commentary. London: M. Pickering/Grand Rapids: Eerdmans, 1996.

Bukkens, Sandra G. F. "The Nutritional Value of Edible Insects." *Ecology of Food and Nutrition* (New York) 36 (1997): 287–319.

Bultmann, Rudolf K. *The History of the Synoptic Tradition.* Oxford: Blackwell, [2]1968 ([2]1931).

Burkitt, F. C. *Evangelion da-Mepharreshe: The Curetonian Version of the Four Gospels.* Cambridge: Cambridge University, 1904.

Calvin, John. *Commentarius in harmoniam evangelicam.* Corpus reformatorum 73. K. G. Bretschneider, ed. Bad Feilnbach, Germany: Schmidt Periodicals GMBH, 1990 (1891).

—. *Commentary on a Harmony of the Evangelists: Matthew, Mark, and Luke.* William Pringle, trans. Grand Rapids: Eerdmans, 1949.

Carter, Warren. *Matthew and the Margins: A Sociopolitical and Religious Reading.* The Bible and Liberation. Maryknoll, NY: Orbis, 2000.

Casey, Maurice. *An Aramaic Approach to Q: Sources for the Gospels of Matthew and Luke.* SNTSMS 122. Cambridge: Cambridge University, 2002.

Castelli, Elizabeth A. *Imitating Paul: A Discourse of Power.* Louisville: Westminster John Knox, 1991.

Chamblin, Knox. "Gospel and Judgment in the Preaching of John the Baptist." *TynBul* 13 (1963): 7–15.

—. "John the Baptist and the Kingdom of God." *TynBul* 15 (1964): 10–16.

Charlesworth, James H. "John the Baptizer and Qumran Barriers in Light of the *Rule of the Community.*" In: *The Provo International Conference on the Dead Sea Scrolls.* STDJ 30. D. W. Parry and E. Ulrich, eds. Leiden: Brill, 1999. 353–75.

Chouliara-Raïos, Hélène. *L'Abeille et le miel en Égypte d'après les Papyrus Grecs.* Ioannina: Philosophike Schole Panepistemiou Ioanninon, 1989.

Clark, Elizabeth A. *Reading Renunciation: Asceticism and Scripture in Early Christianity.* Princeton: Princeton University, 1999.

Clausen, Lucy W. *Insect: Fact and Folklore.* New York: Macmillan, 1954.

Cleary, Michael. "The Baptist of History and Kerygma." *ITQ* 54 (1988): 211–27.

Colbert, M.D., Don. *What Would Jesus Eat?* Nashville: Thomas Nelson, 2002.

Cole, R. Alan. *The Gospel according to Mark: An Introduction and Commentary.* TNTC 2. Grand Rapids: Eerdmans, ²1989 (1961).

Comby, Bruno. *Délicieux insectes: Les protéines du futur...* Geneva: Éditions Jouvence, 1990.

Condit, Ira J. *The Fig.* New Series of Plant Science Books 19. Waltham, MA: Chronica Botanica, 1947.

Conring, Barbara. *Hieronymus als Briefschreiber: Ein Beitrag zur spätantiken Epistolographie.* Studien und Texte zu Antike und Christentum 8. Tübingen: Mohr Siebeck, 2001.

Cowan, Frank. *Curious Facts in the History of Insects, Including Spiders and Scorpions: A Complete Collection of the Legends, Superstitions, Beliefs, and Ominous Signs Connected with Insects, together with Their Uses in Medicine, Art, and as Food and a Summary of Their Remarkable Injuries and Appearances.* Philadelphia: Lippincott, 1865.

Cramer, Friedrich. *Der heilige Johannes im Spiegel der französischen Pflanzen- und Tierbezeichnungen: Ein Beitrag zur Kenntnis der volkstümlichen Namengebung.* Giessener Beiträge zur romanischen Philologie Zusatzheft 8. Giessen: Selbstverlag des Romanischen Seminars, 1932.

Crane, Eva. *The Archaeology of Beekeeping.* Ithaca, NY: Cornell University, 1983.

—. *Bees and Beekeeping: Science, Practice and World Resources.* Ithaca, NY: Comstock, 1990.

—. "History of Honey." In: *Honey: A Comprehensive Survey.* E. Crane, ed. London: Heinemann, 1975. 439–88.

Crane, Eva et al. "Biological Properties of Honey." In: *Honey: A Comprehensive Survey* (ed. E. Crane). 258–66.

Cranfield, C. E. B. *The Gospel according to St. Mark.* CGTC. Cambridge: Cambridge University, 1959.

Croy, N. Clayton. *The Mutilation of Mark's Gospel.* Nashville: Abingdon, 2003.

Curtis, Robert I. *Ancient Food Technology.* Technology and Change in History 5. Leiden: Brill, 2001.

Dabeck, P. "'Siehe, es erschienen Moses und Elias' (Mt 17, 3)." *Bib* 23 (1942): 175–89.

Dalby, Andrew. *Siren Feasts: A History of Food and Gastronomy in Greece.* London/New York: Routledge, 1997 (1996).

Dalman, Gustaf. *Orte und Wege Jesu.* Schriften des Deutschen Palästina-Instituts 1. Gütersloh: C. Bertelsmann, ³1924. ET: *Sacred Sites and Ways: Studies in the Topography of the Gospels.* London: SPCK/New York: Macmillan, 1935.

Daly, Lloyd W. *Aesop without Morals: The Famous Fables, and a Life of Aesop.* New York: T. Yoseloff, 1961.

Daniélou, Jean. *The Work of John the Baptist.* Baltimore: Helicon 1966.

Daube, David. "A Quartet of Beasties in the Book of Proverbs." *JTS* n.s. 36 (1985): 380–6.

Davies, Malcolm and Jeyaraney Kathirithamby. *Greek Insects.* New York: Oxford University Press, 1986.

Davies, Margaret. *Matthew.* Readings: A New Biblical Commentary. Sheffield: JSOT Press, 1993.

Davies, S. L. "John the Baptist and Essene Kashruth." *NTS* 29 (1983): 569–71.

Davies, W. D. and Dale C. Allison, Jr. *A Critical and Exegetical Commentary on the Gospel according to Saint Matthew.* ICC. Edinburgh: T. & T. Clark, 1988.

Deane, Anthony C. "The Ministry of John the Baptist." *The Expositor* 8 (1917): 420–31.

DeFoliart, Gene R. "Insects as Food: Why the Western Attitude Is Important." *Annual Review of Entomology* (Palo Alto, CA) 44 (1999): 21–50.

—. "Insects as Human Food." *Crop Protection* (Guildford, England) 11 (1992): 395–9.

Diamond, Cora. "Eating Meat and Eating People." In: eadem, *The Realistic Spirit: Wittgenstein, Philosophy, and the Mind.* Representation and Mind. Cambridge, MA: MIT Press, 1991. 319–34.

Dibelius, Martin. *Die Formgeschichte des Evangeliums.* Tübingen: Mohr (Siebeck) ²1933 (1919). ET: *From Tradition to Gospel.* SL 124. B. L. Woolf, trans. New York: Scribner, 1965.

—. *Die urchristliche Überlieferung von Johannes dem Täufer.* FRLANT 15. Göttingen: Vandenhoeck & Ruprecht, 1911.

Donahue, John R. and Daniel J. Harrington. *The Gospel of Mark.* SP 2. Collegeville, MN: Liturgical Press, 2002.

Douglas, Mary. "The Abominations of Leviticus." In: eadem, *Purity and Danger: An Analysis of Concepts of Pollution and Taboo.* New York: Praeger, 1966. 41–57.

Driver, S. R. "Excursus on Locusts." In: *The Books of Joel and Amos.* H. C. O. Lanchester, ed. Cambridge: Cambridge University, ²1915. 84–93.

Edwards, James R. *The Gospel according to Mark.* Pillar New Testament Commentary. Leicester: Apollos/Grand Rapids: Eerdmans, 2002.

Eisler, Robert. "The Baptist's Food and Clothing." In: idem, *The Messiah Jesus and John the Baptist according to Flavius Josephus' Recently Rediscovered 'Capture of Jerusalem' and Other Jewish and Christian Sources.* New York: L. MacVeagh, 1931 (1929–30).

Erasmus von Rotterdam. *Desiderii Erasmi Roterodami, Opera Omnia.* J. Le Clerc, ed. Lugduni Batavorum (Leiden): Petri Vander, 1703–06 = Hildesheim: Olms, 1961–62.

—. *Novum Instrumentum, Basel 1516.* H. Holeczek, ed. Stuttgart-Bad Cannstatt: Fromman-Holzboog, 1986.

—. *Paraphrasis in Marcum.* ET: *Paraphrase on Mark.* Erika Rummel, trans. Toronto: University of Toronto, 1988.

Ernst, Josef. *Johannes der Täufer: Interpretation, Geschichte, Wirkunsgeschichte.* BZNW 53. Berlin: de Gruyter, 1989.

Essig, Edward O. *Insects and Mites of Western North America: A Manual and Textbook.* New York: Macmillan, ²1958.

Evans, Craig F. "The Central Section of St. Luke's Gospel." In: *Studies in the Gospels: Essays in Memory of R. H. Lightfoot.* D. E. Nineham, ed. Oxford: Blackwell, 1955. 37–53.

—. *Saint Luke.* TPINTC. London: SCM/Philadelphia: TPI, 1990.

Evans, Howard Ensign. "Year of the Locust." In: idem, *Life on a Little-Known Planet.* Chicago: University of Chicago, 1984 = New York: Lyons & Burford, 1993. 195–226.

Faierstein, Morris M. "Why Do the Scribes Say that Elijah Must Come First?" *JBL* 100 (1981): 75–86.

Faultless, Julian. "The Two Recensions of the Prologue to John in Ibn al-Ṭayyib's *Commentary on the Gospels.*" In: *Christians at the Heart of Islamic Rule: Church Life and Scholarship in ᶜAbbasid Iraq.* David Thomas, ed. Leiden: Brill, 2003. 177–98.

Faure, Jacob C. *The Phases of Locusts in South Africa.* London: Imperial Institute of Entomology, 1932 = *Bulletin of Entomological Research* 23 (1932): 293–405 + Plates.

Fehrle, Eugen. *Zur Geschichte der griechischen Geoponica.* Leipzig: Teubner, 1913.

Feichtinger, Barbara. *Apostolae apostolorum: Frauenaskese als Befreiung und Zwang bei Hieronymus.* Studien zur klassischen Philologie 94. Frankfurt am Main: Lang, 1995.

Filson, Floyd V. *A Commentary on the Gospel according to St. Matthew.* HNTC. New York: Harper, 1960.

Fiore, Benjamin. *The Function of Personal Example in the Socratic and Pastoral Epistles.* AnBib 105. Rome: Biblical Institute Press, 1986.

Firmage, Edwin. "Zoology." Art. *ABD*, 6.1109–67.

Fitzmyer, Joseph A. *The Gospel according to Luke: Introduction, Translation, and Notes.* AB 28. Garden City, NY: Doubleday, 1981–85.

Flannery, Timothy F. *The Future Eaters: An Ecological History of the Australasian Lands and People.* New York: Braziller, 1995.

Fraade, Steven D. "Ascetical Aspects of Ancient Judaism." In: *Jewish Spirituality: From the Bible through the Middle Ages.* Arthur Green, ed. World Spirituality 13. New York: Crossroad, 1986. 253–88.

France, R. T. *The Gospel according to Matthew: An Introduction and Commentary.* Grand Rapids: Eerdmans, 1986.

—. *The Gospel of Mark.* Doubleday Bible Commentary. New York: Doubleday, 1998.

—. *The Gospel of Mark: A Commentary on the Greek Text.* NIGTC. Carlisle, U.K.: Paternoster/Grand Rapids: Eerdmans, 2002.

Fraser, H. Malcolm. *Beekeeping in Antiquity.* London: University of London, [2]1951.

Frerichs, W. W. "Grasshoppers." Art. *IDB*, 2.470.

Frey, Jörg. "Die Bedeutung der Qumranfunde für das Verständnis des Neuen Testaments." In: *Qumran: Die Schriftrollen vom Toten Meer.* M. Fieger et al., eds. NTOA 47. Freiburg: Freiburg Schweiz/Göttingen: Vandenhoeck & Ruprecht, 2001. 129–208.

Friesen, Steven J. "Poverty in Pauline Studies: Beyond the So-called New Consensus." *JSNT* 26/3 (2004): 323–61.

Frizzell, Lawrence. "Elijah the Peacemaker: Jewish and Early Christian Interpretations of Malachi 3:23–24." *SIDIC* 35/2–3 (2002): 24–30.

García Soler, María José. *El arte de comer en la antigua Grecia.* Madrid: Biblioteca Nueva, 2001.

Garella, Rich. "Interactions with Our Insect Friends" (© 1995). Online (with photos): http://www.garella.com/rich/insect.htm (on 12 April 2004).

Garland, David E. *Reading Matthew: A Literary and Theological Commentary on the First Gospel.* Reading the NT. New York: Crossroad, 1993.

—. *Zondervan Illustrated Bible Backgrounds Commentary.* Vol. 1: *Matthew, Mark, Luke.* C. E. Arnold, gen. ed. Grand Rapids: Zondervan, 2002.

Garnsey, Peter. *Famine and Food Supply in the Graeco-Roman World: Responses to Risk and Crisis.* Cambridge: Cambridge University, 1988.

—. *Food and Society in Classical Antiquity.* Cambridge: Cambridge University, 1999.

Geddert, Timothy J. *Mark.* Scottdale, PA: Herald, 2001.

Gemoll, Wilhelm. *Untersuchungen über die Quellen, den Verfasser und die Abfassungszeit der Geoponica.* Berliner Studien für classische Philologie und Archäologie 1/1. Berlin: S. Calvary, 1883 = Walluf bei Wiesbaden: M. Sändig, 1972.

Gerstenberger, Erhard S. *Leviticus: A Commentary.* OTL. Louisville: Westminster John Knox, 1996.

Geyser, Albert S. "The Youth of John the Baptist." *NovT* 1 (1956): 70–5.

Gibson, C. L. "John the Baptist in Muslim Writings." *Muslim World* (Hartford, CT) 45 (1955): 334–45.

Gibson, Shimon. *The Cave of John the Baptist: The Stunning Archaeological Discovery that Has Redefined Christian History.* New York: Doubleday, 2004.

Gilbert, Allan S. "The Flora and Fauna of the Ancient Near East." In: *Civilizations of the Ancient Near East.* Jack M. Sasson, ed. New York: Scribner's, 1995. 1.153–74.

Gill, Sam D. *Storytracking: Texts, Stories, and Histories in Central Australia.* New York: Oxford University Press, 1997.

Gilula, Dwora. "Comic Food and Food for Comedy." In: *Food in Antiquity.* J. Wilkins, F. D. Harvey and M. Dobson, eds. Exeter: University of Exeter, 1995. 386–99.

Gnilka, Joachim. *Das Evangelium nach Markus.* EKKNT 2/1–2. Zurich: Benziger/ Neukirchen-Vluyn: Neukirchener, ³1989.

Goodenough, E. R. *Jewish Symbols in the Greco-Roman Period.* New York: Pantheon, 1953-68.

Gordon, David George. *The Eat-A-Bug Cookbook: 33 Ways to Cook Grasshoppers, Ants, Water Bugs, Spiders, Centipedes, and Their Kin.* Berkeley: Ten Speed Press, 1998.

Gordon, Robert P. "Loricate Locusts in the Targum to Nahum III 17 and Revelation IX 9." *VT* 33 (1983): 338–9.

Gorman, Jr., Frank H. *Divine Presence and Community: A Commentary on the Book of Leviticus.* International Theological Commentary. Grand Rapids: Eerdmans, 1997.

Gossen, Hans. "Heuschrecke." Art. PW 8/2.1381–6; PWSup 8.179–81.

Gould, Ezra P. *Critical and Exegetical Commentary on the Gospel according to St. Mark.* ICC. Edinburgh: T. & T. Clark/New York: Scribner's, 1983 (1896).

Gowers, Emily. *The Loaded Table: Representations of Food in Roman Literature.* Oxford: Clarendon/Oxford: Oxford University, 1993.

Graf, Georg. *Geschichte der christlichen arabischen Literatur.* Studi e testi 133. Vatican City: Biblioteca apostolica vaticana, 1944–53.

Grant, Robert M. "The Heresy of Tatian." *JTS* n.s. 5 (1954): 62–8.

—. "Tatian and the Bible." *StPatr* 1 (1957): 297–306.

Grégoire, Henri. "Les Sauterelles de Saint Jean-Baptiste: texte épigraphique d'une épître de S. Isidore de Péluse." *Byzantion* 5 (1929–30): 109–28.

Griffith, Sidney H. "Asceticism in the Church of Syria: The Hermeneutics of Early Christian Monasticism." In: *Asceticism* (ed. Wimbush and Valantasis). 220–45.

Guelich, Robert A. *Mark 1–8:26.* WBC 34A. Dallas: Word, 1989.

Gundry, Robert H. *Mark: A Commentary on His Apology for the Cross.* Grand Rapids: Eerdmans, 1993.

—. *Matthew: A Commentary on His Handbook for a Mixed Church under Persecution.* Grand Rapids: Eerdmans, ²1994.

Güting, Eberhard W. "The Relevance of Literary Criticism for the Text of the New Testament: A Study of Mark's Traditions on John the Baptist." In: *Studies in the Early Text of the Gospels and Acts: The Papers of the First Birmingham Colloquium on the Textual Criticism of the New Testament.* D. G. K. Taylor, ed. Text-critical Studies 1. Atlanta: Society of Biblical Literature, 1999. 142–67.

Häfner, Gerd. *Der verheissene Vorläufer: Redaktionskritische Untersuchung zur Darstellung Johannes des Täufers im Matthäus-Evangelium.* SBB 27. Stuttgart: Katholisches Bibelwerk, 1994.

Hagner, Donald A. *Matthew 1–13.* WBC. Dallas: Word, 1993.

Hänsler, Heinrich. "Noch einmal 'Honig im hl. Lande.'" *ZDPV* 35 (1912): 186–99.

Hare, Douglas R. A. *Mark.* Westminster Bible Companion. Louisville: Westminster John Knox, 1996.

—. *Matthew.* Interpretation. Louisville: John Knox, 1993.

Harrington, Daniel J. *The Gospel of Matthew.* SP 1. Collegeville, MN: Liturgical Press, 1991.

Harrison, Roland K. *Leviticus: An Introduction and Commentary.* Downers Grove, IL: Inter-Varsity, 1980.

—. "Palm Tree." Art. *ISBE*, 3.649.

Hartley, John E. *Leviticus.* WBC 4. Dallas: Word, 1992.

Hartmann, Michael. *Der Tod Johannes des Täufers: Eine exegetische und rezeptions-geschichtliche Studie auf dem Hintergrund narrativer, intertextueller und kulturanthropologischer Zugänge.* SBB 45. Stuttgart: Katholisches Bibelwerk, 2001.

Hehn, Victor. *Kulturpflanzen und Haustiere in ihrem Übergang aus Asien nach Griechenland und Italien sowie in das übrige Europa: Historisch-linguistische Studien.* Otto Schrader, ed. Berlin: Gebrüder Borntraeger, [8]1963 (1870). ET: *Cultivated Plants and Domesticated Animals in Their Migration from Asia to Europe: Historico-linguistic Studies.* Amsterdam: John Benjamins, 1976 (1885).

Heinrici, C. F. Georg. *Des Petrus von Laodicea Erklärung des Matthäusevangeliums.* Leipzig: Dürr, 1908.

Hellwing, Salo (Shlomo). "Human Exploitation of Animal Resources in the Early Iron Age Strata at Tel Beer-sheba." In: *Beer-Sheba II: The Early Iron Age Settlements.* Ze'ev Herzog, ed. Publications of the Institute of Archaeology 7. Tel Aviv: Tel Aviv University, 1984. 105–15.

Hendel, Ronald. "The Exodus in Biblical Memory." *JBL* 120 (2001): 601–22.

Hentschel, Georg. *Die Elijaerzählungen: Zum Verhältnis von historischem Geschehen und geschichtlicher Erfahrung.* ETS 33. Leipzig: St. Benno, 1977.

Hess, J. J. "Beduinisches zum Alten und Neuen Testament." *ZAW* 35 (1915): 120–36.

Hill, David. *The Gospel of Matthew.* NCB. London: Oliphants, 1972 = Grand Rapids: Eerdmans, 1981.

Hirschfeld, Yizhar. "Food: Christian Perspectives." Art. *Encyclopedia of Monasticism* (ed. W. M. Johnston). 1.483–5.

Hjelt, Arthur. *Die altsyrische Evangelienübersetzung und Tatians Diatessaron.* Leipzig: Deichert, 1901.

Hollenbach, Paul W. "John the Baptist." Art. *ABD*, 3.887–99.

—. "Social Aspects of John the Baptizer's Preaching Mission in the Context of Palestinian Judaism." *ANRW* 2/19/1 (1979): 850–75.

Holt, Vincent M. *Why Not Eat Insects?* Hampton/Middlesex: Classey, 1967 (1885).

Hooker, Morna D. *The Gospel according to Saint Mark.* BNTC. London: A & C Black/Peabody, MA: Hendrickson, 1991.

Horsley, Richard A. *Hearing the Whole Story: The Politics of Plot in Mark's Gospel.* Louisville: Westminster John Knox, 2001.

Houtman, C. "Elijah." Art. *DDD*, 282–5.

Hudson, Nicola A. "Food in Roman Satire." In: *Satire and Society in Ancient Rome.* Susan H. Braund, ed. Exeter Studies in History 23. Exeter: University of Exeter, 1989. 69–87.

Hui, Archie W. D. "John the Baptist and Spirit-Baptism." *EvQ* 71 (1999): 99–115.

Hünemörder, Christian. "Heuschrecke." Art. *DNP*, 5.526–8.

Hurowitz, Victor A. "אכל in Malachi 3:11–Caterpillar." *JBL* 121 (2002): 327–30.
—. "Joel's Locust Plague in Light of Sargon II's Hymn to Nanaya." *JBL* 112 (1993): 597–603.
Hurtado, Larry W. *Mark.* Good News Commentary. San Francisco: Harper & Row, 1983.
—. *Mark.* New International Biblical Commentary. Peabody, MA: Hendrickson, 1989.

Infoshop.org. "Italian Anarchists Protest McDonalds in Bergamo." Online: http://www.infoshop.org/news4/mcd_italy.html (on 8 April 2004).
Isman Murray B. and Martin S. Cohen. "Kosher Insects." *American Entomologist* 41 (Summer 1995): 100–2.
Israel, Richard J. "The Promised Land of Milk and Date Jam: The Problems of Bees and Honey in the Bible and the Talmud." *National Jewish Monthly* (Washington) 87/3 (1972): 26–30.

Jackson, F. J. Foakes and Kirsopp Lake. *The Beginnings of Christianity.* London: Macmillan, 1920.
Jacob, Irene and Walter Jacob. "Flora." Art. *ABD*, 2.803–17.
Jeremias, Joachim. "Ἠλ(ε)ίας." Art. *TDNT*, 2.928–41.
Johnson, Sherman E. *A Commentary on the Gospel according to St. Mark.* HNTC. New York: Harper, 1960 = Peabody, MA: Hendrickson, 1990.
Johnson, Jr., S. Lewis. "The Message of John the Baptist." *BSac* 113 (1956): 30–6.
Jones, James L. "References to John the Baptist in the Gospel according to St. Matthew." *AThR* 41 (1959): 298–302.
Joosse, Peter. "Barhebraeus' ܟܬܒܐ ܕܒܘܬܝܪܐ (*Butyrum Sapientiae*): A Description of the Extant Manuscripts." *Le Muséon* 112 (1999): 417–58.
Joüon, Paul. "Le costume d'Elie et celui de Jean Baptiste." *Bib* 16 (1935): 74–81.
Juel, Donald H. *The Gospel of Mark.* Interpreting Biblical Texts. Nashville: Abingdon, 1999.

Kaplan, Aryeh. *The Living Torah: The Five Books of Moses, A New Translation Based on Traditional Jewish Sources.* Jerusalem/New York: Maznaim, [2]1981.
Kazmierski, Carl R. *John the Baptist: Prophet and Evangelist. Metaphor and Social Context in Matthew's Gospel.* Collegeville, MN: Liturgical Press, 1996.
Keener, Craig S. *A Commentary on the Gospel of Matthew.* Grand Rapids: Eerdmans, 1999.
Kelhoffer, James A. "Did John the Baptist Eat Like a Former Essene? Locust-Eating in the Ancient Near East and at Qumran." Forthcoming in *Dead Sea Discoveries*.
—. "'How Soon a Book' Revisited: ΕΥΑΓΓΕΛΙΟΝ as a Reference to 'Gospel' Materials in the First Half of the Second Century." *ZNW* 95/1–2 (2004): 1–34.
—. "John the Baptist's 'Wild Honey' and the Ambiguity of Certain References to 'Honey' in Antiquity." Forthcoming in *Greek, Roman and Byzantine Studies*.
—. "'Locusts and Wild Honey' (Mark 1:6c and Matt 3:4c): The *Status Quaestionis* concerning the Diet of John the Baptist." *Currents in Biblical Research* 2 (2003): 104–27.
—. *Miracle and Mission: The Authentication of Missionaries and Their Message in the Longer Ending of Mark.* WUNT 2.112. Tübingen: Mohr Siebeck, 2000.
—. "The Witness of Eusebius' *ad Marinum* and Other Christian Writings to Text-Critical Debates concerning the Original Conclusion to Mark's Gospel." *ZNW* 92 (2001): 78–112.
Keller, Otto. *Die Antike Tierwelt.* Leipzig: W. Engelmann, 1909–13.

Khalifé, Louis. "Étude sur l'histoire rédactionnelle des deux textes parallèles: Lv. 11 et Dt. 14, 1–21." *Melto* 2 (1966): 57–72.

Kieferndorf, Philipp. "Seine Speise war Heuschrecken?" *Vegetarische Warte* 54 (1921): 188–9.

Kirk, Albert and Robert E. Obach. *A Commentary on the Gospel of Matthew.* New York: Paulist, 1978.

Klauck, Hans-Josef. *Apocryphal Gospels: An Introduction.* Edinburgh: T & T Clark, 2003 (2002).

Klijn, A. F. J. *Jewish-Christian Gospel Tradition.* VCSup 17. Leiden: Brill, 1992.

Klostermann, August. *Das Markusevangelium nach seinem Quellenwerthe für die evangelische Geschichte.* Göttingen: Vandenhoeck & Ruprecht, 1867.

Klostermann, Erich. *Das Markusevangelium.* HNT 3. Tübingen: Mohr (Siebeck), ⁵1971 (1919).

Koester, Helmut. *Ancient Christian Gospels: Their History and Development.* London: SCM/Philadelphia: TPI, 1990.

—. *Introduction to the New Testament.* Berlin: de Gruyter/Philadelphia: Fortress, ²1995.

Kopf, L. "al-Damīrī, Muḥammad b. Mūsā b. ʿĪsā Kamāl al-Dīn." Art. *The Encyclopaedia of Islam.* H. A. R. Gibb et al., eds. Leiden: Brill, ²1960. 2.107–8.

Kraeling, Carl H. *John the Baptist.* New York: Scribner, 1951.

Krauss, Samuel. "Honig in Palästina." *ZDPV* 32 (1909): 151–64.

—. *Talmudische Archäologie.* Grundriss der Gesamtwissenschaft des Judentums. Leipzig, 1910–12 = Hildesheim: Olms, 1966.

—. "Zur Kenntnis der Heuschrecken in Palästina." *ZDPV* 50 (1927): 244–9.

Krentz, Edgar. "None Greater among Those Born from Women: John the Baptist in the Gospel of Matthew." *CurTM* 10 (Dec. 1983): 333–8.

Kuény, G. "Scènes apicoles dans l'Ancienne Égypte." *JNES* 9 (1950): 84–93.

Kutsch, Ernst. "Heuschreckenplage und Tag Jahwes in Joel 1 und 2." *TZ* 18 (1962): 81–94.

Lagrange, M.-J. *Évangile selon Saint Marc.* ÉBib. Paris: Gabalda, ⁵1929 (1911). Reprinted, 1966.

Lamarche, Paul. *Évangile de Marc: Commentaire.* ÉBib n.s. 33. Paris: Gabalda, 1996.

Lambrecht, Jan. "John the Baptist and Jesus in Mark 1.1–15: Markan Redaction of Q?" *NTS* 38 (1992): 357–84.

Lane, George. "An Account of Gregory Bar Hebraeus Abu al-Faraj and His Relations with the Mongols of Persia." *Hugoye: Journal of Syriac Studies* 2/2 (1999); online: http://syrcom.cua.edu/Hugoye/Vol2No2/HV2N2GLane.html (on 30 April 2004).

Lane, William L. *The Gospel of Mark.* NICNT. Grand Rapids: Eerdmans, 1974.

LaVerdiere, Eugene. *The Beginning of the Gospel: Introducing the Gospel according to Mark.* Collegeville, MN: Liturgical Press, 1999.

Layton, Bentley. "Social Structure and Food Consumption in an Early Christian Monastery: The Evidence of Shenoute's *Canons* and the White Monastery Federation A.D. 385–465." *Le Muséon* 115 (2002): 25–55.

Ledger, John. "The Eighth Plague Returneth! The Locusts Are Coming!" *African Wildlife* (Linden, South Africa) 41 (1987): 197–210.

Lenski, C. H. *The Interpretation of St. Mark's Gospel.* Minneapolis: Augsburg, 1964.

Lerner, Berel Dov. "Timid Grasshoppers and Fierce Locusts: An Ironic Pair of Biblical Metaphors." *VT* 49 (1999): 545–8.

Levine, Daniel B. "Acorns and Primitive Life in Greek and Latin Literature." *Classical and Modern Literature* 9 (1989): 87–95.

Leyser, Conrad. *Authority and Asceticism from Augustine to Gregory the Great.* Oxford Historical Monographs. Oxford: Clarendon/Oxford: Oxford University, 2000.

Lightstone, Jack. *Mishnah and the Social Formation of the Early Rabbinic Guild: A Socio-Rhetorical Approach.* Studies in Christianity and Judaism/Études sur le christianisme et le judaïsme 11. Waterloo, Ontario: Wilfrid Laurier University, 2002.

Lindeskog, Gösta. "Johannes der Täufer: Einige Randbemerkungen zum heutigen Stand der Forschung." *ASTI* 12 (1983): 55–83.

Loane, Marcus L. *John the Baptist as Witness and Martyr.* Grand Rapids: Zondervan, 1969.

Lohfink, Gerhard. *Die Himmelfahrt Jesu: Untersuchungen zu den Himmelfahrts- und Erhöhungstexten bei Lukas.* SANT 26. Munich: Kösel, 1971.

Lohmeyer, Ernst. *Das Evangelium des Markus.* Meyer I.2. Göttingen: Vandenhoeck & Ruprecht, [17]1967.

—. *Das Urchristentum.* Vol. 1: *Johannes der Täufer.* Göttingen: Vandenhoeck & Ruprecht, 1932.

—. "Zur evangelischen Überlieferung von Johannes dem Täufer." *JBL* 51 (1932): 300–19.

Löhr, Hermut. "Speisenfrage und Tora im Judentum des Zweiten Tempels und im entstehenden Christentum." *ZNW* 94 (2003): 17–37.

Loisy, Alfred. *L'Évangile selon Marc.* Paris: Émile Nourry, 1912.

Lührmann, Dieter. *Das Markusevangelium.* HNT 3. Tübingen: Mohr Siebeck, 1987.

Lupieri, Edmondo F. "John the Baptist in New Testament Traditions and History." *ANRW* 2/26/1 (1993): 430–61.

—. "John the Baptist: The First Monk. A Contribution to the History of the Figure of John the Baptist in the Early Monastic World." In: *Monasticism: A Historical Overview.* Word and Spirit 6. Still River, MA: St. Bede's, 1984. 11–23.

—. "John the Gnostic: The Figure of the Baptist in Origen and Heterodox Gnosticism." *StPatr* 19 (1989): 322–7.

—. "'The Law and the Prophets Were until John': John the Baptist between Jewish Halakhot and Christian History of Salvation." *Neot* 35 (2001): 49–56.

—. *The Mandaeans: The Last Gnostics.* Grand Rapids: Eerdmans, 2002 (1993).

Luz, Ulrich. *Matthew: A Commentary.* Hermeneia. Minneapolis: Augsburg Fortress, 1990–2001 (1985).

Macina, Robert. "Jean le Baptiste était-il Élie?: Examen de la tradition néotestamentaire." *Proche Orient chrétien* (Jerusalem) 34 (1984): 209–32.

Madsen, David B. "A Grasshopper in Every Pot." *Natural History* (New York) 98/7 (1989): 22–5.

Mahan, L. Kathleen and Sylvia Escott-Stump, eds. *Krause's Food, Nutrition & Diet Therapy.* Philadelphia: W. B. Saunders, [10]2000.

Malbon, Elizabeth Struthers. *Hearing Mark: A Listener's Guide.* Harrisburg, PA: TPI, 2002.

Malek, Jaromir. "The Locusts on the Daggers of Ahmose." In: *Chief of Seers: Egyptian Studies in Memory of Cyril Aldred.* Elizabeth Goring et al., eds. Studies in Egyptology. London/New York: Kegan Paul International, 1997. 207–19.

Mann, C. S. *Mark.* AB 27. Garden City, NY: Doubleday, 1986.

Manson, T. William. "John the Baptist." *BJRL* 36 (1953–54): 395–412.

Marcus, Joel. *Mark 1–8: A New Translation with Introduction and Commentary.* AB 27. New York: Doubleday, 2000.

Margoliouth, D. S. Review of A.-S. Marmardji, *Diatessaron de Tatien* (1935). In: *JTS* 38 (1937): 76–9.

Marmardji, A.-S. *Diatessaron de Tatien.* Beirut: Imprimerie catholique, 1935.

Marshall, I. Howard. *The Gospel of Luke: A Commentary on the Greek Text.* NIGTC. Grand Rapids: Eerdmans, 1978.

Marx, [no first name given]. "Die Nahrung Johannes des Täufers: Eine Antwort auf den Artikel von Philipp Kieferndorf." *Vegetarische Warte* 55 (1922): 1–5.

Marxsen, Willi. "John the Baptist." In: idem, *Mark the Evangelist: Studies on the Redaction History of the Gospel.* Nashville: Abingdon, 1969 (1956, [2]1959). 30–53.

Masseron, Alexandre. *Saint Jean Baptiste dans l'art.* Paris: Arthaud, 1957.

Mayor, Adrienne. "Mad Honey! Bees and the Baneful Rhododendron." *Archaeology* 48/6 (Nov.–Dec. 1995): 32–40.

McGowan, Andrew B. *Ascetic Eucharists: Food and Drink in Early Christian Ritual Meals.* New York: Oxford University Press, 1999.

McNeile, Alan H. *The Gospel according to St. Matthew.* London: Macmillan, 1915 = Grand Rapids: Baker, 1980.

Meier, John P. "John the Baptist in Matthew's Gospel." *JBL* 99 (1980): 383–405.

—. *A Marginal Jew: Rethinking the Historical Jesus.* Vol. 2: *Mentor, Message and Miracles.* New York: Doubleday, 1991.

Meinardus, Otto F. A. "The Relics of St. John the Baptist and the Prophet Elisha: An Examination of the Claims of Their Recent Invention in Egypt." In: *Coptic Studies.* FS Mirrit Boutros Ghali. Leslie S. B. MacCoull, ed. Cairo: Society for Coptic Archaeology, 1979. 26–63.

Menzel, Peter and Faith D'Aluisio. *Man Eating Bugs: The Art and Science of Eating Insects.* Berkeley: Ten Speed Press, 1998.

Metzger, Bruce M. *The Early Versions of the New Testament: Their Origin, Transmission, and Limitations.* Oxford: Clarendon, 1977.

Metzsch, von, Friedrich-August. *Johannes der Täufer: Seine Geschichte und seine Darstellung in der Kunst.* Munich: Callwey, 1989.

Meyer, Heinrich August Wilhelm. *Critical and Exegetical Hand-book to the Gospel of Matthew.* New York: Funk & Wagnalls, 1884 ([6]1876; 1858).

Michaels, J. Ramsey. "Paul and John the Baptist: An Odd Couple?" *TynBul* 42 (1991): 245–60.

Michaelis, Wilhelm. "μέλι." Art. *TDNT*, 4.552–4.

Milgrom, Jacob. "The Biblical Diet Laws as an Ethical System." In: idem, *Studies in Cultic Theology and Terminology.* SJLA 36. Leiden: Brill, 1983. 104–18.

—. "Ethics and Ritual: The Foundations of the Biblical Dietary Laws." In: *Religion and Law: Biblical-Judaic and Islamic Perspectives.* E. B. Firmage et al., eds. Winona Lake, IN: Eisenbrauns, 1990. 159–91.

—. *Leviticus 1–16: A New Translation with Introduction and Commentary.* AB 3. New York: Doubleday, 1991.

Miller, Robert J. "Elijah, John, and Jesus in the Gospel of Luke." *NTS* 34 (1988): 611–22.

Mitchell, Margaret M. *The Heavenly Trumpet: John Chrysostom and the Art of Pauline Interpretation.* HUT 40. Tübingen: Mohr Siebeck, 2000.

Molin, Georg. "Elijahu: Der Prophet und sein Weiterleben in den Hoffnungen des Judentums und der Christenheit." *Judaica* 8 (1952): 65–94.

Moloney, Francis J. *The Gospel of Mark: A Commentary.* Peabody, MA: Hendrickson, 2002.

Moran, William L. "The Literary Connection between Lv 11,13–19 and Dt 14,12–18." *CBQ* 28 (1966): 271–7.

Morony, Michael G. "Michael the Syrian as a Source for Economic History." *Hugoye: Journal of Syriac Studies* 3/2 (2000), online: http://syrcom.cua.edu/Hugoye/Vol3No2/HV3N2Morony.html (on 8 April 2004).

Morris, Leon. *The Gospel according to Matthew.* Grand Rapids: Eerdmans, 1992.

—. *Luke: An Introduction and Commentary.* Grand Rapids: Eerdmans, ²1988 (1974).

Morrison, Reg. *Australia: The Four Billion Year Journey of a Continent.* New York: Facts on File Publications, 1990 (1988).

Moskala, Jirí. "Categorization and Evaluation of Different Kinds of Interpretation of the Laws of Clean and Unclean Animals in Leviticus 11." *BR* 46 (2001): 5–41.

Müller, Christoph Gregor. "Kleidung als Element der Charakterzeichnung im Neuen Testament und seiner Umwelt: Ein Streifzug durch das lukanische Erzählwerk." *SNTSU* 28 (2003): 187–214.

—. *Mehr als ein Prophet: Die Charakterzeichnung Johannes des Täufers im lukanischen Erzählwerk.* Herders biblische Studien 31. Freiburg: Herder, 2001.

Müller, Ulrich B. *Johannes der Täufer: Jüdischer Prophet und Wegbereiter Jesu.* Leipzig: Evangelische Verlagsanstalt, 2002.

Mulvaney, John and Johan Kamminga. *Prehistory of Australia.* Washington, DC: Smithsonian Institution Press, ²1999.

Murphy, Catherine M. *John the Baptist: Prophet of Purity for a New Age.* Collegeville, MN: Liturgical Press, 2003.

Murphy O'Connor, Jerome. "John the Baptist and Jesus: History and Hypotheses." *NTS* 36 (1990): 359–74.

Nestle, Eberhard. "Zum Mantel aus Kamelshaaren." *ZNW* 8 (1907): 238.

Neufeld, Edward. "Apiculture in Ancient Palestine (Early and Middle Iron Age) within the Framework of the Ancient Near East." *UF* 10 (1978): 219–47.

Nevo, David. "The Desert Locust, *Schistocerca gregaria*, and Its Control in the Land of Israel and the Near East in Antiquity, with Some Reflections on Its Appearance in Israel in Modern Times." *Phytoparasitica: Israel Journal of Plant Protection Sciences* 24 (1996): 7–32.

Nineham, Dennis E. *The Gospel of St. Mark.* Pelican Gospel Commentaries. New York: Seabury, 1968 (1963).

Nolan, Mary Lee. "Pilgrimages, Christian: Western Europe." Art. *Encyclopedia of Monasticism* (ed. W. M. Johnston). 2.1024–8.

Nolland, John. *Luke.* WBC 35. Dallas: Word, 1989–93.

Noth, Martin. *Leviticus: A Commentary.* OTL. Philadelphia: Westminster, ²1977.

Öhler, Markus. *Elia im Neuen Testament: Untersuchungen zur Bedeutung des alttestamentlichen Propheten im frühen Christentum.* BZNW 88. Berlin: de Gruyter, 1997.

Osborne, Catherine. "Ancient Vegetarianism." In: *Food in Antiquity.* J. Wilkins, D. Harvey and M. Dobson, eds. Exeter: University of Exeter, 1995. 214–24.

Ott, Jonathan. "The Delphic Bee: Bees and Toxic Honeys as Pointers to Psychoactive and Other Medicinal Plants." *Economic Botany* (New York) 52/3 (1998): 260–6.

Ozimek L. et al. "Nutritive Value of Protein Extracted from Honey Bees." *Journal of Food Science* (Chicago) 50 (1985): 1327–9, 1332.

Pallis, Alexandros. *A Few Notes on the Gospels according to St. Mark and St. Matthew: Based Chiefly on Modern Greek.* Liverpool: Liverpool Booksellers, 1903.

Palmoni, Y. "Locust." Art. *IDB*, 3.144–8.

Patte, Daniel. *The Gospel according to Matthew: A Structural Commentary on Matthew's Faith.* Philadelphia: Fortress, 1987.

Pattie, James O. *The Personal Narrative of James O. Pattie, of Kentucky: During an Expedition from St. Louis through the Vast Regions between that Place and the Pacific Ocean.* Cincinnati: E. H. Flint, 1833 = Chicago: Donnelly, 1930.

Perry, Ben Edwin. *Studies in the Text History of the Life and Fables of Aesop.* Philological Monographs 7. Haverford, PA: American Philological Association, 1936.

Pesch, Rudolf. "Anfang des Evangeliums Jesu Christi: Eine Studie zum Prolog des Markusevangeliums (Mk 1, 1–15)." In: *Das Markus-Evangelium.* R. Pesch, ed. Wege der Forschung 411. Darmstadt: Wissenschaftliche Buchgesellschaft, 1979. 311–55.

—. *Das Markusevangelium I. Teil: Einleitung und Kommentar zu Kap. 1,1–8,26.* HTKNT 2.1. Freiburg: Herder, ⁴1984.

Peter, Heinrich. *Johannes der Täufer in der urchristlichen Überlieferung.* Marburg: H. Bauer, 1911.

Petersen, William L. "The Genesis of the Gospels." In: *New Testament Textual Criticism and Exegesis.* FS Joël Delobel. BETL 161. Adelbert Denaux, ed. Leuven: Peeters, 2002. 33–65.

—. "Tatian's Diatessaron." In: Koester, *Ancient Christian Gospels.* 403–30.

—. *Tatian's Diatessaron: Its Creation, Dissemination, Significance, and History in Scholarship.* VCSup 25. Leiden: Brill, 1994.

Pierre, Marie-Joseph. "Lait et miel, ou la douceur du verbe." *Apocrypha* 10 (1999): 139–76.

Plummer, Alfred. *The Gospel according to St. Mark.* CGTSC. Cambridge: Cambridge University, 1915.

Pope, Marvin H. "Of Locusts and Locust Eggs." *JBL* 93 (1974): 293.

Pothecary, Sarah. "Strabo, the Tiberian Author: Past, Present and Silence in Strabo's *Geography.*" *Mnemosyne* 55 (2002): 387–438.

Powell, J. Enoch. *The Evolution of the Gospel: A New Translation of the First Gospel with Commentary and Introductory Essay.* New Haven: Yale University, 1994.

Pryor, John W. "John the Baptist and Jesus: Tradition and Text in John 3.25." *JSNT* 66 (1997): 15–26.

Purcell, Nicholas. "Eating Fish: The Paradoxes of Seafood." In: *Food in Antiquity.* J. Wilkins, F. D. Harvey and M. Dobson, eds. Exeter: University of Exeter, 1995. 132–49.

Rawlinson, A. E. J. *St Mark.* WC. London: Methuen, ⁶1960 (1925).

Reim, Helmut. *Die Insektennahrung der australischen Ureinwohner: Eine Studie zur Frühgeschichte menschlicher Wirtschaft und Ernährung.* Städtisches Museum für Völkerkunde (Leipzig) Veröffentlichungen 13. Berlin: Akademie-Verlag, 1962.

Reumann, John. "The Quest for the Historical Baptist." In: *Understanding the Sacred Text.* J. Reumann, ed. Valley Forge, PA: Judson, 1972.

Rhoads, David M. "Narrative Criticism: Practices and Prospects." In: *Characterization in the Gospels: Reconceiving Narrative Criticism.* D. Rhoads and K. Syreeni, eds. Sheffield: Sheffield Academic, 1999. 264–85.

Richter, Georg. "'Bist du Elias?' (Joh. 1, 21)." *BZ* n.s. 6 (1962): 79–92, 238–56.

Robinson, John A. T. "The Baptism of John and the Qumran Community." Reprinted in: idem, *Twelve New Testament Studies*. SBT 34. Naperville, IL: A. R. Allenson, 1962. 11–27.

—. "Elijah, John and Jesus: An Essay in Detection." *NTS* 4 (1958): 263–81.

Rothschild, Clare Komoroske. *Luke-Acts and the Rhetoric of History: An Investigation of Early Christian Historiography*. WUNT 2.175. Tübingen: Mohr Siebeck, 2004.

Roumbalou, Maria. "Hermits: Eastern Christian." Art. *Encyclopedia of Monasticism* (ed. W. M. Johnston). 1.579–83.

Sabbatucci, Dario. "Dieta Carnea e Vegetarianesimo." In: *Homo edens: Regimi, miti e pratiche dell'alimentazione nella civiltà del Mediterraneo*. Oddone Longo and Paolo Scarpi, eds. Milan: Diapress/Documenti, 1989. 243–4.

Sacks, Kenneth S. *Diodorus Siculus and the First Century*. Princeton: Princeton University, 1990.

Saller, Richard. "Martial on Patronage and Literature." *CQ* 33 (1983): 246–57.

Sanders, E. P. *Jesus and Judaism*. London: SCM/Philadelphia: Fortress, 1985.

Sandy, D. Brent. "John the Baptist's 'Lamb of God' Affirmation in Its Canonical and Apocalyptic Milieu." *JETS* 34 (1991): 447–59.

Schlatter, Adolf. *Johannes der Täufer*. W. Michaelis, ed. Basel: Friedrich Reinhardt, 1956.

Schlosser, Eric. *Fast Food Nation: The Dark Side of the All-American Meal*. Boston: Houghton Mifflin, 2001.

Schmidt, Karl L. *Der Rahmen der Geschichte Jesu: Literarkritische Untersuchungen zur ältesten Jesusüberlieferung*. Darmstadt: Wissenschaftliche Buchgesellschaft, 1969 (1919).

Schmidt-Nielsen, Knut. *Desert Animals: Physiological Problems of Heat and Water*. Oxford: Clarendon, 1964.

Schnackenburg, Rudolf. *The Gospel of Matthew*. Grand Rapids: Eerdmans, 2002 (1985–87).

Schochet, Elijah Judah. *Animal Life in Jewish Tradition: Attitudes and Relationships*. New York: Ktav, 1984.

Schuster, Mauriz. "Mel." Art. PW, 15.364–84.

Schütz, Roland. *Johannes der Täufer*. ATANT 50. Zurich/Stuttgart: Zwingli, 1967.

Schweizer, Eduard. *The Good News according to Mark*. Richmond, VA: John Knox, 1970 ([12]1968).

—. *The Good News according to Matthew*. Atlanta: John Knox, 1975.

Scobie, Charles H. H. *John the Baptist*. Philadelphia: Fortress, 1964.

Seidl, Theodor. "Heuschreckenschwarm und Prophetenintervention: Textkritische und syntaktische Erwägungen zu Am 7:2." *BN* 37 (1987): 129–38.

Senior, Donald. *Matthew*. ANTC. Nashville: Abingdon, 1998.

Shaver, Brenda J. "The Prophet Elijah in the Literature of the Second Temple Period: The Growth of a Tradition." Diss., University of Chicago, 2001.

Shaw, Brent D. "'Eaters of Fish, Drinkers of Milk': The Ancient Mediterranean Ideology of the Pastoral Nomad." *Ancient Society* (Louvain) 13–14 (1982–83): 5–31.

Shaw, Teresa M. *The Burden of the Flesh: Fasting and Sexuality in Early Christianity*. Minneapolis: Fortress, 1998.

Sheridan, Susan Guise. "Scholars, Soldiers, Craftsmen, Elites?: Analysis of French Collection of Human Remains from Qumran." *Dead Sea Discoveries* 9 (2002): 199–248.

Sheridan, S. G., J. Ullinger and J. Ramp. "Anthropological Analysis of the Human Remains from Khirbet Qumran: The French Collection." Forthcoming in: *The Archaeology of Qumran II.* Jean-Baptiste Humbert and Jan Gunneweg, eds. Presses Universitaires de Fribourg, Suisse and the École Biblique et Archéologique Française.

Sickenberger, Joseph. "Über die dem Petrus von Laodicea zugeschriebenen Evangelien-kommentare." *TQ* 86 (1904): 10–19.

Silberman, L. H. "Honig." Art. *Biblisch-historisches Handwörterbuch: Landeskunde, Geschichte, Religion, Kultur, Literatur.* Bo Reicke and Leonhard Rost, eds. Göttingen: Vandenhoeck & Ruprecht, 1962–79. 2.747.

Simonsen, D. "Milch und Honig: (Eine Erwiderung)." *ZDPV* 33 (1910): 44–6.

Simoons, Frederick J. *Eat Not This Flesh: Food Avoidances from Prehistory to the Present.* Madison: University of Wisconsin, [2]1994.

Slater, William J., ed. *Dining in a Classical Context.* Ann Arbor: University of Michigan, 1991.

Smith, James V. "Resurrecting the Blessed Hyperechius." Diss., Loyola University Chicago, 2003.

Smith, Robert H. *Matthew.* ACNT. Minneapolis: Augsburg, 1989.

Snyman, A. H. "Analysis of Mt 3.1 – 4.22." *Neot* 11 (1977): 19–31.

Sokol, Moshe. "Maimonides on Freedom of the Will and Moral Responsibility." *HTR* 91 (1998): 25–39.

Soler, Jean. "The Semiotics of Food in the Bible." In: *Food and Drink in History: Selections from the Annales, Économies, Sociétés, Civilisations, Volume 5.* R. Forster and O. Ranum, eds. Baltimore: Johns Hopkins University, 1979. 126–38.

Sparkes, B. A. "The Greek Kitchen." *JHS* 82 (1962): 121–37.

Stafford, Jennifer M. "Avian Food Selection with Application to Pesticide Risk Assessment: Are Dead and Desiccated Insects a Desirable Food Source?" M.S. Thesis (Biology), Utah State University, 2001.

Staubli, Thomas. *Die Bücher Levitikus, Numeri.* Neuer Stuttgarter Kommentar, Altes Testament 3. Stuttgart: Katholisches Bibelwerk, 1996.

Steinmann, Jean. *Saint John the Baptist and the Desert Tradition.* New York: Harper, 1958.

Strack, H. L. and P. Billerbeck. *Kommentar zum Neuen Testament aus Talmud und Midrasch.* Munich: Beck, 1922–61.

Sutton, Mark Q. *Insects as Food: Aboriginal Entomophagy in the Great Basin.* Ballena Press Anthropological Papers 33. Menlo Park, CA: Ballena, 1988.

Svartvik, Jesper. *Mark and Mission: Mk 7:1–23 in Its Narrative and Historical Contexts.* ConBNT 32. Stockholm: Almqvist & Wiksell, 2000.

Swanton, John R. *The Indian Tribes of North America.* Smithsonian Institution Bureau of American Ethnology 145. Washington: Smithsonian Institution Press, 1969 (1952).

Swete, H. B. *The Gospel according to St. Mark.* London: Macmillan, [3]1913 (1898) = Grand Rapids: Kregel, 1977.

Tatum, W. Barnes. *John the Baptist and Jesus: A Report of the Jesus Seminar.* Sonoma, CA: Polebridge, 1994.

Taylor, Joan E. *The Immerser: John the Baptist within Second Temple Judaism.* Studying the Historical Jesus. London: SPCK/Grand Rapids: Eerdmans, 1997.

Taylor, Ronald L. *Butterflies in My Stomach, Or: Insects in Human Nutrition.* Santa Barbara, CA: Woodbridge, 1975.

Taylor, Ronald L. and Barbara J. Carter. *Entertaining with Insects, Or: The Original Guide to Insect Cookery.* Yorba Linda, CA: Salutek, 1996 (1976).

Taylor, Vincent. *The Gospel according to Saint Mark.* Grand Rapids: Baker, [2]1966.

Thompson, Dorothy. "Athenaeus in His Egyptian Context." In: *Athenaeus and His World: Reading Greek Culture in the Roman Empire.* D. Braund and J. Wilkins, eds. Exeter: Exeter University, 2000. 77–84.

Thompson, John A. "Joel's Locusts in the Light of Near Eastern Parallels." *JNES* 14 (1955): 52–5.

—. "Translation of the Words for Locust." *Bible Translator* 25 (1974): 405–11.

Tilly, Michael. *Johannes der Täufer und die Biographie der Propheten: Die synoptische Täuferüberlieferung und das jüdische Prophetenbild zur Zeit des Täufers.* BWANT 7/17. Stuttgart: W. Kohlhammer, 1994.

Tinambunan, E. R. L. "Elijah according to the Fathers of the Church." *Carmelus* (Rome) 49 (2002): 85–116.

Trilling, Wolfgang. "DieTäufertradition bei Matthäus." *BZ* 3 (1959): 271–89.

Trocmé, Étienne. *L'Évangile selon Saint Marc.* CNT 2. Geneva: Labor et Fides, 2000.

Trublet, Jacques. "Alimentation et sainteté: Lévitique 11 Deutéronome 14." *Christus* 29 (1982): 209–17.

Trumbower, Jeffrey A. "The Role of Malachi in the Career of John the Baptist." In: *Gospels and the Scriptures of Israel.* C. A. Evans and W. R. Stegner, eds. JSNTSup 104. Sheffield: Sheffield Academic, 1994. 28–41.

Turner, C. H. *The Gospel according to St. Mark: Introduction and Commentary.* London: SPCK, 1928.

Tzedakis, Yannis and Holley Martlew. *Minoans and Mycenaeans: Flavours of Their Time, National Archaeological Museum, 12 July–27 November 1999.* Athens: Kapon, 1999.

UBS Committee on Translations. *Fauna and Flora of the Bible.* Helps for Translators 11. London/New York: United Bible Societies, [2]1980.

Valavanolickal, Kuriakose A. *The Use of the Gospel Parables in the Writings of Aphrahat and Ephrem.* Arbeiten zur Religion und Geschichte des Urchristentums 2. Frankfurt an Main: Lang, 1996.

Van Buren, E. D. *The Fauna of Ancient Mesopotamia as Represented in Art.* AnOr 18. Rome: Pontificium institutum biblicum, 1939.

Van der Valk, Marchinus. *Researches on the Text and Scholia of the Iliad.* Leiden: Brill, 1963–64.

Van Iersel, Bas M. F. *Mark: A Reader-Response Commentary.* JSNTSup 164. Sheffield: Sheffield Academic, 1998.

Van Leeuwen, Cornelis. "The 'Northern One' in the Composition of Joel 2,19–27." In: *The Scriptures and the Scrolls.* F. García Martínez et al., eds. VTSup 49. Leiden: Brill, 1992. 85–99.

Vickery, Kenton F. *Food in Early Greece.* Chicago: Ares, 1980 (1936).

Vielhauer, Philipp. "Tracht und Speise Johannes des Täufers: Bisher unveröffentlicht." In: idem, *Aufsätze zum Neuen Testament.* TB 31. Munich: Chr. Kaiser, 1965. 47–54.

Von Tischendorf, Constantin. *Novum Testamentum Graece: Ad Antiquissimos Testes Denuo Recensuit.* Leipzig: Giesecke & Devrient, [8]1869.

Vööbus, Arthur. *Early Versions of the New Testament: Manuscript Studies.* Papers of the Estonian Theological Society in Exile 6. Stockholm: Estonian Theological Society in Exile, 1954.

—. *History of Asceticism in the Syrian Orient: A Contribution to the History of Culture in the Near East.* CSCO 184, 197, 500. Louvain: Secrétariat du Corpus SCO, 1958–88.

Wakefield, Elmer G. and Samuel C. Dellinger. "Diet of the Bluff Dwellers of the Ozark Mountains and Its Skeletal Remains." *Annals of Internal Medicine* 9 (1936): 1412–18.

Walker Bynum, Caroline. *Holy Feast and Holy Fast: The Religious Significance of Food to Medieval Women.* Berkeley: University of California, 1987.

Walsh, Jerome T. "Elijah (Person)." Art. *ABD*, 2.463–6.

Ward, Bernard. *Healing Foods from the Bible.* Boca Raton, FL: Globe Communications, 1996.

Webb, Robert L. *John the Baptizer and Prophet: A Socio-Historical Study.* JSNTSup 62. Sheffield: JSOT Press, 1991.

Weiss, Bernhard. *A Commentary on the New Testament.* Vol. 1: *Matthew–Mark.* New York: Funk & Wagnalls, 1906 ([8]1892).

Weis, E. "Johannes der Täufer (Baptista), der Vorläufer (Prodromos)." Art. *Lexikon der christlichen Ikonographie.* Engelbert Kirschbaum et al., eds. Rome/Freiburg: Herder, 1968–76. 7.164–90.

Wellhausen, Julius. *Das Evangelium Marci.* Berlin: G. Reimer, [2]1909.

Wettstein, Johann Jakob. *Novum Testamentum Graecum.* Amstelaedam: Ex officina Dommeriana, 1751–52 = Graz, Austria: Akademische Druck- u. Verlagsanstalt, 1962.

White, Ellen G. H. *Counsels on Diet & Foods.* Washington: Review and Herald, 1938.

—. *Testimonies for the Church.* Mountain View, CA: Pacific Press, [4]1948.

White, Jr., Jonathan W. "Composition of Honey." In: *Honey: A Comprehensive Survey* (ed. E. Crane). 157–206.

White, Jr., Jonathan W. et al. "Composition of Honey IV: The Effect of Storage on Carbohydrates, Acidity, and Disease Content." *Journal of Food Science* (Chicago) 26 (1961): 63–71.

White, K. D. "Farming and Animal Husbandry." In: *Civilization of the Ancient Mediterranean* (ed. M. Grant and R. Kitzinger). 1.211–45.

Whiting, John D. "Jerusalem's Locust Plague: Being a Description of the Recent Locust Influx into Palestine, and Comparing Same with Ancient Locust Invasions as Narrated in the Old World's History Book, the Bible." *The National Geographic Magazine* 28/6 (1915): 511–50.

Wilkins, John. *The Boastful Chef: The Discourse of Food in Ancient Greek Comedy.* New York: Oxford University Press, 2000.

Williamson, Jr., Lamar. *Mark.* IBC. Atlanta: John Knox, 1983.

Wills, Lawrence M. *The Quest of the Historical Gospel: Mark, John, and the Origins of the Gospel Genre.* London/New York: Routledge, 1997.

Wimbush, Vincent L. and Richard Valantasis, eds. *Asceticism.* New York: Oxford University Press, 1995.

Windisch, Hans. "Die Notiz über Tracht und Speise des Täufers Johannes und ihre Entsprechungen in der Jesusüberlieferung." *ZNW* 32 (1933): 65–87.

Wink, Walter. *John the Baptist in the Gospel Tradition.* SNTSMS 7. Cambridge: Cambridge University, 1968.

Witherington III, Ben. *The Gospel of Mark: A Socio-Rhetorical Commentary.* Grand Rapids: Eerdmans, 2001.

Wolff, Christian. "Zur Bedeutung Johannes des Täufers im Markusevangelium." *TLZ* 102 (1977): 857–65.

Wordsworth, Christopher. *The New Testament of Our Lord and Saviour Jesus Christ: In the Original Greek, with Notes and Introductions.* London: Rivingtons, [2]1861–62.

Wucherpfennig, Ansgar. *Heracleon Philologus: Gnostische Johannesexegese im zweiten Jahrhundert.* WUNT 142. Tübingen: Mohr Siebeck, 2002.

Yamasaki, Gary. *John the Baptist in Life and Death: Audience-Oriented Criticism of Matthew's Narrative.* JSNTSup 167. Sheffield: Sheffield Academic, 1998.
Yamauchi, Edwin M. "Ancient Ecologies and the Biblical Perspective." *Journal of the American Scientific Affiliation* 32 (1980): 193–203.
Young, Frances M. *Biblical Exegesis and the Formation of Christian Culture.* Cambridge: Cambridge University, 1997.
Young, Richard A. "Didn't John the Baptist Snack on Locusts?" In: idem, *Is God a Vegetarian? Christianity, Vegetarianism, and Animal Rights.* Chicago: Open Court, 1999. 90–101.

Zahn, Theodor. *Das Evangelium des Markus.* Leipzig: A. Deichert, 1910.
—. *Das Evangelium des Matthäus.* Leipzig: A. Deichert, [4]1922 (1903) = Wuppertal: R. Brockhaus, 1984.
Zeitlin, Solomon. "The Hoax of the 'Slavonic Josephus.'" *JQR* 39 (1948): 171–80.

Reference Works

Alexander, Patrick H. et al., eds. *The SBL Handbook of Style: For Ancient Near Eastern, Biblical, and Early Christian Studies.* Peabody, MA: Hendrickson, 1999.
Allenbach, Jean, ed. *Biblia Patristica: Index des citations et allusions bibliques dans la littérature patristique.* Paris: C.N.R.S., 1975.
Altaner, Berthold. *Patrology.* New York: Herder and Herder, 1960 (1931).

Berkowitz, Luci et al. *Thesaurus Linguae Graecae: Canon of Greek Authors and Works.* New York: Oxford University Press, [3]1990, with addenda and corrigenda online at: http://www.tlg.uci.edu/ (on 3 Nov. 2003; s.v. "A&C to printed Canon").
Borgen, Peder et al., eds. *The Philo Index: A Complete Greek Word Index to the Writings of Philo of Alexandria.* Leiden: Brill, 2000.
Brand Miller, Janette et al. *Tables of Composition of Australian Aboriginal Foods.* Canberra, Australia: Aboriginal Studies Press, 1993.

Claesson, Gösta. *Index Tertullianeus.* Paris: Études augustiniennes, 1974–75.

Dalby, Andrew. *Food in the Ancient World: A–Z.* London/New York: Routledge, 2003.
DeFoliart, Gene R., ed. "Food-insects.com." Online: http://www.food-insects.com (on 8 April 2004).
Denis, Albert-Marie. *Concordance Grecque des Pseudépigraphes d'ancien Testament.* Louvain-la-Neuve: Université Catholique de Louvain, 1987.
Di Berardino, Angelo, ed. *Encyclopedia of the Early Church.* 2 Vols. Adrian Walford, trans. New York: Oxford University Press, 1992.

Elpel, Thomas J., ed. "The Food Insects Newsletter." Online: http://www.hollowtop.com/finl_html/finl.html (on 8 April 2004).

Food and Agriculture Organization of the United Nations: Food Policy and Nutrition Division. *Food Composition Tables for the Near East.* Z. I. Sabry and R. L. Rizek, eds. FAO Food and Nutrition Paper 26. Rome: Food and Agriculture Organization, 1982.

Four Winds Food Specialists. *Ethnic Foods Nutrient Composition Guide: Hard-to-Find Items, Selected Foreign Terms, Scientific Names.* Sunnyvale, CA: Four Winds Food Specialists, [2]2001.
Freedman, David Noel, ed. *Eerdmans Dictionary of the Bible.* Grand Rapids: Eerdmans, 2000.

Gelb, I. J. et al., eds. *Assyrian Dictionary of the Oriental Institute of the University of Chicago.* Chicago: University of Chicago Oriental Institute, 1956–.
Green, Joel B. et al., eds. *Dictionary of Jesus and the Gospels.* Downers Grove, IL: InterVarsity, 1992.
Grendler, Paul F. *Encyclopedia of the Renaissance.* New York: Scribner's, 1999.

Hornblower, Simon and Antony Spawforth, eds. *The Oxford Classical Dictionary.* Oxford: Oxford University, [3]1996.

Jastrow, Marcus. *A Dictionary of the Targumim, The Talmud Babli and Yerushalmi, and the Midrashic Literature.* New York: Judaica, 1989 (1971).
Jennings, William and Ulric Gantillon. *Lexicon to the Syriac New Testament (Peshiṭta).* Eugene, OR: Wipf and Stock, 2001 (1926).
Johnston, William M., ed. *Encyclopedia of Monasticism.* Chicago: Fitzroy Dearborn, 2000.

Kannengiesser, Charles. *Handbook of Patristic Exegesis: The Bible in Ancient Christianity.* The Bible in Ancient Christianity 1–2. Leiden: Brill, 2004.
Kazhdan, Alexander P. *Oxford Dictionary of Byzantium.* New York: Oxford University Press, 1991.
Kittel, Gerhard and Gerhard Friedrich, eds. *Theological Dictionary of the New Testament.* Grand Rapids: Eerdmans, 1964–76.

Lampe, G. W. *A Patristic Greek Lexicon.* Oxford: Oxford University, 1969.
Leeming, H. and K. Leeming, eds. *Josephus' Jewish War and Its Slavonic Version: A Synoptic Comparison.* Arbeiten zur Geschichte des antiken Judentums und des Urchristentums 46. Leiden: Brill, 2003.
Liddell, Henry G., Robert Scott, H. S. Jones and Roderick McKenzie. *A Greek-English Lexicon with a Supplement 1968.* Oxford: Clarendon, [9]1992.

National Academy of Sciences. *Dietary Reference Intakes for Energy, Carbohydrate, Fiber, Fat, Fatty Acids, Cholesterol, Protein, and Amino Acids (Macronutrients).* Washington, DC: National Academy Press, 2002. Online: http://books.nap.edu/books/0309085373/html/index.html (on 8 April 2004).

Payne Smith, Robert and Jessie Payne Smith Margoliouth. *A Compendious Syriac Dictionary.* Winona Lake, IN: Eisenbrauns, 1998 (1903).

Quasten, Johannes. *Patrology.* 4 Vols. Westminster, MD: Christian Classics, 1986 (1950–53).

Rengstorf, Karl H., ed. *A Complete Concordance to Flavius Josephus.* Leiden: Brill, 1973–83.

Steedman, Alison, ed. *Locust Handbook.* Kent, UK: Natural Resources Institute, Overseas Development Administration, [3]1990.

Swanson, Reuben J., ed. *New Testament Greek Manuscripts: Variant Readings.* Vol. 1: *Matthew*, 1995. Sheffield: Sheffield Academic, 1995.

—. *New Testament Greek Manuscripts: Variant Readings.* Vol. 2: *Mark*, 1995. Sheffield: Sheffield Academic, 1995.

United States Department of Agriculture (USDA). *National Nutrient Database for Standard Reference, Release 16–1.* Online: http://www.nal.usda.gov/fnic/foodcomp (on 17 May 2004).

Uvarov, Boris P. *Grasshoppers and Locusts: A Handbook of General Acridology.* Cambridge: Cambridge University, [2]1966–77 (1928).

Van der Toorn, Karel et al. *Dictionary of Deities and Demons in the Bible: DDD.* Leiden: Brill/Grand Rapids: Eerdmans, [2]1999.

Vauchez, Andre. *Encyclopedia of the Middle Ages.* Chicago/London: Fitzroy Dearborn, 2000.

Washburn, David L. *A Catalog of Biblical Passages in the Dead Sea Scrolls.* Text-Critical Studies 2. Atlanta: Society of Biblical Literature, 2002.

Wiles, James W. *A Scripture Index to the Works of St. Augustine in English Translation.* Lanham: University Press of America, 1995.

Index of References

1. Hebrew Bible

2. Other Jewish Sources (Pre-Modern)

Artapanus   40 n.11

Assumption of Moses
10.3–4   120 n.80

b. Ḥullin
63b (II.10.B)   57 n.62
65a (IV.1.A)   57, 119–120
    n.78
65a (IV.2.B)   58
65a–66a (IV.3.C–
    IV.5.C)   58
66a–67a (V.1–2)   57

Baruch
1:20   84 n.19
5:7   120 n.80

3 Baruch 16.3   42–43 n.20

1 Enoch
1.6   120 n.80
90.31   129

2 Enoch
8.1–4   96, 98 n.62
8.5–6 (J)   96 n.55
22.8–9 (J)   96

2 Esdras
2:19   84 n.19
4:24   40–41 n.16

Ezekiel the Tragedian
144–146   40 n.11

4 Ezra 6.26   129

Joseph and Aseneth
16.8–23   88 n.31

Josephus
  Ant.
    2.6.5 (§118)   82 n.5
    2.14.4 (§306)   40 n.11, 42 n.20
    3.1.6 (§28)   82 n.5

10.10.2 (§190)   185
14.7.4 (§124)   82 n.5
18.5.2 (§§116–
    119)   4 n.7, 117 n.67
  B.J.
    1.9.1 (§184)   82 n.5
    2.7.2 (§110)   176 n.150
    2.7.3 (§111)   176 n.150
    2.8.8 (§143)   54 n.54
    4.8.3 (§468)   28 n.115, 88,
        97–98
    4.9.7 (§536)   42–43 n.20
  Vita 2 §11   23 n.89, 33
        n.135, 126–128,
        133, 183 n.172,
        185, 198

Jubilees
  1.7   84 n.19
  48.5   40 n.11

Judith 2:20   40 n.14

Letter of Aristeas   45, 53, 56, 60,
        196
  109   95 n.51
  112   95, 97 n.59
  128–172   51
  144b–146a   51, 52, 107
        n.28, 119

Lives of the Prophets
  4:14   185

2 Maccabees
  5:21–27   183 n.172, 185
  5:21–26   125–126
  5:27   126, 133, 174,
        176 n.148, 198

*Martyrdom and
Ascension of Isaiah*
  2:7–11   183 n.172
  2.7–10   126
  2.11   126, 133, 142
        n.31, 198

3. Greco-Roman Sources

4. New Testament

5. Other Christian Literature

Index of Modern Authors

Index of Subjects

Wissenschaftliche Untersuchungen zum Neuen Testament
Alphabetical Index of the First and Second Series

Bolyki, János: Jesu Tischgemeinschaften. 1997.
Volume II/96.

Bosman, Philip: Conscience in Philo and Paul.
2003. *Volume II/166.*

Bovon, François: Studies in Early Christianity.
2003. *Volume 161.*

Brocke, Christoph vom: Thessaloniki – Stadt
des Kassander und Gemeinde des Paulus.
2001. *Volume II/125.*

Brunson, Andrew: Psalm 118 in the Gospel of
John. 2003. *Volume II/158.*

Büchli, Jörg: Der Poimandres – ein paganisier-
tes Evangelium. 1987. *Volume II/27.*

Bühner, Jan A.: Der Gesandte und sein Weg im
4. Evangelium. 1977. *Volume II/2.*

Burchard, Christoph: Untersuchungen zu
Joseph und Aseneth. 1965. *Volume 8.*

– Studien zur Theologie, Sprache und Umwelt
des Neuen Testaments. Ed. von D. Sänger.
1998. *Volume 107.*

Burnett, Richard: Karl Barth's Theological
Exegesis. 2001. *Volume II/145.*

Byron, John: Slavery Metaphors in Early
Judaism and Pauline Christianity. 2003.
Volume II/162.

Byrskog, Samuel: Story as History – History as
Story. 2000. *Volume 123.*

Cancik, Hubert (Ed.): Markus-Philologie. 1984.
Volume 33.

Capes, David B.: Old Testament Yaweh Texts in
Paul's Christology. 1992. *Volume II/47.*

Caragounis, Chrys C.: The Development of
Greek and the New Testament. 2004.
Volume 167.

– The Son of Man. 1986. *Volume 38.*

– see *Fridrichsen, Anton.*

Carleton Paget, James: The Epistle of Barnabas.
1994. *Volume II/64.*

Carson, D.A., O'Brien, Peter T. and *Mark
Seifrid* (Ed.): Justification and Variegated
Nomism.
Volume 1: The Complexities of Second
Temple Judaism. 2001. *Volume II/140.*
Volume 2: The Paradoxes of Paul. 2004.
Volume II/181.

Ciampa, Roy E.: The Presence and Function of
Scripture in Galatians 1 and 2. 1998.
Volume II/102.

Classen, Carl Joachim: Rhetorical Criticsm of
the New Testament. 2000. *Volume 128.*

Colpe, Carsten: Iranier – Aramäer – Hebräer –
Hellenen. 2003. *Volume 154.*

Crump, David: Jesus the Intercessor. 1992.
Volume II/49.

Dahl, Nils Alstrup: Studies in Ephesians. 2000.
Volume 131.

Deines, Roland: Die Gerechtigkeit der Tora im
Reich des Messias. 2004. *Volume 177.*

– Jüdische Steingefäße und pharisäische
Frömmigkeit. 1993. *Volume II/52.*

– Die Pharisäer. 1997. *Volume 101.*

– and *Karl-Wilhelm Niebuhr (Ed.):* Philo und
das Neue Testament. 2004. *Volume 172.*

Dettwiler, Andreas and *Jean Zumstein (Ed.):*
Kreuzestheologie im Neuen Testament.
2002. *Volume 151.*

Dickson, John P.: Mission-Commitment in
Ancient Judaism and in the Pauline
Communities. 2003. *Volume II/159.*

Dietzfelbinger, Christian: Der Abschied des
Kommenden. 1997. *Volume 95.*

*Dimitrov, Ivan Z., James D.G. Dunn, Ulrich
Luz* and *Karl-Wilhelm Niebuhr* (Ed.): Das
Alte Testament als christliche Bibel in
orthodoxer und westlicher Sicht. 2004.
Volume 174.

Dobbeler, Axel von: Glaube als Teilhabe. 1987.
Volume II/22.

Du Toit, David S.: Theios Anthropos. 1997.
Volume II/91

Dübbers, Michael: Christologie und Existenz im
Kolosserbrief. 2005. *Volume II/191.*

Dunn , James D.G. (Ed.): Jews and Christians.
1992. *Volume 66.*

– Paul and the Mosaic Law. 1996. *Volume 89.*

– see *Dimitrov, Ivan Z.*

Dunn, James D.G., Hans Klein, Ulrich Luz and
Vasile Mihoc (Ed.): Auslegung der Bibel in
orthodoxer und westlicher Perspektive. 2000.
Volume 130.

Ebel, Eva: Die Attraktivität früher christlicher
Gemeinden. 2004. *Volume II/178.*

Ebertz, Michael N.: Das Charisma des Gekreuzigten. 1987. *Volume 45.*

Eckstein, Hans-Joachim: Der Begriff Syneidesis
bei Paulus. 1983. *Volume II/10.*

– Verheißung und Gesetz. 1996. *Volume 86.*

Ego, Beate: Im Himmel wie auf Erden. 1989.
Volume II/34

Ego, Beate, Armin Lange and *Peter Pilhofer
(Ed.):* Gemeinde ohne Tempel – Community
without Temple. 1999. *Volume 118.*

Eisen, Ute E.: see *Paulsen, Henning.*

Ellis, E. Earle: Prophecy and Hermeneutic in
Early Christianity. 1978. *Volume 18.*

– The Old Testament in Early Christianity.
1991. *Volume 54.*

Endo, Masanobu: Creation and Christology.
2002. *Volume 149.*

Ennulat, Andreas: Die 'Minor Agreements'.
1994. *Volume II/62.*

Ensor, Peter W.: Jesus and His 'Works'. 1996.
Volume II/85.

Eskola, Timo: Messiah and the Throne. 2001.
Volume II/142.
– Theodicy and Predestination in Pauline
Soteriology. 1998. *Volume II/100.*
Fatehi, Mehrdad: The Spirit's Relation to the
Risen Lord in Paul. 2000. *Volume II/128.*
Feldmeier, Reinhard: Die Krisis des Gottessoh-
nes. 1987. *Volume II/21.*
– Die Christen als Fremde. 1992. *Volume 64.*
Feldmeier, Reinhard and *Ulrich Heckel* (Ed.):
Die Heiden. 1994. *Volume 70.*
Fletcher-Louis, Crispin H.T.: Luke-Acts:
Angels, Christology and Soteriology. 1997.
Volume II/94.
Förster, Niclas: Marcus Magus. 1999.
Volume 114.
Forbes, Christopher Brian: Prophecy and
Inspired Speech in Early Christianity and its
Hellenistic Environment. 1995. *Volume II/75.*
Fornberg, Tord: see *Fridrichsen, Anton.*
Fossum, Jarl E.: The Name of God and the
Angel of the Lord. 1985. *Volume 36.*
Foster, Paul: Community, Law and Mission in
Matthew's Gospel. *Volume II/177.*
Fotopoulos, John: Food Offered to Idols in
Roman Corinth. 2003. *Volume II/151.*
Frenschkowski, Marco: Offenbarung und
Epiphanie. Volume 1 1995. *Volume II/79 –*
Volume 2 1997. *Volume II/80.*
Frey, Jörg: Eugen Drewermann und die
biblische Exegese. 1995. *Volume II/71.*
– Die johanneische Eschatologie. Volume I.
1997. *Volume 96.* – Volume II. 1998.
Volume 110.
– Volume III. 2000. *Volume 117.*
Frey, Jörg and *Udo Schnelle (Ed.):* Kontexte
des Johannesevangeliums. 2004.
Volume 175.
Freyne, Sean: Galilee and Gospel. 2000.
Volume 125.
Fridrichsen, Anton: Exegetical Writings. Edited
by C.C. Caragounis and T. Fornberg. 1994.
Volume 76.
Garlington, Don B.: 'The Obedience of Faith'.
1991. *Volume II/38.*
– Faith, Obedience, and Perseverance. 1994.
Volume 79.
Garnet, Paul: Salvation and Atonement in the
Qumran Scrolls. 1977. *Volume II/3.*
Gese, Michael: Das Vermächtnis des Apostels.
1997. *Volume II/99.*
Gheorghita, Radu: The Role of the Septuagint
in Hebrews. 2003. *Volume II/160.*
Gräbe, Petrus J.: The Power of God in Paul's
Letters. 2000. *Volume II/123.*

Gräßer, Erich: Der Alte Bund im Neuen. 1985.
Volume 35.
– Forschungen zur Apostelgeschichte. 2001.
Volume 137.
Green, Joel B.: The Death of Jesus. 1988.
Volume II/33.
Gregory, Andrew: The Reception of Luke and
Acts in the Period before Irenaeus. 2003.
Volume II/169.
Gundry Volf, Judith M.: Paul and Perseverance.
1990. *Volume II/37.*
Hafemann, Scott J.: Suffering and the Spirit.
1986. *Volume II/19.*
– Paul, Moses, and the History of Israel. 1995.
Volume 81.
Hahn, Johannes (Ed.): Zerstörungen des
Jerusalemer Tempels. 2002. *Volume 147.*
Hannah, Darrel D.: Michael and Christ. 1999.
Volume II/109.
Hamid-Khani, Saeed: Relevation and Con-
cealment of Christ. 2000. *Volume II/120.*
Harrison; James R.: Paul's Language of Grace
in Its Graeco-Roman Context. 2003.
Volume II/172.
Hartman, Lars: Text-Centered New Testament
Studies. Ed. von D. Hellholm. 1997.
Volume 102.
Hartog, Paul: Polycarp and the New Testament.
2001. *Volume II/134.*
Heckel, Theo K.: Der Innere Mensch. 1993.
Volume II/53.
– Vom Evangelium des Markus zum viergestal-
tigen Evangelium. 1999. *Volume 120.*
Heckel, Ulrich: Kraft in Schwachheit. 1993.
Volume II/56.
– Der Segen im Neuen Testament. 2002.
Volume 150.
– see *Feldmeier, Reinhard.*
– see *Hengel, Martin.*
Heiligenthal, Roman: Werke als Zeichen. 1983.
Volume II/9.
Hellholm, D.: see *Hartman, Lars.*
Hemer, Colin J.: The Book of Acts in the Setting
of Hellenistic History. 1989. *Volume 49.*
Hengel, Martin: Judentum und Hellenismus.
1969, ³1988. *Volume 10.*
– Die johanneische Frage. 1993. *Volume 67.*
– Judaica et Hellenistica.
Kleine Schriften I. 1996. *Volume 90.*
– Judaica, Hellenistica et Christiana.
Kleine Schriften II. 1999. *Volume 109.*
– Paulus und Jakobus.
Kleine Schriften III. 2002. *Volume 141.*
Hengel, Martin and *Ulrich Heckel* (Ed.): Paulus
und das antike Judentum. 1991. *Volume 58.*

Hengel, Martin and *Hermut Löhr* (Ed.):
Schriftauslegung im antiken Judentum und
im Urchristentum. 1994. *Volume 73.*

Hengel, Martin and *Anna Maria Schwemer:*
Paulus zwischen Damaskus und Antiochien.
1998. *Volume 108.*

– Der messianische Anspruch Jesu und die
Anfänge der Christologie. 2001. *Volume 138.*

Hengel, Martin and *Anna Maria Schwemer*
(Ed.): Königsherrschaft Gottes und himm-
lischer Kult. 1991. *Volume 55.*

– Die Septuaginta. 1994. *Volume 72.*

Hengel, Martin; Siegfried Mittmann and *Anna
Maria Schwemer* (Ed.): La Cité de Dieu /
Die Stadt Gottes. 2000. *Volume 129.*

Herrenbrück, Fritz: Jesus und die Zöllner. 1990.
Volume II/41.

Herzer, Jens: Paulus oder Petrus? 1998.
Volume 103.

Hoegen-Rohls, Christina: Der nachösterliche
Johannes. 1996. *Volume II/84.*

Hofius, Otfried: Katapausis. 1970. *Volume 11.*

– Der Vorhang vor dem Thron Gottes. 1972.
Volume 14.

– Der Christushymnus Philipper 2,6-11. 1976,
[2]1991. *Volume 17.*

– Paulusstudien. 1989, [2]1994. *Volume 51.*

– Neutestamentliche Studien. 2000. *Volume 132.*

– Paulusstudien II. 2002. *Volume 143.*

Hofius, Otfried and *Hans-Christian Kammler:*
Johannesstudien. 1996. *Volume 88.*

Holtz, Traugott: Geschichte und Theologie des
Urchristentums. 1991. *Volume 57.*

Hommel, Hildebrecht: Sebasmata. Volume 1 1983.
Volume 31 – Volume 2 1984. *Volume 32.*

Hvalvik, Reidar: The Struggle for Scripture and
Covenant. 1996. *Volume II/82.*

Johns, Loren L.: The Lamb Christology of the
Apocalypse of John. 2003. *Volume II/167.*

Joubert, Stephan: Paul as Benefactor. 2000.
Volume II/124.

Jungbauer, Harry: „Ehre Vater und Mutter".
2002. *Volume II/146.*

Kähler, Christoph: Jesu Gleichnisse als Poesie
und Therapie. 1995. *Volume 78.*

Kamlah, Ehrhard: Die Form der katalogischen
Paränese im Neuen Testament. 1964. *Volume 7.*

Kammler, Hans-Christian: Christologie und
Eschatologie. 2000. *Volume 126.*

– Kreuz und Weisheit. 2003. *Volume 159.*

– see *Hofius, Otfried.*

Kelhoffer, James A.: The Diet of John the
Baptist. 2005. *Volume 176.*

– Miracle and Mission. 1999. *Volume II/112.*

Kieffer, René and *Jan Bergman (Ed.):* La Main de
Dieu / Die Hand Gottes. 1997. *Volume 94.*

Kim, Seyoon: The Origin of Paul's Gospel.
1981, [2]1984. *Volume II/4.*

– Paul and the New Perspective. 2002.
Volume 140.

– "The 'Son of Man'" as the Son of God.
1983. *Volume 30.*

Klauck, Hans-Josef: Religion und Gesellschaft
im frühen Christentum. 2003. *Volume 152.*

Klein, Hans: see *Dunn, James D.G..*

Kleinknecht, Karl Th.: Der leidende Gerechtfer-
tigte. 1984, [2]1988. *Volume II/13.*

Klinghardt, Matthias: Gesetz und Volk Gottes.
1988. *Volume II/32.*

Koch, Michael: Drachenkampf und Sonnenfrau.
2004. *Volume II/184.*

Koch, Stefan: Rechtliche Regelung von
Konflikten im frühen Christentum. 2004.
Volume II/174.

Köhler, Wolf-Dietrich: Rezeption des Matthäusevangeliums in der Zeit vor Irenäus. 1987.
Volume II/24.

Köhn, Andreas: Der Neutestamentler Ernst
Lohmeyer. 2004. *Band II/180.*

Kooten, George H. van: Cosmic Christology in
Paul and the Pauline School. 2003.
Volume II/171.

Korn, Manfred: Die Geschichte Jesu in
veränderter Zeit. 1993. *Volume II/51.*

Koskenniemi, Erkki: Apollonios von Tyana in
der neutestamentlichen Exegese. 1994.
Volume II/61.

Kraus, Thomas J.: Sprache, Stil und historischer
Ort des zweiten Petrusbriefes. 2001.
Volume II/136.

Kraus, Wolfgang: Das Volk Gottes. 1996.
Volume 85.

– and *Karl-Wilhelm Niebuhr* (Ed.): Früh-
judentum und Neues Testament im Horizont
Biblischer Theologie. 2003. *Volume 162.*

– see *Walter, Nikolaus.*

Kreplin, Matthias: Das Selbstverständnis Jesu.
2001. *Volume II/141.*

Kuhn, Karl G.: Achtzehngebet und Vaterunser
und der Reim. 1950. *Volume 1.*

Kvalbein, Hans: see *Ådna, Jostein.*

Kwon, Yon-Gyong: Eschatology in Galatians.
2004. *Volume II/183.*

Laansma, Jon: I Will Give You Rest. 1997.
Volume II/98.

Labahn, Michael: Offenbarung in Zeichen und
Wort. 2000. *Volume II/117.*

Lambers-Petry, Doris: see *Tomson, Peter J.*

Lange, Armin: see *Ego, Beate.*

Lampe, Peter: Die stadtrömischen Christen in
den ersten beiden Jahrhunderten. 1987,
[2]1989. *Volume II/18.*

Landmesser, Christof: Wahrheit als Grundbegriff neutestamentlicher Wissenschaft. 1999. *Volume 113.*
– Jüngerberufung und Zuwendung zu Gott. 2000. *Volume 133.*
Lau, Andrew: Manifest in Flesh. 1996. *Volume II/86.*
Lawrence, Louise: An Ethnography of the Gospel of Matthew. 2003. *Volume II/165.*
Lee, Pilchan: The New Jerusalem in the Book of Relevation. 2000. *Volume II/129.*
Lichtenberger, Hermann: see *Avemarie, Friedrich.*
Lichtenberger, Hermann: Das Ich Adams und das Ich der Menschheit. 2004. *Volume 164.*
Lierman, John: The New Testament Moses. 2004. *Volume II/173.*
Lieu, Samuel N.C.: Manichaeism in the Later Roman Empire and Medieval China. ²1992. *Volume 63.*
Lindgård, Fredrik: Paul's Line of Thought in 2 Corinthians 4:16-5:10. 2004. *Volume II/189.*
Loader, William R.G.: Jesus' Attitude Towards the Law. 1997. *Volume II/97.*
Löhr, Gebhard: Verherrlichung Gottes durch Philosophie. 1997. *Volume 97.*
Löhr, Hermut: Studien zum frühchristlichen und frühjüdischen Gebet. 2003. *Volume160.*
– : see *Hengel, Martin.*
Löhr, Winrich Alfried: Basilides und seine Schule. 1995. *Volume 83.*
Luomanen, Petri: Entering the Kingdom of Heaven. 1998. *Volume II/101.*
Luz, Ulrich: see *Dunn, James D.G.*
Mackay, Ian D.: John's Raltionship with Mark. 2004. *Volume II/182.*
Maier, Gerhard: Mensch und freier Wille. 1971. *Volume 12.*
– Die Johannesoffenbarung und die Kirche. 1981. *Volume 25.*
Markschies, Christoph: Valentinus Gnosticus? 1992. *Volume 65.*
Marshall, Peter: Enmity in Corinth: Social Conventions in Paul's Relations with the Corinthians. 1987. *Volume II/23.*
Mayer, Annemarie: Sprache der Einheit im Epheserbrief und in der Ökumene. 2002. *Volume II/150.*
McDonough, Sean M.: YHWH at Patmos: Rev. 1:4 in its Hellenistic and Early Jewish Setting. 1999. *Volume II/107.*
McGlynn, Moyna: Divine Judgement and Divine Benevolence in the Book of Wisdom. 2001. *Volume II/139.*
Meade, David G.: Pseudonymity and Canon. 1986. *Volume 39.*

Meadors, Edward P.: Jesus the Messianic Herald of Salvation. 1995. *Volume II/72.*
Meißner, Stefan: Die Heimholung des Ketzers. 1996. *Volume II/87.*
Mell, Ulrich: Die „anderen" Winzer. 1994. *Volume 77.*
Mengel, Berthold: Studien zum Philipperbrief. 1982. *Volume II/8.*
Merkel, Helmut: Die Widersprüche zwischen den Evangelien. 1971. *Volume 13.*
Merklein, Helmut: Studien zu Jesus und Paulus. Volume 1 1987. *Volume 43.* – Volume 2 1998. *Volume 105.*
Metzdorf, Christina: Die Tempelaktion Jesu. 2003. *Volume II/168.*
Metzler, Karin: Der griechische Begriff des Verzeihens. 1991. *Volume II/44.*
Metzner, Rainer: Die Rezeption des Matthäusevangeliums im 1. Petrusbrief. 1995. *Volume II/74.*
– Das Verständnis der Sünde im Johannesevangelium. 2000. *Volume 122.*
Mihoc, Vasile: see *Dunn, James D.G..*
Mineshige, Kiyoshi: Besitzverzicht und Almosen bei Lukas. 2003. *Volume II/163.*
Mittmann, Siegfried: see *Hengel, Martin.*
Mittmann-Richert, Ulrike: Magnifikat und Benediktus. *1996. Volume II/90.*
Mußner, Franz: Jesus von Nazareth im Umfeld Israels und der Urkirche. Ed. von M. Theobald. 1998. *Volume 111.*
Niebuhr, Karl-Wilhelm: Gesetz und Paränese. 1987. *Volume II/28.*
– Heidenapostel aus Israel. 1992. *Volume 62.*
– see *Deines, Roland*
– see *Dimitrov, Ivan Z.*
– see *Kraus, Wolfgang*
Nielsen, Anders E.: "Until it is Fullfilled". 2000. *Volume II/126.*
Nissen, Andreas: Gott und der Nächste im antiken Judentum. 1974. *Volume 15.*
Noack, Christian: Gottesbewußtsein. 2000. *Volume II/116.*
Noormann, Rolf: Irenäus als Paulusinterpret. 1994. *Volume II/66.*
Novakovic, Lidija: Messiah, the Healer of the Sick. 2003. *Volume II/170.*
Obermann, Andreas: Die christologische Erfüllung der Schrift im Johannesevangelium. 1996. *Volume II/83.*
Öhler, Markus: Barnabas. 2003. *Volume 156.*
Okure, Teresa: The Johannine Approach to Mission. 1988. *Volume II/31.*
Onuki, Takashi: Heil und Erlösung. 2004. *Volume 165.*
Oropeza, B. J.: Paul and Apostasy. 2000. *Volume II/115.*

Ostmeyer, Karl-Heinrich: Taufe und Typos. 2000. *Volume II/118.*

Paulsen, Henning: Studien zur Literatur und Geschichte des frühen Christentums. Ed. von Ute E. Eisen. 1997. *Volume 99.*

Pao, David W.: Acts and the Isaianic New Exodus. 2000. *Volume II/130.*

Park, Eung Chun: The Mission Discourse in Matthew's Interpretation. 1995. *Volume II/81.*

Park, Joseph S.: Conceptions of Afterlife in Jewish Insriptions. 2000. *Volume II/121.*

Pate, C. Marvin: The Reverse of the Curse. 2000. *Volume II/114.*

Peres, Imre: Griechische Grabinschriften und neutestamentliche Eschatologie. 2003. *Volume 157.*

Philonenko, Marc (Ed.): Le Trône de Dieu. 1993. *Volume 69.*

Pilhofer, Peter: Presbyteron Kreitton. 1990. *Volume II/39.*

– Philippi. Volume 1 1995. *Volume 87. –* Volume 2 2000. *Volume 119.*

– Die frühen Christen und ihre Welt. 2002. *Volume 145.*

– see *Ego, Beate.*

Plümacher, Eckhard: Geschichte und Geschichten. Aufsätze zur Apostelgeschichte und zu den Johannesakten. Herausgegeben von Jens Schröter und Ralph Brucker. 2004. *Volume 170.*

Pöhlmann, Wolfgang: Der Verlorene Sohn und das Haus. 1993. *Volume 68.*

Pokorný, Petr and *Josef B. Souček:* Bibelauslegung als Theologie. 1997. *Volume 100.*

Pokorný, Petr and *Jan Roskovec* (Ed.): Philosophical Hermeneutics and Biblical Exegesis. 2002. *Volume 153.*

Porter, Stanley E.: The Paul of Acts. 1999. *Volume 115.*

Prieur, Alexander: Die Verkündigung der Gottesherrschaft. 1996. *Volume II/89.*

Probst, Hermann: Paulus und der Brief. 1991. *Volume II/45.*

Räisänen, Heikki: Paul and the Law. 1983, [2]1987. *Volume 29.*

Rehkopf, Friedrich: Die lukanische Sonderquelle. 1959. *Volume 5.*

Rein, Matthias: Die Heilung des Blindgeborenen (Joh 9). 1995. *Volume II/73.*

Reinmuth, Eckart: Pseudo-Philo und Lukas. 1994. *Volume 74.*

Reiser, Marius: Syntax und Stil des Markusevangeliums. 1984. *Volume II/11.*

Rhodes, James N.: The Epistle of Barnabas and the Deuteronomic Tradition. 2004. *Volume II/188.*

Richards, E. Randolph: The Secretary in the Letters of Paul. 1991. *Volume II/42.*

Riesner, Rainer: Jesus als Lehrer. 1981, [3]1988. *Volume II/7.*

– Die Frühzeit des Apostels Paulus. 1994. *Volume 71.*

Rissi, Mathias: Die Theologie des Hebräerbriefs. 1987. *Volume 41.*

Roskovec, Jan: see *Pokorný, Petr.*

Röhser, Günter: Metaphorik und Personifikation der Sünde. 1987. *Volume II/25.*

Rose, Christian: Die Wolke der Zeugen. 1994. *Volume II/60.*

Rothschild, Clare K.: Luke Acts and the Rhetoric of History. 2004. *Volume II/175.*

Rüegger, Hans-Ulrich: Verstehen, was Markus erzählt. 2002. *Volume II/155.*

Rüger, Hans Peter: Die Weisheitsschrift aus der Kairoer Geniza. 1991. *Volume 53.*

Sänger, Dieter: Antikes Judentum und die Mysterien. 1980. *Volume II/5.*

– Die Verkündigung des Gekreuzigten und Israel. 1994. *Volume 75.*

– see *Burchard, Christoph*

Salier, Willis Hedley: The Rhetorical Impact of the Sēmeia in the Gospel of John. 2004. *Volume II/186.*

Salzmann, Jorg Christian: Lehren und Ermahnen. 1994. *Volume II/59.*

Sandnes, Karl Olav: Paul – One of the Prophets? 1991. *Volume II/43.*

Sato, Migaku: Q und Prophetie. 1988. *Volume II/29.*

Schäfer, Ruth: Paulus bis zum Apostelkonzil. 2004. *Volume II/179.*

Schaper, Joachim: Eschatology in the Greek Psalter. 1995. *Volume II/76.*

Schimanowski, Gottfried: Die himmlische Liturgie in der Apokalypse des Johannes. 2002. *Volume II/154.*

– Weisheit und Messias. 1985. *Volume II/17.*

Schlichting, Günter: Ein jüdisches Leben Jesu. 1982. *Volume 24.*

Schnabel, Eckhard J.: Law and Wisdom from Ben Sira to Paul. 1985. *Volume II/16.*

Schnelle, Udo: see *Frey, Jörg.*

Schutter, William L.: Hermeneutic and Composition in I Peter. 1989. *Volume II/30.*

Schwartz, Daniel R.: Studies in the Jewish Background of Christianity. 1992. *Volume 60.*

Schwemer, Anna Maria: see *Hengel, Martin*

Scott, James M.: Adoption as Sons of God. 1992. *Volume II/48.*

– Paul and the Nations. 1995. *Volume 84.*

Shum, Shiu-Lun: Paul's Use of Isaiah in Romans. 2002. *Volume II/156.*

Siegert, Folker: Drei hellenistisch-jüdische Predigten. Teil I 1980. *Volume 20* – Teil II 1992. *Volume 61.*

– Nag-Hammadi-Register. 1982. *Volume 26.*

– Argumentation bei Paulus. 1985. *Volume 34.*

– Philon von Alexandrien. 1988. *Volume 46.*

Simon, Marcel: Le christianisme antique et son contexte religieux I/II. 1981. *Volume 23.*

Snodgrass, Klyne: The Parable of the Wicked Tenants. 1983. *Volume 27.*

Söding, Thomas: Das Wort vom Kreuz. 1997. *Volume 93.*

– see *Thüsing, Wilhelm.*

Sommer, Urs: Die Passionsgeschichte des Markusevangeliums. 1993. *Volume II/58.*

Souček, Josef B.: see *Pokorný, Petr.*

Spangenberg, Volker: Herrlichkeit des Neuen Bundes. 1993. *Volume II/55.*

Spanje, T.E. van: Inconsistency in Paul? 1999. *Volume II/110.*

Speyer, Wolfgang: Frühes Christentum im antiken Strahlungsfeld. Volume I: 1989. *Volume 50.*

– Volume II: 1999. *Volume 116.*

Stadelmann, Helge: Ben Sira als Schriftgelehrter. 1980. *Volume II/6.*

Stenschke, Christoph W.: Luke's Portrait of Gentiles Prior to Their Coming to Faith. *Volume II/108.*

Sterck-Degueldre, Jean-Pierre: Eine Frau namens Lydia. 2004. *Volume II/176.*

Stettler, Christian: Der Kolosserhymnus. 2000. *Volume II/131.*

Stettler, Hanna: Die Christologie der Pastoralbriefe. 1998. *Volume II/105.*

Stökl Ben Ezra, Daniel: The Impact of Yom Kippur on Early Christianity. 2003. *Volume 163.*

Strobel, August: Die Stunde der Wahrheit. 1980. *Volume 21.*

Stroumsa, Guy G.: Barbarian Philosophy. 1999. *Volume 112.*

Stuckenbruck, Loren T.: Angel Veneration and Christology. 1995. *Volume II/70.*

Stuhlmacher, Peter (Ed.): Das Evangelium und die Evangelien. 1983. *Volume 28.*

– Biblische Theologie und Evangelium. 2002. *Volume 146.*

Sung, Chong-Hyon: Vergebung der Sünden. 1993. *Volume II/57.*

Tajra, Harry W.: The Trial of St. Paul. 1989. *Volume II/35.*

– The Martyrdom of St.Paul. 1994. *Volume II/67.*

Theißen, Gerd: Studien zur Soziologie des Urchristentums. 1979, [3]1989. *Volume 19.*

Theobald, Michael: Studien zum Römerbrief. 2001. *Volume 136.*

Theobald, Michael: see *Mußner, Franz.*

Thornton, Claus-Jürgen: Der Zeuge des Zeugen. 1991. *Volume 56.*

Thüsing, Wilhelm: Studien zur neutestamentlichen Theologie. Ed. von Thomas Söding. 1995. *Volume 82.*

Thurén, Lauri: Derhethorizing Paul. 2000. *Volume 124.*

Tolmie, D. Francois: Persuading the Galatians. 2005. *Volume II/190.*

Tomson, Peter J. and *Doris Lambers-Petry* (Ed.): The Image of the Judaeo-Christians in Ancient Jewish and Christian Literature. 2003. *Volume 158.*

Trebilco, Paul: The Early Christians in Ephesus from Paul to Ignatius. 2004. *Volume 166.*

Treloar, Geoffrey R.: Lightfoot the Historian. 1998. *Volume II/103.*

Tsuji, Manabu: Glaube zwischen Vollkommenheit und Verweltlichung. 1997. *Volume II/93*

Twelftree, Graham H.: Jesus the Exorcist. 1993. *Volume II/54.*

Urban, Christina: Das Menschenbild nach dem Johannesevangelium. 2001. *Volume II/137.*

Visotzky, Burton L.: Fathers of the World. 1995. *Volume 80.*

Vollenweider, Samuel: Horizonte neutestamentlicher Christologie. 2002. *Volume 144.*

Vos, Johan S.: Die Kunst der Argumentation bei Paulus. 2002. *Volume 149.*

Wagener, Ulrike: Die Ordnung des „Hauses Gottes". 1994. *Volume II/65.*

Wahlen, Clinton: Jesus and the Impurity of Spirits in the Synoptic Gospels. 2004. *Volume II/185.*

Walker, Donald D.: Paul's Offer of Leniency (2 Cor 10:1). 2002. *Volume II/152.*

Walter, Nikolaus: Praeparatio Evangelica. Ed. von Wolfgang Kraus und Florian Wilk. 1997. *Volume 98.*

Wander, Bernd: Gottesfürchtige und Sympathisanten. 1998. *Volume 104.*

Watts, Rikki: Isaiah's New Exodus and Mark. 1997. *Volume II/88.*

Wedderburn, A.J.M.: Baptism and Resurrection. 1987. *Volume 44.*

Wegner, Uwe: Der Hauptmann von Kafarnaum. 1985. *Volume II/14.*

Weissenrieder, Annette: Images of Illness in the Gospel of Luke. 2003. Volume II/164.

Welck, Christian: Erzählte ‚Zeichen'. 1994. *Volume II/69.*

Wiarda, Timothy: Peter in the Gospels . 2000.
    Volume II/127.
Wilk, Florian: see *Walter, Nikolaus.*
Williams, Catrin H.: I am He. 2000.
    Volume II/113.
Wilson, Walter T.: Love without Pretense. 1991.
    Volume II/46.
Wischmeyer, Oda: Von Ben Sira zu Paulus.
    2004. *Volume 173.*
Wisdom, Jeffrey: Blessing for the Nations and
    the Curse of the Law. 2001. *Volume II/133.*
Wucherpfennig, Ansgar: Heracleon Philologus.
    2002. *Volume 142.*

Yeung, Maureen: Faith in Jesus and Paul. 2002.
    Volume II/147.
Zimmermann, Alfred E.: Die urchristlichen
    Lehrer. 1984, ²1988. *Volume II/12.*
Zimmermann, Johannes: Messianische Texte
    aus Qumran. 1998. *Volume II/104.*
Zimmermann, Ruben: Christologie der Bilder
    im Johannesevangelium. 2004. *Volume 171.*
–   Geschlechtermetaphorik und Gottes-
    verhältnis. 2001. *Volume II/122.*
Zumstein, Jean: see *Dettwiler, Andreas*
Zwiep, Arie W.: Judas and the Choice of
    Matthias. 2004. *Volume II/187.*

For a complete catalogue please write to the publisher
Mohr Siebeck • P.O. Box 2030 • D–72010 Tübingen/Germany
Up-to-date information on the internet at www.mohr.de